ESG in the Boardroom

A Guidebook for Directors

Katayun I. Jaffari • Stephen A. Pike

Editors

AMERICAN**BAR**ASSOCIATION

Business Law Section

Printed in the United States of America.

26 25 24 23 22   5 4 3 2

ISBN: 978-1-63905-051-2

Discounts are available for books ordered in bulk. Special consideration is given to state bars, CLE programs, and other bar-related organizations. Inquire at Book Publishing, ABA Publishing, American Bar Association, 321 N. Clark Street, Chicago, Illinois 60654-7598.

www.shopABA.org

Contents

Foreword

Almost ten years ago, I had the privilege to sit in a room at an American Bar Association (ABA) meeting with a number of great governance minds. Our leader, John Stout, the then chair of the Corporate Governance Committee of the Business Law Section (BLS), raised a brand new topic not discussed at the Business Law Section before—Sustainability. His right hand at the time was Sheri Ellis, whom John will tell you was the engine that made everything in the Committee run, and she made sure our meeting ran well.

I was surrounded by not just John Stout but a few others, including John Olson of Gibson, Dunn & Crutcher LLP, John White of Cravath, Swaine & Moore LLP and a former Director of the Division of Corporation Finance (yes that's a lot of Johns) and Laurence Hazell from Standard & Poor's. The conversation was something no one was discussing at the time—Sustainability and the Board of Directors' role. The dialogue was fascinating. I was in that room because I had been to the launch of SASB, the Sustainability Accounting Standards Board, in New York City just recently. As a corporate securities lawyers from Philadelphia, I went to the SASB launch thanks to Nancy Cleveland who, before anyone else I know, reached out and said, "Kathy, sustainability and ESG are topics your clients will care about because investors will care about these topics." As a matter of fact, we wrote one of the first articles regarding materiality and the disclosure regime a year before.

Thus, the ABA BLS launched the Governance and Sustainability Subcommittee, a joint committee of the Corporate Governance Committee and the Federal Regulation of Securities Committee of the Business Law Section of the ABA. There was no way I was going run the subcommittee without Nancy, and she jumped on the train; for that we are eternally grateful. It was Nancy who was our teacher. She had to convince many lawyers that sustainability and ESG were important topics to our clients and here to stay. Fortunately, we had the support of Fed Reg, thanks to David Lynn, the then chair of the Federal Regulation of Securities Committee. With David on board, the three of us were on a roll. We provided training, education and a platform for the dialogue with continuing legal education programs and written thought leader pieces. We educated the lawyers who took the topic further.

Now, here we are, launching our much-anticipated guidebook. This guidebook has come to fruition thanks to Bruce Dravis, Chair of the Corporate Governance Committee when I conceived the idea of a guidebook, and who encouraged me to pursue its creation. This guidebook would never have happened but for my Co-Editor Stephen Pike, who has fortunately joined me as Co-Chair of our newly minted ESG Subcommittee. His efforts to bring this book to fruition were invaluable and for that I am eternally grateful.

To Stephen, Nancy, John, Bruce, Sheri, David, Frank Placenti, the current Chair of the Corporate Governance Committee, and every single contributor to this book, I personally extend my gratitude. While there are so many to list, I want to thank Tanuja Dehne, Leah Seligmann, and Laurel Peacock who taught me a great deal about sustainability. And of course, I am eternally grateful to all of our subcommittee members, speakers, and champions of the ESG topic.

With gratitude,

Kathy Jaffari

Preface

ESG, Sustainability, Corporate Social Responsibility—the terms that have become a dynamic and critical focus of corporate governance in recent years. ESG, CSR, and sustainability have presented boards of directors with challenges that, in the past, would have been considered out of the scope of board responsibilities and certainly beyond the realm of shareholder primacy. Today, when discussions of "corporate purpose" are commonplace, boards of directors must address ESG, CSR, and sustainability issues and take into account the interests of not just shareholders but all other stakeholders, including employees and the communities in which the business operates. While many shareholders are pursuing an ESG agenda, increases in climate change litigation globally and regulatory and legislative requirements are requiring boards to oversee the management of ESG risks. The momentum pushing ESG issues to the forefront of corporate governance is rapidly increasing.

The ESG challenges for today's and tomorrow's boards are and may continue to be complicated and it is with that perspective that we set out to carefully explore what happens when governance meets sustainability. Our book serves as a "point-in-time" snapshot of intelligent and current thinking about the intersection of governance and sustainability; it is a guide to provide insight to directors with respect to ESG matters.

Our intention was not to create a textbook or a learned treatise on ESG issues. Rather, our intention is to provide a practical guidebook for corporate directors to assist their learning regarding ESG issues and to offer a wealth of practical insights from a team of sustainability and governance professionals who authored the chapters that you are about to read. Because the ESG landscape is evolving in a dynamic manner, we asked our authors to provide their perspectives and assessments as to where we are today and practical insights and guidance that might be most helpful for corporate directors. Their views are not unitary. It is our intention to provide a diversity of viewpoints in order to offer you a more holistic view of the ESG and sustainability landscape. Unlike a puzzle, each chapter does not neatly fit into place without overlap. This is intentional as we have endeavored to bring together a range of perspectives about issues that are lacking precise legal definition or characterization. Hence, you will find the benefits of providing perspectives that are not siloed.

We begin the book with a lexicon of ESG and sustainability terms so that corporate directors have a baseline to understand the conversation.

Part I of this book provides a foundational introduction to what is sustainability in the context of corporate governance and how it has evolved. In Part II the role of the Board is examined. Our authors address fiduciary duties and corporate purpose; a focus on a director's duties specifically addressing the challenges and opportunities of ESG, including the role of audit committees; a discussion as to how boards can approach sustainability; and bringing the reader into the boardroom, a chapter filled with questions for directors to ask.

Part III of the book provides a snapshot of the ESG landscape looking at the drivers of sustainability and who are the stakeholders in the conversation, as well as a review of shareholder activism, and how can boards can manage the dynamic landscape. In this part of the book, there is also an introduction into sustainable investing and impact investing.

Part IV deals with how ESG affects corporate strategy and risk oversight—mission-critical responsibilities of the boards of directors. Our authors look at legislation; reporting requirements, both mandatory and voluntary; sustainability ratings; and litigation and risk management.

Finally, in Part V of the book, specific areas of ESG are explored including corporate culture, human capital management, environmental resources management, the UN sustainable development goals and other international sustainability initiatives, and an overview of B corporations.

We hope that you find the information provided in these chapters informative as you develop and apply your working knowledge of ESG and sustainability. We believe that these insights will provide you with a solid grasp of the ESG landscape that is quickly evolving and growing.

Stephen Pike

Acknowledgments

This Guidebook is simply that—a guide to introduce corporate directors to the world of ESG and sustainability. ESG is a constantly changing and evolving area. This guidebook was written at a point in time. Law, regulations, and rules are changing as this guidebook goes to publication. The intent of this resource is not to provide a comprehensive "end" to the conversation but rather to provide a resource that introduces, guides and teaches corporate director about the current issues around ESG and sustainability. The guidebook provides a snapshot in time with issues to consider and resources to turn to. It's the beginning of the conversation, not the end.

This guidebook was "crowdsourced" with chapters prepared by individual contributors who are members of Governance and Sustainability Subcommittee of the American Bar Association Corporate Governance Committee. The authors are identified in the individual chapters which if desired can be read alone and separate from each other. Each contributor would want the you, the reader, to know that this Guidebook is not intended to provide, or to substitute for, legal advice and that the views expressed herein are their own and not those of their respective firms or clients.

The editors wish to acknowledge and extend their sincere appreciation to the dedicated and highly-skilled authors who contributed to this Guidebook and to thank Frank M. Placenti, the Chair of the Corporate Governance Committee for his support. In particular, the editors would like to thank and acknowledge John Stout for his forethought and intelligence in creating the Governance and Sustainability Committee many years ago before any other legal scholars considered the importance of ESG in the boardroom, as well as to Nancy Cleveland who taught many of us about the importance of ESG and sustainability. She taught us that sustainability was the capacity of a corporation to endure in light of limited resources. Although she was challenged by many lawyers, she taught us all well at the American Bar Association. Finally, we would like to thank the dedicated staff of the American Bar Association who assisted in the preparation and publication of this Guidebook.

Your Editors,

Katayun I. Jaffari and Stephen A. Pike

Lexicon of ESG and Sustainability
by Nancy S. Cleveland

Sustainability, like many complex subjects, is the proverbial alphabet soup of terminology. Not only has the concept of sustainability cultivated myriad and nuanced words and phrases, but there is also a plethora of organizations, replete with their own parade of acronyms, which have evolved to incorporate sustainability into the way we do business.

In this opening chapter, you will find a glossary of terminology and organizations to help you make sense of it all. You can read it for grounding as you begin your journey through this book and come back to it for reference as needed.

We have tried to limit the contents of this chapter to those terms and organizations that are relevant to the subject matter of this book. Hopefully, we have not missed anything critical or burdened you with excess.

Terminology		
Common Acronym	**Terminology**	**Meaning**
	Adaptive system	The adaptive system is an informal organizational operating system. It reflects how employees get things done by building an internal network of connections and influence with others in the organization who are outside the employee's direct report chain of command, department, or business unit.

Terminology		
	Alternative transportation fuels	Alternative transportation fuels are bio-diesel, compressed natural gas, hydrogen, liquefied natural gas, liquefied petroleum gas, ethanol, and methanol. Hybrid and electric vehicles are referred to as alternative fuel vehicles because they utilize electricity in place of gasoline to eliminate some or all fossil fuel impacts.
	Anthropogenic	An effect that is caused or influenced by human activity. In sustainability, this term is used in connection with environmental pollutants or pollution (i.e., climate change) caused by humans.
	Anticompetitive practices	Anticompetitive practices refer to business activities that artificially restrict or eliminate competition by exploiting market position to the disadvantage of competitors, customers, and suppliers. The result is higher prices, less choice for consumers, reduced output, market inefficiencies, or misallocation of resources (or combinations of these effects). Examples of anticompetitive practices include cartels, collusion, conspiracy, mergers, predatory pricing, price discrimination, price fixing agreements, exclusive dealing, geographic market restrictions, refusal to deal/sell, resale price maintenance, and tied selling.
AUM	Assets under management	The aggregate of all assets being managed by a financial services company, often divided into aggregates per asset class.

Terminology		
	B Corp	B Corps are for-profit companies certified by the nonprofit B Lab to meet rigorous standards of social and environmental performance, accountability, and transparency. Basic requirements to become a B Corp are: • completing and scoring at least 80 out of 200 points on B Lab's Impact Assessment, • incorporating language that permits the company to address societal goals into legal formation documents, and • signing the B Corp Declaration of Interdependence and Term Sheet. • Companies must reapply every two years to maintain certification. See also Benefit Corporation.
	Benefit Corporation	A benefit corporation (sometimes also referred to as a public benefit corporation) is a for-profit legal form that permits companies to work toward societal goals, while increasing shareholder value, without risking a breach of fiduciary duty lawsuit. This legal form creates a solid foundation for long-term mission alignment and value creation, putting shareholders on notice that the company will not maximize shareholder returns where expenditures are needed to address environmental and social impacts of business operations. Benefit corporations and B Corps are often used interchangeably to describe this type of for-profit company. While they share many similarities and are complementary, there are differences. Benefit corporations are legal business entities, whereas B Corps are designated by certification. A benefit corporation can be certified as a B Corp, but does not have to be. There are other ways to satisfy the requirements of being a benefit corporation. Likewise, a B Corp can be a benefit corporation, but it can also be an LLC, C corporation, or other type of legal business entity. See also B Corp.

Terminology		
	Bioaccumulation	The process by which toxins accumulate in living tissue, such as in plants, fish, or people. Toxins can come from ingestion or direct contact with contaminated air, water, or food. Toxins accumulate to the extent the organism is unable to process and discharge a particular toxin.
	Biocapacity	The ability of a biologically productive area, such as Earth's ecosystem, to supply resources and absorb wastes. Biocapacity can increase or decrease over time with changes in demand or as a result of technological advances.
	Biodiversity	This term refers to the biological diversity of life on Earth. Human influences, among other things, have caused the total number of species on the planet to decrease. This raises concerns about the effect of reduced biodiversity on economics, medicine, and the ability of ecosystems to remain viable. World Wildlife Fund's Inventory and the IUCN Red List are resources that document biodiversity losses.
	Biomimicry	Applying lessons learned from the study of nature and its methods and systems to technology, product, and methodology design.
	Biosphere	Coined in 1875 by Eduard Suess, the biosphere is that part of a planet's outer shell—including air, land, and water—within which life occurs, and which biotic processes alter or transform. From the broadest geophysiological point of view, the biosphere is the global ecological system integrating all living beings and their relationships, including their interaction with the elements of the lithosphere (rocks), hydrosphere (water), and atmosphere (air).
	Board diversity	Directors have a variety of skills, expertise, and experiences and fairly reflect and represent the race and ethnicity, gender and sexual identification, religion, disability, socioeconomic status, veteran status, and age of a company's primary markets.

Terminology		
	Board independence	Independent members of a board of directors have no ownership interest in the company they serve, are not related to or otherwise affiliated with any members of the management team, and have minimal or no business dealings with the company to avoid conflicts of interest. The determination of independence is more pro-scribed for publicly traded companies, where factors are determined based on legal requirements and stock exchange rules. Some stock exchanges require that a set percentage or a majority of public company directors be independent.
	Borrow, Use, Return	The borrow, use, return model, sometimes called "cradle-to-cradle," follows a circular, closed-loop system of industrial production and consumption. The model is as follows: • Borrow: extraction of energy and raw materials with minimal harm to the environment • Design and Use: phase out use of toxic and bioaccumulating substances and design products that are energy- and water-efficient • Return: recirculate or decompose biological materials to natural ecosystems
	Business behavioral norms	Business behaviors norms are the unwritten social and behavioral expectations of a business environment outside of or in addition to written codes of conduct or legal requirements. Sometimes, these can run counter to written expectations and undermine the desired corporate culture.
	Butterfly effect	In chaos theory, the butterfly effect is the sensitive dependence on initial conditions in which a small change in one state of a deterministic nonlinear system can result in large differences in a later state. The term is closely associated with the work of mathematician and meteorologist Edward Lorenz. Source: Wikipedia (https://en.wikipedia.org/wiki/Butterfly_effect).

Terminology		
.	Buycot	The inverse of a boycott. Consumers consciously use their buying power to support companies whose actions and/or goals they support.
	Carbon accounting	The process of measuring all greenhouse gases emitted by an entity.
	Carbon emissions scopes	The Greenhouse Gas (GHG) Protocol Corporate Standard classifies a company's GHG emissions into three "scopes." Scope 1 emissions are direct emissions from owned or controlled sources. Scope 2 emissions are indirect emissions from the generation of purchased energy. Scope 3 emissions are all indirect emissions (not included in scope 2) that occur in the value chain of the reporting company, including both upstream and downstream emissions.
	Carbon footprint	The total amount of greenhouse gases (GHGs) emitted by or attributed to an entity, as the result of its activities over a given period of time. All GHGs are converted to carbon dioxide equivalents, summed, and expressed as carbon dioxide. NOTE: Sometimes, the term GHG footprint is used for this meaning and carbon footprint is used to refer only to total emissions of carbon dioxide.
	Carbon neutral	The condition of having a zero carbon footprint, that is, no carbon emissions created by or attributable to an organization. This may be achieved on an accounting basis by purchasing carbon credits or offsets to negate actual emissions.
	Carbon pricing	Carbon pricing charges emitters for their carbon dioxide (CO_2) emissions. The charge, or carbon price, is the cost to emit one ton of CO_2 into the atmosphere. Carbon pricing is usually imposed either as a carbon tax or a requirement to purchase permits to emit, generally known as cap-and-trade.
	Carbon sink	A carbon sink is a natural or artificial reservoir that absorbs and stores a carbon-containing chemical compound for an indefinite period. Examples of natural sinks for carbon dioxide are the oceans and plants. Examples of artificial sinks are landfills and carbon capture and storage facilities.

Terminology		
	Child labor	Engaging children to perform work in a business or industry, especially which is inhumane or violate laws prohibiting employment below a specified minimum age. It is often defined as work that is mentally, physically, socially, or morally dangerous and harmful to children, including work that impairs or deprives a child of the opportunity or ability to get an education.
	Circular economy	The circular economy is a generic term for an industrial economy that is, by design or intention, restorative and in which material flows are of two types, biological nutrients, designed to re-enter the biosphere safely, and technical nutrients, which are designed to circulate at high quality without entering the biosphere.
	Climate change	Climate change is a change in the statistical distribution of weather patterns when that change lasts for an extended period of time (i.e., decades to millions of years). Climate change may refer to a change in average weather conditions, or in the time variation of weather around longer-term average conditions (i.e., more or fewer extreme weather events). Climate change is caused by factors such as biotic processes, variations in solar radiation received by Earth, plate tectonics (leading to volcanic eruptions), and human activities that contribute significantly to global warming. Source: Wikipedia (https://en.wikipedia.org/wiki/Climate_change).
Climate VaR	Climate Value-At-Risk	Climate VaR is a financial model created by MSCI designed to provide a forward-looking and return-based valuation assessment to measure climate-related risks and opportunities in an investment portfolio. The fully quantitative model offers deep insights into how climate change could affect company valuations.

Terminology		
	Conflict minerals	Conflict minerals are natural resources extracted in war-torn regions and sold to finance armed conflict and human rights abuses, most notably in the eastern provinces of the Democratic Republic of the Congo. The use of conflict minerals is increasingly scrutinized within organizational supply chains. In the US, minerals that are regulated as conflict minerals are Tantalum, Tin, Tungsten, and Gold.
	Coopetition	A practice of competitors cooperating and working with each other for a limited purpose on a project, joint venture, or co-marketing basis. Coopetition is often used to break through a market barrier when no one competitor can do so alone. Once the barrier is removed, competition resumes in the newly created open market space.
CR	Corporate Responsibility	A corporate initiative to assess and take responsibility for the company's effects on the environment, and its impact on social welfare. It applies to the company efforts that go beyond what may be required by regulators or environmental protection groups.
CSR	Corporate Social Responsibility	A corporate initiative to assess and take responsibility for the company's impact on social welfare, particularly in the communities where the company is located.
	Cradle-to-cradle	A phrase invented by Walter R. Stahel in the 1970s and popularized by William McDonough and Michael Braungart in their 2002 book of the same name, cradle-to-cradle is a framework to create production techniques that are efficient and waste-free. All material inputs and outputs are seen either as technical or biological nutrients. Technical nutrients can be recycled or reused with no loss of quality, and biological nutrients are composted or consumed. See Borrow, Use, Return definition.

Terminology		
	Cradle-to-grave	By contrast to cradle-to-cradle, cradle-to-grave refers to taking responsibility for the disposal of goods produced, but not necessarily by putting products' unused constituent components back into service. See Take, Make, Waste definition.
	Deforestation	The clearing or intentional destruction or removal of virgin forests for agricultural, commercial, housing, or firewood use, without replanting and allowing time for the forest to regenerate itself before or because an alternative use is established. Because forests are carbon sinks, deforestation contributes to the greenhouse effect. It can also lead to desertification.
	Desertification	Conversion of a grassland or an arid land (often magnified by droughts) into a desert through actions such as overgrazing, repeated burning, intensive farming, and stripping of vegetation through deforestation.
DJSI	Dow Jones Sustainability Index	A financial index that measures corporate sustainability initiatives by evaluating how a publicly traded company recognizes in its business strategy risks and opportunities that arise from sustainability issues. Companies are assessed and selected for inclusion in the DJSI based on their long-term economic, social, and environmental asset management plans.
	Downcycle	A term coined by William McDonaugh and Michael Braungart to describe a process of converting materials and products into new materials, but of lesser quality, each time they reach the end of a useful life cycle until there is no lower value reuse and disposal is required.

Terminology		
	Earth Overshoot Day	Earth Overshoot Day is the day in each calendar year when human demand for natural resources and the carbon dioxide emissions we create in a calendar year exceeds the planet's annual ability to regenerate resources and reabsorb the carbon emissions generated. The first Overshoot Day was calculated in the 1970s, and the date has come earlier and earlier each year. Earth Overshoot Day for 2010 was August 21st; for 2021, July 29th. Overshoot Day is calculated annually by the Global Footprint Network.
	Ecological footprint	The total ecological impact (the amount of land, food, water, and other resources) needed to sustain a person or organization. For large populations (such as countries), the total productive capacity of the Earth is sometimes used. For example, on average, the population of the US consumes so many resources that were the rest of the world's population to consume at the same level, so several more Earths would be needed to meet the demand.
	Economic capital	From a planetary perspective, this is the value created by the distribution of revenue derived from the use of natural and human capital. In traditional business terms, it often refers to the distribution of revenue at an organization's disposal for funding business operations and creating profits. From a sustainability perspective, this business concept is expanded to consider the value created from all the ways in which revenue is distributed. Economic capital can be spent on operations or to generate revenue or profits, or held to support access to credit. It can also be used to create additional social and environmental capital.

Terminology		
	Economic sustainability	Economic sustainability relates to an organization's direct impacts on the economy. This extends beyond the important baseline of making sure that an organization is profitable. Economic sustainability concerns how an organization distributes its revenue. Is the organization's distribution of revenues among employees, management, shareholders, and the community reasonable? Does the organization promote and support local economic development through community partnerships or hiring? Is the organization transparent about its financial health, ownership, investments, and advocacy? These are some of the considerations that go into an analysis of economic sustainability.
	Ecosystem	An ecosystem is a dynamic and interdependent community of organisms that interact with each other and their physical environment. An ecosystem can include people, animals, plants, and microorganisms, as well as the environmental conditions that support them.
	Ecosystem services	Functions and benefits provided by the Earth's ecosystem such as food, raw materials, medicines, hydro energy, clean air and water, pest and disease control, soil regeneration, shade, wind, tidal currents, plant pollination, nutrient cycles, and human art, recreation, and enjoyment. Sometimes, these benefits are grouped into four categories: provisioning, regulating, supporting, and cultural.
	Energy management	The process of systematic planning, sourcing, and distribution of energy resources to meet consumption needs while taking into account environmental and economic impacts.
	Environmental footprint	The total of an entity's carbon, waste, and water footprints.

Terminology		
	Environmental justice	Environmental justice refers to inequalities in use and access to environmental resources, such as clean air and water and healthy living conditions. Clean and healthy environments are often reserved for wealthier peoples, giving poorer people less access to clean resources or healthy living conditions. Environmental Justice proponents seek to promote more equal access or distribution of resources and to halt or lower the impact humans have on environmental services, particularly in areas inhabited by poor or disenfranchised people.
	Environmental sustainability	Environmental sustainability includes, and goes beyond being compliant with environmental regulations and laws. Activities include work to reduce energy, carbon, water, and waste. There may be activities to preserve biodiversity. An organization may work to develop and sell Earth- and people-friendly products and services. Generally, environmental sustainability is the practice of identifying the past, current, and potential negative environmental impacts of an organization, and working to eliminate or avoid them. At its best, environmental sustainability creates positive or regenerative impacts, such as creating more renewable energy than is used.
ESG	Environmental, Social, Governance	ESG refers to the business processes, customs, policies, and laws that define expectations for environmental protection, social norms, and good governance.
	Equator Principles	Developed in 2002 by a group of banks, these guidelines are a framework for addressing environmental and social risks in project financing. The purpose of the principles is to screen projects for adverse environmental or human effects in order to safeguard communities and natural habitats. Financial institutions who sign-on to the principles agree not to finance projects that fail to meet these screens. These principles classify projects into three categories depending on these effects and the need to address them.

	Terminology	
	Externalities	Externalities are effects of services, products, or production on those who are not involved in the buyer/seller relationship that occur when unintended consequences from the market behaviors affect an uninvolved third party. They can be either negative (pollution or waste clean-up fees that a community must bear even though it was caused by an individual person or entity) or positive (The Clean Water Act generates positive effects for many who are not regulated by it).
	Forced labor	Forced labor refers to any form of modern slavery, and includes human trafficking, which is the act of moving people from place to place for the purpose of forced labor. The common denominator in all forced labor is the use of fraud or physical and/or psychological force or coercion to exploit and enslave a person. Forced labor includes debt bondage, in which individuals are forced to work to pay off a debt under terms and conditions that make repayment impossible. Victims are among the most vulnerable populations: • women and girls who are sexually exploited; • migrants who are trapped in debt bondage; and • sweatshop workers who are exploited through low or inadequate-in-kind compensation such as food and shelter.
	Fossil fuels	Fossil fuels are fuels formed by natural processes such as anaerobic decomposition of buried dead organisms. The age of the organisms and their resulting fossil fuels is typically millions of years, and sometimes exceeds 650 million years. Fossil fuels contain high percentages of carbon and include coal, petroleum, and natural gas. Source: Wikipedia (https://en.wikipedia.org/wiki/Fossil_fuel).

Terminology		
	Governance	Governance refers to the processes, practices, and relationships by which an organization is controlled and directed. It is the manner in which rights and responsibilities are distributed for making decisions and building a company's culture. An organization's means of governance include values, policies, and accountability and transparency requirements.
	Green building	A comprehensive process for building design and construction with the objective of minimizing adverse environmental impacts, including reducing a building's energy consumption, while contributing to the health and productivity of building occupants. A common metric for green buildings is the LEED (Leadership in Energy and Environmental Design) certification developed by the US Green Building Council (USGBC). See https://www.usgbc.org.
	Greenhouse effect	The greenhouse effect is the process by which radiation from a planet's atmosphere warms the planet's surface to a temperature above what it would be in the absence of its atmosphere. If a planet's atmosphere contains radiatively active gases (i.e., greenhouse gases), the atmosphere radiates energy in all directions. Part of this radiation is directed toward the surface, warming it. Source: Wikipedia (https://en.wikipedia.org/wiki/Greenhouse_effect).
	Greenhouse Gas Protocol	The Greenhouse Gas (GHG) Protocol, developed by World Resources Institute (WRI) and World Business Council on Sustainable Development (WBCSD), sets the global standard for how to measure, manage, and report GHG emissions. Companies and organizations around the world are using GHG Protocol standards and tools to manage their emissions and become more efficient, resilient, and prosperous organizations. See http://www.ghgprotocol.org/.

Terminology		
GHGs	Greenhouse Gases	Gases that contribute to the greenhouse effect by absorbing infrared radiation and trapping heat in the atmosphere. Some GHGs such as carbon dioxide are emitted to the atmosphere through both natural processes and human activities. Others are created and emitted solely through human activities. The gases considered for calculating a carbon footprint are carbon dioxide, methane, nitrous oxide, hydrofluorocarbons, perfluorocarbons, and sulfur hexafluoride.
	Greenwashing	This term merges the concepts of green (environmentally sound) and whitewashing (to conceal or gloss over wrongdoing). Greenwashing is any form of marketing or public relations that links an organization to a positive association with environmental or social issues for an unsustainable product, service, or practice, or wrongly leads the public to believe that one truly green product, service, or practice is representative of all the organization's products, services, or practices.
	Hazardous waste	Hazardous waste is waste that is dangerous or potentially harmful to public health or the environment. Hazardous wastes can be liquids, solids, gases, or sludges, and are ignitable, reactive, corrosive, or toxic. They can be discarded commercial products, like cleaning fluids or pesticides, the by-products of manufacturing processes, or contaminated biological materials. Many of these wastes are subject to regulations affecting their handling, transfer, and disposal. Source: US Environmental Protection Agency (https://www.epa.gov/hw/learn-basics-hazardous-waste).
	Human rights	Human rights are those fundamental rights, freedoms, and standards of treatment to which all people are entitled. They are listed in the United Nations' Universal Declaration of Human Rights. They include such basic, recognized rights as life, liberty, and security of a person, and freedom from slavery and torture. They also include more modern-day rights, such as the rights to privacy, freedom of movement, opinion and expression, decent working conditions, and education.

Terminology		
	Indoor air pollutants	Indoor air pollutants are airborne contaminants inside buildings including the off-gases from furniture, carpets, and wall coverings, dust, mold, and other harmful particulates.
	Institutional investor	An institutional investor is an entity that pools money to purchase securities, real property, and other investment assets or originate loans. Institutional investors include banks, insurance companies, pensions, hedge funds, REITs, investment advisors, endowments, and mutual funds. Operating companies which invest excess capital in these types of assets may also be included in the term. Activist institutional investors may also influence corporate governance by exercising voting rights in their investments.
	Intangible assets	Intangible assets are nonmonetary assets that have no physical substance. They are resources that a business controls and expects will deliver economic benefits. Traditional examples include brand equity, intellectual property, trade secrets, and goodwill. Emerging concepts and circumstances include refined ways of thinking about goodwill such as reputation (e.g., based on operations and supply chain management), social license to operate (e.g., based on transparency, trust, and accountability), and ability to innovate (e.g., based on collaboration and business partnerships). See also definitions of social capital, natural capital, and economic capital.

Terminology		
	Integrated Bottom Line	A process, described by Theo Ferguson, for integrating financial, environmental, and social costs and benefits into a unified measure of business activity. Conventional objectives of profitability, competitive advantage, efficiency, and economic growth are judged successful by their compatibility with biodiversity, ecological sustainability, equity, community support, and maximized well-being for a variety of stakeholders. An Integrated Bottom Line differs from a Triple Bottom Line in that all measures are combined into one balance sheet and income statement (instead of separated in three, different ones). For example, short-term, sustainable resource use is encouraged to maximize efficiency because it is factored into accounts payable. Ecosystem restoration is entered as long-term debt. Market forces are tempered by distribution equity, and social forces are elevated through premiums placed on human capital. Business plans can be redesigned so that qualitative outcomes have equal or greater measure to quantitative goals.
	Integrated Reporting	The International Integrated Reporting Council (IIRC) defines the integrated report as "a concise communication about how an organization's strategy governance, performance and prospects, in the context of its external environment, lead to the creation of value in the short, medium and long term." Its goal is to give a holistic view of a company, based on performance, business model, and strategy in the context of a company's material social and environmental issues.

Terminology		
	Kyoto Protocol	The Kyoto Protocol is an international treaty, which extends the 1992 United Nations Framework Convention on Climate Change (UNFCCC) that commits State Parties to reduce greenhouse gas emissions. It is based on the premise that (a) global warming exists and (b) man-made carbon dioxide emissions have caused it. The Kyoto Protocol was adopted in Kyoto, Japan, on 11 December 1997 and entered into force on 16 February 2005. There are currently 192 parties to the Protocol. The Kyoto Protocol implemented the objective of the UNFCCC to fight global warming by reducing greenhouse gas concentrations in the atmosphere to "a level that would prevent dangerous anthropogenic interference with the climate system" (Art. 2). The Protocol is based on the principle of common but differentiated responsibilities: it puts the obligation to reduce current emissions on developed countries on the basis that they are historically responsible for the current levels of greenhouse gases in the atmosphere.
LEED	Leadership in Energy & Environmental Design	LEED is a set of rating systems for the sustainable design, construction, operation, and maintenance of commercial buildings, homes, and neighborhoods. There are four levels of building certification: Platinum, Gold, Silver, and Certified. The US Green Building Council (USGBC) developed LEED. The Green Building Certification Institute (GBCI) manages accreditation of individuals and certification of buildings under the LEED programs.
LCA	Life cycle assessment	The collection and examination of the overall impacts of a product or service from materials sourcing to production to distribution to disposal. LCA focusses on the energy inputs and outputs and the materials used in order to gauge social, economic, and environmental impacts of the product or service. An LCA is also being developed for social and socioeconomic production and consumption impacts on workers, local communities, consumers, society, and all other value chain actors.

Terminology		
	Limits to Growth	The idea that there are natural thresholds that cannot be exceeded without risking the health of the entire system. Limits are essential to the idea that natural capital must be conserved. The concept is also at the heart of several prominent economic theories and many people's inability to regard change or conservation as necessary since they don't recognize that limits exist on natural capital. Limits to Growth was a 1972 book by Donella and Dennis Meadows and Jørgen Randers, modeling the consequences of a rapidly growing world population. It prompted many changes in the 1970s with regard to resource use in order to avoid the projections in the book. The most recent updated version was published in June 2004 by Chelsea Green Publishing Company under the name Limits to Growth: The 30-Year Update.
	Living wage	A living wage is a wage that is high enough to support basic needs. The wage is calculated based on a number of factors, including location, taking into account geographic variations in the cost of living, family size, and the number of working adults in the family.
	Low carbon economy	An economy based on low carbon power sources that therefore has a minimal output of greenhouse gas emissions. Source: Wikipedia (https://en.wikipedia.org/wiki/Low-carbon_economy Sometimes). This is also referred to as decarbonization or decarbonized economy.
	Materiality (sustainability reporting)	For purposes of reporting under various voluntary sustainability reporting frameworks, materiality is the concept of identifying, prioritizing, and reporting on sustainability-related issues and impacts that are most relevant and of greatest importance to the stakeholder audience of the report. Isolating issues in this way allows an organization to focus its resources and the attention of its stakeholder audience on the most significant sustainability issues for the particular organization. The determination of what is material will depend on the audience and the framework under which information is being reported.

Terminology		
	Materiality (SEC disclosures)	For SEC reporting purposes and under the voluntary SASB standards, information is deemed to be material if there is "a substantial likelihood" that a "reasonable investor" would view the information as "significantly alter[ing] the 'total mix' of information made available." TSC Indus. v. Northway, Inc., 426 U.S. 438, 449 (1976).
	Materiality assessment	The process of having management and various stakeholders identify and prioritize an organization's most significant sustainability issues. The process clearly identifies convergence and divergence on issues between stakeholders and management. The convergence issues typically form the core focus of an organization's sustainability strategy.
MDGs	Millennium Development Goals	The Millennium Development Goals, established by declaration at the United Nations Millennium Summit in 2000, are eight goals with measurable targets and clear deadlines for improving the lives of the world's poorest people. To meet these goals and eradicate poverty, leaders of 189 countries signed the historic millennium declaration. They sunsetted in 2015 and were superceded by the Sustainable Development Goals.
	Millenium ecosystem assessment	A United Nations-funded study of the state of ecosystem services around the world. It is the most extensive and accurate study of its kind. Launched in 2001 and completed in March 2005, the Millennium Ecosystem Assessment reports on habitat status, fishing, coral reefs, forests, water use, atmospheric carbon and temperature, weather, land use, and population. More than 1300 scientists from 95 countries synthesized research, data, and models from a variety of sources to develop a set of 15 reports as well as scenarios. Accelerating changes humans have made to the ecosystem are creating high risks for people and businesses as well as some opportunities. See https://www.millenniumassessment.org.

Terminology		
	Natural capital	From a planetary perspective, this is the stock of natural resources that yields a flow of valuable ecosystem goods and services into the future. For business organizations, natural capital is a valuation concept that measures the organization's use of natural resources and the effect of that use on the availability of those resources into the future. Environmental destruction or degradation decreases an organization's natural capital, while restoration, substitution, or regenerative activities increase it.
	Natural resources	Natural resources are things that exist in nature that have value because they are necessary or useful to humans. They can include both renewable and nonrenewable resources.
	Net Zero	A target of negating greenhouse gases produced by human activity, by reducing emissions and absorbing carbon dioxide from the atmosphere.
NGO	Nongovernmental organization	A nonprofit group or organization that is run neither by business or by government and is created to realize particular social or economic pursuits, through research, activism, training, promotion, advocacy, lobbying, or community service.
	Nonrenewable	Any material (including a source of energy) that cannot be replenished in full, at the same quality, within the period of time during which it will be used up.
	Off-gassing	Off-gassing (sometimes called out-gassing) is when a substance releases chemicals in gaseous form under normal conditions of temperature and pressure. Many chemicals released during the off-gassing process are potentially harmful to human health when inhaled or absorbed through the skin and mucus membranes. Examples of off-gassing substances are paints, adhesives, certain fabrics, and many plastics, fire retardants, and cleaning chemicals. Many of these are volatile organic compounds, some of which are potentially hazardous, particularly in enclosed spaces.

Terminology		
	Oversight of sustainability	Oversight of sustainability activities by a board of directors means that the company has established operational, financial, risk management, and reporting processes which ensure that the board receives the information it needs to effectively address significant environmental, social, and governance issues.
	Overview Effect	The overview effect is a cognitive shift in awareness reported by some astronauts during spaceflight, often while viewing the Earth from outer space. It is the experience of seeing firsthand the reality of the Earth in space, which is immediately understood to be a tiny, fragile ball of life, "hanging in the void," shielded and nourished by a paper-thin atmosphere. From space, national boundaries vanish, the conflicts that divide people become less important, and the need to create a planetary society with the united will to protect this "pale blue dot" becomes both obvious and imperative. Source: Wikipedia (https://en.wikipedia.org/wiki/Overview_effect).
	Paris Agreement	The Paris Agreement is an international agreement within the United Nations Framework Convention on Climate Change (UNFCCC) related to reduction of GHG emissions, and climate change adaptation and finance. Created at the 21st Conference of the Parties of the UNFCCC in Paris in 2015, the agreement went into effect on November 4, 2016. Signatory nations pledged to measure, monitor, and reduce their greenhouse gas emissions.
	Patient capital	Investment strategies that provide social and environmental returns in addition to financial returns with an emphasis on returns over the long term. While a longer investment horizon and/or a smaller financial return may be inherent in individual patient capital investments, neither of these conditions are required of patient capital investments.
	Planetary boundary	A planetary boundary is a limit that defines the safe operating space for humanity with respect to the Earth system and its associated biophysical subsystems and processes.

		Terminology
	Precautionary Principle	An approach to determining whether a given process or policy should be pursued or continued based on an analysis of the social, economic, or environmental risks associated with that activity. Not all risks are known when a new practice is introduced or a current one is reexamined, and the ethical approach in light of implied or expected (but not confirmed) negative impacts is to stop such practices as a precaution until more is known about the impacts. The Precautionary Principle has been used in many health- and environment-related issues, such as food safety, industrial manufacturing, product recalls, and the approval or recall of pharmaceuticals.
PRI	Principles for Responsible Investment	Six PRIs developed by the investment community under the aegis of the United Nations Principles for Responsible Investment (UNPRI), a UN-supported network of international investors, in the belief that sustainability issues can affect the performance of investment portfolios, and must be given appropriate consideration by investors. The principles provide a voluntary framework by which all investors can incorporate sustainability issues into their decision-making and operational practices.
PBC	Public Benefit Corporation	See Benefit Corporation.
	Reporting assurance	An independent, third-party review of the processes used to generate the information contained a report, resulting in an objective, written statement supporting the integrity of that information. A negative finding would result in either no assurance or a qualified statement.
	Reputational capital	Reputational capital is part of an organization's social capital. It is a qualitative measure of a company's intangible assets such as ethics, integrity, and trustworthiness.

Terminology		
	Resilience	Resilience in a business context is an organization's ability to recognize, quickly respond to, and recover from disruptions or rapid changes and resulting risks. Resilience includes the capacity to identify the hidden opportunities in risk events to make advances, realize competitive advantage, or identify solutions that produce new revenue.
	Scope 1 carbon emissions	Scope 1 carbon emissions include all greenhouse gas emissions that come from directly sources owned or controlled by an organization.
	Scope 2 carbon emissions	Scope 2 carbon emissions include all indirect greenhouse gas emissions that occur because of an organization's consumption of purchased electricity, heat, or steam.
	Scope 3 carbon emissions	Scope 3 emissions are all indirect upstream and downstream greenhouse gas emissions (not included in scope 2) that occur in an organization's value chain for its benefit (e.g., emissions associated with the production, distribution, use, and disposal of its products).
	Shareholder activism	Shareholder activism is the process of dialogue between company executives and shareholders who file resolutions seeking change. Investor pressure on corporate executives often garners media attention, which adds even more pressure on corporations. Shareholder activism, also known as shareholder advocacy, first gained momentum during the 1970s when religious investors formed a coalition (the Interfaith Center on Corporate Responsibility) to advocate for socially responsible changes in corporate policies. When activism relates to sustainability, it serves to educate the public on often-ignored social, environmental, and governance issues and can lead companies to improve their behavior and become more sustainable.
	Sin stock	A sin stock is the ownership interest in a company that engages in activities or creates or sells products that are viewed as contributing to a social ill or sin. What activities or products meet this definition is in the eye of the beholder. Examples are alcohol, tobacco, gambling, firearms, human trafficking, and mercenaries.

Terminology		
	SMART framework	The SMART framework is an acronym of criteria that are useful in guiding certain decisions. The SMART framework is often used in the context of setting goals and choosing metrics. In that context, the SMART criteria are: • Specific: clear and focused • Measurable: quantifiable or qualitatively indicates progress; comparable • Achievable: agreed upon and aligned with organizational goals • Realistic: cost-effective and within resource constraints • Time-bound: completed within a specific timeframe
	Social capital	A business's value derived from human assets, stakeholder relationships, business practices, reputation, and other intangibles associated with the way the organization engages with or treats people.
	Social justice	Social justice is an interactive process, not an outcome, in which members of a community seek: • fair (re)distribution of resources, opportunities, and responsibilities; • challenge the roots of oppression and injustice; • empower all people to exercise self-determination and realize their full potential; and • build social solidarity and community capacity for collaborative action (School of Social Welfare, University of California, 2011). It is based on the principle that all individuals, groups, and communities are equal and thus are entitled regardless of gender, race, wealth, sexuality, or heritage to receive fair and just treatment.

Terminology		
	Social license to operate	Refers to the level of acceptance or approval by society of an organization and its operations. The term was coined in the late 1990s by Canadian mining executive Jim Cooney. In the 1980s, local communities started to pressure companies to integrate more sustainable practices into their operations. The change in corporate culture resulting from social pressure gained much attention and ultimately led to the idea that companies need to acquire "social permission" beyond meeting legal requirements in order to operate a business successfully.
SROI	Social Return on Investment	The measure of an investment's ability to produce social value in a community or broader society. An attempt to monetize social value in order to help investors assess potential investments based on returns outside of traditional financial measures.
	Social sustainability	Social sustainability refers to how an organization treats and engages with the people connected to the organization. Efforts to promote employee and supplier diversity and equal opportunity show the organization values inclusiveness. Good governance and ethics practices show management's commitment to living the organization's stated values. Product responsibility and workforce development and wellness programs show concern for customers and employees. Two-way stakeholder engagement shows that an organization respects and at least hears the voice of those most relevant to the health of the organization. Community needs-based philanthropy reveals an organization's sense of responsibility for the local community's well-being.
SRI	Socially Responsible Investing or Sustainable, Responsible, Impact	Whether intended to mean Socially Responsible Investing or Sustainable, Responsible, Impact, this term refers to an investment strategy that considers both financial return and the ways in which the investment will promote or bring about a change for the betterment of society and, in the latter case, the planet.

Terminology		
	Stakeholder engagement	Stakeholder engagement is the process by which an organization involves people who may be affected by, or who can influence, its decisions. Companies engage their stakeholders in dialogue to find out what social and environmental issues matter most to them. They do this to improve decision-making and accountability. An underlying principle of stakeholder engagement is that stakeholders' input is valuable and better informs the decision-making process. This differentiates stakeholder engagement from communication processes that seek to issue a message or sway groups to agree with a decision that is already made.
	Stakeholders	Any party (internal or external to an organization) that can influence or be influenced by an organization's activities. The degree of influence determines how key a party is to the organization. Stakeholders are not necessarily directly involved with doing the organization's work. For example, World Wildlife Federation works to protect wildlife. If an organization's activities have a big enough impact on wildlife, World Wildlife Federation could become a stakeholder.
	Sullivan principles	The Sullivan principles are the names of two corporate codes of conduct, developed by the African-American preacher Rev. Leon Sullivan, promoting corporate social responsibility: • The original Sullivan principles were developed in 1977 to apply economic pressure on South Africa in protest of its system of apartheid. The principles eventually gained wide adoption among US-based corporations. • The new global Sullivan principles were jointly unveiled in 1999 by Rev. Sullivan and United Nations Secretary General Kofi Annan. The new and expanded corporate code of conduct, as opposed to the originals' specific focus on South African apartheid, was designed to increase the active participation of corporations in the advancement of human rights and social justice at the international level. Source: Wikipedia (https://en.wikipedia.org/wiki/Sullivan_principles).

Terminology		
	Supplier diversity	Supplier diversity is a business strategy to ensure that a company is purchasing its important materials, products, and services from as diverse a base of suppliers as possible to support economic development, promote competition, expand purchasing channels, and improve innovation capacity.
	Sustainability	A simple dictionary definition of sustainability is the "capacity to endure." Implicit in that definition is the concept of thriving into the future. The capacity to endure requires balancing short- and long-term perspectives to managing risks and seizing opportunities that arise from current conditions and trends. To do this, one has to examine, balance, and integrate social, environmental, and economic considerations. At its core, sustainability is about value creation and innovation. Here are a few definitions of sustainability in the context of operating a business: The Dow Jones Sustainability Index: "Corporate Sustainability is a business approach that creates long-term shareholder value by embracing opportunities and managing risks deriving from economic, environmental and social developments." Andrew Savitz in the Triple Bottom Line: "A sustainable company is one that creates profit while protecting the environment and improving the lives with whom it interacts." An Eloquent Anonymous Person: "A sustainable organization engages in the simultaneous pursuit of economic prosperity, environmental stewardship, and social responsibility."
SMS	Sustainability Management System	A documented set of processes and practices that memorialize how an organization plans, manages, collects data on, implements, communicates about, and improves its sustainability performance. It follows the traditional "Plan-Do-Check-Act" framework of most management systems.

Terminology		
	Sustainable design	The process of developing products, services, and organizations that comply with the principles of economic, social, and ecological sustainability. There are many principles of sustainable design, including a customer-centric approach, dematerialization, transmaterialization, and biomimicry.
	Sustainable development	Development that meets the needs of the present without compromising the ability of future generations to meet their own needs.
SDGs	Sustainable Development Goals	SDGs are a global development framework of 17 interlinked global goals established in 2015 by the United Nations General Assembly. The goals are designed to achieve a better and more sustainable future for the world by the year 2030 as part of a United Nations (UN) Resolution called the 2030 Agenda. The SDGs succeed the UN's Millennium Development Goals which ended in 2015. The 17 SDGs are: (1) No Poverty, (2) Zero Hunger, (3) Good Health and Well-being, (4) Quality Education, (5) Gender Equality, (6) Clean Water and Sanitation, (7) Affordable and Clean Energy, (8) Decent Work and Economic Growth, (9) Industry, Innovation and Infrastructure, (10) Reducing Inequality, (11) Sustainable Cities and Communities, (12) Responsible Consumption and Production, (13) Climate Action, (14) Life Below Water, (15) Life On Land, (16) Peace, Justice, and Strong Institutions, (17) Partnerships for the Goals.
	Sustainable materials management	A systemic approach to using and reusing materials and resources most productively and sustainably throughout their life cycles, from the point of resource extraction through material disposal. Sustainable materials management seeks to minimize the amount of materials used and all the associated environmental impacts, as well as accounts for economic efficiency and social considerations.

Terminology		
	Systems	Systems are a set of elements or parts that are coherently organized and interconnected in a pattern or structure. This pattern or structure thus produces a characteristic set of behaviors, often classified as its "function" or "purpose" that form a united whole (Meadows, 2008).
	Systems thinking	The practice of looking at a pattern, structure, or organized set of elements or parts (a system) to understand, analyze, and act based upon the relationships among those elements or parts and with other systems. Systems thinking is used in solving complex problems as a method of anticipating and avoiding unintended consequences. Unintended consequences most often occur when components of the system are acted upon in isolation.
	Take, Make, Waste	The Take, Make, Waste model, sometimes called "cradle-to-grave," follows a linear system of industrial production and consumption. The model is as follows: • Extract (dig up, cut down, or drill out) natural resources • Manufacture and process into usable products • Sell the products • Buy and use the products • Dispose of the materials remaining at the end of the product's useful life in the trash or recycling • Haul the disposed materials to landfills, incinerators, or recycling centers
	Take-back program	A "producer responsibility" approach to facilitating reuse or recycling whereby consumers return used products back to the company that produced them. Laws mandating company take back programs attempt to create incentives for companies to incorporate reusability/recyclability considerations into their initial product design.

		Terminology	
	Total cost accounting	Total cost accounting is a financial tool used to provide a more complete assessment of the true profitability of an entity by taking into account a wider range of direct and indirect costs and savings. It uses longer time horizons that reflect the full economic or commercial life of the project, incorporates the time value of money, reveals hidden costs, and considers uncertain or less quantifiable costs.	
	Tragedy of the Commons	A situation where individuals acting independently and rationally according to their own self-interest behave contrary to the best interests of the whole group by depleting a commonly held resource (e.g., the environment, a pasture, the atmosphere). The phrase was originally coined by William Forster Lloyd and later used by Garrett Hardin in a 1968 article by the same name.	
TBL	Triple Bottom Line	An expansion of the traditional measurement and reporting framework for businesses that takes into account environmental, social, and economic performance in addition to financial performance. See other definitions for social sustainability, environmental sustainability, economic sustainability in the glossary.	
	UN Global Compact	The United Nations Global Compact is a strategic policy initiative for businesses that are committed to aligning their operations and strategies with ten universally accepted principles in the areas of human rights, labor, environment, and anti-corruption.	
	Unintended consequences	Results from actions that were not expected or intended. Unintended consequences are often negative and are due to systems being more complex and interconnected than we may realize—especially environmental and social systems. The Precautionary Principle is an attempt at helping individuals, organizations, and societies to be more mindful of the effects of their decisions before taking action or making changes. It is being increasingly adopted by organizations around the world.	

Terminology		
	Upcycle	A term coined by William McDonaugh and Michael Braungart. The process of converting an industrial nutrient (material) into something of similar or greater value in its second life. Aluminum and glass, for example, can usually be upcycled into the same quality of aluminum and glass as the original products. Upcycling is sometimes referred to as creative reuse.
	Value chain	A value chain is a set of activities that a firm operating in a specific industry performs in order to deliver a valuable product or service for the market. The concept comes from business management and was first described and popularized by Michael Porter in his 1985 best-seller, Competitive Advantage: Creating and Sustaining Superior Performance. The appropriate level for constructing a value chain is the business unit, not division or corporate level. Products pass through a chain of activities in order, and at each activity the product gains some value. The chain of activities gives the products more added value than the sum of added values of all activities.
VDM	Value Driver Model	The Value Driver Model (VDM) is a tool developed jointly by the United Nations Global Compact and UN Principles for Responsible Investment for determining and communicating the value of sustainability to business. It was designed to enhance investors' understanding of how sustainability can protect and drive performance and financial value for a company. The VDM provides a framework for companies to better understand and communicate how sustainability strategies and performance translate into measurable financial value.
	Waste footprint	The total amount of waste generated by an entity, which takes into account all waste streams: recyclables, landfill waste, compostables, and super-recyclables.

Terminology		
	Waste management	The process of reducing the negative effects of waste on the environment and society, including human health and well-being.
	Water footprint	The total amount of water used or consumed by an entity.
	Water management	Water management is the control, movement, protection, use, and preservation of fresh water resources to minimize damage to life and property and maximize availability for essential needs.
	Zero waste	The goal of developing products and services, managing their use and deployment, and creating recycling systems and markets in order to eliminate the volume and toxicity of waste and materials and conserve and recover all resources. Implementing zero waste eliminates all discharges to land, water, or air that may be a threat to planetary, human, animal, or plant health. Many cities and states already have set zero-waste goals.

Organizations		
Common Acronym	**Organization**	**Description**
BSR	Business for Social Responsibility	BSR™ is an organization of sustainable business experts that works with its global network of the world's leading companies to build a just and sustainable world. With offices in Asia, Europe, and North America, BSR™ provides insight, advice, and collaborative initiatives to help its member companies see a changing world more clearly, create long-term business value, and scale impact. Source: BSR website.
	Business Round Table	Business Roundtable is an association of chief executive officers of America's leading companies working to promote a thriving US economy and expanded opportunity for all Americans through sound public policy. Source: Business Round Table website.
CDP	CDP	Formerly known as the Carbon Disclosure Project, the CDP is an international organization of institutional investors promoting greater transparency around corporate management of climate change issues. The CDP annually invites the world's largest corporations to publicly disclose their greenhouse gas emissions and climate change management strategies. Through the CDP's supply chain initiative, large companies request that their suppliers report greenhouse gas emissions and climate change management strategies. Source: CDP website.
CECP CIF	CECP's CEO Investor Forum	CECP's CIF empowers CEOs on their journey to refocus investor expectations toward the long term and supports the work of investor relations, corporate sustainability, corporate social responsibility, corporate communications, and the corporate secretary. Source: CECP website.

Organizations		
CECP SII	CECP's Strategic Investor Initiative	The Strategic Investor Initiative is a coalition of thought leaders committed to the long-term movement. Collectively, SII is developing a new platform for leading companies to create, convey, and deliver long-term plans to long-term investors. SII's vision is to spark the movement of trillions of dollars of capital to companies demonstrating performance excellence over the long term. SII provides tools and resources designed to introduce and support market behaviors that ultimately deliver sustained long-term value for all stakeholders. Source: CECP website.
CECP	Chief Executives For Corporate Purpose	CECP is a CEO-led coalition that believes that a company's social strategy—how it engages with key stakeholders including employees, communities, investors, and customers—determines company success. Founded in 1999 by actor and philanthropist Paul Newman and other business leaders to create a better world through business, CECP has grown to a movement of more than 200 of the world's largest companies that represent $11.3 trillion in revenues, $23.8 billion in societal investment, 17.4 million employees, and $15 trillion in assets under management. CECP helps companies transform their social strategy by providing customized connections and networking, counsel and support, benchmarking and trends, and awareness building and recognition. Source: CECP website.
	Climate Action 100+	Climate Action 100+ is an investor-led initiative to ensure the world's largest corporate greenhouse gas emitters take necessary action on climate change. Source: Climate Action 100+ website.

Organizations		
	Climate Majority Project	Majority Action is a nonprofit, nonpartisan organization that merged in 2018 with the 50/50 Climate Project to launch the Climate Majority Project and continue the work of educating and engaging investors on the critical role of corporate governance in confronting climate change. The Climate Majority Project works to harness the power of investors to promote climate responsibility on corporate boards and accelerate economy-wide decarbonization. Working with some of the world's largest institutional investors to encourage public companies to adopt responsible corporate governance practices and implement long-term strategies in line with the scale of climate challenge, it uses original research, investor education, corporate engagement, and public communications. Source: Climate Majority Project website.
Ceres	Coalition of Environmentally Responsible Economies	Ceres is a nonprofit organization working to transform the economy to build a just and sustainable future for people and the planet. It works with influential capital market leaders to solve sustainability challenges. Through its networks and global collaborations of investors, companies, and nonprofits, Ceres drives action and inspires equitable market-based and policy solutions throughout the economy. Source: Ceres website.
COP	Conference of the Parties	COP is the supreme decision-making body of the United Nations Framework Convention on Climate Change (UNFCC). All States that are Parties to the Convention are represented at the COP, at which they review the implementation of the Convention and any other legal instruments that the COP adopts and take decisions necessary to promote the effective implementation of the Convention, including institutional and administrative arrangements. Source: UNFCCC website.

Organizations		
CAROL	Corporate Alliance for the Rule of Law	This is a corporate advocacy group to support, promote, and strengthen the rule of law as the foundation for social and economic development and the protection of personal freedoms. Source: Corporate Alliance for the Rule of Law website.
	EcoVadis	Founded in 2007, EcoVadis is a provider of business sustainability ratings, with a global network of more than 75,000 rated companies. Source: EcoVadis website.
	Equileap	Headquartered in Amsterdam, Equileap is a provider of data and insights on gender equality in the corporate sector. Equileap researches and ranks over 3,500 public companies around the world using a unique and comprehensive Gender Equality Scorecard™ with 19 criteria, including the gender balance of the workforce, senior management and board of directors, as well as the pay gap, parental leave, and sexual harassment. Source: Equileap website.
FLA	Fair Labor Association	FLA is a collaborative effort of universities, civil society organizations, and socially responsible companies dedicated to protecting workers' rights around the world. It is an international organization, headquartered in Washington, DC, with offices in China and Switzerland. FLA places the onus on companies to voluntarily meet internationally recognized labor standards wherever their products are made. Source: FLA website.
FASB	Financial Accounting Standards Board	FASB is a private, nonprofit organization whose primary purpose is to establish and improve generally accepted accounting principles (GAAP) within the US in the public's interest. The Securities and Exchange Commission (SEC) designated the FASB as the organization responsible for setting accounting standards for public companies in the US. The FASB replaced the American Institute of Certified Public Accountants' (AICPA) Accounting Principles Board (APB) on July 1, 1973. Source: FASB website.

Organizations		
FCTLGlobal	Focusing Capital on the Long-Term	FCLTGlobal's mission is to rebalance capital markets to support a long-term, sustainable economy. It is a nonprofit organization supported by leading companies and investors worldwide that develops research and practical tools to drive long-term value creation for companies, savers, and communities. Source: FCTLGlobal website.
US SIF	Forum for Sustainable and Responsible Investment	US SIF works to advance sustainable investing across all asset classes. Its mission is to rapidly shift investment practices toward sustainability, focusing on long-term investment and the generation of positive social and environmental impacts. Its members, representing $5 trillion in assets under management or advisement, include investment management and advisory firms, mutual fund companies, research firms, financial planners and advisors, broker-dealers, banks, credit unions, community development organizations, nonprofit associations, and asset owners. US SIF is supported in its work by the US SIF Foundation, a 501(C)(3) organization that undertakes educational, research, and programmatic activities to advance the mission of US SIF. Source: US SIF website.
GIIN	Global Impact Investing Network	GIIN is a nonprofit 501c(3) organization dedicated to increasing the scale and effectiveness of impact investing. The GIIN builds critical infrastructure and supports activities, education, and research that help accelerate the development of a coherent impact investing industry. Source: GIIN website.
GRI	Global Reporting Initiative	GRI is an international organization that operates one of the world's most widely used public reporting standards for triple-bottom-line sustainability, focusing on human rights, labor, environment, and corporate governance. Source: GRI website.

Organizations		
HCMC	Human Capital Management Coalition	HCMC is a cooperative effort among a diverse group of asset owners to further elevate human capital management as a critical component in company performance. The Coalition engages companies and other market participants with the aim of understanding and improving how human capital management contributes to the creation of long-term shareholder value. Source: HCMC website.
	IFRS Foundation	IFRS Foundation is a not-for-profit, public interest organization established to develop a single set of high-quality, understandable, enforceable, and globally accepted accounting standards—IFRS Standards—and to promote and facilitate adoption of the standards. IFRS Standards are set by the IFRS Foundation's standard-setting body, the International Accounting Standards Board. Source: IFRS Foundation website.
ISS	Institutional Shareholder Services, Inc.	Founded in 1985, Institutional Shareholder Services group of companies (ISS) empowers investors and companies to build for long-term and sustainable growth by providing high-quality data, analytics, and insight. ISS is a provider of corporate governance and responsible investment solutions, market intelligence, fund services, and events and editorial content for institutional investors and corporations, globally. Source: ISS website.
ICCR	Interfaith Center for Corporate Responsibility	In operation for 50 years, ICCR pioneered the use of shareholder advocacy to press companies on environmental, social, and governance issues. The coalition of over 300 global institutional investors currently represents more than $4 trillion in managed assets. Source: ICCR website.
IASB	International Accounting Standards Board	IASB is an independent, private-sector body that develops, approves, and promotes international financial reporting standards (IFRS) for firms in many countries outside the US. The IASB was established in 2001 and operates under the oversight of the IFRS Foundation.

Organizations		
IIRC	International Integrated Reporting Council	IIRC) is a global coalition of regulators, investors, companies, standard setters, the accounting profession, and NGOs. The coalition promotes communication about value creation as the next step in the evolution of corporate reporting. Its mission is to establish integrated reporting and thinking within mainstream business practice as the norm in the public and private sectors. The IIRC's vision is to align capital allocation and corporate behavior to wider goals of financial stability and sustainable development through the cycle of integrated reporting and thinking. Source: IIRC website.
ILO	International Labor Organization	ILO is a United Nations agency whose mandate is to advance social and economic justice through setting international labor standards. Founded in October 1919 under the League of Nations, it is the first and oldest specialized agency of the United Nations. The ILO's international labor standards are broadly aimed at ensuring accessible, productive, and sustainable work worldwide in conditions of freedom, equity, security, and dignity. Source: Wikipedia (https://en.wikipedia.org/wiki/International_Labour_Organization).
	Majority Action	Majority Action is a nonprofit, nonpartisan organization that empowers shareholders to hold corporations accountable to high standards of corporate governance, social responsibility, and long-term value creation. Majority Action merged in 2018 with the 50/50 Climate Project. See Climate Majority Project. Source: Majority Action website.
MSCI	MSCI Inc.	MSCI Inc., is an American finance company, serving as a global provider of equity, fixed income, hedge fund stock market indexes, multi-asset portfolio analysis tools, and ESG products. Source: MSCI website.

Organizations		
NOAA	National Oceanic and Atmospheric Administration	NOAA is an American scientific agency within the US Department of Commerce focused on the conditions of the oceans and the atmosphere. Formed in 1970. Source: Wikipedia.
NGFS	Network of Central Banks and Supervisors for Greening the Financial System	The Central Banks and Supervisors Network for Greening the Financial System is a group of Central Banks and Supervisors who exchange experiences, share best practices, contribute to the development of environment and climate risk management in the financial sector, and mobilize mainstream finance to support the transition toward a sustainable economy. Its purpose is to define and promote best practices to be implemented within and outside of the Membership of the NGFS and to conduct or commission analytical work on green finance. Source: NGFS website.
OGCI	Oil & Gas Climate Initiative	OGCI is a CEO-led initiative that aims to accelerate the industry response to climate change. OGCI member companies explicitly support the Paris Agreement and its aims. As leaders in the industry, accounting for almost 30% of global-operated oil and gas production, OGCI aims to leverage its collective strength and expand the pace and scope of the industry's transitions to a low-carbon future. Source: OGCI website.
	One Planet Sovereign Wealth Fund Framework	Following the 2015 Paris Agreement to collectively mitigate the effects of climate change, the One Planet Summit was held on 12 December 2017, which was followed by the Climate Finance Day, recognizing the important role played by this sector. Given both their influence and long-term investment horizons, Sovereign Wealth Funds are uniquely positioned to promote long-term value creation and sustainable market outcomes. Accordingly, the "One Planet Sovereign Wealth Fund Working Group" was established at the event to accelerate efforts to integrate financial risks and opportunities related to climate change in the management of large, long-term asset pools. Source: OnePlanet SWF website.

Organizations		
OSCI	Open-Source Climate Initiative	OS-C is establishing an Open-Source collaboration community to build a software platform that will dramatically boost global capital flows into climate change mitigation and resilience. Through a nonprofit, noncompetitive organization, OS-C will aggregate the best available data, modeling and computing, and data science worldwide into an AI-enhanced physical-economic model that functions like an operating system, enabling powerful applications for climate-integrated investing in a world where the future will be very different from the past. Source: OS-C website.
	RE100	RE100 is a global initiative bringing together influential businesses driving the transition to 100% renewable electricity. Led by the Climate Group and in partnership with CDP, RE 100's mission is to accelerate change toward zero-carbon grids at scale. Source: RE 100 website.
	Refinitiv	Refinitiv, an LSEG (London Stock Exchange Group) business, is a provider of financial markets data and infrastructure (including ESG investing, sustainable finance review, and managing ESG risk), with $6.25 billion in revenue, over 40,000 customers and 400,000 end-users across 190 countries. Source: Refinitiv website.
	RepRisk	RepRisk AG is an environmental, social, and corporate governance data science company based in Zurich, Switzerland, specializing in ESG and business-conduct risk research, and quantitative solutions. The company runs an online due-diligence database that allows clients to monitor and assess the risk exposure of companies, infrastructure projects, sectors, and countries related to 28 ESG issues. The issues are mapped to the 10 principles of the United Nations Global Compact, the Sustainability Accounting Standards Board (SASB) Materiality Map, and the United Nations Sustainable Development Goals (SDGs). Source: Wikipedia (https://en.wikipedia.org/wiki/RepRisk).

Organizations		
RBA	Responsible Business Alliancea	Founded in 2004, the Responsible Business Alliance, formerly the Electronic Industry Citizenship Coalition (EICC), is a nonprofit organization comprising electronics, retail, auto, and toy companies committed to supporting the rights and well-being of workers and communities worldwide affected by the global supply chain. RBA members commit and are held accountable to a common Code of Conduct and utilize a range of RBA training and assessment tools to support continual improvement in the social, environmental, and ethical responsibility of their supply chains. Source: RBA website.
	RobecoSAM	In business for over 25 years, RobecoSAM is one of the original ESG rating natives, and is known for its work on Sustainable Investing. RobecoSAM is the ingredient brand Robeco uses to designate selected SI intelligence and SI research and tooling, as well as its impact funds. Source: Robeco website.
SBTi	Science Based Targets initiative	SBTi is a partnership between CDP, the United Nations Global Compact, World Resources Institute (WRI), and the World Wide Fund for Nature (WWF). The SBTi call to action is one of the We Mean Business Coalition commitments. SBTi drives ambitious climate action in the private sector by enabling companies to set science-based emissions reduction targets. Science-based targets show companies how much and how quickly they need to reduce their greenhouse gas (GHG) emissions to prevent the worst effects of climate change. Source: SBTi website.
SASB	Sustainability Accounting Standards Board	SASB is an independent 501(c)3 nonprofit organization with a mission to develop sustainability-accounting standards that help public companies disclose relevant, material information to investors. Source: SASB website.

Organizations		
SDSN	Sustainable Development Solutions Network	SDSN mobilizes global scientific and technological expertise to promote integrated, practical solutions for sustainable development, including the implementation of the Sustainable Development Goals (SDGs) and the Paris Climate Agreement, through education, research, policy analysis, and global cooperation. Source: SDSN website.
SFPA	Sustainable Food Policy Alliance	SFPA seeks to accelerate the pace of change in the food industry through individual company leadership and collective support for public policies that raise the bar and inspire further action in this critical journey. Source: SFPA website.
	Sustainalytics	Sustainalytics, a Morningstar Company, provides high-quality, analytical environmental, social, and governance (ESG) research, ratings and data to institutional investors and companies. Source: Sustainalytics website.
TCFD	Task Force on Climate-Related Financial Disclosures	TCFD was established by the Financial Stability Board, an international body that monitors and makes recommendations about the global financial system, to develop recommendations for more effective climate-related disclosures. The TCFD has established a reporting framework for organizations to disclose clear, comparable, and consistent information about the risks and opportunities presented by climate change in order to promote more informed investment, credit, and insurance underwriting decisions and, in turn, enable stakeholders to understand better the concentrations of carbon-related assets in the financial sector and the financial system's exposures to climate-related risks. Source: TCFD website.

Organizations		
IPSF	The International Platform on Sustainable Finance	On October 18, 2019, the European Union launched together with relevant authorities of Argentina, Canada, Chile, China, India, Kenya, and Morocco the International Platform on Sustainable Finance. The platform is a forum for dialogue between policymakers, with the overall aim of increasing the amount of private capital being invested in environmentally sustainable investments. Source: European Commission website.
	TruValue Labs	TruValue Labs applies artificial intelligence to uncover ESG data to identify both risks and opportunities at the speed of current events. It quantifies company ESG performance by mining unstructured text from external sources, going beyond traditional company-disclosed ESG risk information. Source: TruValue Labs website.
UNEP	United Nations Environment Programme	UNEP is the leading global environmental authority that sets the global environmental agenda, promotes the coherent implementation of the environmental dimension of sustainable development within the United Nations system, and serves as an authoritative advocate for the global environment. Source: UNEP website.
UNFCCC	United Nations Framework Convention on Climate Change	The UNFCCC secretariat (UN Climate Change) is the United Nations entity tasked with supporting the global response to the threat of climate change. The UNFCCC has near-universal membership (197 Parties) and is the parent treaty of the 2015 Paris Agreement. It was established in 1992. Source: UNFCCC website.
UNPRI	United Nations Principles for Responsible Investment	UNPRI is a United Nations-supported network of international investors working together toward the development of a more sustainable global financial system. The six Principles for Responsible Investment developed by UNPRI provide a voluntary framework by which all investors can incorporate sustainability issues into their decision-making and operational practices. Source: UNPRI website.

Organizations		
SEC	US Securities and Exchange Commission	SEC is a government agency created by Congress. Its primary responsibilities are to regulate the securities markets, enforce federal securities laws, and protect investors. It also oversees corporate takeovers. Its mission is to protect investors and maintain fair and efficient capital markets.
USGBC	US Green Building Council	USGBC, co-founded by Mike Italiano, David Gottfried, and Rick Fedrizzi in 1993, is a private 501(c)(3), membership-based nonprofit organization that promotes sustainability in building design, construction, and operation. Source: USGBC website.
WMBC	We Mean Business Coalition	WMBC is a global nonprofit coalition working with businesses to take action on climate change by catalyzing business leadership to drive policy ambition and accelerate the transition to a zero-carbon economy. Source: WMBC website.
WEF	World Economic Forum	WEF engages political, business, cultural and other leaders of society to shape global, regional and industry agendas. It was established in 1971 as a not-for-profit foundation and is headquartered in Geneva, Switzerland. It is independent, impartial, and not tied to any special interests. Its activities are shaped by a unique institutional culture founded on the stakeholder theory, which asserts that an organization is accountable to all parts of society. Source: WEF website.
WRI	World Resources Institute	WRI is a global research nonprofit organization established in 1982 with funding from the MacArthur Foundation under the leadership of James Gustave Speth. WRI's activities are focused on seven areas: food, forests, water, energy, cities, climate, and ocean. Source: Wikipedia (https://en.wikipedia.org/wiki/World_Resources_Institute).

Organizations		
WWF	Worldwide Fund for Nature	WWF is an international nongovernmental organization founded in 1961 that works in the field of wilderness preservation and the reduction of human impact on the environment. It was formerly named the World Wildlife Fund, which remains its official name in Canada and the US. WWF is the world's largest conservation organization, with over five million supporters worldwide, working in more than 100 countries and supporting around 3,000 conservation and environmental projects. They have invested over $1 billion in more than 12,000 conservation initiatives since 1995. Source: Wikipedia (https://en.wikipedia.org/wiki/World_Wide_Fund_for_Nature).

PART I

Chapter 1
Sustainability Meets Governance

John H. Stout

Introduction: Sustainability as an Ecosystem

Sustainability has been described as "a global concern for meeting our current society's interests and needs without compromising the interests and needs of future generations."

Today's important, very basic, challenge for Boards as they consider "sustainability" is how to collaborate with management in the incorporation of relevant sustainability elements into corporate strategy and effective Board oversight.

Originally, sustainability had a primarily environmental focus. That focus has evolved and expanded dramatically to include Environmental Social Governance (ESG), Corporate Social Responsibility (CSR), Diversity Equity and Inclusion (DE&I), Rule of Law (ROL), and Social Justice and Human Rights.

> ESG is a dynamic ecosystem.

Also within the breadth of this ecosystem are corporate purpose and values, and human rights; environmental impacts, such as carbon emissions and climate change; worker health and safety, including human trafficking, forced labor, child labor; and technology and its applications and ethics.

As Boards and management develop and evaluate corporate strategies that reflect the company's values, embrace relevant sustainability initiatives, and deliver long-term financial value, Directors must be aware of stakeholder concerns and demands, customer and supplier conduct necessitating rigorous supply chain oversight, governance standards and practices, and compliance with domestic and international laws and regulations which are continuing to legalize many elements of the sustainability ecosystem.

Sustainability and the Rule of Law

The Rule of Law is not usually referenced in sustainability discussions. Nonetheless, the events of 2020 and 2021, both domestic and international, underscore a focus on the Rule of Law as a critical component of the sustainability ecosystem. Sharp political divisions magnified by the print, TV, and online platforms, over the appointment of federal, state, and local judges, the passage and promotion of laws reflecting these divisions regarding voting rights, basic human rights, and various public policy issues, the January 6 assault on Congress, the appearance of armed protesters at and within the halls of state governments, the violence which has attended many public protests, increasing crime, and the misuse of the state and federal court systems, on the part of those who sought to overturn the results of the 2020 presidential election, all evidence a significant, growing disrespect for the Rule of Law.

> The Rule of Law is the critical element of corporate sustainability.

The Rule of Law is essential to the well-being and sustainability of society as well as the conduct of business within that society and the social interaction of members of that society. Clearly, the ability of the U.S. economy to survive, thrive, and attract worldwide investment, as well as the ability of U.S. companies to do business worldwide, is dependent on the Rule of Law. It is essential that challenges to the Rule of Law be addressed by our businesses, as well as our citizens, as a critical element of the sustainability ecosystem.

In that regard, the American Bar Association has long advocated for the Rule of Law, as have a number of organizations domestically and internationally. The Business Law Section of the ABA recently formed a Working Group to address the Rule of Law and the responsibility of business lawyers and their clients to call out challenges to, advocate for, and support the Rule of Law. The Chubb Insurance Company has long had a foundation which supports and advocates for the Rule of Law and has more recently supported the formation of a Rule of Law corporate advocacy group, the Corporate Alliance for the Rule of Law (CAROL). Chubb was joined by six major corporations. CAROL continues to seek the participation of other corporations. The U.S., the United Nations, the World Justice Project (WJP) and the American Civil Liberties Union are also long-time advocates for the Rule of Law which is a core founding principle of each. It is concerning that the 2021 WJP Rule of Law Index shows a continued decline in the United States' adherence to the Rule of Law. This decline does not bode well for the Rule of Law as a core element of the sustainability of U.S. society.

Sustainability and Corporate Integrity

As a society, the U.S. is experiencing an extended period of corporate integrity failures, many of which call into question the effectiveness of the Boards and Directors of these companies. There have always been major failures of corporate integrity throughout U.S. history. However, beginning in the late 1900s and early 2000s, corporate integrity failures spawned two significant pieces of legislation: the *Sarbanes Oxley Act* and the *Dodd Frank Act*. We also have seen increased pressure from regulators on lawyers, accountants, consultants, and employees (through whistleblower protections) to address integrity failures.

> In the last 20 plus years, we have seen the losses of billions of dollars of corporate value attributable to corporate integrity failures, losses which ultimately rest with the Boards of these corporations. Boards have yet to adequately fulfill their responsibilities to hold management accountable, and accept their own accountability, for these losses, jeopardizing the company's sustainability and prospects for long-term value creation.
>
> If governance means anything, it must mean that the governing bodies and the individuals who serve on those bodies, and (i) select the CEO and approve senior management, (ii) select the Directors who comprise the Board and its committees, (iii) approve corporate strategy, key corporate policies, and significant corporate transactions, and (iv) oversee and establish corporate risk identification and mitigation systems and policies must, through the choices they make and the execution of their oversight responsibilities, accept assurance of their company's integrity as their number one responsibility.

Sustainability and Corporate Purpose

Recently, the subject of corporate purpose has become a matter of substantial interest focused on whether the purpose of the corporation should be focused principally on increasing shareholder value ("shareholder primacy"), or on interests of key corporate stakeholders including shareholders, employees, suppliers, customers, financiers, communities, and the society in general ("stakeholder primacy"). Many of the stakeholder primacy advocates acknowledge that the interests of shareholders are important when focused on value creation, but not necessarily primary. Lawrence Fink, CEO of BlackRock, has given an initial push to this discussion. In his letters over the past several years to the CEOs of companies in which BlackRock has invested. In his recently released 2021 letter, Mr. Fink has stated that BlackRock wants those corporations to focus on key elements of sustainability: purpose, social impact, and long-term value creation, specifically calling out carbon emissions and climate change.

In 2020, the Business Roundtable restated its view on the purpose of the corporation to endorse a stakeholder focus. Clearly, one aspect of the stakeholder primacy view has been to address concerns about "short termism," which in many circles had become a problematic aspect of shareholder primacy. Interestingly, other large institutional investors, including Calpers, Calsters, TIAA, Vanguard, and State Street, have also endorsed a broader view of corporate purpose and the importance of environmental and other sustainability initiatives. A corporate strategy that includes a strong commitment to selected elements of the sustainability ecosystem necessitates a governance perspective beyond a primary focus on shareholder value creation.

Not to be missed in this discussion of corporate purpose is the significant rise of "benefit corporations" as a corporate form which requires the statement of a public or social benefit and affords Directors special protection when they place such a benefit on a par with, or higher than, shareholder value creation.

Sustainability and Corporate Strategy

Crystal clear in reflecting on the many aspects of sustainability is the critical importance of embedding relevant sustainability elements into corporate strategy, and, in the view of a number of important institutional investors, including a particular focus on carbon emissions and the risks and impact of climate change on corporate operations. Further, investors are seeking increased accountability from Boards and management for corporate results through metrics linking strategy and performance with executive compensation. With companies increasingly facing the demands of investors, stakeholders, regulators, and ratings organizations for information and data relating to sustainability policies, strategies, goals, metrics, and achievements, there is increased attention from regulators and investors on the accuracy and completeness of such information. Recently, the Securities and Exchange Commission announced the creation of a 22-member Climate and ESG Task Force within its Enforcement Division, citing investor reliance on climate- and ESG-related disclosures. The Task Force will look for disclosure-related misconduct on the part of companies as well as disclosure and compliance-related issues on the part of investment advisors and funds.

Investor expectations underscore the need for Boards to reconsider Board composition and Director skills as they populate Boards and Board committees, particularly Governance (Board composition), Compensation (executive compensation, agreements, and plans), and Audit (risk and disclosure), and consider whether additional committees should be formed to assist Boards with their oversite and strategy responsibilities pertaining to companies' sustainability initiatives.

Sustainability and a Robust, Clearly Articulated Corporate Governance System

Critical to integrating sustainability into corporate purpose and strategy is a governance system that articulates the Board's commitment to the corporation's purpose and values addressed through governance principles which articulate:

- The Board's responsibility for a company culture based on strong values which include sustainability, integrity, ethics, compliance with, and support for, the Rule of Law, backed by a rigorous, functioning system of processes and procedures which assure compliance.
- Board organization and leadership which includes well-thought-out independent Board leadership, executive sessions, and independent committees established to enable the Board to effectively discharge its oversight responsibilities.
- Position descriptions for Directors and senior management which will form the basis for performance evaluations.

- Committee charters and committee member and chair position descriptions which will form the basis for evaluation of the committees, committee members, and leadership.
- The importance of Board composition and refreshment, including Director diversity, term limits, age limits, skill sets, as well as provision for voluntary or requested resignations of Directors in order to serve the interests of the Board and company as needs arise.
- Director conflicts of interest relative to their engagements and commitments with respect to service and transactions which are outside of their Board service.
- Commitment to executive sessions, candor in the exercise of Director responsibilities and service, access to all company information and materials important to the exercise of their responsibilities, and commitment to keeping all company information confidential.
- Protocols regarding communication with shareholders, stakeholders, employees, customers, suppliers, and others.
- Compliance with company governing documents, policies, and laws and regulations to which the company is subject.
- A commitment to best governance practices in the discharge of their duties as Directors, continuing education respecting the company, its industry, Board practices, sustainability strategies, metrics, disclosures, and other matters to assist Director performance.
- A commitment to meaningful company engagement with the various elements of the sustainability ecosystem.

Sustainability and Effective Board Oversight

Critical to assuring the values, purpose, integrity, and the sustainability of the company, as well as long-term value creation, is the effective performance of the Board's oversight responsibilities, entailing the use of tactics, strategies, and tools at the Board's disposal, including:

- *Director Selection*. Selection of Directors who are (i) committed to the company and its values, (ii) literate with respect to technology used by and applicable to the company's business, (iii) familiar with various aspects of the sustainability ecosystem applicable to the company, (iv) aware of the company's strategy, and qualified to assess and contribute to that strategy, and (v) who understand and use best governance practices in performing their duties.
- *CEO/Management Selection/Approval*. Selection, evaluation, and compensation of a CEO and approval of senior management who are committed to establishing and maintaining a culture which is dedicated to the corporation's core values, sustainability, ethics, integrity, and long-term value creation.
- *Board Organization*. Authorizing Board committees required to assist the Board in its governance and oversight responsibilities, including governance, compensation,

audit, and others such as risk, technology, and sustainability/ESG/CSR based on the Board's needs and priorities.

- *Board Leadership.* Selection of an independent Board chair and committee leadership critical to the Boards' accomplishment of its oversight and strategy responsibilities; capable of ensuring productive Board and committee meetings and agendas; an effective culture of mutual respect and candor, robust discussion and collaboration among Directors', vigorous discussions with management on risk, strategy and other matters of importance; and in the case of the Chair, maintaining a proper balance of collaboration and oversight between the Board and management, and lastly, presiding at executive sessions of the Board, and shareholder and stakeholder meetings, as appropriate,

- *Robust Compliance Systems and Processes.* The challenge of assisting the Board with its responsibilities, in a time of increasing corporate complexity, sustainability demands, and pressures from activist stakeholders, mandates that a Board, in association with management, develop a talent rich, extremely well-funded compliance function. Such a system must incorporate:

  (i) A skilled legal department to assure company (supplier and customer) compliance with its own governing documents, values, policies, and applicable laws and regulations; supplemented as needed by external counsel.

  (ii) A compliance organization separate from, or included within, the legal department, capable of looking broadly at compliance matters, internally and externally, and beyond the bounds of laws and regulations applicable to or affecting the corporation.

  (iii) An Internal Audit Group with sufficient talent, independence, financial resources, and scope, to continuously examine all corporate functions, departments, and committees pertaining to corporate performance, culture, risks and mitigation, integrity, sustainability goals and practices, and stakeholder complaints. The Internal Audit Group should function as the Board's and management's "eyes and ears," a tremendously valuable and often under-utilized, and under-funded tool, to help Directors meet their responsibilities. Boards must use this tool more effectively.

  (iv) External auditors, engaged by the Board, to independently assess the company's financial accounting systems, internal controls, application of proper accounting standards, quality of accounting and internal audit personnel, and accuracy and adequacy of financial and related disclosures.

  (v) Such outside resources as the Board and committees deems necessary for the fulfillment of their oversight responsibilities.

- *Rigorous Evaluation of Boards, Committees, and Directors.* Rigorous CEO, Board, committee, and Director evaluation is a valuable, underutilized tool that Boards must use to assure their collective performance and that of their individual Directors. Boards and committees must meet the standards of exceptional performance, setting annual objectives for their work, and assessing their performance. As Boards and investors rightly expect continuous improvement and exceptional performance from management and their companies, so must Boards, committees, and Directors hold themselves to continuous improvement and standards of performance excellence.

- *Oversight over Company Disclosures; Policies and Political Contributions.* Directors must be aware of the many ways in which corporate information is disclosed (e.g., executive comments, press releases, required reports to regulators, press reports, corporate transactions, litigation, etc.). Oversight over company financial, business, and sustainability disclosures is a critical issue for Boards as inaccurate, incomplete, and misleading disclosures continue to have implications for a company's reputation with shareholders, stakeholders, regulators, and rating organizations, and will increasingly result in legal liability.

  Increasingly, companies are publishing sustainability reports. Directors should be aware of the reporting platform selected by the company from the many available. Different investors prefer different platforms, and there are currently demands from investors and regulators for greater harmonization of sustainability reporting standards. The company's choice of a platform shapes the information the company makes available regarding its initiatives, priorities, and achievements.

  The merger of the Sustainability Accounting Standard Boards (SASB), and the International Integrated Reporting Council (IIRC), creating the Value Reporting Foundation, reflects a movement toward greater harmonization of sustainability disclosure standards of which companies and their Boards must be aware.

  Lastly, Boards must oversee political comments in various forums by company executives, and political contributions. Given the extremely volatile political climate in the U.S. and abroad, politically related activities and contributions to candidates and parties have had significant public and online repercussions among employees, investors, suppliers, customers, and other stakeholders. Similarly, corporate endorsement of pledges propounded by various activist groups has implications for companies' strategies, and falls within the Board's oversight responsibilities.

- *Monitoring External Sources of Information; Know Your Investors, Proxy Advisors, Activists, and Critics.* Directors must monitor external information sources relevant to the company and its business, such as analyst reports; releases by proxy advisors pertaining to their voting practices; competitors' comments and advertising; news articles, blogs, investor websites and outreach engagement communications; activist communications and announcements; chat rooms, other forms of social commentary, investors, activists, securities traders, legislators, regulators, governance commentators and industry associations; and ratings of rating organizations, as well as the commentary and criteria which are the basis of their ratings.

- *Risk Assessment.* Continuous oversight over the execution of company strategy, and assessment of enterprise risk, is an essential element of corporate sustainability and long-term value creation. While risk identification, assessment, and mitigation is the business of all company personnel, every internal group, and many external relationships with advisors, consultants, suppliers, customers, etc., the Board, as the company's governing body, has a critical role in assuring that appropriate systems and processes are in place and functioning.

Risks are internal and external. Again, a strong Internal Audit Group working with the legal and compliance functions will be of invaluable assistance to the Board and its committees in the performance of its risk oversight responsibilities. Boards should also be aware of the situations, activities, and conduct, which have adversely impacted other companies within and without their industry—values, integrity and ethical failures, flawed cultures, overly aggressive goals and financial rewards, passive Boards, and executives and Boards downplaying the seriousness of critical situations, ignoring human and business risks for business, and personal financial gain, ignoring warnings (the Florida Condominium collapse, the California wildfires disaster), and thinking that "it can't happen here." These are among the many consequences of ineffective risk oversight that Boards must avoid.

Take-Aways for Board Members

- Directors should continually improve their sustainability literacy; make it a key focus of Board composition and education.
- Review corporate values; include corporate integrity and sustainability.
- Know the key stakeholders, competitors, and regulators sustainability views and practices.
- Focus oversight on sustainability strategy, practices, and disclosures.
- Understand key elements in sustainability ratings applicable to their company.
- Evaluate their company's sustainability strategies, focus, and results relative to their peers and those in relevant industry associations.
- Oversee sustainability disclosures for completeness, accuracy, and value to stake-holders; avoid embellishment and "greenwashing."
- Integrate sustainability goals, strategies, and performance into executive compensation.
- Utilize oversight tools to assure effective oversight: Board committees; internal audit; and independent third-party review.
- Assess compliance and risk oversight systems and processes; make sure they are effective and functioning.
- Collaborate with management on company strategy and goal setting, as well as risks and opportunities posed by the sustainability ecosystem, and rigorously assess management and Board performance.
- Know the person/group within management responsible for sustainability initiatives enterprise-wide; assess the performance and effectiveness of that person/group.

Chapter 2
The Evolution of Corporate Sustainability

William Jannace

Background

An Inflection Point

As the world has suffered through the COVID-19 pandemic and the U.S. is navigating social injustice issues, it is time to reflect on corporate sustainability as seen both domestically in the U.S. and internationally such as at the 2020 and 2021 World Economic Forums (WEFs). Is this an inflection point and tectonic shift in the corporate governance paradigm or rather a continuation of the evolution of the basic fundamentals of corporate governance; the role and interactions of the board, the management, and shareholders, albeit in a far different world and capital markets environment[1] than when Professors Berle and Means

---

1. There was a record $269.5bn green issuance for 2020. Liam Jones, *Record $269.5bn Green Issuance for 2020: Late Surge Sees Pandemic Year Pip 2019 Total by $3bn*, CLIMATE BONDS INITIATIVE (Jan. 24, 2021), https://www.climatebonds.net/2021/01/record-2695bn-green-issuance-2020-late-surge-sees-pandemic-year-pip-2019-total-3bn.

postulated their theory on corporate law[2] and Professor Milton Friedman articulated his thoughts on shareholder capitalism?[3]

> The theme of the 2020 WEF was "Stakeholders for a Cohesive and Sustainable World."

The theme of the 2020 WEF was "Stakeholders for a Cohesive and Sustainable World." In addition to world leaders from government and business, the 2020 WEF conference included Greta Thunberg, who traveled the world in 2019 warning about the perils of climate change.[4] The backdrop for that conference was unfortunately the devastating Australian wildfires which provided more impetus to address what people have characterized as an existential threat to humanity—climate change. Most recently, The Intergovernmental Panel on Climate Change ("IPCC") 6th Assessment Report, Climate Change 2021: The Physical Science Basis, provided a sobering assessment of the prospects of the planet's climate. The report also sounded a cautionary optimistic tone if quick action is taken to achieve zero net carbon emissions.[5]

The WEF 2021 agenda noted that the pandemic demonstrated that no institution or individual alone can address the economic, environmental, social, and technological challenges of our complex, interdependent world. The pandemic has accelerated systemic changes that were apparent before its inception. The fault lines that emerged in 2020 appeared as critical inflection points in 2021. The time to rebuild trust and to make crucial choices is rapidly approaching as the need to reset priorities and the urgency to reform systems grow stronger around the world. It is essential for leaders and nations to work together for a more inclusive, cohesive, and sustainable future as soon as possible in 2021.[6]

Announcements and initiatives that arose before and after the WEF meetings clearly articulate that participants in the capital markets–corporate governance ecosystem such as asset owners, asset managers, investee companies and their employees, stakeholders, and governments are prioritizing sustainability through the integration of environmental, social, and governance (ESG) factors into policies, practices, and investments.[7] The

---

2. A description of a separation of ownership and control in America's largest companies was a well-known feature of Adolf Berle and Gardiner Means' 1932 book The Modern Corporation and Private Property. Diffuse share ownership and the managerial autonomy which tends to follow from it would become hallmarks of American corporate governance. See Brian Cheffins, *The Rise and Fall (?) of the Berle-Means Corporation*, HARVARD LAW SCHOOL FORUM ON CORPORATE GOVERNANCE (Aug. 6, 2018), https://corpgov.law.harvard.edu/2018/08/06/the-rise-and-fall-of-the-berle-means-corporation/.

3. Milton Friedman, *The Social Responsibility of Business Is to Increase Its Profits*, N.Y. Times mag., Sept. 13, 1970, http://umich.edu/~thecore/doc/Friedman.pdf.

4. Joumanna Bercetche, *Has 'Davos Man' Now Morphed Into 'Davos Everyone'?*, CNBC (Jan. 21, 2020) https://www.cnbc.com/2020/01/21/has-davos-man-now-morphed-into-davos-everyone.html.

5. IPCC WORKING GROUP I, *Climate Change 2021: The Physical Science Basis*, IPCC (Aug. 6, 2021), https://www.ipcc.ch/report/sixth-assessment-report-working-group-i/.

6. *The Davos Agenda 2021*, WORLD ECONOMIC FORUM, https://weforum.org/focus/the-davos-agenda-2021.

7. Among other initiatives, The Task Force on Climate-related Financial Disclosures (TCFD), the UN's Principles for Responsible Investment, the Vatican's 2019 statement advocating carbon pricing regimes, and the Climate Finance Partnership, have been promulgated to address climate change and to further sustainability. TASK FORCE ON CLIMATE-RELATED FINANCIAL DISCLOSURES, https://www.fsb-tcfd.org/; PRINCIPLES FOR RESPONSIBLE INVESTING, https://www.unpri.org/; Ben van Beurden, et al., *Vatican Dialogues: Participant Statement on Climate Pricing*, TOTAL ENERGIES (June 14, 2019), https://www.total.com/news/vatican-dialogues-participant-statement-carbon-pricing; *Climate Finance Partnership*, INTERNATIONAL CLIMATE INITIATIVE (Dec. 2021), https://www.international-climate-initiative.com/en/details/project/climate-finance-partnership-20_I_395-3178; Larry Fink, *Larry Fink's 2021 Letter to CEOs*, BLACKROCK, https://www.blackrock.com/corporate/investor-relations/larry-fink-ceo-letter.

announcements reflected a continuation of investment trends that have developed for nearly two centuries: Socially Responsible Investing (SRI), Corporate Social Responsibility (CSR), Impact Investing, and Sustainability.[8]

The Change

During an earlier era of corporate governance, with dispersed share ownership dominated by retail participation, shareholder activism often resulted in Delaware courts opining on the role of boards, particularly in the context of mergers and acquisitions and other value-creating transactions. Corporate governance during this period was dominated by corporate raiders (e.g., dissident shareholders) and their advisors on one side and besieged corporations and their advisors on the other side. With the end of the "hostile takeover and leveraged buyout"[9] era in the early 1990s coupled with the rise of permanent ownership in corporate America through passive index investing,[10] new concepts pertaining to longer-term value creation through ESG, CSR and SRI (collectively referred to as "Corporate Sustainability") came to the forefront of corporate governance priorities and dialogue. Today, these are considered mainstream concepts with respect to the asset–owner–manager–investee company ecosystem. For those new to the field of corporate governance and investing, these acronyms are mainstream pillars of value creation.

In the 1980s, during the era of great takeovers, elements of the SRI industry were attempting to push companies and in some instances countries, in the instance of apartheid in South Africa,[11] toward better corporate behavior. In this regard, SRI had historically been the remit of organizations with religious mandates qualitatively focused rather than subject to investment-oriented disciplines and nowhere as pervasive across every stratum of the corporate governance–investment value creation chain as it is today. The growth in ESG assets under management was made possible, in part, through the end of defined benefit

---

8. Sustainable or socially responsible investing have their roots dating back more than 200 years ago to investment practices of the Methodists. Others suggest that it dates back to Sharia investing. The issue of governance, however, began with the beginning of corporations, dating back to the East India Company, the Hudson's Bay Company, the Levant Company, and other major chartered companies during the 16th and 17th centuries. See William Donovan, *The Origins of Socially Responsible Investing*, THE BALANCE (Apr. 23, 2020), https://www.the balance.com/a-short-history-of-socially-responsible-investing-3025578; Nicholas J. Price, *What is the History of Corporate Governance and How Has It Changed?*, DILIGENT: INSIGHTS (Oct. 3, 2018), https://insights .diligent.com/corporate-governance/what-is-the-history-of-corporate-governance-and-how-has-it-changed/

9. State legislators countered takeovers with anti-takeover statutes at the state level. That, coupled with the junk bond market discredited due to regulatory scrutiny and an economic downturn, discouraged future merger activity. See Id.

10. Some argue that passive investing and sustainability are incompatible because sustainable investing requires active choices and so cannot be done purely passively. See David Blitz and Wilma de Groot, *Passive Investing and Sustainability Are Incompatible*, ROBECO: INVESTING (updated Jan. 16, 2019), https://www.robeco.com/en/insights /2018/09/passive-investing-and-sustainability-are-incompatible.html.

11. The Sullivan Principles espoused corporate social responsibility to apply economic pressure in South Africa in response to its apartheid system of racial segregation. The UN adopted an updated version of the principles' corporate code of conduct for companies as part of the UN's Global Compact. Press Release, United Nations, Good Corporate Citizenship, Business Reputations, Intimately Tied, Secretary-General Tells Corporate Leaders (Nov. 2, 199) (on file with the United Nations). See also Jessica Ann Levy, *Black Power in the Boardroom: Corporate America, The Sullivan Principles, and the Anti-Apartheid Struggle*, 21 ENT. & SOC. 170, 170-209 (2020). https://www .cambridge.org/core/journals/enterprise-and-society/article/black-power-in-the-boardroom-corporate-america-the -sullivan-principles-and-the-antiapartheid-struggle/4DBC22EF8E9F936C1C151F844894CAD4. (published electronically by CAMBRIDGE UNIVERSITY PRESS on behalf of the BUSINESS HISTORY CONFERENCE)

plans[12] and the rise of defined contribution plans that provided a pool of permanent liquidity in the capital markets, helped make SRI mainstream and thus ushered in the modern Corporate Sustainability movement.

Numerous investment names and acronyms have been subsumed in one manner or another under the rubric of ESG . Whether it be "Sin Stocks," "Best in Class,"[13] "Values-Based Investing," "Conscience Investing," "Green Investing," "Impact Investing," "Gender Lens," and "Fossil Fuel-Free," today Corporate Sustainability covers these investment themes and categories in varying degrees from a more holistic and analytical perspective to make capital allocation decisions across the entire investment spectrum. From targeted reactionary focus on negative screening for traditional "Sin Stocks" from a few Corporate Sustainability pioneers, modern Corporate Sustainability is now a pillar of global capital markets and corporate governance, and as discussed in more detail in other chapters of this book, impacting the debate on fossil fuels including: divestment and exit versus voice, gradual and incremental decarbonization, fundamental stock research and credit ratings and the integration of ESG factors into such ratings, required disclosures for stock exchange listing standards, global accounting and sustainability disclosure standards, multinational corporations being forced to balance stakeholder and shareholder demands, some corporations choosing to be constituted as Benefits Corporations (and some being asked via proxy proposal in 2021 to consider reincorporating as ones) and some becoming Certified B Corporations,[14] and most recently the role of derivatives in sustainable finance.[15]

The Modern CSR Movement—Overview

The Demand Side of Corporate Sustainability

Investment Funds

The modern CSR movement has its genesis in Article 23 of the 1948 United Nations Universal Declaration on Human Rights,[16] which called for the right to: employment, favorable work conditions, equal pay for equal work, and the right to join trade unions.

---

12. EMPLOYEE BENEFITS SECURITY ADMINISTRATION, *Financial Factors in Selecting Plan Investments*, FEDERAL REGISTER (June 30, 2020), https://www.federalregister.gov/documents/2020/06/30/2020-13705/financial-factors-in -selecting-plan-investments.

13. The Dreyfus Third Century Fund was established in 1972. It was seeking companies that "show evidence in the conduct of their business, relative to other companies in the same industry or industries, of contributing to the enhancement of quality of life in America—'Best in Class' in SRI by the 1990s." See Blaine Townsend, *From SRI to ESG: The Origins of Socially Responsible and Sustainable Investing*, 1 J. IMP. & ESG INVST. 10, 10–25, (2020). https:// www.bailard.com/wp-content/uploads/2020/09/History-Socially-Responsible-Investing-and-ESG-Investing.pdf.

14. Certified B Corporations—or "B Corps," is a standards-based designation like "organic" or "fair trade." Any company can become a Certified B Corporation through the nonprofit B Lab's third-party certification process, whereas only companies incorporated in states that have passed benefit corporation legislation can become benefit corporations. Abigail Barnes et al., *A Legislative Guide to Benefit Corporations: Create Jobs, Drive Social Impact, and Promote the Economic Health of Your State*, PATAGONIA INC. with VERMONT LAW SCHOOL and THE YALE ENVIRONMENTAL LAW ASSOCIATION (2018), http://benefitcompanybar.org/wp-content/uploads/2018/07/Legislative -Guide-B-Corps_Final.pdf.

15. Karol Lanoo & Apostolos Thomadakis, *Derivatives in Sustainable Finance: Enabling the Green Transition*, CENTRE FOR EUROPEAN POLICY STUDY (2020), https://www.isda.org/a/KOmTE/Derivatives-in-Sustainable-Finance.pdf.

16. UNITED NATIONS DRAFT COMMITTEE, *Universal Declaration of Human Rights*, UNITED NATIONS (Dec. 10, 1948), https://www.un.org/sites/un2.un.org/files/udhr.pdf.

During the social upheavals and activist movements of the 1960s and 1970s, the concept of socially responsible corporate behavior gained traction.[17] In this regard, in 1971, the Pax World sustainable fund was established by United Methodist ministers seeking to avoid investing church funds in companies contributing to the Vietnam War, by aligning its investments with its values and urging companies to adhere to a standard of social and environmental responsibility.

At the time the fund was launched, the traditional model of shareholder-centric corporate law was premised on the concept of the business of business is business, whereby profit making was dichotomized from CSR. During this period, corporate governance could be characterized as corporation-specific and idiosyncratic rather than the broader and more stakeholder-centric concept it has evolved into today with potential attendant societal impact and systemic risk implications.[18] In this regard, due to the size of the capital markets during this pre-globalization period, ESG and related fiduciary duty responsibilities could be viewed through the prism of the individual corporation and its conduct in obtaining shareholder value without broader stakeholder-centric considerations pervasive today. The lack of permanent shareholder ownership and resulting stewardship capabilities and responsibilities was also a factor in corporate governance being more idiosyncratic in nature at that time.

The Regulatory Environment

Privatization, deregulation, corporate takeovers, and leveraged buyouts financed by junk bonds in the 1980s led to an explosion of CSR awareness and activism in the 1990s, as globalization and communications technology accelerated flows of capital, information, and people across borders. Permanent shareholders via indexing and other funds subject to federal securities laws[19] and regulations and guidance, most notably from the Department of Labor (DOL),[20] began exercising voting authority as a means of increasing shareholder value. A major factor behind this was the DOL's 1988 "Avon Letter," which provided that in general, the fiduciary act of managing plan assets which are shares of corporate stock

---

17. Michael E. Porter & Mark R. Kramer, *Creating Shared Value*, Harv. Bus. Rev., Jan.–Feb. 2011, https://hbr .org/2011/01/the-big-idea-creating-shared-value.

18. *See* PRI Association & UNEP Financial Initiative, *Universal Ownership Why Environmental Externalities Matter to Institutional Investors*, UNEP Financial Initiative, (March 2011), http://www.unepfi.org/fileadmin/documents /universal_ownership_full.pdf.

19. In 2020, the U.S. Securities and Exchange Commission (SEC) published supplementary guidance via a policy statement regarding the proxy voting responsibilities of investment advisers under Rule 206(4)-6 under the Investment Advisers Act of 1940 (Advisers Act). The SEC previously issued guidance discussing how fiduciary duty and Rule 206(4)-6 under the Advisers Act relate to an investment adviser's exercise of voting authority on behalf of clients. In the policy statement, the SEC stated that the adviser should consider whether its policies and procedures, including any with respect to automated voting of proxies, are reasonably designed to ensure that it exercises voting authority in its client's best interest. See Securities and Exchange Commission, *Supplement to Commission Guidance Regarding Proxy Voting Responsibilities of Investment Advisors*, SEC: Rules & Policy (July 22, 2020), https://www.sec.gov/rules/policy/2020/ia-5547.pdf.

20. The DOL has addressed proxy voting requirements through Interpretive Bulletins (IBs) and Field Assistance Bulletins (FABs).

would include the voting of proxies appurtenant to those shares of stock.[21] The DOL's position was that votes should be considered plan assets and that fiduciaries are also required to monitor and document proxy voting.[22] During the Obama administration, the DOL issued guidance on how fiduciaries can use ESG factors in the context of investment decision-making, proxy voting, and shareholder engagement and the limits on the use of such factors. In 2015 and 2016, it issued IBs 2015-01 and 2016-01, affirming the position that plan fiduciaries may consider ESG factors in investment decision-making if the ESG factors have a direct relationship to the economic and financial value of the plan's investment.

State Law and Other Stakeholders

In addition, state corporate law imposes fiduciary duties on corporate boards. Most recently, corporate law has started to focus on sustainability. For example, the Delaware Certification of Adoption of Transparency and Sustainability Standards Act[23] became effective in 2018, to support sustainability practices by providing Delaware-governed entities a platform for demonstrating their commitment to corporate and social responsibility and sustainability. It was an acknowledgment that sustainability and responsibility embody business practices and systems that are designed to foster innovation and long-term growth while promoting business practices intended to provide societal benefits.

Furthermore, informed stakeholders—customers, employees, suppliers, civil society organizations and other nongovernmental organizations (NGOs), media, and today non-shareholder social media activists—demanded transparency and accountability from corporations particularly with respect to their supply chains and their support of initiatives to address climate change, among others, in a growing litany of ESG proxy proposals, rewarding companies that contributed positively to social and environmental well-being and punishing firms that ignored or neglected the negative externalities of their business practices or were perceived to be on the wrong side of history.

Environmental Pressure

In the 1980s, environmental concerns continued to incentivize growth for sustainable investing. The catalytic moment was the Exxon Valdez oil spill in Alaska which ushered in a permanent Sustainable Investing Shareholder movement that changed its modus operandi from reactive to proactive. As a result, the Coalition of Environmentally Responsible Economies (CERES) was founded which brings together investors, business leaders, and public-interest

---

21. See Employee Benefits Security Administration: Labor, *Interpretive Bulletin Relating to the Fiduciary Standard Under ERISA in Considering Economically Targeted Investments*, Federal Register (Oct. 26, 2015), https://www .federalregister.gov/documents/2015/10/26/2015-27146/interpretive-bulletin-relating-to-the-fiduciary-standard -under-erisa-in-considering-economically. See also, Employee Benefits Security Administration, *US Labor Department Provides Updated Guidance On Proxy Voting By Employee Benefits Plans*, U.S. Department of Labor (Dec. 28, 2016), https://www.dol.gov/newsroom/releases/ebsa/ebsa20161228. The DOL further clarified that ESG factors can be a proper component of appropriate fiduciary investment decision-making. In 2018, the DOL issued FAB 2018-01, which if not rescinding previous guidance, provided a more cautious and nuanced approach to the use of ESG factors.
22. James McRitchie, *Fiduciary Duty to Announce Votes (Part 2): Historical Background*, Corporate Governance: CorpGov.net (May 28, 2014), https://www.corpgov.net/2014/05/fiduciary-duty-announce-votes-part-2-historical -background/.
23. Certification of Adoption and of Transparency and Sustainability Standards Act, 81 Del. Laws, c. 279, §1. https://delcode.delaware.gov/title6/c050e/index.html.

groups to speed the adoption of sustainable business practices and the transition to a low-carbon economy.[24] CERES continues to advocate for action to address climate change.[25]

The Role of Index Funds

CEOs of the largest global asset management firms have put portfolio company executives on notice that their short-term focus can be a barrier to long-term growth. BlackRock's 2016 corporate governance letter to CEOs advised that the culture of quarterly earnings focus is contrary to the long-term approach BlackRock needed and that it was asking every CEO to lay out for shareholders each year a strategic framework for long-term value creation.[26] Its 2018 letter to corporations emphasized that a corporation had a social purpose as well.[27] In its 2020 letter to its clients, BlackRock announced that it would: make sustainability integral to portfolio construction and risk management; exit investments that present a high sustainability-related risk, such as thermal coal producers; launch new investment products that screen fossil fuels; and strengthen its commitment to sustainability and transparency in its investment stewardship activities.[28] Its 2021 letter highlighted issues critical to creating durable value such as capital management, long-term strategy, purpose, and climate change.[29]

The "Big Three" of indexing—Vanguard, BlackRock, and State Street—have been encouraging publicly traded companies to adopt and regularly disclose long-term strategic plans and governance practices. The CEOs of major public companies and institutional investment firms have signed up to The Common Sense Principles 2.0 which is a revised set of principles designed to provide a basic framework for sound, long-term-oriented governance.[30] In 2019, CECP's Strategic Investor Initiative (SII) released a template for companies seeking to develop and communicate effective long-term strategic plans that help inform investment, voting, and engagement decisions. This enhanced communication and transparency includes the development of long-term plans, supported by the SII initiative.[31]

> The CECP's SII was established to help shift trillions in investor assets to companies that move away from a myopic focus on short-term corporate results and adopt and communicate long-term strategies that integrate financially material ESG factors into their business operations.

24. *About Us*, Ceres, https://www.ceres.org/about-us.

25. Press Release, Ceres, 40 Investors with Nearly $1 Trillion Join Other Leaders to Urge U.S. Financial Regulators to Act on Climate Change as Systemic Financial Risk (July 21, 2020) (on file with Ceres).

26. Larry Fink, *Larry Fink's 2016 Letter to CEOs*, Blackrock, https://www.blackrock.com/corporate/investor-relations/2016-larry-fink-ceo-letter

27. Larry Fink, *Larry Fink's 2018 Letter to CEOs: A Sense of Purpose*, Blackrock, https://www.blackrock.com/corporate/investor-relations/2018-larry-fink-ceo-letter.

28. Larry Fink, *Larry Fink's 2020 Letter to CEOs: A Fundamental Reshaping of Finance*, Blackrock, https://www.blackrock.com/corporate/investor-relations/2020-larry-fink-ceo-letter.

29. Larry Fink, *Larry Fink's 2021 Letter to CEOs*, Blackrock, https://www.blackrock.com/corporate/investor-relations/larry-fink-ceo-letter.

30. Aabha Sharma & Howard Dicker, *Commonsense Principles 2.0: A Blueprint for U.S. Corporate Governance?*, Harvard Law School Forum on Corporate Governance (Oct. 18, 2018), https://corpgov.law.harvard.edu/2018/10/30/commonsense-principles-2-0-a-blueprint-for-u-s-corporate-governance/#:~:text=The%20Commonsense%20Principles%202.0%20puts,and%20care%20to%20the%20 company.

31. *Strategic Investor Initiative Releases New Framework for Companies Seeking to Develop Long-Term Plans*, Global Newswire (Apr. 22, 2019), https://www.globenewswire.com/news-release/2019/04/22/1807455/0/en/Strategic-Investor-Initiative-Releases-New-Framework-for-Companies-Seeking-to-Develop-Long-Term-Plans.html.

Focusing Capital on the Long-Term (FCTLGlobal) is an initiative for advancing practical actions to focus business and markets on the long term. FCLTGlobal's mission is to develop practical structures, metrics, and approaches for longer-term behaviors in the investment and business worlds. FCLTGlobal's founders and members advocate for adoption of these structures and metrics within the investment community and in corporate boardrooms.[32]

> In August 2019, the U.S. Business Roundtable published a new statement on the purpose of a corporation, with signatories committed to delivering value for all stakeholders (communities, employers, suppliers), not just to shareholders.

In August 2019, the U.S. Business Roundtable (BRT) published a new statement (BRT Statement) on the purpose of a corporation. The letter was signed by 181 CEOs of some of the largest U.S. companies including J.P. Morgan, Johnson & Johnson, and Ford and committed to delivering value for all stakeholders (communities, employers, suppliers), not just to company shareholders.[33] In 2020, the BRT established a Special Committee of the BRT Board of Directors to advance racial equity and justice solutions resulting in policy endorsements and corporate initiatives designed to advance racial equity and justice and increase economic opportunity in America.[34] It is worth noting that a recent study found, among other things, that almost one-hundred BRT Companies that updated their corporate governance guidelines since the release of the BRT Statement generally did not add any language that improves the status of stakeholders and in fact most of them chose to retain in their guidelines a commitment to shareholder primacy.[35]

Take-Aways for Board Members

Stewardship Trends, the Interaction of Corporate Sustainability Supply, Demand and Regulatory Realities—A Perfect Storm!

As this publication comes to press, the model is still evolving due to the fallout from the pandemic and social unrest in the U.S. and abroad. Although the challenges from the pandemic may seem unprecedented in the short term, the long-term deployment of resources and change in corporate perspectives, e.g., a continued push toward decarbonization and use of renewable energy sources, and the emphasis of the "S" (and has been suggested

---

32. FCLT GLOBAL, https://www.fcltglobal.org/.

33. *Business Roundtable Redefines the Purpose of a Corporation to Promote an Economy That Serves All Americans*, BUSINESS ROUNDTABLE (Aug. 19, 2019), https://www.businessroundtable.org/business-roundtable-redefines-the-purpose-of-a-corporation-to-promote-an-economy-that-serves-all-americans.

34. *Business Roundtable CEOs Announce Corporate Actions, Public Policy Recommendation to Advance Racial Equity and Justice, Increase Economic Opportunity in America*, BUSINESS ROUNDTABLE (Oct. 15, 2020), https://www.businessroundtable.org/business-roundtable-ceos-announce-corporate-actions-public-policy-recommendations-to-advance-racial-equity-and-justice-increase-economic-opportunity-in-america.

35. Lucian A. Bebchuck & Roberto Tallarita, *Will Corporations Deliver Value to All Stakeholders?*, 75 VAND. L. REV. (forthcoming May 2022). https://papers.ssrn.com/sol3/papers.cfm?abstract_id=3899421.

an additional "E" for Employee to the ESG construct)[36] in the ESG paradigm in the short term may help supplement the traditional social safety nets provided by governments and afford them the opportunities to deploy their resources to address these crises and place their respective countries and companies in the long term on a more sustainable path of development and inclusive prosperity.

While this may entail sacrificing some profits in the short term, the pandemic may provide companies with the opportunity to put into practice the tenets of stakeholder capitalism they have ascribed to in writing.[37] While stakeholder capitalism will need to stand the test of time during good and bad markets and economic cycles, it may be a step in the right direction, despite any weaknesses in the short term.[38] At the same time, corporations need to be mindful that the Corporate Sustainability movement is not monolithic in that there are different perspectives on stakeholder capitalism with some still ascribing to shareholder primacy. For example, while some hedge fund activists have targeted firms over climate risk, there are still others that focus on shareholder returns in the belief that stakeholder capitalism provides license to corporations to waste corporate assets and wealth under the guise of CSR.[39]

During this time of the pandemic, we have also all been reminded of the reach and extent of social injustice and systemic racism in the U.S. While we have a long way to go if we are to rebuild a more inclusive society and economy, the private sector as noted above has begun the process[40] of expanding its remit by expanding the traditional concept of ESG and CSR to include Corporate Social Justice.[41] This expansion has been backed by financial commitments to various corporate-led initiatives.

Matters for Boards to Consider

Shareholder proxy proposals in 2021 have and continue to be ESG-centric and large shareholders are increasing their support for climate-related proposals, but investors are

---

36. Former Chief Justice of the Delaware Supreme Court, Leo Strine, advocated a rebalancing of shareholders and workers' rights, calling on those promoting ESG to make it EESG, with the added "E" standing for employees. See Michael Skapinker, *Boosting Corporate Social Good Will Not Protect the Workers*, Financial Times: Opinion, Work & Careers (Oct. 7, 2019), https://www.ft.com/content/d106dc54-e698-11e9-9743-db5a370481bc.

37. See *Business Roundtable Redefines the Purpose of a Corporation to Promote an Economy That Serves All Americans*, Business Roundtable (Aug. 19, 2019), https://www.businessroundtable.org/business-roundtable-redefines-the-purpose-of-a-corporation-to-promote-an-economy-that-serves-all-americans.

38. A 2020 study reviewed data from companies of some of the BRT signatories and found little evidence (so far) that the BRT statement altered corporate behavior. According to the study, the latest data on incentives suggest shareholders still come to take precedent. See *Academics Make an Empirical Case Against Stakeholderism*, The Economist: Business (March 14, 2020), https://www.economist.com/business/2020/03/12/academics-make-an-empirical-case-again-stakeholderism.

39. Mark R. DesJardine et al., *Why Activist Hedge Funds Target Socially Responsible Firms: The Reaction Costs of Signaling Corporate Social Responsibility*. acad. maNage. J. (2020), https://tinyurl.com/yd2v6tey.

40. A group of investors from the Racial Justice Investing (RJI) Coalition has developed and circulated for endorsement an Investor Statement of Solidarity and Call to Action to Address Systemic Racism. See Julie Wokaty, *Investors Commit Address Systemic Racism Through Their Portfolios, Corporate Engagements and Policy Advocacy*, Interfaith Center on Corporate Responsibility: Julie Wokaty's Blog (June 18, 2020), https://www.iccr.org/investors-commit-address-systemic-racism-through-their-portfolios-corporate-engagements-and-policy.

41. Lily Zheng, *We're Entering the Age of Corporate Social Justice*, Harv. Bus. Rev. (June 15, 2020), https://hbr.org/2020/06/were-entering-the-age-of-corporate-social-justice.

withholding support for boards that have not made progress on diversity, accountability, and responsiveness to climate change, among other things.[42]

While ESG investing has and continues to attract investment fund flow (with proposed regulations potentially increasing such flow),[43] it is far more nuanced than all stakeholders realize or acknowledge. It has performed better than funds that do not integrate such factors into their investments by losing less not making more. Issues of whether we are in an ESG Bubble have also been raised, and board deliberations about enhancing their firms' CSR posture should be viewed through that prism as some shareholders remain skeptical and traditional shareholder activism remains.[44] In a low-interest-rate environment, corporations have been able to issue debt to buy-back stocks and raise dividends, raising enterprise value in some instances, and placating shareholders focusing on balance sheet activism. Can this continue if interest rates rise? Will this incentivize more sustainability measures by corporations or more activism by shareholders potentially derailing sustainability measures as they might be forced to focus on short-term price performance?

While the above trends and their impacts are tangible and are known by companies and their boards, the potential impact of a new and enhanced regulatory regime remains unclear as the Biden administration's "whole-of-government" approach resulting from executive orders[45] and related regulatory initiatives to address climate change are in the process of being implemented. Given the known trends of shareholder stewardship, traditional activism, ESG investment popularity (the demand and supply sides of Corporate Sustainability), and the unknown impact of pending legislation and the current regulatory initiatives to address "greenwashing," it is incumbent upon boards to be proactive and view their responsibilities through the broadest prism of corporate governance, risk, and Corporate Sustainability and address these potential risks and opportunities to their enterprise value in terms of short-term and long-term horizons while seeking to analyze them holistically as part of a long-term sustainability strategy, to better discern risks on the

---

42. James J. Miller, *2021 Proxy Season Issues and Early Voting Trends*, Harvard Law School Forum on Corporate Governance (May 20, 2021), https://corpgov.law.harvard.edu/2021/05/20/2021-proxy-season-issues -and-early-voting-trends/.

43. The investment advisory industry is more focused on ESG and may be subject to more requirements (see Financial Factors in Selecting Retirement Plan Investment Act, whereby plans would have to consider ESG factors in a prudent manner consistent with their fiduciary obligations, the same legal standard that ERISA already applies to non-ESG investment factors. *Financial Factors in Selecting Plan Investment*, Federal Register (Nov. 13, 2020), https://www.federalregister.gov/documents/2020/11/13/2020-24515/financial-factors-in-selecting -plan-investments. See also the Sustainable Investment Policies Act of 2021 that would amend the Investment Advisers Act of 1940 to require large asset managers to establish Sustainable Investment Policies. https://www .govtrack.us/congress/bills/116/hr8960).

44. Ryan Ermey, *Ignore ESG Funds 'At Your Peril,' Experts Say: Sustainable Funds Outperformed Peers in 2020*, Grow: Acorns + CNBC (May 4, 2021), https://grow.acorns.com/investing-in-esg-funds-doesnt-mean-sacrificing -returns/.; Tom Lauricello & Jess Liu, *Sustainable Funds Weather Downturns Better Than Peers*, Morningstar (June 15, 2020), https://www.morningstar.com/articles/988114/sustainable-funds-weather-downturns -better-than-peers.

45. In May 2021, the Biden administration issued an executive order to strengthen the U.S. financial system against climate-related risks. See *Fact Sheet: President Biden Directs Agencies to Analyze and Mitigate the Risk Climate Change Poses to Homeowners and Consumers, Businesses and Workers, and the Financial System and Federal Government*, The White House: Briefing Room. (May 20, 2021), https://www.whitehouse.gov/briefing -room/statements-releases/2021/05/20/fact-sheet-president-biden-directs-agencies-to-analyze-and-mitigate -the-risk-climate-change-poses-to-homeowners-and-consumers-businesses-and-workers-and-the-financial -system-and-federal-government/.

horizon, and their ability to navigate change. For example, current board members, corporate leadership, and capital markets and investment leadership have risen to positions of authority during the American-led rules-based international system (i.e., the Bretton Woods System), making it easier to discuss and aspire to Corporate Sustainability for the world. As the world order has evolved, more multipolar and complex, will Sustainability and Stakeholder Capitalism be circumscribed by this new reality? How will companies and their boards that espouse Corporate Sustainability navigate the "S" in ESG in a globalized world of interconnected supply chains that have and are prone to ethical lapses and human rights abuses and subject to shareholder and non-shareholder opprobrium? In a world where commerce and national security have been conflated (e.g., cyber attacks, and ransomware), board competency skills and refreshment are vital as companies navigate the demand by shareholders for investee company focus on sustainability in an environment susceptible to cyber and climate risk. To say that a company is on board with Corporate Sustainability without palpable actions and reactions to support it may not be sufficient at all times and under all circumstances.

Issues of corporate governance and overreach date back over 400 years,[46] and corporate governance with today's emphasis on sustainability may suffer from the same issues. It is a process of ever-evolving iterations, with one-step forward and two-step back, and constant vigilance is needed to ensure progress. But as the saying goes: Do not let the perfect be the enemy of the good, as the alternatives may be worse.

---

46. Shareholder Activism at the Dutch East India Company 1622–1625: Redde Rationem Villicationis Tuae! Give an Account of Your Stewardship! file:///C:/Users/wjann.000/Downloads/SSRN-id1496871.pdf.

PART II

Chapter 3

An Introduction to Directors' Fiduciary Duties, Corporate Purpose, and Stakeholder Interests

Bruce Dravis

Before the COVID-19 pandemic, the term "sustainability" had attained a certain cachet in the business and investment world. "Sustainability" was a corporate shorthand that conveyed both forward-looking virtue and fiscal prudence, bespeaking a blend of save-the-planet earnestness with bean-counting technocratic probity and planning. Academic research indicated that companies that adopted sustainability policies became more valuable than companies that did not.[1]

---

1. Robert G. Eccles et al., *The Impact of Corporate Sustainability on Organizational Processes and Performance*, 60 MANAGE. SCI. 2835–57 (2014) (herein, "Eccles"); see discussion *infra* notes 32–37 and accompanying text.

The basic sentiment of sustainability is hard to attack. Who would actively promote *un*sustainability?[2]

As noted in previous chapters, "ESG"—Environmental, Social, and Governance—is the abbreviation for a broad set of sustainability issues investors want corporate managers to address, and that investment and social activists press with policymakers. ESG has served as a catch-all description for addressing a host of corporate behaviors that have the potential to impose negative externalities in such areas as human rights, the environment, community relations, workplace safety, and the like.

There is no single ESG or unified ESG position for all companies in all circumstances—but the underlying basic ESG case is that when you take a long view, some things in life are more important than generating profit as calculated under Generally Accepted Accounting Principles (GAAP).

Even pre-pandemic corporate leaders began to speak of the corporation's role in addressing its "stakeholders," a change from the rubric of "shareholder primacy," which represented a change in language if not necessarily in actual practice.[3] Various companies adopted operating policies that included ESG components.[4]

Then, the social and economic disruption created by the 2020–2021 pandemic reframed the question of what sustainability means for individual companies and for the economy as a whole.

By June 2020, a mere 5 months after the first case of COVID-19 was reported in the U.S., unemployment had begun to moderate after reaching levels not seen since the Great Depression of the 1930s[5] following bi-partisan Congressional approval of $2 trillion

---

2. But see, e.g., *Notice of Proposed Rulemaking on Financial Factors in Selecting Plan Investments Amending "Investment Duties" Regulation at 29 CFR 2550.404a-1*, U.S. Department of Labor (June 23, 2020), https://www.dol.gov/agencies/ebsa/about-ebsa/our-activities/resource-center/fact-sheets/financial-factors-in-selecting-plan-investments; *Labor Dept. Seeks to Restrict Social Goals in Retirement Investing*, N.Y. TIMES, June 24, 2020, https://www.nytimes.com/2020/06/24/business/labor-retirement-investing.html ("The Labor Department is seeking a new federal regulation that could discourage retirement funds from making investments based on environmental, social and governance considerations."). At the time the Labor Department rules were proposed, Labor Secretary Eugene Scalia set out his views on the matter in the Wall Street Journal (see Eugene Scalia, *Retirees' Security Trumps Other Social Goals*, WALL STREET J. (2020), https://www.wsj.com/articles/retirees-security-trumps-other-social-goals-11592953329), prompting rebuttal from the CEO of the UN-sponsored Principles for Responsible Investment, see Reynolds, *ESG Is Risk Management, Not an Asset Class*, WALL STREET J. (2020), https://www.wsj.com/articles/esg-is-risk-management-not-an-asset-class-11593453762?mod=searchresults&page=1&pos=2. The Biden administration announced that it would not enforce the newly adopted ESG rules and would rewrite and formally propose replacement rules (*The Labor Department Will Not Enforce Two Trump-Era Rules Regulating Retirement Plans*, N.Y. TIMES, Mar. 11, 2021, https://www.nytimes.com/2021/03/11/business/the-labor-department-will-not-enforce-two-trump-era-rules-regulating-retirement-plans.html).

3. See discussion *infra* notes 10–24 and accompanying text.

4. See, e.g., *Microsoft Will Be Carbon Negative by 2030*, MICROSOFT (Jan. 16, 2020), https://blogs.microsoft.com/blog/2020/01/16/microsoft-will-be-carbon-negative-by-2030/; Bloomgarden, *Corporate Responsibility Is Taking on a New Meaning*, FORBES (Jan. 2, 2019), https://fortune.com/2019/01/02/corporate-social-responsibility-sustainability-transparency/ (reporting on *Building a More Just Marketplace: The 2018 Rankings of America's Most JUST Companies*, https://justcapital.com/reports/americas-most-just-companies-2018/).

5. *Don't Cheer Too Soon. Keep an Eye on the Core Jobless Rate*, N.Y. TIMES, June 15, 2020, https://www.nytimes.com/2020/06/15/upshot/jobless-rate-misleading-virus.html.

in fiscal stimulus[6] and the deployment of trillions more in Federal Reserve support for the economy.[7] At the time this chapter was written (mid-2021), no victory over COVID-19 has been declared, but the 2021 effort to end the disruption to daily life has included additional fiscal stimulus of $1.9 trillion and a mass vaccination program.[8]

> The 2020–2021 pandemic revealed that collective problems that exist at global scale require resources beyond those that can be easily mustered under the current rules for the American economic system.

The 2020–2021 pandemic revealed that collective problems that exist at global scale require resources beyond those that can be easily mustered under the current rules for the American economic system. Unless one assumes that current rules governing the economy are adequate to address the need for a durable economy—a risky assumption, given that the economy staved off crashes in 2008 and 2020 only through the injection of trillions of dollars of government funds—it is inevitable that those rules will change. The need for such change is already visible, and the call for such change has already begun.[9]

At the company level, businesses that seemed solid pre-pandemic discovered weaknesses such as broken business models, inadequate liquidity, disconnected supply chains, and workforce dislocations. Some businesses suffered more than others, but all were affected.

Even before the pandemic, investors, managers, lawyers, and policymakers continuously debated corporate governance doctrines on the fiduciary duties of directors, the purpose of

---

6. National Public Radio, *What's Inside the Senate's $2 Trillion Coronavirus Aid Package* (Mar. 26, 2020), https://www.npr.org/2020/03/26/821457551/whats-inside-the-senate-s-2-trillion-coronavirus-aid-package. Between new spending and tax breaks, the Wall Street Journal estimated the coronavirus price tag at $3.3 trillion as of June 3, 2020 (see Kate Davidson & Paul Kiernan, *Coronavirus Stimulus Funds Are Largely Depleted After Nine Weeks*, WALL STREET J. (2020), https://www.wsj.com/articles/coronavirus-stimulus-funds-are-largely-depleted-after-nine-weeks-11591185600.

7. Fed actions included expanded quantitative easing ("Between mid-March and mid-June, the Fed's portfolio of securities held outright grew from $3.9 trillion to $6.1 trillion."); lending to securities firms under the Primary Dealer Lending Facility; and backstopping repo, commercial paper, and money market fund markets. See Brookings Institute, *What's the Fed Doing in Response to the COVID-19 Crisis? What More Could It Do?* (June 12, 2020, updated June 19, 2020), https://www.brookings.edu/research/fed-response-to-covid19/. See also *The Fed Goes All in with Unlimited Bond-Buying Plan*" N.Y. TIMES, Mar. 23, 2020, https://www.nytimes.com/2020/03/23/business/economy/coronavirus-fed-bond-buying.html.

8. See *Here are the highlights of Biden's $1.9 trillion 'American Rescue Plan.'* N.Y. TIMES, Jan. 14, 2021, https://www.nytimes.com/2021/01/14/us/biden-american-rescue-plan.html.

9. See, e.g., Ceres Accelerator for Sustainable Capital Markets, *Addressing Climate as a Systemic Risk: A Call to Action for U.S. Financial Regulators* (June 1, 2020), https://www.ceres.org/news-center/press-releases/sweeping-new-report-provides-us-financial-regulators-key-action-steps, advocating for regulatory changes regarding systemic risk caused by climate change. See also Ceres Accelerator for Sustainable Capital Markets, *Blueprint for Responsible Policy Engagement on Climate Change* (July 16, 2020), https://www.ceres.org/resources/reports/blueprint-responsible-policy-engagement-climate-change; *The Pandemic Is Showing Us How Capitalism Is Amazing, and Inadequate*, N.Y. TIMES, Nov. 14, 2020 ("The nine months of the pandemic have shown that in a modern state, capitalism can save the day—but only when the government exercises its power to guide the economy and act as the ultimate absorber of risk. The lesson of Covid capitalism is that big business needs big government, and vice versa."), https://www.nytimes.com/2020/11/14/upshot/coronavirus-capitalism-vaccine.html; *Inside the Global Fight to Save Capitalism*, Politico, Dec. 11, 2020, https://www.politico.com/newsletters/global-translations/2020/12/11/inside-the-global-fight-to-save-capitalism-491124.

the corporation, and the relationship of the corporation to other stakeholders. Evolution of governance doctrines is part of how business adapts to changing times and circumstances.

Changes to the rules to make the economy more durable can, and almost certainly will, build upon the insights and experience of investors, companies, and business thought leaders developed by adopting sustainability practices from the pre-COVID era. Individual companies and investors implementing sustainability strategies have gained experience with the fine details and trade-offs involved. That granular knowledge represents hands-on understanding of the mechanics and potential unintended consequences of what is needed to create a truly durable economy post-COVID.

The role of corporate governance—the process by which private sector actors assemble and deploy capital, labor, and other resources to provide goods and services in the economy—has been vital in the pre-COVID era, both as companies adopt ESG strategies and as they communicate within the broader culture what is required for a sustainable future to emerge.

Fiduciary Duties, Corporate Purpose, and Stakeholder Interests

Shareholder Primacy

While "shareholder primacy" is not a statutory requirement, it is a doctrine that has been broadly accepted by investors and operating companies. "The United States is a 'shareholder primacy' jurisdiction, meaning that the primary focus of corporations is to return profits to shareholders. If stakeholder needs are considered, they are a secondary concern."[10]

The usual shorthand for shareholder primacy is that companies should "maximize shareholder value." As a first principle, requiring corporations to make money is not crazy: A company that does not make enough money to stay in business is not in a position to do anything else. The principle of shareholder primacy is usually attributed to Milton Freidman, an economist whose belief in unregulated working of market forces resonates strongly with those who benefit from the operation of market forces, or have ideological axes to grind. Those who feel unprotected by market forces or are left behind by them have less enthusiasm for Friedman or his worldview.

Focusing on benefits to shareholders is certainly consistent with Delaware law. Under the Delaware General Corporation Law (DGCL) as interpreted by the Delaware Court of Chancery and the Delaware Supreme Court, the board of directors of a company owes fiduciary duties to the "corporation and its shareholders" and the Delaware Chancery Court has noted that a corporation that chooses the for-profit Delaware corporate form binds its directors to "the fiduciary duties and standards that accompany that form. Those standards include acting to promote the value of the corporation for the benefit of its stockholders."[11]

10. American Bar Association Task Force for Sustainable Development, *Information for the United States Concerning Legal Perspectives on an Annual Board Statement of Significant Audiences and Materiality* (herein, "ABA Response"), https://d306pr3pise04h.cloudfront.net/docs/issues_doc%2FCorporate_Governance%2Flegal-memo%2Fus.pdf (part of the 2015 "Sustainability & the Fiduciary Duty of Boards of Directors" report by the United Nations Global Compact, https://www.unglobalcompact.org/library/3791).
11. ebay Domestic Holdings, Inc. v. Newmark, 16 A.3d 1 (Del. Ch. 2010).

> Directors of a for-profit Delaware corporation are permitted to approve the use of corporate assets to provide benefits to constituencies other than the shareholders, during the corporation's active operation as a going concern, but such "non-stockholder constituencies and interests can be considered . . . only instrumentally, in other words, when giving consideration to them can be justified as benefitting the stockholders."

The doctrine of shareholder primacy has had three great virtues, pre-pandemic. One is administrative ease—the doctrine provides a simplifying and clarifying function, by making the metrics for success quantifiable and measurable, either as reported in GAAP or reflected in the company's share price in the market.

Second, even though Delaware embraces "a republican model of corporate democracy giving the board strong power to pursue its own vision of what is best for stockholders,"[12] it is shareholders who have the ultimate corporate authority. "[O]nly stockholders can bring derivative actions. In addition, only stockholders have the right to vote for directors, to approve certificate amendments, to amend the bylaws, and to vote on important transactions such as mergers. In sum, under Delaware corporation law, no constituency other than stockholders is given any power."[13]

Finally, shareholder primacy aligns with the pursuit of alpha returns—non-risk-adjusted financial gains. For the disaggregated and atomistic investors and companies pursuing economic gain, shareholder primacy directs that the fruits of victory go to the shareholders (at least, after bonuses to management are paid).

In the capital markets, pursuit of alpha by investors, traders, and speculators produces a positive economic impact by providing liquidity for stocks and other financial instruments as individual holders, pursuing individual near-term and long-term goals, use individual strategies to evaluate, acquire, and divest securities, and engage in a day-by-day (or for algorithms, nanosecond-by-nanosecond) process of buying and selling.

Short-sighted investment can pay off in the short term. Business behaviors that shift costs onto employees, customers, or the public at large can be profitable to the business owners, executives, and investors in the short term. Undertaking risky business practices can generate profits in the short term. Famously, this attitude was summarized in July 2007 by former Citigroup CEO Charles Prince, who said, "As long as the music is playing, you've got to get up and dance," just before Citigroup's market capitalization of $250 billion was whittled to $8 billion.[14]

What the pandemic has revealed is that a shareholder primacy economy is a Formula One Car Economy. An economy designed for maximum performance in a fast-moving and highly competitive environment is not designed to come to a sudden stop, or to be durable when a crisis occurs.

ESG contemplates that a time will come when the music stops, or at least slows. And even if individual market participants do not want to recognize it, or want to maximize

---

12. The Dangers of Denial: The Need for a Clear-Eyed Understanding of the Power and Accountability Structure Established by the Delaware General Corporation Law, Leo E. Strine, Jr. (Strine).

13. Strine at footnotes 78–83 (footnotes omitted).

14. See *Citigroup's Chuck Prince Wants to Keep Dancing, and Can You Really Blame Him?* Time, July 10, 2007, https://business.time.com/2007/07/10/citigroups_chuck_prince_wants/.

profits now by evading paying the costs that will inevitably fall due, the dancers in every economic class will need to have jobs and food and shelter and medicine. The value of the institutions and activities that create those necessities of life will be measured differently if the accounting is fully burdened with all of the associated costs.

The core question on sustainability then becomes, if collective action to create a common good is desirable, or even necessary, how does the existing law on the ownership and investment of capital support or interfere with the ability of the free market to address sustainability?

Corporate Purpose and Fiduciary Duty

As a legal matter, "corporate purpose" is different from a corporate "vision statement" or "mission statement." There is also within the business community in recent years a "corporate purpose" debate whether corporations exist solely to benefit investors or society as a whole.[15]

Vision statements and mission statements adopted by corporations can have tremendous value as tools for establishing a company's core business objective and acting as a foundational statement for the values in the corporate culture. In turn, the quality of corporate culture (the explicit and implicit rules and behaviors of a company's personnel) can make or break the durability and sustainability of a company. A good corporate culture is valuable to good governance—bad corporate culture tends to tolerate or even encourage abusive behaviors that ultimately undermine the governance and operation and even success of a company.[16]

Corporate purpose, by contrast to a corporate mission statement or vision statement, is a legally required element of the corporation's Certificate of Incorporation, the document by which the corporation is established in Delaware. To form a Delaware corporation, the promoters must file a Certificate of Incorporation that sets out the "nature of the business or purposes to be conducted or promoted. It shall be sufficient to state, *either alone or with other businesses or purposes*, that the purpose of the corporation is to engage in any lawful act or activity for which corporations may be organized under the General Corporation Law of Delaware, and by such statement all lawful acts and activities shall be within the purposes of the corporation, except for express limitations, if any" (*emphasis added*).[17]

The corporation's objective may be "to conduct or promote any lawful business or purposes, except as may otherwise be provided by the Constitution or other law of this

---

15. In 2019, The Business Roundtable adopted a "Statement on the Purpose of a Corporation" (Aug. 19, 2019), https://www.businessroundtable.org/business-roundtable-redefines-the-purpose-of-a-corporation-to-promote-an-economy-that-serves-all-americans, by which the Statement's 181 corporate signatories announced a commitment to operate their respective companies to "deliver value to all [stakeholders], for the future success of our companies, our communities and our country." Thereafter, the World Economic Forum issued "The Universal Purpose of a Company in the Fourth Industrial Revolution" (Dec. 2, 2019), https://www.weforum.org/agenda/2019/12/davos-manifesto-2020-the-universal-purpose-of-a-company-in-the-fourth-industrial-revolution/, which called also for corporations to be responsible to corporate stakeholders and not merely shareholders. Without binding specific companies to take specific actions for the benefits of specific stakeholders, these statements stand as evidence of a general concern in the business community that the invisible hand, acting alone, is not providing sufficient social benefit.

16. National Association of Corporate Directors (NACD), *Report of the NACD Blue Ribbon Commission on Culture as a Corporate Asset* (2017), https://www.nacdonline.org/insights/publications.cfm?ItemNumber=48252.

17. DGCL Section 102(a)(3).

State."[18] The "any lawful purpose" language operates as something of a savings clause to prevent any other statement of corporate purpose in the charter from acting as a limitation on corporate power or authority, in the event that the business or circumstances confronting the corporation change or as the business evolves.[19]

The DGCL was amended in 2013 to permit creation of an entity called a benefit corporation or "B-Corp," which is defined as "a for-profit corporation . . . that is intended to produce a public benefit or public benefits and to operate in a responsible and sustainable manner. To that end, a public benefit corporation shall be managed in a manner that balances the stockholders' pecuniary interests, the best interests of those materially affected by the corporation's conduct, and the public benefit or public benefits identified in its certificate of incorporation."[20]

To form a Delaware B-Corp, the Certificate of Incorporation must "(1) identify within its statement of business or purpose pursuant to §102(a)(3) of this title *one or more specific public benefits to be promoted* by the corporation; and (2) state within its heading that it is a public benefit corporation" (emphasis added).[21]

While both for-profit Delaware corporations and Delaware B-Corps are governed by a board of directors, and directors of both types of organizations owe to the corporation and to the shareholders the fiduciary duties of care and loyalty, and are obligated to act on an informed basis, in good faith and in the honest belief that their actions are "in the best interests of the company," B-Corp directors are allowed to balance their duties to shareholders against obligations to the non-shareholder constituencies identified in the B-Corp charter.[22]

A B-Corp board can approve the use of corporate assets to promote non-shareholder benefits directly, in accordance with the B-Corp's "public benefit" charter provisions.[23] By contrast, directors of a for-profit Delaware corporation are permitted to approve the use of corporate assets to provide benefits to constituencies other than the shareholders, during the corporation's active operation as a going concern, but such "non-stockholder constituencies and interests can be considered … only instrumentally, in other words, when giving consideration to them can be justified as benefitting the stockholders."[24] Expenditures for charitable giving, community improvement, employee benefits, or operation of the company along lines that address ESG issues do not violate the principle of shareholder primacy, so long as such activities and expenditures are made as part of the board's business judgment that they ultimately benefit shareholders.

---

18. DGCL Section 101(b).

19. Strine, *supra* note 77 and accompanying text.

20. DGCL Section 362.

21. DGCL Section 362.

22. See *New DGCL Amendments and Market Developments Continue to Shift Balance in Decision on Whether to Convert to a Public Benefit Corporation*, https://blog.freshfields.us/post/102gabm/new-dgcl-amendments-and-market-developments-continue-to-shift-balance-in-decision.

23. DGCL Section 365.

24. Strine, *supra* note 33 and accompanying text.

Stakeholders

Although shareholders, employees, customers, and society at large can at various times and in various contexts be considered as "stakeholders" in how the way a corporation is run, each of those groups has a specific relationship to the corporation, with distinct and different capacities to make legal or economic claims on the corporation.[25]

> Although shareholders, employees, customers, and society at large can at various times and in various contexts be considered as "stakeholders" in how the way a corporation is run, each of those groups has a specific relationship to the corporation, with distinct and different capacities to make legal or economic claims on the corporation.

Research suggests improved corporate valuations accrue to corporations that prioritize "understanding the needs of their stakeholders, making investments in managing these relationships, and reporting internally and externally on the quality of their stakeholder relationships."[26]

Contrary to the expectations of critics who contended that sustainability was "a form of agency cost" in which managers derived "private benefits from embedding environmental and social policies in the company's strategy" or would result in a lack of competitiveness from a higher cost structure,[27] a survey of 180 companies across various industries (dividing between 90 "High-Sustainability" and 90 "Low-Sustainability" companies) over a period of 18 years between 1993 and 2010 found that companies in the High-Sustainability group received significantly higher market valuations than did those in the Low-Sustainability group.[28]

In fact, integration of such issues into a company's business model and strategy may be a source of competitive advantage for a company in the long run.[29] Moreover, improved stakeholder engagement may be an intangible asset "in the form of strong long-term relationships, which can become sources of competitive advantage ... [W]hen a corporation is able to credibly commit to contracting with its stakeholders on the basis of mutual trust and cooperation and a longer-term horizon—as opposed to contracting in an attempt to curb opportunistic behavior—then the corporation will experience reduced agency costs, transactions costs, and costs associated with team production."[30]

In other words, following through on a sustainability strategy may improve a company's strategic thinking and execution.[31]

Even within a regime of shareholder primacy, boards and managements have the discretion to pursue business strategies that can incur additional near-term costs to a company without immediate corresponding returns. "Though U.S. law has no mandate to consider

---

25. See, e.g., the adoption by the board of Prudential Financial, Inc. of a matrix setting out various stakeholder interests the company considers. *Prudential's Multi-stakeholder Framework Reinforces Board Commitment to Investors, Employees, Customers and Society* (Dec. 19, 2019), https://news.prudential.com/prudentials-multi-stakeholder-framework-reinforces-board-commitment-to-investors-employees-customers-and-society.htm.
26. Eccles, *supra* note 4, at 10.
27. *Id.* at 2.
28. *Id.* at 18.
29. *Id.* at 19.
30. *Id.* at 9.
31. *Id.* at 19. See also Singer, *Five Ways a Sustainability Strategy Provides Clarity During a Crisis*, Harvard Law School Forum on Corporate Governance (July 6, 2020), https://corpgov.law.harvard.edu/lawfirm/the-conference-board/.

stakeholder needs, directors have discretion to include stakeholders concerns in their deliberations. So long as their decisions serve a rational business purpose, directors may consider and act on issues concerning the company's impacts on non-shareholders."[32]

Research and development budgets of drug and technology companies, for example, represent a near-term use of corporate cash aimed at generating longer-term product revenues. Companies are also entitled to make expenditures without immediate-term payoffs, such as achieving carbon neutrality or removing vendors from the supply chain if those vendors abuse human rights.

As companies take individual actions to insulate themselves from the consequences of various ESG risks, their collective experience is creating a body of knowledge on the most effective implementations of sustainability policies. The perspectives of these companies, in turn, can be shared among business and investors on how best to address the collective threats faced by all businesses and all investors in society, including but not limited to climate change.

From that shared perspective, shareholders and stakeholders will have the chance to work with policymakers on how best to develop a framework for a post-COVID private economy that works in concert with public entities to address collective threats that operate at global scale.

Almost inevitably, those actions will require taking steps to change the laws to coordinate public and private sector actions on problems that threaten the durability of the economy. To believe in an outcome in which continued environmental and social degradation occurs, because business and society fail to change a legal structure in which atomistic decisions by self-interested actors pursue economic gains without regard to consequences to others, is to believe in a helplessness that is not part of the historic American character.

Markets and Market Failures

The corporate and securities laws are a complex and interlocking set of laws that define property rights.

These laws set boundaries and conditions respecting the rights of investors to own shares in private for-profit institutions with limited liability and perpetual life. These laws also establish the rights of corporate managers and boards to use corporate assets or distribute them to shareholders;[33] the obligations of corporate managers to disclose financial and operating information about the companies they operate;[34] and the terms under which markets to trade corporate shares operate.[35] As economist and former Labor Secretary Robert Reich notes, government makes and enforces the rules of the game in the economy, and when it does so, "Government doesn't 'intrude' on the 'free market.' It creates the market."[36]

---

32. ABA Response, *supra* note 16, Answer 11.

33. These are principally the laws and regulations of the state in which a corporation is formed, as interpreted by the common law developed by the courts of that jurisdiction, which for public companies is most often Delaware.

34. These are principally the state and federal securities laws, as interpreted by state and federal courts and the rules of the Securities and Exchange Commission (SEC).

35. These are principally the Securities Exchange Act of 1934, plus the rules of the SEC and the rules of the exchanges themselves.

36. Robert B. Reich, *Saving Capitalism For The Many, Not The Few 5* (2015), quoted in David J. Berger, *In Search of Lost Time: What If Delaware Had Not Adopted Shareholder Primacy?* (2017), https://papers.ssrn.com/sol3/papers.cfm?abstract_id=2916960.

At present, disaggregated and atomistic investors and companies pursue the economic opportunities within their grasp, in most cases without a need to consider the impacts on others.

The claim that the invisible hand of the marketplace will move business activities to maximize the common good is an ideology disguised as a cliché.[37] The claim is belied every day by the experience of those the market leaves behind.

Properly structured markets provide price discovery and economic efficiency, but the fact is that the markets also fail in consistent and identifiable ways. One of those failures is the tendency of market forces to underinvest in the common good—be it police, firemen, lighthouses, or public health. In consequence, government uses taxes to purchase the public goods that the market will not supply, or uses regulation to prohibit practices that the market will not quickly self-police, such as pollution, fraud, or the production of contaminated food or drugs.[38]

Once a risk is big enough—represented as a public good that the market would not or could not buy, or self-regulation that the market would not undertake—it can even become a systemic risk to the operation of the economy. The lack of public health infrastructure to handle the 2020 pandemic is the most recent example.

But COVID also exposed a smallness of imagination in the business and investing world respecting sustainability, an undue and undeserved respect for the ability of markets to address systemic risk:

- Institutional investors can use diversification to address portfolio risk—but not systemic risk like a pandemic.[39]

- Operating companies can use sustainability strategies to address company-specific risk, which is helpful company by company—but not systemic risk.

For "sustainability" to be an effective macroeconomic strategy, the private sector and the public sector will ultimately need to collaborate to rethink at least some of the rules of capitalism. The benefits to individual companies or investors from piecemeal company-by-company efforts can still be undermined by collective risks that exist at global scale.

---

37. Even Adam Smith, originator of the concept of the "invisible hand" of the marketplace, contended that the government had a role in the economy for the provision of "those public institutions and those public works, which, although they may be in the highest degree advantageous to a great society, are, however, of such a nature, that the profit could not repay the expense to any individual or small number of individuals, and which it therefore cannot be expected that any individual or small number of individuals should erect or maintain." Adam Smith, WEALTH OF NATIONS (1776) (Book V, part III).

38. Vast literature exists on the topics of negative externalities and the under-provision of public goods in laissez faire markets. Particularly lucid is John Cassidy, HOW MARKETS FAIL (2010).

39. "[Modern Portfolio Theory (MPT)] says that while investors can diversify idiosyncratic risk, they are at the market's whim with systemic risk. In other words, MPT postulates that investments are buffeted by beta (the market's risk and return) but how investors invest does not affect beta. However, we know from research studies that the impact of exposure to those systemic risks—market beta—is more powerful in determining investment returns than any manager's ability to extract differentiated returns owing to their skill (managerial alpha). That creates the MPT paradox. If it is accepted that MPT cannot affect beta, then an investor is in a bind: what we can affect matters much less than what MPT tells us we cannot." Jim Hawley & Jon Lukomnik, *Guest Viewpoint* IPE MAG., Oct. 2018, https://www.ipe.com/guest-viewpoint-jim-hawley-and-jon-lukomnik/10026861.article.

In the end, addressing such risks will require government-scale resources and coordination of public sector and private sector efforts. Until that time arrives, companies and investors can only do their best to address ESG matters under the existing corporate laws and doctrines.

Take-Aways for Board Members

Boards should:

- Require management to consider ESG in long-term strategy, and to document how it has specifically addressed ESG in planning.
- Use ESG as one of the frameworks for board oversight of corporate strategy and for reviewing the assumptions and facts used by management in developing corporate strategy.
- Assign concrete and specific tasks to board committees to deal with ESG issues (for example, having the audit committee review how costs and benefits of ESG topics are calculated and reported internally, and to shareholders and customers).

Boards should not:

- Think that ESG is a "fad" or accept claims that it is "already covered" by what the company is doing.
- Adopt a statement about ESG for public relations purposes, without the intention or resources to follow through.
- Expect to receive the benefits of the Business Judgment Rule on ESG matters unless the board affirmatively takes action, after deliberating in good faith and with due care.

Chapter 4
Directors' Duties Regarding Sustainability and ESG

Peter P. Tomczak

Sustainability and environmental, social, and governance (ESG) issues have come to dominate global headlines and discourse. Communities and governments are increasingly aware of and grappling with complex problems presented by humanity's impact on our natural world and our common welfare. So, too, are businesses, as reflected in innumerable interactions among many corporate stakeholders. Stockholders—a diverse group that encompasses large asset managers, labor pension funds, funds specifically targeting sustainable and ethical investments, activists for myriad causes, and individuals—are more frequently asking directors to explain and show, qualitatively and quantitatively, how their for-profit corporations' business models and strategies embrace practices that help tackle significant environmental, societal, and ethical challenges. Employees, too, are voicing their concerns and perspectives. Beyond mere words, stockholders, plus governmental authorities, rating agencies, media and clicktivists, academics, and consumers, are taking actions such as "vote no" campaigns, affirmative regulation, and boycotts to make businesses incorporate the sustainability and ESG principles advocated by those stakeholders.

Directors' decision-making on sustainability and ESG is guided by both what they should do and what they must do. Many sustainability and ESG topics confronting boards of directors are new, but the fundamental obligations of directors to their corporations and stockholders have remained constant. Directors' fiduciary duties are generalized legal principles, applied in highly contextual cases, including those involving sustainability and ESG matters. There is no simple, "one-size-fits-all" approach mandating whether and to what extent directors must adopt and implement sustainability principles, let alone a definitive answer on how directors must address any specific sustainability or ESG issue. Rather, as explained below, directors have broad discretion within the business judgment rule to adopt and implement more sustainable and ethical business practices that enhance the value of the corporation to its stockholders over the long term.

This chapter builds on the previous one, and addresses directors' fiduciary duties to adopt more sustainable principles and practices in establishing the corporation's strategy, and overseeing their implementation in the corporation's business and operations. Fiduciary duties of directors in the United States are generally governed by state, not federal, law. The summary of fiduciary duties set forth in this chapter proceeds from existing Delaware corporate law. The policy debates of what the law should or could be are addressed elsewhere in this book, though they do inform how this area of fiduciary duty law is evolving. Further, Delaware is the state of incorporation for approximately 60 percent of Fortune 500 companies. Its well-developed corporate law jurisprudence, with a large number of written opinions in cases decided by judges with deep experience in corporate governance and resolving disputes among corporate stakeholders, is looked to by states that may have yet to consider particular cutting-edge issues.

The Framework of Directors' Fiduciary Duties

The Role of the Board of Directors

The board of directors is the ultimate governing body of a corporation. In the common law tradition, directors in-effect serve as trustees of the corporation for its owners, the stockholders. Directors collectively manage the business and affairs of the corporation. Among other responsibilities, they: (i) establish overall corporate strategy; (ii) oversee the corporation's risk management and compliance with laws; (iii) select the officers and senior executives of the corporation; (iv) approve major transactions, dividends, and stock buy-back programs; and (v) oversee management in its day-to-day operation of the business, with that line between oversight and management at times being somewhat blurry, in practice. With the increasing importance of sustainability and ESG issues to corporate stakeholders and the perceived economic success of the business, directors more frequently find themselves needing to address sustainability and ESG when fulfilling their proper governance role and in dealing with internal and external parties, in particular stockholders.

> The increasing importance of sustainability and ESG issues to corporate stakeholders and the perceived economic success of the business require directors to address more frequently sustainability and ESG issues in fulfilling their proper governance role.

Directors at all times must satisfy their fiduciary duties. Understanding what these fiduciary duties demand of directors entails identifying what those duties are and to whom they are owed. That analysis also implicates what standard a court would apply in determining whether directors fulfilled their fiduciary duties.

Directors' Fiduciary Duties of Care and Loyalty, and Their Duty to Monitor

Directors owe fiduciary duties of care and loyalty. In brief, the fiduciary duty of care requires directors to make decisions in a careful manner based on all material information reasonably available to them. Directors should assure themselves that they have sufficient information needed to make a decision, though perfection in knowing every fact is not required. Importantly, in doing so, directors are fully protected in relying in good faith on the corporation's books and records, the corporation's officers and employees, and other committees of the board. Further, with particular relevance to sustainability and ESG issues that may be complex and highly technical in nature, directors may rely in good faith on the advice, opinions, and reports of experts (i.e., a person selected with reasonable care as to matters reasonably believed to be within his or her professional or expert competence). Sound process is key in establishing compliance with the duty of care. Directors should be able to demonstrate their active engagement in deliberations, attendance at and the length of meetings, and the materials, advice, and reports considered in making a decision. Toward this end, appropriate minutes and records of board decision-making should be kept.

The fiduciary duty of loyalty requires directors to act in good faith and with an honest belief that their decision or action is in the best interests of the corporation and its stockholders. Directors cannot place their personal interests ahead of those of the corporation and its stockholders. A director is said to be "interested" when he or she has a material financial or other interest in a decision that is different from that of the stockholders or, in the transactional context, the director stands on both sides of the transaction. In addition, a director risks breaching his or her duty of loyalty if he or she acts in a way suggesting that he or she is beholden to, or dominated or controlled by, one who is "interested" in the decision or transaction. To avoid possibly violating their duty of loyalty, directors should remain alert to their actual or apparent interestedness or lack of independence, and disclose all facts relevant to any potential conflict of interest of the director to the appropriate governing body. In certain situations, full disclosure and the implementation of procedural safeguards may significantly reduce or eliminate a director's risk of violating his or her duty of loyalty.

One obligation that flows from the duties of care and loyalty has particular significance in approaching sustainability and ESG issues: the duty to monitor. These oversight duties are commonly referred to as *Caremark* duties after the landmark 1996 Delaware Court of Chancery decision[1] that expressly recognized them. It is axiomatic that corporations may only conduct lawful business by lawful means. In *Caremark*, the court further recognized that corporations had greater incentives to enact effective ethics and compliance programs in order to promote the corporation's compliance with laws in light of (i) the increasing use of criminal sanctions and corporate criminal liability to punish corporations' violations of law, and (ii) the reductions in fines available under the U.S. Sentencing Guidelines. As the court in *Caremark* explained:

> [I]t would . . . be a mistake to conclude . . . that corporate boards may satisfy their obligation to be reasonably informed concerning the corporation, without assuring themselves that information and reporting systems exist in the organization that are reasonably designed to provide to senior management and to the board itself timely,

---

1. *In re* Caremark Int'l Inc. Deriv. Litig., 698 A.2d 959 (Del. Ch. 1996).

accurate information sufficient to allow management and the board, each within its scope, to reach informed judgments concerning both the corporation's compliance with law and its business performance.[2]

With such a system in place, directors must then monitor and oversee in good faith the corporation's compliance with laws.

Claims for violations of the duty to monitor have been filed by stockholders in the wake of major corporate scandals for violations of a wide assortment of criminal laws and regulatory rules. The underlying infractions have ranged from unlawful payments to physicians in *Caremark* itself, to money laundering, bribery conduct, off-label marketing practices for pharmaceuticals, cartel behavior, human slavery in the corporate supply chain, mining accidents, cybersecurity breaches, serial sexual harassment by a senior officer, misclassification of employees as independent contractors, and food safety failures.

Yet, despite their broad application to diverse compliance violations, even in light of certain recent decisions involving prime risks for single-product companies or profoundly deficient corporate governance practices in which defendants' motions to dismiss were denied, *Caremark* claims remain among the most difficult to plead and prove for plaintiff stockholders. The duty to monitor therefore does not punish mere business risk-taking, even if those business decisions may be criticized with the benefit of hindsight for having resulted in substantial financial losses. If the corporation has a charter provision exculpating directors for breaches of the duty of care, directors are not monetarily liable unless they acted disloyally or in bad faith (i.e., intentionally or knowingly) in not satisfying their fiduciary duties, having "utterly failed to implement any reporting or information system or controls," or "having implemented such a system or controls, consciously failed to monitor or oversee its operations thus disabling themselves from being informed of risks or problems requiring their attention."[3] A showing of bad faith would have profound consequences, including avoiding the protections of exculpatory charter provisions against certain monetary claims against directors, and precluding directors from potential indemnification. To be clear, though, "[b]ad oversight is not bad-faith oversight."[4]

Each director owes these fiduciary duties individually. However, the entire board should be engaged on the many ESG issues that may materially impact the corporation's overall business, strategy, culture, and financial performance, as well as the corporation's overall approach to ESG issues and aggregate risk tolerance. More technical or discrete ESG issues that demand particular expertise or detailed analysis may be better assigned to an appropriate committee of the board of directors to oversee. And the audit, compensation, nominating and governance, and other familiar committees certainly will be significantly involved within their respective capacities in addressing multiple ESG issues. ESG issues may be interconnected, and thus the board of directors should establish mechanisms to promote collaboration and discussion among committees tasked with overseeing different ESG issues. In short, boards of directors will need to consider the complexities of corporate governance structures for overseeing ESG.

---

2. *Id.* at 970.
3. Stone v. Ritter, 911 A.2d 362, 370 (Del. 2006).
4. Richardson v. Clark, 2020 Del. Ch. LEXIS 378, *5 (Del. Ch. 2020).

> The entire board should be engaged on the many ESG issues that may materially impact the corporation's overall business, strategy, culture, and financial performance, including to address interconnected ESG issues by establishing mechanisms to promote collaboration among various board committees and senior executives responsible for different ESG topics.

Further, the foregoing fiduciary duties are generalized principles of broad application. Board decisions on the incorporation of sustainability and ESG principles into the corporation's strategy, business model, and operations are not exempt. Under Delaware law, there is no specific duty to be, or not to be, sustainable.[5] So, the answer to what is required of directors in a given board decision on sustainability or ESG will depend on the application of these overarching duties to the particular facts of the case, evaluated by a court pursuant to a standard of review.

To Whom Fiduciary Duties Are Owed

The demands imposed on directors by their fiduciary duties are shaped by not only the nature of the duty but to whom it is owed. In particular, the duty of loyalty requires directors to act in the best interests of the corporation and its stockholders. Directors' fiduciary duties with respect to sustainability thereby implicate the recently reinvigorated debate of the corporation's proper purpose, and stockholder versus stakeholder primacy. That topic was discussed in greater detail in the previous chapter, though it is briefly summarized here toward assisting directors in understanding the scope of their fiduciary duties.

Shareholder Primacy (Delaware)

Delaware law clearly provides for shareholder primacy. As succinctly stated by Delaware Supreme Court Chief Justice Leo E. Strine, Jr., this means that "directors must make stockholder welfare their sole end, and that other interests may be taken into consideration only as a means of promoting stockholder welfare."[6] But this requirement should not be construed as an absolute bar that precludes directors from considering other benefits to the corporation and its various stakeholders. To the contrary, directors may advance non-stockholder stakeholders interests if they benefit the stockholders' pecuniary interests. Though directors may consider other stakeholders when making their decisions, directors must still intend in good faith to maximize long-term interests of the stockholders, and those other stakeholders may only be considered to the extent they coincide with such long-term stockholder value creation. See *infra* §III.B.1 (discussing how focusing on a long-term versus short-term time horizon for stockholder interests may substantially reduce perceived tension with current sustainability and ESG expenditures).

"Stockholders" as a group consist of multiple parties with different financial and non-financial goals, varying levels of risk aversion, and longer or shorter expected time horizons

---

5. Though beyond the scope of this chapter, countries outside of the United States have begun amending the fiduciary duties imposed under their laws to expressly require consideration of sustainability and ESG issues.
6. Leo E. Strine, Jr., *The Dangers of Denial: The Need for a Clear-Eyed Understanding of the Power and Accountability Structure Established by the Delaware General Corporation Law*, 50 Wake Forest L. Rev. 761, 768 (2015).

to earn a return on their investment. In saying that fiduciary duties are owed to the stock-holders, the directors are not required to focus on the idiosyncratic goals of any one stock-holder. Instead, directors should view stockholders by their common status as residual risk bearers who have contributed capital to a presumably perpetual corporate enterprise.

The limits of directors' freedom to base decisions on interests other than the long-term interests of the stockholders is illustrated by the decision in *eBay Domestic Holdings, Inc. v. Newmark*.[7] In that case, the directors of Craigslist adopted certain defensive mechanisms to slow or prevent control of it being acquired by eBay. The Craigslist directors defended their actions as protecting Craigslist's social values and community-centered culture, eschewing proof that this culture resulted in increased profitability for the stockholders. The court rejected the Craigslist directors' argument, holding that fiduciary duties and standards include promoting the value of the corporation for the benefit of its stockholders, and refusing in that context "a corporate policy that specifically, clearly, and admittedly seeks *not* to maximize the economic value of a for-profit Delaware corporation for the benefit of its stockholders—no matter whether those stockholders are individuals of modest means or a corporate titan of online commerce."[8] In sum, "the social beliefs of the managers, no more than their own financial interests, cannot be their end in managing the corporation."[9] A rationale that wholly disregards stockholder value is invalid under Delaware law.

Constituency Statutes (Other U.S. States and Countries)
In contrast to Delaware, most other U.S. states and many other countries expressly allow (indeed, some require) directors to consider the interests of additional corporate stakeholders—employees, suppliers, and the community in which the corporation operates, among others. Adopted by a majority of U.S. states during the 1980s and 1990s primarily to deter corporate raiding and takeovers of local companies, these "constituency statutes" provide directors with a shield against fiduciary liability in taking into account interests of other stakeholders beyond the stockholders. Constituency statutes generally use similar language, though they vary on certain issues such as the full scope of factors that directors may consider, what other stakeholders may be considered, when such expanded factors may be considered (or is it limited to the context for corporate control), and the level of liability protection afforded under the statute.

Outside of the United States, many countries also reject the shareholder primacy model. For example, UK corporate law requires directors to consider a non-exhaustive list of stake-holders in determining, pursuant to their fiduciary duties, the best interests of the com-pany. In Canada, the duty of care includes identifying sustainability risks related to climate change. European countries that have a civil law system follow a variety of stakeholder governance models, with a strong focus on workers' rights and labor's participation at the board level in countries such as France and Germany. A July 2020 study by the European Commission found that in all EU jurisdictions, directors' duties are owed primarily to the company and not to the company's shareholders, and multijurisdictional studies show that

---

7. 16 A.3d 1 (Del. Ch. 2010).
8. *Id.* at 34.
9. Leo E. Strine, Jr., *Our Continuing Struggle with the Idea that For-Profit Corporations Seek Profit*, 47 Wake Forest L. Rev. 135, 151 (2012).

shareholder primacy in companies hinders their long-term contribution to sustainability.[10] Concerned that a short-term mindset among directors still hindered development of sustainable practices, the European Commission study recommended among other things a new EU directive providing an EU-wide formulation of directors' duties and the company's interest, requiring directors (i) to balance, along with shareholder interests, the long-term interests of the company, interests of employees and customers, local and global environment, and society at large, and (ii) to identify and mitigate sustainability risks and impacts arising from the company's business and supply chains.[11]

Public Benefit Corporations (Delaware)

Although Delaware has declined to adopt a constituency statute, it took steps to address growing unease about the shareholder primacy model, and societal and investor demand for companies to adopt sustainability and ESG principles, by creating an innovative form of business organization: the "public benefit corporation," or "PBC."[12] A PBC is a for-profit corporation that seeks to produce a public benefit while operating in a responsible and sustainable manner. The governing statute expressly provides that the directors must balance the stockholders' financial interests, the interests of other stakeholders impacted by the corporation's activities, and the public benefit mission of the PBC as set forth in its certificate of incorporation. Notably, directors are deemed to satisfy their fiduciary duties in balancing these interests and goals if their decision is informed, disinterested, and rational in its balancing of stakeholder interests. A Delaware PBC also must every other year disclose to its stockholders the PBC's promotion of its stated public benefit and the interests of those materially impacted by its activities, including among other information the objectives established by the board of directors in promoting that public benefit, the standards by which progress on those goals will be measured, and an assessment of whether those goals were achieved.[13]

Recently, Delaware lowered the barriers to entry to becoming a PBC, reducing the voting threshold to transform into a PBC, eliminating the triggering of statutory appraisal rights upon doing so, and clarifying and affirming the exculpatory and indemnification protections afforded PBC directors under Delaware law. With these statutory amendments and provisions, and with several PBCs now being publicly traded and larger corporations forming PBC subsidiaries in their group of companies, this alternative form of business organization opens new opportunities to corporations, directors, and stockholders who seek to more transparently and forcefully address sustainability and ESG in their businesses.

* * * * *

---

10. European Commission Directorate-General for Justice and Consumers, *Study on Directors' Duties and Sustainable Corporate Governance* (July 2020), https://op.europa.eu/en/publication-detail/-/publication /e47928a2-d20b-11ea-adf7-01aa75ed71a1/language-en.

11. *Id.* at vii, ix.

12. Although sometimes used interchangeably in colloquial conversation, a PBC is different than a "B Corp." A "B Corp" is not a form of legal entity but a certification by the nonprofit B Lab for having satisfied certain criteria.

13. In addition, the Delaware Certification of Adoption of Transparency and Sustainability Standards Act allows a company to voluntarily seek certification under it for sustainability plans devised by the company's governing body and tailored to the company's business.

Regardless of which corporate law model governs, there are significant practical conse-quences from the increasing focus on sustainability and ESG issues by corporate stake-holders other than stockholders. Many directors have reported that the greatest pressure to address environmental, social, and ethical issues now is being exerted by the company's customers and key supply chain partners. Even under shareholder primacy or with share-holder apathy, directors should not and cannot disregard these concerns. This trend may, in practice, have an equal if not greater influence on companies' adoption of sustainability and ESG principles than the choice of a particular corporate law model.

Standards of Review—Business Judgment and Entire Fairness

Directors' fiduciary duties for sustainability are shaped by both the substantive legal obli-gations owed by the directors, and the standards under which a court would review a claim that the directors' decision violated their fiduciary duties. The starting point for courts in most situations[14] is the business judgment rule. The business judgment rule is not a fiduciary duty; it is a presumption that, in making a business decision, directors acted on an informed basis, in good faith, and in the honest belief that the decision was taken in the interests of the corporation and its stockholders. A plaintiff stockholder challenging a board's decision bears the burden to rebut this presumption by pleading facts that show the directors acted with gross negligence, disloyally, or in bad faith. If the plaintiff cannot do so, then the business judgment will apply, and the court will uphold the directors' decision if it can be attributed to any rational business purpose. The business judgment rule promotes multiple underlying policies, including among others an acknowledgment that courts are suboptimal decision-makers on commercial matters and a respect for stockholders' rights as owners.

If, however, a plaintiff stockholder rebuts the presumptions of the business judgment rule by showing that the directors did not act in an informed manner, in good faith, or in the best interests of the corporation and its stockholders, then the protections of the busi-ness judgment rule will no longer apply. Instead, a court will evaluate the directors' decision under the more onerous and intrusive standard of entire fairness. Under entire fairness, the burden shifts initially to the defendant directors to prove that the decision or transaction was objectively fair, both through fair dealing and at a fair price. At bottom, under entire fairness, the decisions of the directors will no longer be sustained merely because they were rational, as they would be under the more lenient business judgment rule.

Approaching Sustainability and ESG Issues

The Increasing Importance and Complexity of Sustainability and ESG

Directors certainly feel increased pressure to integrate more sustainable and ethical business practices into their decision-making on key corporate actions and strategies. Stockholders and other stakeholders, all with different perspectives, time horizons, and goals, are more

---

14. For certain matters that inherently are subject to the omnipresent risk of directors having a conflict of inter-est, such as the adoption of defensive measures in response to perceived threats to corporate control, Delaware courts have required directors first to demonstrate that they acted reasonably before being entitled the protec-tions of the business judgment rule. These situations are generally beyond the scope of this chapter.

frequently asking directors to explain their approach to sustainability and ESG issues, and agree to targets and plans that implement specific actions advocated. Directors' deliberations often entail consideration of complex and evolving issues, with courses of action that may fundamentally change the company and its business operations. The reverberations of boards' decisions impact corporate stakeholders differently. Sometimes, different stakeholders—or even different members of the same stakeholder group, such as stockholder pension funds and activist funds—advocate for competing principles and goals.

In addition, governmental authorities are increasingly enacting legislation and promulgating rules that embody sustainability or ESG principles. In many jurisdictions, including the United States, these laws are enforced both civilly and criminally, including through the prosecution of corporations and their directors, officers, and employees, and the imposition of monetary and non-monetary sanctions and penalties. What once may have been aspirational goals consigned to private decisions to "do the right thing" are now backed by the force of law that corporations must obey.

Applying the Existing Fiduciary Duty Framework to Sustainability and ESG

Under the existing fiduciary framework of general application, directors have substantial though not unfettered freedom to consider and adopt sustainability and ESG principles in the corporation's overall strategy and business model. Even within the Delaware model of shareholder primacy, directors of for-profit entities are within their business judgment to account for opportunities and risks presented by sustainability if also motivated and justified by the creation of stockholder value. From that touchstone, the application of the business judgment rule flexibly allows directors to pursue courses of action tailored to the specific needs of the business. To avail themselves of the protections of the business judgment rule, directors must act in good faith, in an informed manner, and in the best interests of the corporation and its stockholders. In practice, that means understanding among other things the benefits and costs of sustainable practices, alternative strategies, and their respective impacts upon stockholders and other corporate stakeholders.

> The business judgment rule flexibly allows directors to pursue courses of action tailored to address the business's specific ESG issues and goals, provided directors act in good faith, in an informed manner, and in the best interests of the corporation and its stockholders.

Indeed, the business judgment rule supports multiple underlying policies that apply with equal if not more force in the context of sustainability and ESG. First, the business judgment rule prevents undue substantive second-guessing by courts. Courts, making decisions based on the more limited universe of facts before them, are typically not better positioned than directors and corporate managers to decide complex issues such as how to reduce the corporation's carbon footprint, incorporate the use of sustainable materials and inputs, manage a global supply chain to promote ethical business practices, etc. The variety of responses resulting from a free market for sustainable solutions helps advance the ultimate goals of sustainability and ESG. In addition, by avoiding substituting their judgment for those of the directors, courts exhibit rightful deference to stockholder rights as owners and their choice of who should manage the business and affairs of their company. As noted above, stockholders have been an important driving force for boards to focus on sustainability in the corporation, as those stockholders increasingly see sustainable business models and principles as maximizing long-term stockholder value. Stockholders can thus elect existing or new directors who best represent the stockholders' preferred focus on and strategy for a sustainable and ethical business that complies with applicable laws.

Directors confronting a bewildering array of sustainability and ESG issues should be comforted by the continued vitality of the business judgment rule. Further, toward complying with their fiduciary duties, directors may also find it particularly useful to frame their decisions on sustainability and ESG issues by, among other considerations, both (i) the long-term horizon for creation of corporate and stockholder value, and (ii) their duty to monitor the corporation's compliance with laws.

> Directors should frame their decisions on sustainability and ESG issues by among other considerations both the long-term horizon for creation of corporate and stockholder value, and their duty to monitor the corporation's compliance with laws.

Long-Term Horizon

It is incorrect to assert that stockholder value is intrinsically opposed to sustainability. What was once viewed as purely ethical norm, or even a fringe idea, may evolve into a key issue affecting the economic value of the corporate enterprise. Climate change is just such an example. Decades ago, even with growing acceptance of scientific evidence, the propositions that human activities influenced Earth's climate and would cause a warming of the lower atmosphere were treated as moral or environmental problems. Now, businesses regularly consider the impact of climate change and other consequences of global warming on their business operations and financial results. These businesses also assess their contributions to anthropogenic climate change. They are aware that governmental authorities are beginning to more squarely regulate certain commercial and consumer activities toward limiting the negative consequences of climate change. They are also aware that consumers may prefer competing or substitute products that better embody sustainable and ethical principles with which those consumers identify. Sustainability and ESG therefore become drivers of brand value. Those new legal rules and changing consumer preferences may disrupt the existing business model and operations, and ultimate financial performance, of the company.

Much of the perceived tension between sustainability and stockholder interest is actually a difference between temporal (i.e., short-term versus longer-term) horizons for financial performance. In fact, vocal stockholder proponents of more sustainable and ethical business practices have tied sustainability and ESG to long-term value. The President and CEO of State Street Global Advisors observed, "ESG issues have become much more important for us as long-term investors." Many commentators have pointed to the August 2019 Statement on the Purpose of the Corporation from the Business Roundtable, which was signed by 181 Chief Executive Officers, as a harbinger of the broader rejection of shareholder primacy. The signatories expressed their intention to operate their companies for the benefit of all stakeholders, but they also in the same document confirmed their commitment to creating long-term value for the stockholders. Similarly, in its 2020 Investment Stewardship Global Corporate Governance and Engagement Principles, BlackRock, the world's largest asset manager, stated that its "fiduciary duty to clients is to protect and enhance their economic interest in the companies in which we invest on their behalf . . . Our consideration of these [ESG] factors is consistent with protecting the long-term economic interest of our clients' assets."

The default lifespan of corporations is perpetual. Outside of specific contexts which by their very nature impose a shorter temporal horizon such as a sale of corporate control, the corporation's best interests are determined without regard to a fixed investment horizon, and directors are generally free to establish the time frame for creation of stockholder value. Although different stockholders may have different time horizons to recoup their investment, in light of the corporation's perpetual existence, the fiduciary duties of the directors point toward the creation of value for the residual claimants over the long term.

Accordingly, beyond exceptional settings establishing a shorter timeframe, directors are entitled to account for and take action to enhance the long-term value that would be available to the stockholders. Courts have expressly recognized that "a corporation may take steps, such as giving charitable contributions or paying higher wages, that do not maximize corporate profits currently."[15] This is permissible because "such activities are rationalized as producing greater profits over the long-term" for the corporation and its residual-claimant stockholders.[16] Similarly, expenditures to adopt more sustainable and ethical practices may be undertaken if rationally related to the creation of long-term stockholder value—a justification that exists in all but a small set of sustainability and ESG concerns that are not expected to increase value at all within any time horizon, and may constitute waste.

In practice, many boards of directors and senior management are under significant pressure to deliver short-term returns. Stockholders as a group include both index funds with long-term investment horizons and equally, if not more, vocal active asset managers and activists with shorter-term time investment horizons. The demands of dealing with such stockholders do not alter the legal duties of directors, but do require directors to consider and articulate clearly the trade-offs in sustainability and ESG investments. The corporate strategy and business plan, and communications about them to key corporate stakeholders, should demonstrate how foregone short-term returns and strategies increase long-term stockholder value, and are not merely an excuse for near-term underperformance.

---

15. Frederick Hsu Living Tr. v. ODN Holding Corp., 2017 Del. Ch. LEXIS 67, *44–45 (Del. Ch. 2017) (quoting Leo E. Strine, Jr., *Our Continuing Struggle with the Idea that For-Profit Corporations Seek Profit*, 47 Wake Forest L. Rev. 135, 147 n. 34 (2012), and also citing TW Servs., Inc. v. SWT Acq. Corp., 1989 Del. Ch. LEXIS 19, 1989 WL 20290, *7 (Del. Ch. 1989) (noting that directors "may be sensitive to the claims of other 'corporate constituencies'" in pursuing the stockholders' long-run interests)).

16. Allen v. El Paso Pipeline GP Co., 113 A.3d 167, 180 (Del. Ch. 2014) (quoting Leo E. Strine, Jr., *Our Continuing Struggle with the Idea that For-Profit Corporations Seek Profit*, 47 Wake Forest L. Rev. 135, 147 n. 34 (2012)).

Complying with Their Duty to Monitor

Another way to approach directors' fiduciary duties for sustainability and ESG is through the lens of the duty to monitor. *Caremark* duties are relevant to sustainability and ESG in at least two ways. First, as noted above, sustainability and ESG principles, representing society's expectations for lawful and ethical conduct, become enshrined in laws and regulations. Corporations must comply with those applicable laws. And through corporate information and reporting systems, boards of directors, appropriately within their scope, monitor their corporations' compliance with these laws.

Revelations that corporations violated laws addressing ESG issues often trigger claims by plaintiff stockholders that directors failed to exercise sufficient oversight. Thus, as noted above, plaintiff stockholders have sought to hold directors personally responsible for corporate scandals involving corporate misconduct from bribery, to human slavery in the corporate supply chain, to food safety failures. Further, using the "tools at hand" as urged by Delaware courts, plaintiff stockholders are with equal if not greater frequency seeking to inspect corporate books and records to investigate mismanagement and potential oversight claims. Directors must be mindful of the increasing legal and reputational risks arising from litigation of fiduciary claims and inspection demands. See generally *infra* Chapter 17 (discussing ESG litigation and risk management).

In addition, going beyond what is legally required of the corporation, there is unity between the design and implementation of an effective compliance system and the corporation's commitment to sustainability and ESG. As explained by Chief Justice Leo E. Strine, Jr., Kirby M. Smith, and Reilly S. Steel, sustainability and ESG may be understood as an extension of the directors' *Caremark* duties. Both start with rigorous analysis of a fundamental question: how does a corporation make money? That way must always be lawful. By then going beyond the minimum requirements imposed by the law and embodying sustainable and ethical principles in how the corporation conducts business, directors will cause their corporations to meet both legitimate and reasonable expectations for sustainability and ESG, while concomitantly reducing the risk of violating existing law on issues. Sustainability and ESG therefore may be encompassed within the board's existing structures, policies, and programs for compliance.

Conclusion

Directors are granted substantial freedom to consider and adopt ESG principles and sustainable practices. However, they must at all times satisfy their fiduciary duties to the corporation and the stockholders. How those fiduciary duties apply to directors' decisions on specific sustainability and ESG matters will continue to evolve as boards of directors more frequently address those issues and engage with stockholders and other corporate stakeholders about them. The challenges and opportunities presented by sustainability and ESG are immense, and engaged boards of directors that practice sound decision-making and promote ethical corporate cultures are well positioned to steward the corporations they serve in delivering benefits to all corporate stakeholders and society.

Take-Aways for Board Members

- The board of directors should articulate succinctly the board's approach to sustainability and ESG, as well as how that approach enhances the long-term financial value of the corporation and its stockholders, in satisfaction of the directors' fiduciary duties. The board of directors should review the stated purpose of the corporation, and consider if that purpose, as articulated, should be updated to address sustainability and ESG principles. The board also may want to consider whether, in light of the purpose and goals of the corporation, it should become a public benefit corporation (PBC).

- The board of directors should determine whether the strategic planning and risk management relating to particular sustainability and ESG issues should be overseen by the full board of directors or a particular board committee. To the extent responsibility for such oversight is assigned to one or more committees of the board, it should be appropriately reflected in committee charters and the board should consider how committees will collaborate with one another in order to address interrelated ESG issues. Over a longer-term horizon, the board of directors should also evaluate whether the composition of its members, and responsible committees' members, matches the experience and expertise needed to oversee those material sustainability and ESG issues.

- Given the clear importance of sustainability and ESG to the corporation's stockholders and its long-term financial success, directors should be active in decision-making on sustainability and ESG issues, and monitoring the corporation's progress with respect to these areas. Directors should educate themselves about key ESG and sustainability trends within the corporation's industry, and how the company will be impacted by those trends and developments. Directors should seek out and rely upon input from corporate management, advisers, and experts qualified to address the topic(s) under consideration. The board of directors should establish a process by which management can regularly inform the board of directors of developments in sustainability and ESG that materially impact the corporation's current and future business, and management's responses to them.

- In addressing specific material ESG and sustainability issues, directors should start from first principles. Mindful of applicable law, they should discuss whether their decisions ultimately follow a shareholder primacy or stakeholder governance model. They should evaluate what data and other information are needed for them to make an informed decision on a particular issue, and make arrangements for that data and information to be provided to the board sufficiently in advance of any meeting.

- The board of directors should review the corporation's overall business strategy and enterprise risk management, from both short-term and long-term perspectives, toward understanding how they integrate sustainability principles and address ESG risks.

- The board of directors, in particular the compensation committee of the board of directors, should consider how the corporation's compensation practices foster alignment between long-term stockholder value and sustainable practices.

- Directors should keep abreast of legal developments that may change the scope of their fiduciary duties. There is substantial discussion in the United States and many countries about reshaping fiduciary duties. For example, the Accountable Capitalism Act, introduced on August 15, 2018, would compel certain very large corporations to procure a federal charter, and their directors to balance the pecuniary interests of stockholders and all corporate stakeholders materially affected by the corporation's conduct as well as community and societal factors. Outside of the United States, the European Commission has launched a public consultation to hear and gather data from corporate stakeholders on "sustainable corporate governance," including among other issues the scope of stakeholder interests to be accounted for in directors' fiduciary duties and the integration of sustainability issues into corporate strategy.

- In addition, directors should monitor the evolving disclosure requirements under U.S. federal securities laws and other U.S. and international laws. See *infra* Chapters 14 and 15 (discussing public company mandatory reporting and voluntary reporting, respectively, and discussing disclosure of ESG issues and information). Beyond mandatory disclosure rules, in seeking stockholder action, directors of Delaware corporations must fulfill their fiduciary duty to disclose fully and fairly material information. Directors should be mindful of what categories of facts are in practice considered material and disclosed when seeking stockholder action. Directors should also receive regular updates on material sustainability and ESG litigation involving the company's key ESG risks, industry, and similarly situated competitors. See *infra* Chapter 17 (discussing ESG litigation, including disclosure, conduct, and governance claims involving ESG issues).

- The board of directors should also consider how best to communicate its approach to sustainability to stockholders and other stakeholders, including proxy advisers and ESG rating agencies. This outreach may include publication of a corporate "Statement of Purpose" or "Sustainability Report," but should not end there. Directors of U.S. public companies should understand how the corporation describes their ESG decision-making and oversight processes in its proxy statement, annual report, and/or Sustainability Report. Directors should also plan for longer-running conversations among the board, senior corporate officers, key stockholders, and other corporate stakeholders.

- The board of directors should pay close attention to measuring corporate performance toward achieving sustainability and ESG goals set forth in the overall corporate strategy and communications with corporate stakeholders. Management should explain to the board which quantitative metrics are most suitable to utilize and track given the corporation's business. Directors should consider how existing information and reporting systems can be used in monitoring performance metrics for sustainability and ESG, and any enhancements that would allow the board of directors and management to measure progress.

- Directors should attend meetings (in person or remotely). They should actively participate in the meeting and proactively ask questions of management. Directors should take sufficient time to deliberate upon decisions. The corporate secretary and/or general counsel should keep an appropriate written record of the directors' decision-making.

* * * * *

The author is grateful to Isabella de la Guardia and Cristina Villaroel for their research assistance, and Beatriz Araujo, Eric Klinger-Wilensky, Robert Mascola, and Craig Roeder for their insightful comments. The views expressed herein are the personal views of the author and do not represent the views of Baker & McKenzie LLP or constitute legal advice.

Additional Reading

1. Peter A. Atkins, et al., *Social Responsibility and Enlightened Shareholder Primacy: Views from the Courtroom and Boardroom* (Feb. 4, 2019), https://corpgov.law .harvard.edu/2019/02/21/social-responsibility-and-enlightened-shareholder -primacy-views-from-the-courtroom-and-boardroom/.

2. Business Roundtable, *Statement on the Purpose of a Corporation* (Aug. 2019), https://s3.amazonaws.com/brt.org/BRT-StatementonthePurposeofaCorporation October2020.pdf.

3. Robert G. Eccles & Svetlana Klimenko, *The Investor Revolution*, HARV. BUS. REV., May–June 2019, https://hbr.org/2019/05/the-investor-revolution.

4. SEC Commissioner Allison Herren Lee, *Keynote Address at the 2021 Society for Corporate Governance National Conference—Climate, ESG, and the Board of Directors: "You Cannot Direct the Wind, But You Can Adjust Your Sails"* (June 28, 2021), https://www.sec.gov/news/speech/lee-climate-esg-board-of-directors.

5. PwC, *ESG Oversight: The Corporate Director's Guide* (Nov. 2020), https://www.pwc .com/kr/ko/publications/research-insights/esg-guidebook-layout.pdf.

6. Leo E. Strine, Jr., et al., *Caremark* and ESG, Perfect Together: A Practical Approach to Implementing an Integrated, Efficient, and Effective *Caremark* and EESG Strategy, 106 IOWA L. REV. 1885 (2021) .

7. WBCSD & Baker McKenzie, *Board Directors' Duties and ESG Considerations in Decision-Making* (Nov. 2020), https://www.wbcsd.org/Programs/Redefining-Value /Business-Decision-Making/Governance-and-Internal-Oversight/Resources /Board-directors-duties-and-ESG-considerations-in-decision-making.

Chapter 5

The Role of the Audit Committee in the Board's Management of Sustainability and ESG Issues

Lawrence A. Darby, III

There has been no more striking development in the progressive improvement of disclosure to public securityholders under U.S. federal securities laws and the more gradual recognition of the importance of independent oversight of management in the development of the corporation law jurisprudence of corporate governance than the emergence of the audit committee as a crucial institution in the functioning of the modern business corporation. Beginning in the early 1970s, and following the collapse of speculative excesses in U.S. capital markets in the late 1960s, the Securities and Exchange Commission recommended that publicly traded corporations create an audit committee, and, in 1977, the New York Stock Exchange began to require that all listed companies have an audit committee with independent directors. These developments reflected the growing recognition that disclosure mandates, whether under the securities laws themselves or as part of the companies' obligations under the listing agreement, were not sufficient to fully protect securityholders from management failings, especially as regards the integrity of financial information presented in corporate reports and SEC filings and that stronger oversight by directors from within the public corporation was needed.

The collapse of many "dotcom" companies and most critically the failure of Enron Corporation in 2001 and the concomitant prosecution of Arthur Andersen resulted in the embedding of the audit committee within the structure of corporate governance as a critical bulwark of the integrity of financial disclosures under the federal securities laws with the passage of the Sarbanes Oxley Act of 2002 (SOX).[1] Under SOX, every company listed on a national securities exchange or traded on a national securities association such as NASDAQ is required to have an audit committee.[1] The required audit committee is a committee of the board established for the purpose of overseeing the accounting and financial reporting processes of the issuer and audits of its financial statements and related work.[2] Critical to the functioning of the audit committee is that it is required to be comprised of independent directors.[3] SOX effectively requires that an audit committee include a "financial expert" as committees without the necessary accounting and financial expertise would not be able to carry out their important functions.[4] SOX also affords the audit committee with responsibilities for dealing with the company's auditors and affords the committee specific powers, including the power to engage counsel and consultants to advise it.[5]

When established by the board of directors, audit committees invariably are given "charters" granting them specific authorities and responsibilities, which may vary widely from corporation to corporation. While virtually all audit committees are given responsibility for assuring the integrity of the entity's financial statement disclosures, in practice audit committees typically review the entire range of the entity's financial information disclosures and take steps to ensure the accuracy and adequacy of both the audited financial statements and other financial information presented to the corporation's securityholders or filed with securities regulatory authorities.

Circumstances not entirely dissimilar to the confluence of securities law and governance failures that led to the enactment of SOX are now facing public companies as regards management of sustainability risks, namely the need for improved disclosure of material risks and uncertainties affecting the board's management of ESG issues and the need for improved governance mechanisms for the oversight of the board's performance in addressing these issues.

In 2020, the U.S. Government Accountability Office (GAO) published a report on public companies' disclosure of ESG factors and options to enhance them.[6] The GAO undertook the study because it found investors are increasingly asking public companies to disclose

---

1. SOX Section 301, amending Section 10A of the Securities Exchange Act of 1934 (Exchange Act) to insert paragraph (m).

2. Exchange Act Section 10A(m)(2). As mentioned below, this relatively narrow definition which focuses on reporting processes and the audits of the financial statements themselves has not constrained the functioning of the audit committee in today's corporate environment.

3. Exchange Act Section 10A(m)(3)(A).

4. See SOX Section 407(a). If the issuer does not include a financial expert on the audit committee, it must explain the reason it did not in its public filings. Neither the NYSE nor NASDAQ rules require a financial expert as such, but the NYSE does require that at least one member has accounting or related financial management expertise and NASDAQ requires at least one member to be "financially sophisticated."

5. Exchange Action Section 10A(m)(5).

6. *Government Accountability Office Report on Disclosure of Environmental, Social and Governance Factors and Options to Enhance Them*, GAO-20-530, July 2020 (GAO Report).

information on ESG factors to help them understand risks to the company's financial performance or other issues, such as the impact of the company's business on communities. Securityholders seek information about sustainability factors and their management in order to, among other things, make investment and divestment decisions regarding portfolio composition, protect their long-term investments through monitoring of management of sustainability risks, and inform themselves about sustainability information relevant to shareholder votes.

The GAO Report considered several options to meet the perceived needs of investors for additional ESG information: additional regulatory action (mainly issue-specific rule-making by the SEC including endorsement by the SEC of an ESG Framework in its regulations); additional legislation; additional stock exchange listing requirements; and sporadic private sector initiatives. In principle, the existing disclosure framework of the federal securities laws embraces a requirement for disclosure and discussion of sustainability risks and, for public companies, and there is now a broad understanding that a company's ongoing financial reporting obligations require disclosure of and discussion of sustainability risks. Disappointingly, the GAO Report found that while the quantity and quality of ESG disclosures generally improved in the last few years, most investors interviewed said they sought additional ESG disclosure to address gaps and inconsistencies, among other issues.

To date, the SEC has not adopted a set of comprehensive disclosure standards relating to ESG management and risks. Item 303 of Regulation S-K, Management's Discussion and Analysis of Financial Condition and Results of Operations, has long required disclosure of matters that would have an impact on future operations, including those that have not had an impact in the past. While the SEC has considered requiring specific inclusion of sustainability risks in the MDA discussion, it has so far not done so.[7] In 2016, the SEC issued a Concept Release seeking comments on various topics relating to disclosure requirements, several of which touched on disclosure of sustainability issues, but no action was taken to follow up on these topics. In January 2020, the Commission proposed amendments to the MDA discussion to eliminate duplicative disclosure and modernize and enhance the MDA disclosures. Many had hoped that the amendments and new guidance would specifically address additional sustainability disclosures, but the amendments did not do so.[8] The SEC contented itself with noting that, as part of its reviews of annual and periodic corporate filings and registration statements, the staff may make comments that effectively require additional specific sustainability disclosure by issuers, but these reviews are made on a case-by-case basis and there is no general requirement to discuss sustainability risks.[9] When the August 26, 2020 final rule was adopted, Commissioner Allison Herren Lee issued a

---

7. Regulation S-K, Items 303(a) and 303(b), 17 C.F.R., Part 229.

8. See Securities Act, Release No. 33-10750, 2020 (proposing release) and Securities Act, Release No. 33-10825, 2020.

9. See Jay Clayton (Chairman), *Statement on Proposed Amendments to Modernize and Enhance Financial Disclosures, Other Ongoing Disclosure Modernization Initiatives, Impact of Coronavirus: Environmental and Climate-Related Disclosure*, http://www.sec.gov/news/public-statement/clayton-mda-2020=-01-30. Also, in 2010, the SEC issued Commission Guidance Regarding Disclosure Related to Climate Change (Climate Change Guidance), but it is generally conceded that the Climate Change Guidance did little to improve companies' disclosure practices. The GAO Report also discusses various other efforts undertaken by the SEC's staff since 2010 to improve the quality of ESG disclosures through internal processes, without it may be said much demonstrable effect. See GAO Report 37–38.

statement criticizing the Commission's decision to omit specific disclosure requirements regarding sustainability issues such as climate change and expressed the view that the purported "principles-based approach" to ESG disclosure was likely inadequate and urged reexamination of these issues, especially in view of the large number of comment letters the Commission had received advocating specific ESG disclosure requirements.[10]

Recently Acting Chair Allison Herren Lee stated that the Commission will enhance its focus on climate-related disclosure and begin updating the Commission's 2010 guidance, and the SEC under her leadership created a new position "Senior Policy Advisor for Climate and ESG."[11] It is also notable that the Commission recently announced the formation of an Enforcement Task Force Focused on Climate and ESG issues.[12] Interestingly, in a recent speech at the Corporate Board Member ESG Forum, SEC Commissioner Roisman reiterated his reservations about the SEC issuing prescriptive, line-item disclosure requirements in the ESG space. Commissioner Roisman emphasized that the existing disclosure framework already requires material information one might characterize as "E", "S," or "G," and the SEC has explicitly interpreted its rules to require disclosure of the material effects of climate change. He also expressed agreement with the view that a reason there is not standardized environmental data is that standardization is very hard to do.[13]

None of the major U.S. exchanges has thus far taken any action to mandate specific disclosures. In 2019, the NASDAQ exchange published an ESG Reporting Guide which is nevertheless entirely voluntary.

Notwithstanding the cautious approach of the SEC to mandating specific ESG disclosure requirements, 2019 and last year showed continued dramatic increases in investor pressure for improved ESG disclosure and public corporations have responded accordingly by increased publishing of sustainability reports as part of investor relations and disclosure programs. The Governance and Accountability Institute reported that 90% of S&P 500 companies published sustainability reports in 2019, up from 53% in 2012.[14] Most recently, it has been reported that "activist" investors have formed investment pools to target companies whose ESG performance is perceived to be substantially below what should reasonably be expected for an issuer in its industry.[15]

The U.S. House of Representatives passed in June 2021 a bill entitled the Corporate Governance Improvement and Investor Protection Act, which also purports to respond to SEC inaction, by, among other things, amending the Exchange Act to require the SEC to

---

10. See *Statement of Commissioner Allison Herren Lee regarding Regulation-K and ESG Disclosures: An Unsustainable Silence*, http://www.se.gov/news/public-statement/lee-regulations-k-2020-08026. As noted in Commissioner Lee's statement, there have also been numerous requests by investors petitioning additional rule-making on ESG disclosure.

11. See *Acting Chair Allison Herren Lee's Statement on the Review of Climate Related Disclosure* (Feb. 24, 2021), *Statement by Commissioners Peirce and Roisman on the SEC's Enhanced Climate Change Efforts* (Mar. 5, 2021), and *Press Release Naming Satyam Khanna the Senior Policy Advisor* (Feb. 1, 2021), all https://www.sec.gov.

12. See March 4, 2021 SEC Press Release, https://www.sec.gov.

13. See *Speech by Commissioner Roisman on Addressing Inevitable Costs of a New ESG Disclosure Regime* (June 5, 2021), https://www.sec.gov.

14. See Government and Accountability Institute, *2020 Flash Report* (July 16, 2020), www.ga-institute.com /research-reports/2020.

15. See Richard J. Grossman & Neil P. Stronski, *New Tactics and ESG Themes Change Direction of Shareholder Activism*, Harvard Law School Forum on Corporate Governance (Feb. 26, 2021), https://corpgov.law.harvard .edu/2021/02/06.

adopt rules mandating disclosure by public companies of ESG metrics and the link between the metrics and the issuer's business strategy.[16]

The circumstances are quite different in Europe, a fact which may be especially important for U.S. companies with significant European operations as well as for European issuers. As part of the European Green Deal adopted in December 2019, the European Commission took steps to review provisions of the nonfinancial reporting directives of the Commission and the European Parliament regarding sustainability reporting and disclosure. These steps included an Action Plan on Financing Sustainable Growth Regulation. Recently, the Commission proposed various amendments to its nonfinancial reporting directives which would require the adoption of a first set of reporting standards for sustainability disclosures by October 31, 2022, and a second set of standards specifying complementary information by October 31, 2023.[17]

> Boards need to take decisive action to ensure careful oversight of the corporation's management and reporting of sustainability risks and the accuracy and adequacy of ESG disclosures. The means best suited to this purpose is the enhancement of the audit committee's oversight of both the management of sustainability risks and the accuracy and adequacy of ESG disclosures to securityholders.

With the growing investor pressure for improved ESG disclosure and the impetus for the development of comprehensive sustainability reporting standards along the lines of comprehensive financial accounting standards, boards need to take decisive action to ensure careful oversight of the corporation's management and reporting of sustainability risks and the accuracy and adequacy of ESG disclosures. The means best suited to this purpose is the enhancement of the audit committee's oversight of the management of sustainability risks and of the accuracy and adequacy of ESG disclosures to securityholders and others.[18] While traditionally the role of the audit committee was focused nearly entirely on financial statement review and internal control and auditing issues, more recently it has become clear that the audit committee has an additionally crucial role to play in enterprise risk management.[19]

---

16. H.R. 1187, passed June 17, 2021, https://www.congress.gov.

17. See *Proposal for a Directive of the European Parliament and of the Council, Amending Various Nonfinancial Reporting Directives as Regard Corporate Sustainability* (April 21, 2021), https://eur-lex.europa.eu.

18. While the SEC has not specifically addressed the role of the audit committee in oversight of sustainability risks and disclosures, the Commission has recently taken the somewhat unusual step of issuing a statement emphasizing the importance of the role of audit committees. See Jay Clayton (Chairman), Sagar Teotia (Chief Accountant), and William Hinman (Director, Division of Corporation Finance), *Statement on Role of Audit Committees in Financial Reporting and Key Reminders Regarding Oversite Responsibilities* (Dec. 30, 2019).

19. For a discussion of the traditional role of the audit committee that does recognize potential responsibility for risk management, see A. Al-Baidhani, *Role of Audit Committee in Corporate Governance*, Working Paper, https://www.ssrn.com. Support for an expanded role of the audit committee in enterprise risk management is shown in the surveys conducted by Jeffrey Cohen, Ganesh Krishnamurti, and Arnold Wright in their 2014 paper *Enterprise Risk Management and the Financial Reporting Process: The Experience of Audit Committee Members, CFOS and External Auditors*, https://www.ssrn.com. The audit committee should, however, be wary of undertaking risk management responsibility for corporate action beyond review of corporate disclosure and internal management information gathering and reporting processes. There has been an unfortunate trend in recent years to load up the audit committee with responsibility for various forms of compliance oversight. Imposing too great a burden on already overworked audit committee members may in itself result in inadequate oversight of the most critical corporate disclosure practices.

Strong support for this comes from the auditing profession. For example, in the Deloitte Center for Board Effectiveness preview of audit committee priorities and agenda, one finds the following assessment of the role of the audit committee in overseeing ESG disclosures:

> Although the audit committee's key responsibility with respect to disclosures relates to financial reporting, it has an important role to play in the oversight of the company's other disclosures. That role is increasingly played out in areas in which disclosure is not mandated by current SEC rules, including reporting on the company's environmental, social and governance (ESG) activities . . . Audit committees will be on the "front line" in overseeing whether and the extent to which assurance can be provided as to ESG and other non-financial disclosures.[20]

Similarly, Maura Hodge of KPMG recently wrote:

> How oversight for ESG strategy is handled at the board level is often a matter of preference . . . Yet, no matter where the issues sit at the board level, the intensity of data and information in sustainability reporting brings the audit committee's expertise into play.[21]

Loop, DeNicola, and Berlin of Price Waterhouse Coopers, LLP, recently published a note on *How Does the Board Oversee ESG* which specifically recommended that the audit committee oversee whether the company's ESG disclosures (both qualitative and quantitative) are investor grade and which ESG frameworks and/or standards the company is using as well as whether there are processes and controls in place to ensure the accuracy, comparability, and consistency of the ESG disclosures.[22]

> First, the audit committee needs to review the steps taken by management to identify and manage sustainability risks that are material to understanding the company's financial disclosures to securityholders and to assess the adequacy of these efforts. Second, the committee needs to review the specific ESG-related disclosures the company has made both in its SEC and other regulatory filings as well as its other reports to securityholders for accuracy, completeness, and adequacy of response to expressed stakeholder concerns.

The specific responsibility to be undertaken by the audit committee will necessarily vary from company to company, depending on many factors, including the board's assessment of the importance of ESG issues and reporting to stakeholders and whether other board committees have primary or additional responsibility in regard to the review and management

---

20. See Center for Board Effectiveness, *On the Board's agenda – The Strategic Audit Committee: A 2020 Preview*, https://www2.deloitte.com/us/en/pages/center-for-boardeffectiveness/articles.

21. Maura Hodge, *An Audit Committee Lens on ESG Reporting*, https://home.kpmg.com/socialmedia.

22. Paula Loop et al., *How Does the Board Oversee ESG?* Harvard Law School Forum on Corporate Governance (Dec. 21, 2020), https://www.corpgov.law.edu/2020/12/21.

of sustainability risks. In any case, two themes should be prominent in the assignment of responsibility by the board of directors to the audit committee: First, the committee needs to review the steps taken by management to identify and manage sustainability risks that are material to understanding the company's financial disclosures to securityholders and to assess the adequacy of these efforts. Second, the committee needs to review the specific ESG-related disclosures the company has made both in its SEC and other regulatory filings as well as its other reports to securityholders for accuracy, completeness, and adequacy of response to expressed stakeholder concerns.

Of particular importance as regards the audit committee's scope of responsibility will be the review of any determination by management to adopt one of the frameworks for sustainability disclosures that have been promulgated by standard-setting organizations and of the adherence of the corporation's ESG disclosures to those standards. To date, the most prominent of these is the disclosure standards issued by the Sustainability Accounting Standards Board (SASB), which has published detailed industry-specific disclosure standards that seek to identify the minimal financially material topics and associated metrics for a typical company in an industry.[23] However, because of the growing pressure from institutional investors and others, there is no doubt but that in the near future there will be international global sustainability reporting standards. In September 2020, the influential IFRS Foundation published *a Consultation Paper on Sustainability Reporting* to assess the demand for global sustainability reporting standards, which was widely commented on. In April 2021, the Trustees of the Foundation reported that, assessing the feedback received, they had found an urgent need for global sustainability reporting standards and that as a result they were proposing amendments to the Foundation's Constitution to allow for the creation of a new sustainability reporting standards board under the governance of the Foundation.[24] This development of sustainability reporting standards by such a board will be of greatest importance. Corporate management should be encouraged by the audit committee to instruct the financial statement auditors to pay close attention to standards as they are proposed, and management and the auditors should make every effort to timely report relevant proposals to the members of the audit committee.

When companies adopt specific methodologies for determining metrics specified by the SASB or possibly the new IFRS sustainability standards board, the role of the audit committee in assuring accuracy and adequacy of these disclosures is vital. Price Waterhouse's Governance Insights Center wrote in January 2020 that the audit committee, with its extensive experience in overseeing internal controls, policies and procedures, and reporting, can play a role in understanding the methodologies and policies used to develop

---

23. See *Sustainability Accounting Standards Board, Standards Outcome Report* (June 27, 2013) for a comprehensive description of SASB's process for issue identification and disclosure topic determination and especially *Appendix III: IWG Assessment of Materiality*, https://www.www.sasb.org. In a December 4, 2020, post on the Harvard Law School Forum on Corporate Governance, Defining the Role of the Audit Committee in Overseeing ESG, Deloitte & Touche proposes an ESG maturity model for audit committee responsibilities varying according to whether the company's approach to sustainability reporting is Responsive, Enhanced or Integrated, https://www.deoitte.com.

24. See *Exposure Draft: Proposed Targeted Amendments to the IFRS Constitution to Accommodate an International Sustainability Reporting Standards Board to Set IFRS Sustainability Reporting Standards* (Apr. 26, 2021), https://www.ifrs.org.

the metrics as well as the internal controls in place to assure accuracy, reliability, and consistency of the metrics.[25]

> The audit committee charter should afford the audit committee the specific authority to engage counsel and consultants or other experts to advise it on ESG disclosures and standards development.

Of course, the audit committee's charter or responsibilities and authority given it by the board of directors should include clear provisions both charging the committee with these ESG-related responsibilities and affording the committee the authority and means to carry out its duties, including the authority to engage counsel and possibly consultants or other experts to advise it regarding specific sustainability issues. SOX requires that the audit committee have the authority to engage such counsel and advisors and requires the issuer to provide funding for the committee to compensate them for their services.[26]

The audit committee charter should afford the audit committee with the specific authority to engage counsel and consultants or other experts to advise it on ESG disclosures and standards development and provide for the necessary funding from the issuer. Just as the audit committee will almost always include a member who is a "financial expert" to provide guidance to the committee in its review of financial statement presentation and audit assurances, when sustainability risks are particularly significant to investors, the committee should include a member with the technical background and experience to assist the other members in their review of sustainability disclosures and risks and potentially applicable sustainability reporting.

> When sustainability risks are particularly significant to investors, the audit committee should include a member with the technical background and experience to assist the other members in their review of sustainability disclosures and risks and potentially applicable sustainability reporting.

When the company has determined to disclose detailed quantitative information about sustainability performance and risk factors and especially when these metrics are presented against industry baselines, it may be desirable for the audit committee to engage its own consultant to assist it. Also, in such a case, the committee could encourage management to include in disclosures to securityholders the report of a qualified consultant on the information being presented so that the disclosures are "expertized" for securities disclosure purposes, affording liability protection for all directors and making the committee's task of reviewing the disclosures both more effective and easier.[27]

25. See Price Waterhouse Governance and Insights Center, *Sustainability/ESG Reporting—Why Audit Committees Need to Pay Attention* (January 2020), https://www.pwc.com/us/en/services/governance-insights-center.
26. See Exchange Act Section 10A(m)(5) and (6).
27. "Expertization" of filings under the Securities Act of 1933 alters the burden proof required to establish a due diligence defence of directors. See Section 11(b)(3) of the Securities Act of 1933, https://www.sec.gov.

A final point to be mentioned is that there is an ongoing re-examination of the relevance to corporate performance of perceived obligations to stakeholders other than securityholders that has engaged both corporate leaders including members of the Business Roundtable and the most sanguine academic commentators such as Lucian Bebchuk and former Delaware Supreme Court Justice Leo Strine.[28] The essential elements of debate are whether and to what extent a corporate board should consider the interests, particularly the long-term interests, of "stakeholders" in the corporation, such as employees and indeed other societal interests that may be affected by the externalities from corporate conduct, or whether the board's paramount duty is to securityholders and the appropriateness and effectiveness of corporate action should be judged solely by reference to its consequences for that constituency.

Today's boards of directors are necessarily called upon to consider carefully how to approach the issues framed by this discussion, but it seems of greatest importance in the board's consideration that it receives necessary input on the identification and assessment of the impact of ESG risks on the corporation's various constituencies. No corporate mechanism would appear better suited to that task than a well-functioning audit committee with a clear charter directing it to carry out the assessment of sustainability risks and disclosures with the necessary corporate authorities and financial and technical resources.

Take-Aways for Board Members

The critical take-aways from this review of the role of the audit committee for corporate boards include (1) assigning to the audit committee by inclusion in the audit committee charter responsibility for reviewing and assuring the accuracy and completeness of the corporation's ESG-related disclosures in its public disclosures and regulatory filings; (2) ensuring that, as appropriate, at least one member of the audit committee have specifically relevant ESG-technical background and experience; (3) explicitly providing the committee with authority to engage its own counsel and consultants to advise it on ESG-related disclosure matters and providing for necessary funding; and (4) encouraging management and the company's auditors to ensure that audit committee members are kept abreast of new ESG-related disclosure mandates and especially the potential development of sustainability reporting standards by a newly created IFRS Foundation Sustainability Reporting Standards Board.

---

28. See, e.g., Lucian Bebchuk & Roberto Tallarita, *Shareholderism vs. Stakeholderism – A Misconceived Contradiction. A Comment on the Illusory Promise of Stakeholder Governance*, European Corporate Governance Institute—Law Working Paper 522/2020, https://www.ssrn.com. See also Leo Strine, *Restoration: The Role Stakeholder Governance Must Play in Recreating a Fair and Sustainable American Economy – A Reply to Professor Rock*, U of Penn Inst for Law & Econ Research Paper No. 21-03, https://www.ssrn.com/index.cfm/en/.

Chapter 6
How Can Boards Approach Sustainability?

Kevin M. Coleman, Hope Mehlman, and Beth-ann Roth

Incorporating Sustainability into Company Operations: The Board's Role

The Board of Directors is responsible for both establishing company policy and overseeing how management implements that policy. Once a company recognizes that "sustainability" in some form is—or should be—part of the policy landscape, it becomes the board's job to work with management to define precisely what that means for the company.[1] Having embraced the notion of "sustainability," the challenge becomes to take that notion from being an abstract concept to one that is represented by a precise set of ESG[2]-related actions and goals that relate to the company's own operations, risks, and business objectives.

The board should articulate a set of actions and goals best suited to the company, integrate them into the board's oversight practices, and work with management to ensure implementation. There is no prescribed approach or set of rules. Rather, as with other board duties, the task will be to determine the best governance practices for overseeing

---

1. See generally Veena Ramani, Ceres, *View from the Top: How Corporate Boards Can Engage on Sustainability Performance* (Oct. 2015) https://www.ceres.org/sites/default/files/reports/2017-03/ceres_viewfromthetop.pdf.
2. ESG is an abbreviation for "environmental, social and governance," and constitutes one commonly used acronym intended to embody the concepts associated with sustainability.

the company's implementation of the board's instructions, and then staying informed as to the company's progress.

In order to be able to manage the process, the board should direct management to assign accountability reporting for each of the areas identified as "material" to the business. For example, for each action and goal there should be a specific set of metrics to define improvements to the company's internal operations, and to measure the company's sustainability as compared to its peer group.

Who Owns Sustainability?

The short answer is *everyone*. While boards have oversight duties, a successful sustainability program is a collaborative effort among the board, every level of management, and every business unit in the organization. The board should direct management to embed sustainability policies into its operations and to incorporate the sustainability factors into its regular financial, compliance, risk management, and audit reports to the board. The board, in turn, should incorporate sustainability review into its oversight evaluations across board functions. For a company to embrace sustainability, sustainability must first be made a formal board priority.

Considering Sustainability When Making Board Decisions

In the past, a board was usually expected to consider solely financial considerations when making certain decisions, as finances were viewed as being the principal drivers of shareholder value. Numbers alone were deemed to tell the company's story and constitute the bottom line.

In recent years, it has become increasingly commonplace—including by regulators—to recognize that the *way* a company does business directly impacts its bottom line and, accordingly, must be taken into account in evaluating the company's needs and practices. Looking at the way a company does business through an ESG lens, a "social" or "environmental" benefit might be embedded into the company's product and is the reason it attracts certain buyers. In terms of "governance," with almost any type of business, it is now viewed as common wisdom that a diverse board is likely to bring a more well-reasoned outcome to a board's governance practices, simply by having more voices from a variety of backgrounds at the table, which can potentially bring distinct perspectives to a discussion.

In general, a board's deliberations are protected by a legal doctrine known as the "business judgment rule." Under this rule, board decisions may not be challenged as long as there is evidence of a duly-called meeting at which there was deliberative process where members had an opportunity for discussion and to ask questions and could simultaneously hear one another. Board materials providing board-relevant information and data on the subject matter of the topic are important to help make that record.

Nevertheless, to avoid any question of whether the board is within its bounds to take certain criteria into account when making decisions, it is wise to identify, in some fashion, that sustainability criteria are being made an integral part of the overall landscape. Indeed, because those factors often impact the bottom line, they can—and should when adopted—be characterized as "financially material."[3]

---

3. See *infra* text accompanying note 6.

If a company is organized as a benefit corporation or has a similar registration, then the company already has articles filed with the state corporation commission that identify its mission as being incorporated into operations. The board may rely on that mission to make decisions that incorporate both financial and sustainability criteria consistent with the mission stated in the company's organizing charter.[4] If the company is not legally organized as a benefit corporation or something similar, then the board may determine that it is appropriate to either amend its bylaws or adopt a resolution indicating that whatever sustainability factors the board ultimately adopts should be taken into account in its decision-making.

Identifying Specific Sustainability Priorities

Before the board will grant sustainability a seat at the table, specific relevant issues must be prioritized. Sustainability issues that should be identified for prioritization include "material environmental or social issues that significantly impact operational and business function."[5] Management should identify these material issues based on an analysis of factors most likely to affect the company's growth and business operations. The board can then work with management to determine which policies will best serve the company.

> The company should look at its peers to make certain it is not leaving out factors considered important by its competitors.

A company defines its sustainability program by identifying its principal priorities. It must review those priorities on a regular basis to ensure they reflect the many influences that determine how the sustainability program should look. In addition, the company should look at its peers to make certain it is not leaving out factors considered important by its competitors. Keeping abreast of peer groups is also a way to determine whether it is consistent with business priorities to go above and beyond what the company's peer group is doing in order to set an example and perhaps become a leader in the space, thereby potentially enhancing long-term value.

Once the company identifies its principal priorities, the board should work with management to identify a recognized benchmark against which the board will be able to monitor and measure the company's success in building and maintaining its sustainability program. In many cases, there will be more than one applicable rating or ranking company, and it will likely be important to know where the company stands with respect to each. Those standards can also be considered to help identify the company's principal priorities, so as to be able to monitor progress with respect to its peers and competitors.

---

4. Information on the availability of benefit registrations in various states and the District of Columbia can be found at https://benefitcorp.net/policymakers/state-by-state-status. A company may change its charter to become a benefit company. However, it is not necessary to do so in order to incorporate sustainability criteria into the company's practices.
5. Ramani, *supra* note 1, at 9.

In evaluating which sustainability priorities are central to the company's culture and operations, and at the same time, the company should consider factors such as the following:

- The company's own product line, operations, and customer base will inform a large part of how its sustainability program will take shape. Evaluation will include product impact, as well as the environmental impact of operations. If the product is available internationally, the company should be aware of sustainability standards in the countries into which the product is distributed.

- The business practices of supply-chain providers might be used to decide which vendors the company will choose to reward with contracts for material sourcing and other services.

- Sustainability may also extend beyond the company's own product into areas such as the choices surrounding the selection of its suppliers outside of supply-chain sourcing, such as for office supplies and business consulting. Other examples include internal policies such as workplace policies, diversity and inclusion, executive compensation, workforce development, community engagement, employee mobility and transportation, and transparency in governance.

- Stakeholders such as the company's investors may demand that the company incorporate certain policies into its operations. The company should be aware of the issues important to shareholders and maintain regular channels of communication so that relationships are cordial and constructive. See Chapter 11 for a discussion of how the board can effectively manage those relationships to the mutual benefit of all parties.

There are companies and nonprofit organizations—sometimes referred to as sustainability "advisors" or "consultants"—that can assist the company in every phase of sustainability program design and implementation. They do not dictate how programs must be designed, but rather serve as helpful resources that can be brought into the process as little or as much as the company chooses. An examination of their online materials presents a helpful starting point for categorizing program development. They are also available for more tailored and in-depth fee-based consulting assistance.

The Sustainability Accounting Standards Board (SASB), which is part of the Value Reporting Foundation, is helpful in integrating environmental, social, and governance factors into a financial context. As of this writing, there are 77 sets of industry-specific disclosure standards, "which identify the minimal set of financially material sustainability topics and their associated metrics for the typical company industry" and that are intended to improve "long-term value creation."[6]

While ESG defines the broad categories into which sustainability factors are segmented, in practice the categories tend to be more fluid depending on the resource used and can be broadened or narrowed according to needs of the company. The language used to define the categories can be the company's own, as long as the recipient of the information can determine its purpose.

For example, some consultants break out "governance" as a topic, and leave "environmental" and "social" together as broad categories, even while segmenting out subcategories

---

6. See the discussion of SASB's "Mission" and the link to its industry-specific disclosure standards at https://www.sasb.org/standards/.

for use where appropriate. SASB defines five broad categories as part of its sustainability framework or "dimensions" in a financial context: Environment, Leadership & Governance, Business Model & Innovation, Human Capital, and Social Capital, each of which contains subcategories that break down into a total of 26 discrete topics.[7]

Companies are also increasingly relying on the United Nations Sustainable Development Goals (SDGs) to identify benchmark targets and to identify which of the goals the company has already met. The SDGs consist of 17 goals to which participants throughout the globe aspire.[8] Its stated objective is "to promote prosperity while protecting the planet."

In the end, the board, in its oversight role, should direct that management:

- identify sustainability goals that make sense for the company;
- define the categories into which they fit;
- include input from representatives from the departments that will participate;
- set forth the methodologies proposed to carry out the work needed to reach the goals and the metrics that will apply; and
- confirm that sufficient resources are in place to accomplish those tasks.

Preliminary Work Plan: Initial Sustainability Report

If the set of goals is satisfactory to the board, the board should vote to adopt them preliminarily and direct management to put together a work plan to implement them. The board should set the frequency of review dates to receive presentations from management to assess whether the plan continues to appear to be feasible, is aggressive enough, or needs to be modified. The board should further direct management to advise the board in the event an issue arises prior to the next review about which management believes the board needs to know—i.e., the same as management would do with respect to any other material event that requires disclosure to the board or to a special committee (e.g., the Executive Committee) established for that purpose.

The board might choose to ask that the work plan be in the form of an initial "Sustainability Report" to use as a business plan of sorts to lay out the priorities identified in the preliminary stage.[9] (Reports are also often referred to as "impact reports" and "sustainability impact reports," but can be named or "branded" as the company deems appropriate.) That way, the company will have sufficient time to improve the report and have a revised version ready for when it would normally be issued to stakeholders after an initial period of implementation.

The report should define how each component identified as a sustainability priority will be measured, and should connect sustainability priorities to opportunities, risk, and revenue. Periodic reviews may also include peer analyses so that the company may measure its sustainability performance against others in its industry group. Measurement assessments and peer analyses may require that the company contract with a third-party provider specializing in those assessments.

---

7. SASB's Sustainability Framework and a link to its Materiality Map can be found at https://www.sasb.org /standards-overview/materiality-map/.
8. See https://www.un.org/sustainabledevelopment/. The SDGs "recognize that ending poverty must go hand-in-hand with strategies that build economic growth and address a range of social needs including education, health, social protection, and job opportunities, while tackling climate change and environmental protection."
9. A collection of company sustainability reports can be found at https://www.sustainability-reports.com/.

Resolution to Approve the Adoption of Sustainability Principles

Once the initial sustainability report has been presented in a form acceptable to the board, and the priorities set forth in the report have been put into motion, the board should consider whether to vote to adopt the sustainability factors in their final form. The vote should be memorialized in a resolution in the minutes of meeting. As part of the resolution, the board should authorize the appropriate officers to request—or direct management to produce—an update to the report no less frequently than annually (or whatever the board decides is appropriate under the circumstances).

The board may decide that the report will be solely for the board and internal use, or may require that it also be part of the company's annual report to shareholders. Including this requirement in a resolution adopted by the board helps ensure that the direction of the board appears in the minutes, that the instructions are more likely to be known by management, and that they are carried out as intended. As noted above, it also protects the organization from attempts to discredit the incorporation of sustainability factors into board decision-making.

Proactive Investor Screening Tools

Based on the sustainability factors adopted by the board, the board should discuss with management whether it would be a good strategy to share with stakeholders the company's focus on sustainability and the benefits the company expects to derive as a result. This can serve a number of purposes, including the maintenance of good relationships with the company's investors and their advisers. The enumeration of specific factors and goals can help identify the investment "screens" employed by institutional and individual investors, who often use outside sources to help figure out which companies embody the principles they seek for companies to include in their portfolios. This can be a helpful feature for both shareholders and the research firms that review companies to determine whether they meet certain investment criteria.

By being proactive, the company also sets the stage for good stakeholder communications. Stakeholders get the message that they can engage in a dialog with management, thereby facilitating a relationship. That relationship can later become the basis for a forum within which communications bring about mutually desirable results. Even if the company ends up not putting into place a request from a shareholder, the fact that there is a door open for dialogue creates more of an opportunity for a consensus resolution. That is in contrast to the more contentious alternatives that can arise when dialogue fails—or worse, when dialogue is not even initiated because shareholders believe it would be futile.

Demonstrate the Company's Long-Term Commitment to Sustainability

> The board should take steps to demonstrate that the company is committed to sustainability for the long term.

Besides publishing the company's sustainability report, having board committees dedicated to aspects of sustainability oversight helps make certain that the topic is always at the fore. As a safeguard and "best practice," committees can incorporate sustainability review into their charters. Including an update on sustainability from relevant committees at each regular board meeting will help ensure appropriate board oversight of the company's sustainability practices and disclosures.

The board should decide how best to address sustainability oversight responsibilities; i.e., whether the matters should regularly be reviewed by the board as a whole, or allocated among committees that then report back to the full board in the form of information or decision items. One common practice is to assign primary sustainability oversight responsibility to the board's governance committee, since governance—often a component of sustainability ESG procedures—is already under that committee's oversight.[10] Some boards take this a step further and rename their governance committee to include the term "ESG" or "sustainability."[11] This could serve to demonstrate to both internal and external stakeholders that the company is committed to sustainability; the name of the committee indicates its purpose in a space where the establishment of sustainability committees is not yet a standard operating procedure among the majority of companies.

Some companies assign the "social responsibility" component to the compensation committee. Their responsibilities might include corporate culture, diversity and inclusion, human capital management matters, and workplace safety. This is typically a good fit, especially on those boards where the compensation committee is already looking at full workforce data. Similar to above, some boards rename their compensation committee to reflect this expanded responsibility by including the term "human resources."[12]

Public policy committees are also a good place to house some or all of the board's ESG/sustainability oversight responsibilities.[13] Financial institutions and other companies with

---

10. See, e.g., *Nominating and Governance Committee Charter*, Cardinal Health, Inc. 2 (2020), http://s1.q4cdn .com/687095970/files/doc_downloads/Guidelines/Nominating-and-Governance-Committee-Charter-approved -8.5.2020.pdf; *Nominating and Corporate Governance Committee Charter*, Regions Fin. Corp. 1, 4 (2020), https:// ir.regions.com/~/media/Files/R/Regions-IR/NCG%20Committee%20Charter%20-%20July%202019.pdf.
11. See, e.g., *Corporate Governance, ESG, and Sustainability Committee Charter*, Bank of Am. (2020), http:// investor.bankofamerica.com/static-files/098bb52d-eea3-4ced-bcd1-99e0447423d2; *Nominating & ESG Committee Charter*, Hilton Worldwide Holdings, Inc. (2020), https://ir.hilton.com/~/media/Files/H/Hilton-Worldwide-IR-V3 /committee-composition/nominating-and-esg-committee-charter-2020-final.pdf; *Nominating & ESG Committee Charter*, Nasdaq (2019), http://ir.nasdaq.com/static-files/acb0278d-8216-4bb8-9add-c882b39e3cbe; *Corporate Governance, ESG, and Public Policy Committee Charter*, Western Union Co. (2019), http://s21.q4cdn.com /100551446/files/doc_downloads/gov_documents/2016/Corporate-Governance-and-Public-Policy-Committee -Charter.pdf.
12. See, e.g., *Human Resources and Compensation Committee Charter*, Cardinal Health, Inc. (2020), http:// s1.q4cdn.com/687095970/files/doc_downloads/2020/02/HRCC-Charter-approved-2112020.pdf; *Compensation and Human Resources Committee Charter*, Regions Fin. Corp. (2020), https://ir.regions.com/~/media/Files/R /Regions-IR/CHR%20Committee%20Charter%20-%20July%202019.pdf.
13. See, e.g., *Public Policy and Sustainability Committee Charter*, Coca-Cola Co. 1 (2019), https://d1io3yog0oux5 .cloudfront.net/_1b69e1e69528e5630a2842ce673df6eb/cocacolacompany/db/719/7013/file/public-policy-and -sustainability-committee+%281%29.pdf; *Regulatory and Public Policy Committee Charter*, Microsoft Co. 1–2 (2020), https://view.officeapps.live.com/op/view.aspx?src=https://c.s-microsoft.com/en-us/CMSFiles/Regulatory%20 and%20Public%20Policy%20Committee%20Charter.docx?version=bd327ddd-739f-bc73-99a0-cff70e77075e &lat=47.6833&long=-122.1231.

risk committees might also consider using this committee for that purpose.[14] Some boards establish committees dedicated to sustainability oversight and review.[15] Whatever the name of the committee, the important thing is that there be board oversight of the company's sustainability program.

> The board should consider directing that management establish cross-departmental coopera-tion throughout the company, thereby encouraging the functions involved in the sustainability goals to coordinate their efforts.

In this connection, the board should consider directing that management establish cross-departmental cooperation throughout the company, thereby encouraging the functions involved in the sustainability goals to coordinate their efforts.[16] Such cooperation also helps streamline communications to the board.

Finally, ongoing education for the board and management on the ever-growing body of important issues and impacts relating to sustainability can be useful to ensure that the company is responding appropriately in this space.

Take-Aways for Board Members

- Be proactive! Shareholders look to the company to be knowledgeable, in control of its business, and to be transparent.
- Delegate to management, but set the tone and direction. Guidance comes from the top.
- Identify those members of the board in charge of oversight, and calendar reviews so that the entire board is aware of the program and its evolving progress.

* * * * *

The authors of this chapter would like to thank Claire Young, JD/MBA Candidate at Cumberland School of Law and Brock School of Business at Samford, and Patricia Meadow for their assistance on this chapter.

---

14. See, e.g., *Risk Committee Charter*, Regions Fin. Corp. 4 (2020), https://ir.regions.com/~/media/Files/R/Regions -IR/Risk%20Committee%20Charter%20-%20July%202019.pdf; *Risk and Compliance Committee Charter*, Target Brands, Inc. 2 (2019), https://investors.target.com/static-files/3ff92aaa-a1d8-4fee-a42a-3481828e5ff2.
15. See, e.g., *Sustainability & Corporate Responsibility Committee Charter*, McDonald's Corp. (2016), https:// corporate.mcdonalds.com/content/dam/gwscorp/nfl/corporate-governance-content/board-committees-and -charters/RESTATED_SCR_COMMITTEE_CHARTER_2016.pdf; *ESG Committee Charter*, Marsh & McLennan Cos., Inc. (2020), https://www.mmc.com/content/dam/mmc-web/Files/ESG_Committee_Charter_Final_3.12.20.pdf.
16. See, e.g., *Intel's 2019-2020 Report: Corporate Responsibility at Intel* (2020), https://csrreportbuilder.intel. com/pdfbuilder/pdfs/CSR-2019-20-Full-Report.pdf. Intel calls this "Embedding Corporate Responsibility: . . . We believe that having an integrated strategy and embedding corporate responsibility across the company is the most effective management approach to drive continuous improvements in our performance. We have estab-lished cross-functional Management Review Committees (MRCs) consisting of senior executives who manage corporate responsibility and sustainability activities across the organization" (p. 26).

Chapter 7
Questions for Directors to Ask

Kevin M. Coleman, Hope Mehlman, and Beth-ann Roth

Board Requests for Information:
Process and the Underlying Principles

As noted in the previous chapter, the Board of Directors is responsible for both establishing company policy and overseeing how management implements that policy. When exercising oversight, directors have a fiduciary duty to act in the best interests of the corporation and its shareholders. But how, as a practical matter, is that accomplished?

A board acts as an entity, and—with limited exceptions—makes decisions solely during the course of a meeting of the board at which a quorum is present, and which was called for the purposes set forth in the agenda provided in advance for that meeting. It is presumed that boards make their decisions using sound judgment; as long as directors have no conflicts, and they act with due care and in good faith, the board's decisions are typically protected by the "business judgment rule" and will generally not be reviewable by a court. The key to being protected by the rule is to be able to demonstrate that the board followed a process designed to facilitate appropriate consideration and review of the matters before the board.

> One of the best ways to protect the [board decision-making] process . . . is for board books to contain sufficient materials to demonstrate that the board had before it the information it needed in order to make a reasoned decision.

One of the best ways to protect the process and help ensure that decisions will not be permitted to be second-guessed is for board books to contain sufficient materials to demonstrate that the board had before it the information it needed in order to make a reasoned decision. The materials or the information for many of the agenda items frequently originate with management. However, the board drives its agenda so that the materials prepared by management and staff in advance of board meetings must be responsive to requests made by the board. Some items on the agenda and related documentation in the board book will be for informational purposes, and the agenda generally identifies that fact so that board members know whether they will be voting on a particular item. Likewise, "decision" items are identified as such.

The minutes of meeting then reflect that there was an opportunity for discussion and the expression of divergent views. The minutes indicate the fact that a discussion took place, and that the board reached the decision reflected in the resolution that appears in the minutes. Note that the minutes reflect the *fact* that the discussion took place, versus a summary of the discussion itself. The reason relates to decisions being of the board as an entity so that the decision the quorum reaches as a body is what is relevant, and not the discussion leading up to the decision. For that reason, the conversations that went into the deliberative process are generally not included in the minutes.

Accordingly, the board needs to make specific requests of management so as to ensure that the information it receives for consideration will be sufficient to enable the board to make its decisions. That being said, proactive engagement is not limited to agenda items that require a board decision. Items brought to the attention of the board for its information are just as important for the board's understanding of the company's business and for making a record as those requiring a decision. To facilitate board review of the materials presented to it at the meeting, and to create a record that makes it clear which items are for decision and which are informational, it is a typical practice to identify those alternatives on the face of the agenda itself.

Issues Unique to Sustainability Oversight

Sustainability has become increasingly significant to companies and their stakeholders. However, the factors that constitute sustainability may vary widely from company to company and even among rating agencies, depending on what is being measured and the relative weightings assigned to each.[1] For example, a highly polluting company might end

---

1. See generally Silda Wall Spitzer & John Mandyck, *What Board Need to Know About Sustainability Ratings*, Harv. Bus. Rev., May 2019, https://hbr.org/2019/05/what-boards-need-to-know-about-sustainability-ratings. See also *ESG Risks and Opportunities: Understanding the ESG Landscape*, Donnelley Fin. Solutions (2019), https://www.dfinsolutions.com/sites/default/files/documents/2019-03/dfin_gcm_proxy_whitepaper_ESG_risks_and__oppty_2019223.pdf.

up with a high sustainability rating if its governance practices are stellar so that its rating is high, yet at the bottom of a list from a ratings agency that considers purely environmental factors. But even without mixing ratings, one could end up with an unexpected result: a company that makes an environmentally friendly product could find itself ranked poorly in the environmental category if its manufacturing plant does not manage its operations in a way that exhibits sound environmental stewardship.

It is essential for the board to understand the company's sustainability strategy and where it fits on the spectrum of criteria, and also to guide the conversation to make certain that the board and management agree on the emphasis and what the company is doing to further its efforts. The public nature of sustainability reporting and the ratings assigned to companies on the basis of publicly available information make this consensus even more critical. The "public-arena" accountability that goes hand-in-hand with sustainability—which arguably goes far beyond standard SEC-mandated disclosure—also means that there are potential risks that can arise from events such as products being deemed faulty or uncovering inappropriate workplace practices.

The board should task management with identifying the most appropriate benchmarks to use, and present those to the board for approval, understanding where their peers fit into the equation. Those benchmarks should be set for annual review by management for presentation to the board to confirm their continued viability.

> At a time when individual and institutional investors are increasingly demanding information sufficient for them to assess sustainability risks, it is essential that companies produce meaningful information in order to continue to attract both investors and a high-quality workforce.

That exercise is not simply for optics. At a time when individual and institutional investors are increasingly demanding information sufficient for them to assess sustainability risks, it is essential that companies produce meaningful information in order to continue to attract both investors and a high-quality workforce.

Questions for Management

It is essential that directors ask management sufficiently probing questions so as to elicit answers that clarify the company's sustainability strategy focus. Following are examples of questions that the board should consider posing to management in an effort to define the company's sustainability strategies:

> Does the company have a Chief Sustainability Officer or someone with similar responsibilities or a title that makes it clear who in management has principal oversight of the process?

The Company as a Steward of Sustainability: Current Practices

- *What practices does the company highlight in each of the environmental, social, and governance (ESG) categories?*

  Companies have several opportunities to highlight their various ESG practices. Such disclosures could be made in an annual ESG report, proxy statement, or company website. The board should be aware of what ESG practices the company is discussing publicly.

- *What are the key metrics the company uses to measure its success with respect to its practices? Does the company have in place a methodology to extract data from the measurement process in order to both support its measurements and provide adequate disclosure to stakeholders?*

  It is essential to define the methodologies the company will use to measure whether and to what extent it meets the goals it has set for itself. In addition to defining the methodologies, it will need to produce data that can be incorporated into usable reports that can in turn inform whether to stay a particular course or incorporate changes, whether in the action plan or the stated goal due to feasibility at any given time.

- *Is the company's disclosure of those metrics and assessments relating to what might typically be considered "material" information adequate for investors to make an informed investment decision?*

  Disclosure is the key mechanism for informing potential and existing investors about the company's business, its operations, and—likewise—its sustainability efforts. Due to the impact of sustainability policies and practices on the business's bottom line, it is increasingly critical to have in place accurate, measurable reporting standards so as to meet the needs of both investors and regulators. Some institutional investors define the disclosure standards they wish to see in order to help them analyze companies' sustainability efforts from a common perspective. Examples relating to financial disclosures are recommendations by the Sustainability Accounting Standards Board (SASB) and the Task Force on Climate-Related Financial Disclosures (TCFD). (See Chapter 16 discussing sustainability ratings.)

- *What department or function within the company will be tasked with ensuring that practices are consistent with disclosure, so as not to create a potential violation? Does the company have a Chief Sustainability Officer or someone with similar responsibilities or a title that makes it clear who in management has principal oversight of the process?*

  As with other areas of oversight, it is critical to have someone be responsible for assessing whether practices align with disclosure. Failure to do so potentially creates a private right of action or regulatory liability, even when the omission itself would not have constituted a regulatory violation.

- ***What can the board and its committees do to help?***

Demonstrating to management and leadership teams that the board is supporting ESG/sustainability initiatives can go a long way toward enhancing the relationship with management and remaining on the receiving end of frequent and complete information. Working with management to get their opinions and ideas of how the board can improve in this area may also provide insights not previously considered.

Sustainability Oversight

- ***Does the company have a centralized sustainability oversight department, or does each department work independently to ensure accountability within the company's sustainability programs?***

Companies should be careful about working in silos, particularly with respect to issues relating to ESG, which typically require input from many departments. If there is not a centralized sustainability oversight department, the individual departments must have a plan on how to work collaboratively.

- ***What department has primary responsibility for creating and maintaining the company's sustainability report?***

Although many groups will play a role in publishing an annual ESG/sustainability report, there should be one group that is primarily responsible for the report. This helps to ensure accountability and that the report will be published timely.

External Sustainability Advisors and Standards Boards

- ***Has the company engaged external sustainability "advisors"?***

In certain instances, it might make sense for a company to bring in a consultant to provide expertise. If such a firm has been engaged, the consultant should consider providing a presentation (or multiple presentations) to the board on their findings and progress.

The Company as an Investment: How the Company Scores Based on ESG Investing Criteria

> Having a robust investor engagement program is extremely useful in understanding shareholders' expectations. It also provides companies an opportunity to discuss its ESG practices and disclosures with investors.

- ***What ESG screens include the company as an investment?***

Some investors establish investment "screens" that either preclude them from investing in certain industries/sectors/activities (such as alcohol, tobacco, firearms, or the fossil fuel industry), or require that they seek out certain positive characteristics in a company (such as board diversity). Companies should determine (and boards should know) where the company fits with respect to specific screens.

- *What investment screens does the company "pass" for ESG-focused invest-ment portfolios?*

  If a company knows which screens it currently "passes," it has a better understand-ing of which actions it should (or should not) take going forward. This helps to ensure that the company will not "fail" one of these screens in the future.

- *Does the company invite its investors to engage in order for management to keep abreast of issues of importance and address concerns where possible and on a timely basis?*

  Having a robust investor engagement program is extremely useful in understanding shareholders' expectations. It also provides companies an opportunity to discuss its ESG practices and disclosures with investors.

- *Where does the company rank on each of its strategies with the various rating agencies, and where does it come out in a combined rating system?*

  There are many firms providing ESG ratings and rankings on companies, which are, in turn, used by investors when making voting decisions. The board should have an idea of where the company stands in ESG ratings and rankings, particularly those issued by the most prevalent ESG rating agencies.

Future Sustainability Strategies

- *What areas is the company targeting for future sustainability initiatives, and is there a strategy to address how the company will reach those targets?*

  To properly oversee ESG practices and disclosures, the board must understand where the company has room for enhancement and the strategic plan on how to make such enhancements.

Risk Assessment and Management

- *To what risks is the company subject as a result of its sustainability focus, and how does the company identify those risks?*

  It is important to gain an understanding of how the risks are being identified and measured. Directors should understand where they arise in the company's business/operations and the mechanisms used to identify them.

- *How does the company characterize and prioritize sustainability and ESG risks (financial materiality/relevance/importance/significance/reputation)?*

  The board should understand how the company is characterizing and prioritizing ESG risks (as well as opportunities). The answer to the question should help guide how the company is responding to such risks and opportunities and which disclo-sures *must* be made.

- *Which sustainability and ESG risks has the company identified as being most important/material to it in the short term? The medium term? The long term?*

  This high-level question will also necessitate a discussion on what the company considers "short," "medium," and "long term." Companies differ in the time horizons used in sustainability goal setting. It is generally recommended that environmental goals be set using a 20-year time horizon. Changes tend to be incremental, causing sustainability and environmental goals to take longer to accomplish and realize.

- *How are the company's sustainability and ESG risks incorporated into its broader risk management efforts?*

  Determine whether sustainability/ESG risks fit appropriately into the existing risk management framework the company uses, or whether accommodations or alterations need to be made.

- *Does the company have a clear, articulated vision on how the long-term strategic plan considers the risks and opportunities of sustainability?*

  If the answer to this question is ambiguous, a remedial step the company could take is to launch a disclosure strategy that focuses on the stakeholder needs, aligns business value with sustainability, and uses prominent sustainability standards to steer meaningful disclosure.[2]

- *What is the chance that demand for the company's products and services would be impacted due to climate change or customer demand for more sustainable products? How would this affect the company's business model?*

  Changes in demand are most likely to occur as the world transitions to a "green" or lower-emission model and as consumer preferences shift toward companies that have a publicly known sustainability focus.[3] Answers to this question may prompt a reassessment of a company's business model.[4]

- *What mechanism(s) will be used to keep the board apprised of identified sustainability and ESG risks?*

  This ensures proper escalation of issues, as well as appropriate governance practices in keeping with the board's broader oversight responsibilities. This could include quarterly reports to a particular board committee, periodic presentations to the full board, and/or one-on-one discussions with directors having expertise in this area.

---

2. *Sustainability and the Board: What Do Directors Need to Know in 2018?*, Deloitte Global (Mar. 2018), https://www2.deloitte.com/content/dam/Deloitte/global/Documents/Risk/gx-sustainability-and-the-board.pdf; see generally *Incorporating Sustainability into Long-Term Strategy*, State Street Global Advisors (Feb. 2019), https://www.ssga.com/investment-topics/environmental-social-governance/2019/02/incorporating-sustainability-into-long-term-strategy.pdf.
3. Remi Rosmarin, *Sustainability Sells: Why Consumers and Clothing Brands Alike Are Turning to Sustainability as a Guiding Light*, Bus. Insider, Apr. 22, 2020, https://www.businessinsider.com/sustainability-as-a-value-is-changing-how-consumers-shop.
4. Sarah Keyes & Alan Willis, *Climate Change Briefing: Questions for Directors to Ask*, Chartered Professional Accountants (2017), https://www.nrcan.gc.ca/sites/www.nrcan.gc.ca/files/energy/energy-resources/Climate_Change_Briefing_Questions_for_Directors_to_Ask_-_August_2017.pdf.

- ***How might current or potential future government regulations affect the company or its supply chain in essential operating jurisdictions?***

  Companies potentially deal with an ever-changing regulatory environment, depending on the business and its locations. Different jurisdictions, particularly internationally, have varied approaches to addressing ESG issues. Boards must be aware of how different regulations can potentially impact operation. These regulations might include carbon emission limits, efficiency standards, employee working guidelines, or environmental permits.

Take-Aways for Board Members

- Sound board processes are one of the company's best insurance policies. Make sure board books contain sufficient background information to demonstrate that board members had access to information adequate to inform them about the decisions they are asked to make. Identify on the agenda itself those items on which the board is being asked to vote.
- Work with management to decide what sustainability criteria is appropriate for the company to use to form the basis of its work, and to benchmark its progress.
- Assign responsibility for sustainability to a specific department or function, such as a Chief Sustainability Officer, and include that person on the agenda for each board meeting in order for the board to stay current on the company's positioning and progress, as well as to be kept up to date on associated risks.
- Know how external sustainability advisors rank the company, even if it means subscribing to their services. Identify a target for improvement, and track whether the company is succeeding in attracting new ESG investment capital.

* * * * *

The authors of this chapter would like to thank Claire Young, J.D/MBA Candidate at Cumberland School of Law and Brock School of Business at Samford; Mary Wheeler, Assistant General Counsel, Regions Bank; and Patricia Meadow for their assistance with this chapter.

PART III

Chapter 8
What Are the Drivers of Sustainability?

Hope Mehlman, Kevin M. Coleman, and Nancy S. Cleveland

Introduction

Today, more than ever, companies and directors are feeling the heat to make advancements with respect to corporate sustainability—both from the need to differentiate for competitive advantage and from increasing awareness of *and pressure to address* environmental, social, and governance (ESG) issues.[1] The primary driving forces behind the push for sustainability, aside from the stakeholders, can generally be described in two overarching groups: macro drivers and business drivers.

Macro Drivers

Corporate sustainability macro drivers, the influential variables or events that affect a company's strategy from the top-down, are closely tied to global, national, and local developments.[2] Global developments that can threaten how companies operate can include: changes in weather, sea levels, etc.; social and economic inequality; and events such as

---

1. *Key Drivers of Sustainability – Role of Stakeholders and Business Drivers*, TURNKEY GROUP LTD (Sept. 8, 2017), https://www.turnkeygroup.net/key-drivers-sustainability-role-stakeholders-business-drivers/ (hereinafter *Key Drivers of Sustainability*).
2. Adam Hayes, *Driver*, INVESTOPEDIA (July 14, 2020), https://www.investopedia.com/terms/d/driver.asp#:~:text= Macro%20drivers%20are%20influential%20fiscal,used%20in%20bottom%2Dup%20analysis.

humanitarian crises in countries in which part of a company's supply chain (e.g., labor or raw materials) is located. From this, the broad categories for global developments can be used as a roadmap for describing the macro drivers of sustainability. Thus, the various macro drivers of sustainability include climate change, population growth, and an increased focus on human well-being.

Climate Change

Empirical data shows that the planet is warming (and at greater rates than before) due to excess atmospheric carbon dioxide and other greenhouse gases.[3] With environmental sustainability in mind, directors need to balance both companies' current and future operating demands. Because of more "immediate" issues, such as disease, inflation, and economic factors, directors will need to overcome the temptation to push the problem down the road.

> Climate change, in relation to corporate sustainability, could impact many, if not all, parts of a company's supply chain and operations and "can be inextricably linked to corporate strategy, risk, opportunity, financial performance and shareholder value."

An increase in temperature, however, is only the beginning of the problem. Temperature rising leads to other effects including changes in precipitation patterns; increased droughts, floods, and heatwaves; stronger hurricanes; and continuous rise of sea levels.[4] Further, access to raw materials may be significantly impacted if the effects of climate change continue to increase.[5] Therefore, climate change, in relation to corporate sustainability, could impact many, if not all, parts of a company's supply chain and operations and "can be inextricably linked to corporate strategy, risk, opportunity, financial performance and shareholder value."[6] Put bluntly, management's and the board's "effectiveness in recognizing and addressing climate change issues is likely fundamental to achieving long-term business goals and value creation."[7]

---

3. Mohan Munasighe, *Addressing the Sustainable Development and Climate Change Challenges Together: Applying the Sustainomics Framework*, 2 Procedia Soc. Behav. Sci. (2010), https://doi.org/10.1016/j.sbspro .2010.05.005.

4. *The Effects of Climate Change*, Nat'l Aeronautics & Space Admin., https://climate.nasa.gov/effects/ (last visited Aug. 15, 2020).

5. Lindsay Delevingne et al., *Climate Risk and Decarbonization: What Every Mining CEO Needs to Know*, McKinsey & Co. (Jan. 28, 2020), https://www.mckinsey.com/business-functions/sustainability/our-insights/climate -risk-and-decarbonization-what-every-mining-ceo-needs-to-know#. According to a 2020 McKinsey & Company article, companies' ability to extract raw materials could be impacted due to water stress (droughts and floods), sea-level rise, and shifting demand for materials. *Id.*

6. Sarah Keyes & Alan Willis, *Climate Change Briefing: Question for Directors to Ask*, Chartered Professional Accountants (2017), https://www.nrcan.gc.ca/sites/www.nrcan.gc.ca/files/energy/energy-resources/Climate _Change_Briefing_Questions_for_Directors_to_Ask_-_August_2017.pdf. "The reduction of carbon footprints, including where supply chains occupy a significant portion of that footprint, has become a key issue for many companies." Carmen X. W. Lu et al., *The Other "S" in ESG: Building a Sustainable and Resilient Supply Chain*, Wachtell, Lipton, Rosen & Katz (Aug. 14, 2020), https://corpgov.law.harvard.edu/2020/08/14/the-other-s-in-esg -building-a-sustainable-and-resilient-supply-chain/.

7. Keyes & Willis, supra note 6.

Companies should develop, and boards should oversee, a corporate environmental strategy to aid in mitigating risk and seizing opportunities.[8] This may include setting climate-related goals and targets;[9] internal carbon pricing;[10] improving corporate energy efficiency;[11] or employing environmentally conscious financing mechanisms.[12]

Population Growth

As the world population grows,[13] humans are demanding and consuming more and more resources and placing "severe environmental stress" on the planet.[14] The effects of this environmental stress can manifest through "the growing loss of biodiversity, increasing greenhouse gas emissions, increasing deforestation worldwide, stratospheric ozone depletion, acid rain, loss of topsoil, and shortages of water, food, and fuel-wood in many parts of the world."[15]

Not only is the world population increasing, but trends in the budding middle class are creating a demographic shift.[16] The growing middle class, especially in Asia, which is projected to have five billion people by 2030,[17] will have major implications for "consumption patterns, hard and soft infrastructure provision, and living standards."[18] With the increased demand and heightened consumption of consumer goods, energy food,

---

8. *Business Strategies to Address Climate Change*, Ctr. For Climate & Energy Solutions, https://www.c2es.org /content/business-strategies-to-address-climate-change/ (last visited Aug. 18, 2020); Mo Ghoneim, *Keep Your Corporate Environmental Strategy a Priority, Even in Times of Uncertainty*, Forbes (Apr. 2, 2020), https://www .forbes.com/sites/forbescommunicationscouncil/2020/04/02/keep-your-corporate-environmental-strategy-a-priority-even-in-times-of-uncertainty/#2e631f582aeb.

9. As of the end of 2019, over 680 companies worldwide have committed to setting emissions targets since 2015. See *Release: Companies with More Greenhouse Gas Emissions than France and Spain Combined Reducing Emissions by 35%, in Line with the Paris Agreement*, World Resources Inst. (Dec. 4, 2019), https://www.wri.org/news/2019/12 /release-companies-more-greenhouse-gas-emissions-france-and-spain-combined-reducing#:~:text=More%20 than%20680%20companies%20in,to%20the%20initiative%20for%20validation.

10. Internal carbon pricing "places a monetary value on greenhouse gas emissions, which businesses can then factor into investment decisions and business operations." *Internal Carbon Pricing*, Ctr. For Climate & Energy Solutions, https://www.c2es.org/content/internal-carbon-pricing/ (last visited Aug. 18, 2020).

11. This might entail upgrades to building systems, including lighting; heating, ventilation, and air conditioning; and water management. Companies may also consider implementing alternative energy solutions such as solar panels.

12. Certain financial institutions offer unique debt products that incorporate climate change. For example, the interest rates the company pays will fluctuate based on attainment (or non-attainment) of climate goals. See *Interview by Brian Sullivan and the Fast Money traders, Tim Seymour, Jeff Mills, Dan Nathan and Guy Adami with Jean-Yves Fillion, CEO, BNP Paribas USA* (Jan. 17, 2020), https://www.cnbc.com/video/2020/01/17/bnp -paribas-usa-ceo-jean-yves-fillion-on-markets-and-sustainability.html.

13. According to Pew Research, global population exploded from 2.5 billion in 1950 to over 7.7 billion in mid-2019. Anthony Cilluffo & Neil G. Ruiz, *World's Population Is Projected to Nearly Stop Growing by the End of the Century*, Pew Research Ctr. (June 17, 2019), https://www.pewresearch.org/fact-tank/2019/06/17/worlds-population-is -projected-to-nearly-stop-growing-by-the-end-of-the-century/. This was an increase of 1–2% each year. *Id.*

14. Nat'l Acad. of Scis. et al., Key Determinants of Population Growth 5 (National Academies Press 1993), https:// www.nap.edu/read/9148/chapter/5.

15. *Id.*

16. Commerzbank, Insights: Five Drivers of Sustainable Trade (Mar. 2015), https://www.oxan.com/media/1317/insights _sustainable_trade.pdf.

17. *Id.*

18. Juan Guerra, *Emerging Middle Classes*, ERM Group (2017), https://www.erm.com/sustainabilityreport2017 /megatrends/emerging-middle-classes/.

and land resources,[19] companies will have the opportunity and challenge of meeting this heightened demand, but they should do so while safeguarding the lasting sustainability of the people and planet.

Human Rights, Social Justice, and Well-Being

Another macro driver of sustainability is an increased focus on human rights and well-being across the world. Locally, companies should ensure the health and safety of their workers, something that has become even more evident during the COVID-19 pandemic.[20] Companies should not only provide a workplace free from physical harm, but also ensure the mental health[21] and fair and equitable treatment of their employees.

To better ensure that companies (and their suppliers) are treating employees and other people in the supply chain humanely, many organizations across the globe have adopted and publicly disclosed Human Rights Statements[22] and/or Supplier Codes of Conduct.[23] In many instances, these documents set an expectation of how the company and its suppliers, respectively, must treat its employees.

As communication capabilities have improved through technological developments, the world is more sensitive and aware of humanitarian issues, such as the number of people who lack access to clean water, education, electricity, and employment. This heightened sensitivity to social justice drives businesses to consider how they play a role in making the world better to live in.

To further complicate matters, climate change, population growth, and human rights and well-being macro drivers are interconnected and cannot be thought of in a vacuum or in silos. As climate change becomes more severe and the population continues to grow, these issues are poised to worsen the problems that threaten human well-being (e.g., food and water scarcity). Because of the risks and opportunities created by such macro drivers, in addition to pressure from stakeholders, companies (and the boards that oversee them) should respond actively.

Business Drivers

When businesses successfully embrace sustainability, they do more than ensure integrity within operations and supply chains: they fundamentally integrate sustainability practices into the core business strategy.[24] Embedding sustainability practices into the business allows companies to generate cost savings through reduction of energy and water usage, capture new customers by using sustainability as a differentiation tool, and optimize operation.[25]

---

19. *Resources & Consumption*, Population Matters, https://populationmatters.org/the-facts/resources-consumption (last visited Aug. 18, 2020). "We are currently using up the renewable resources of 1.7 Earths. . . ." *Id.*

20. David Katz & Laura A. McIntosh, *Corporate Governance Update: EESG and the COVID-19 Crisis*, Wachtell, Lipton, Rosen & Katz (May 31, 2020), https://corpgov.law.harvard.edu/2020/05/31/corporate-governance-update -eesg-and-the-covid-19-crisis/.

21. See *id.*

22. See *Company Policy Statements on Human Rights*, Bus. & Human Rights Res. Ctr., https://www.business -humanrights.org/en/company-policy-statements-on-human-rights (last visited Aug. 18, 2020).

23. See *In-Depth Study: Supplier Codes of Conduct*, Red Flag Group (June 4, 2014), https://redflaggroup.com /type/articles/in-depth-study-supplier-codes-of-conduct/.

24. See Commerzbank, supra note 16.

25. *Key Drivers of Sustainability, supra* note 1.

Given that corporate sustainability is dramatically increasing in importance, it is essential to understand the driving forces behind this trend. The three business drivers of corporate sustainability identified in this chapter include globalization, increased interdependency, and increased stakeholder demand.

> Embedding sustainability practices into the business allows companies to generate cost savings through reduction of energy and water usage, capture new customers by using sustainability as a differentiation tool, and optimize operations.

Globalization

Globalization is "the rapid expansion and integration of business activities across borders in response to dramatic technology and government policy changes in the latter part of the 20th century."[26] Put simply, globalization is the process of the world's becoming progressively more connected. The clear result of globalization is that sustainability demands attention from multiple countries and perspectives, and cannot be addressed by isolated institutions.[27]

Globalization is an essential business driver of sustainability because all sectors increasingly rely on international mobility to operate. In particular, as global supply chains continue to grow, it makes sense for companies to view their practices as interconnected and to work together to enhance sustainable practices across the planet.[28] Therefore, if businesses do not adopt more sustainable processes, businesses worldwide could be negatively impacted.

Increased Interdependence

While globalization is generally seen as a positive thing, its downsides are less obvious. One such downside is increased interdependence. This form of interdependence occurs in all sectors and, as mentioned above, is most evident through supply chain tracing. Supply chains are ripe with opportunities for improving sustainability.

The COVID-19 pandemic has generated lasting effects across the globe, especially (in the context of corporate sustainability) by shining a spotlight on companies' ESG practices and operations[29] and by highlighting the need for companies to ensure they have established "resilient, sustainable, legally compliant and ethical supply chains."[30] The lessons learned from the COVID-19 pandemic are broadly applicable to the potential disruption of supply chains. For example, just as a virus unexpectedly disrupted companies' supply chains, so could atypical weather patterns and related flooding. Therefore, it is important for

---

26. *What Do We Mean by "Sustainable Globalization?"*, PR NEWS (Nov. 24, 2008), https://www.prnewsonline.com/what-do-we-mean-by-sustainable-globalization/ (quoting THE SUSTAINABLE ENTERPRISE FIELDBOOK: WHEN IT ALL COMES TOGETHER, (Jeana Wirtenberg ed., Greenleaf Publishing Limited 2009) (2008)).
27. Sai Tang et al., *What Are the Implications of Globalization on Sustainability?—A Comprehensive Study* (Apr. 22, 2020), https://doi.org/10.3390/su12083411.
28. Dave Blanchard, *How to Manage a Global Supply Chain*, INDUS. WEEK (Aug. 14, 2012), https://www.industryweek.com/supply-chain/article/21958031/how-to-manage-a-global-supply-chain.
29. See Tony DeSpirito, *How a Global Pandemic Could Accelerate the ESG Imperative*, BLACKROCK (Apr. 13, 2020), https://www.blackrock.com/institutions/en-us/insights/market-pulse/pandemic-acceleration-for-esg.
30. Lu et al., *supra* note 6.

companies to understand their supply chains and the possible weaknesses therein.[31] For those companies wishing to set climate goals and reduce their carbon footprint, it is imperative to consider how much the supply chain is contributing to the companies' overall emissions.[32]

When suppliers, manufacturers, and producers all work together to create a finished good, the process of altering the raw good results in a loss of control by any one person or organization. This loss of control can lead to operational problems through supply chain friction and decreased efficiency. Interdependence, as displayed in supply chains, is a key driver of sustainability because it gives businesses an opportunity to mitigate risks, enhance operational efficiency, and reduce their carbon footprints.[33] Better awareness of where and how an essential element of a company's supply chain is sourced enables businesses to better prepare for any potential disruptions.

Stakeholder Demand for Increased Sustainability

In addition to business and economic reasons for companies to embrace sustainability as a strategic objective, stakeholders—employees,[34] customers,[35] and shareholders[36]—are also voicing their demand for increased sustainability and related disclosures. External and internal concerns, however, take many forms, and the language and actions employed to demand more sustainability are equally diverse. For example, employees are the stakeholders typically most concerned with the use of plastic, single-use products in the breakroom and reducing the company's carbon footprint.[37]

> Companies, at the direction of the board and stakeholders, should acknowledge their responsibility to the world and the people in it.

---

31. *Id.*

32. *Id.* The emissions produced from a company's supply are factored into the company's "Scope 3" emissions. See *Corporate Value Chain (Scope 3) Standard*, GREENHOUSE GAS PROTOCOL, https://ghgprotocol.org/standards /scope-3-standard (last visited Aug. 18, 2020); FAQ, GREENHOUSE GAS PROTOCOL, https://ghgprotocol.org/sites /default/files/standards_supporting/FAQ.pdf (last visited Aug. 18, 2020).

33. Lu et al., *supra* note 6.

34. Camille Hogg, *Sustainability Has Become an Employee Expectation—Here's What Your Business Can Do About It*, PEAKON (Mar. 10, 2020), https://peakon.com/us/blog/peakon/employee-expectations-2020/; see Brian D'Souza, *Amazon Employees Are Demanding Climate Action. The Company Is Silencing Them*, THE RISING (Feb. 3, 2020), https://therising.co/2020/02/03/amazon-sustainability-silencing-employees-climate-action/.

35. Remi Rosmarin, *Sustainability Sells: Why Consumers and Clothing Brands Alike Are Turning to Sustainability as a Guiding Light*, BUS. INSIDER (Apr. 22, 2020), https://www.businessinsider.com/sustainability-as-a-value-is -changing-how-consumers-shop.

36. E.g., Era Anagnosti et al., *BlackRock Calls for Enhanced Sustainability Disclosure and Accountability for Directors*, WHITE & CASE (Jan. 27, 2020), https://www.whitecase.com/publications/alert/blackrock-calls-enhanced -sustainability-disclosure-and-accountability-directors. "BlackRock is now calling on the public companies it invests in to publish disclosure in line with the Sustainability Accounting Standards Board (SASB) and the Task Force on Climate-related Financial Disclosures (TCFD), and will 'hold board members accountable' where companies and boards are not producing effective sustainability disclosures or implementing frameworks for managing sustainability issues." *Id.* (quoting Larry Fink, *A Fundamental Reshaping of Finance*, BLACKROCK, https://www .blackrock.com/corporate/investor-relations/larry-fink-ceo-letter (last visited Aug. 18, 2020)).

37. Hogg, *supra* note 34.

Customers and consumers often have the same concerns as employees, with the added threat of taking their business elsewhere if certain standards are not met.[38] There is much value to be found in meeting these demands from employees and consumers, failure to meet such demands may result in, risks to reputation and brand if not met. Institutional shareholders are also expecting the companies in which they invest to make progress on incorporating ESG practices and disclosures.[39] And this desire for corporate sustainability has only increased over the years.[40] Companies, at the direction of the board and stakeholders, should acknowledge their responsibility to the world and the people in it.

Take-Aways for Board Members

- Internal and external pressure for strong sustainability practices and disclosures is growing among various stakeholders.

- Adoption of robust sustainability practices may lead to better corporate performance and value creation.

- Boards should oversee management's development of corporate strategies both to seize opportunities and mitigate sustainability risks.

* * * * *

The authors of this chapter would like to thank Claire Young, J.D./MBA Candidate at Cumberland School of Law and Brock School of Business at Samford, and Patricia Meadow for their assistance on this chapter.

---

38. See Renae Reints, *Consumers Say They Want More Sustainable Products. Now They Have the Receipts to Prove It*, FORTUNE (Nov. 5, 2019), https://fortune.com/2019/11/05/sustainability-marketing-consumer-spending/.
39. Anagnosti et al., *supra* note 36; *Incorporating Sustainability into Long-Term* Strategy, STATE STREET GLOBAL ADVISORS, https://www.ssga.com/investment-topics/environmental-social-governance/2019/02/incorporating -sustainability-into-long-term-strategy.pdf.
40. Terri Toyota, *Sustainability Is Now Mission Critical for Businesses. Here's Why*, WORLD ECON. FORUM (Sept. 24, 2018), https://www.weforum.org/agenda/2018/09/sustainability-is-now-mission-critical-for-businesses-heres-why/.

Chapter 9
Who Are the Stakeholders?

Paul Wehrmann

Introduction

Directors of a business corporation are likely quite familiar, or will become quite familiar as a directorship progresses, with the traditional duties of a director and to whom those duties are owed. The underlying principle of those duties is that directors serve the corporation and its shareholders with the ultimate goal of maximizing shareholder value. Although its application can become very complicated in practice, this underlying principle is rather simple in theory. The relationship is basically that of two groups: the directors and the shareholders, with the direction of the corporation being driven by the rules of that relationship. And those rules are principally driven by financial outcomes. Sustainability takes that binary dynamic and expands it in virtually every direction. Those directions are addressed in various ways throughout this guidebook, but a basic question for directors regarding sustainability is "Who are the stakeholders?"

> A stakeholder of a business may be broadly viewed as any person, entity, or group that affects or is affected by that business.

What Is a Stakeholder?

Before answering that question, one might well ask, "*What* is a 'stakeholder'?" A stakeholder of a business may be broadly viewed as any person, entity, or group that affects or is affected by that business. This is clearly casting a wide net that may at first seem overly broad. However, it is important that a director focusing on sustainability understand that a stakeholder is not the same as a shareholder. Indeed, shareholders are but one subset of stakeholders, albeit an important one. All shareholders are stakeholders, but not all stakeholders are shareholders. As many activist shareholder proposals indicate, the lines can blur as to whether a shareholder is acting narrowly as a shareholder or more expansively as a stakeholder. Proposals concerning climate change, workplace and management diversity, and political contributions are some of the examples of shareholding being a conduit for change beyond the traditional shareholder concerns of management control and financial performance. As evidenced by these proposals, a narrow focus on shareholders should be shed in the sustainability context. Why is there such an emphasis on inclusion? It can be said that the essence of sustainability is making business decisions in a way that takes into account their holistic effect on local, regional, and global society, as well as those who are doing business, directly and indirectly, with the company.

> The essence of sustainability is making business decisions in a way that takes into account their holistic effect on local, regional, and global society, as well as those who are doing business, directly and indirectly, with the company.

Key Stakeholders: Employees, Management, and Shareholders

So, who affects or is being affected? A good place to start is with employees and contractors. Their ability to support and care for themselves and their families is based on good stewardship of the enterprise. If the company acts in an unsustainable manner, their jobs may go away, likely along with their ability to afford healthcare. Retirement income may be tied to long-term company performance. For many, their lives may be lost or tragically altered by mismanagement.

Management is also a key stakeholder. They have all the same interests as employees and contractors but with the added layer of having responsibility for business decisions. They also have to bear and manage risks of reputational harm and potential liability. Those risks run to the directors as well, but with broader responsibility and greater potential for liability. Moving to the top of the organizational chart, there are the shareholders or owners. The effect of company action on them is almost entirely financial, but still significant.

Key Stakeholders: Customer, Suppliers, and Creditors

Outside the company walls, virtually every enterprise will have the same core of key stakeholders. Whether engaged in, for example, retail sales, government contracting, or business services, customers, suppliers, and lenders and other creditors are essential. There are, of course, variants, and lines of distinction among these stakeholder groups may not always be bright, particularly in financial services and pensions. The customers, suppliers, and creditors of a hedge fund may coalesce into one.

Customers will have a vested interest in a business and its sustainability. They will want to have continued access to the goods or services provided, but will also want to know that those goods are safe and, increasingly, produced in socially responsible ways. Customers rely on businesses standing behind their work and being available in the event of problems. Vendors and suppliers rely on revenue from sales to the business and want their goods and services not to be misused. Chemical manufacturers do not want their products illegally drained into waterways. Business consultants do not want their reports used to support mistreatment of workers or antitrust violations. Lenders and other creditors have provided financing in the anticipation of survival of the business and enough financial and overall success to make them whole. These lenders and other creditors may be banks, equipment financiers, private equity funds, factoring services, governmental agencies, venture capital funds, suppliers, vendors, professional service providers, and individuals.

> Beyond this core of key external stakeholders common to virtually every business and affected by most of the decisions of that business (customers, suppliers, creditors), there is a landscape of stakeholders that may exist for certain businesses, but not for others, or for only certain business decisions, but not for others.

Other Stakeholders

Beyond this core of key external stakeholders common to virtually every business and affected by most of the decisions of that business (customers, suppliers, creditors), there is a landscape of stakeholders that may exist for certain businesses, but not for others, or for only certain business decisions, but not for others. Probably the most common of these are communities. A small community may be greatly damaged by the closure of a significant employer, such as a manufacturing plant. That same community may be only minimally affected, if at all, by the decision of that same manufacturing plant to switch from one equipment financier to another. The decisions on where to open new grocery stores may have little impact on a large community but may have a great impact on a smaller one. The removal of a coffee shop chain from a major city may have a quite different impact on the local community than the removal of that same coffee shop from a small town. Any disposal of hazardous waste, whether intentional or accidental, will affect the community where that disposal occurred.

Governmental agencies will be stakeholders in the vast majority of businesses. From issuing certificates of occupancy to standards for a safe workplace to regulation of securities offerings, governments at all levels are tasked with ensuring that business enterprises are operating in ways that are safe and legitimate. At the same time, they must balance regulation with encouraging business success and growth, not only for their own sakes but also as drivers of tax revenue. A lack of focus on sustainability may often lead to the necessity of governmental intervention. A preventable explosion of a cargo ship or the commission of extensive fraud simply cannot be ignored by governmental agencies.

Nongovernmental, self-regulatory agencies may be key stakeholders for certain ventures, particularly for licensed professionals. Local state bar associations exist for the purpose of regulating the practice of law in various states. According to its website, the role of the Financial Industry Regulatory Authority (FINRA) is "to protect America's investors by making sure the broker-dealer industry operates fairly and honestly."[1] "Fairness" and "honesty" could equally be stated to be goals of sustainability.

On a broader scale, nonregulatory trade groups and associations are often stakeholders for particular businesses and industries, or particular aspects of various businesses. The American Chemical Society, with its mission "to advance the broader chemistry enterprise and its practitioners for the benefit of Earth and its people" and its vision "to improve people's lives through the transforming power of chemistry,"[2] would have a significant stake in the operations of a vertically integrated plastics company but likely no discernible interest in a staffing agency. Similarly, the National Restaurant Association is unlikely to be a stakeholder in an aeronautics engineering firm but almost certainly would be in a fast-food chain. The American Library Association may have an interest in a publisher's sourcing of paper but very little interest in its choice of office space.

In certain businesses, industries, and geographical regions, trade and labor unions are stakeholders. Their interests should be very much aligned with those of the employees, their members. Their status as stakeholders may vary across both function and location, depending on the unionized status of the workforce employed. A homebuilder may have as a stakeholder a union of construction workers in Nevada, but not a plumbers' union in Nevada (if the homebuilder uses non-unionized Nevada plumbers) and not a construction workers' union in other states where its homes are located but where it uses non-unionized labor.

Charities and nongovernmental organizations (NGOs) may be key stakeholders for very specific purposes. The American Society for the Prevention of Cruelty to Animals and the Humane Society of the United States may be able to have great effect on the treatment of animals used in motion pictures, but no effect on greenlighting decisions. An NGO focused on Ghana may be affected by Ghanaian gold production but not by South African gold production.

Political groups need also be considered as potential stakeholders. From political parties to political action committees to nonprofit advocacy organizations, certain enterprise actions may be of great interest to these entities. And companies can be profoundly affected by the work of these groups. A business could be harmed or even fail if malfeasance of a former officer comes to light as the result of opposition research by an adversarial political action committee in that former officer's political campaign. The Sierra Club may use carrots and sticks to influence the choice of energy used to power a production facility, as the National Rifle Association may with regard to workplace safety policies.

The media is in a unique position to influence public perception. Every business should strive to garner favorable news coverage and avoid negative coverage. A positive relationship with the media can help to build the brand of a business; an antagonistic relationship can hurt it. To such extent, the media is a stakeholder.

Academia should be considered as a stakeholder. This is obviously true for technology firms whose products require licenses to innovations developed in university labs. On a broader scale, it is quite possible that decisions taken by directors and the results of those

---

1. https://www.finra.org/about (last visited May 24, 2021).
2. https://www.acs.org/content/acs/en/about.html?sc=180808_GlobalFooter_od (last visited May 24, 2021).

decisions may not only become the topics of case studies in business and law schools but also spur commentary or calls for change in academic publications and classrooms.

Social groups may rise to the level of stakeholders. Secular fraternal service organizations, such as Rotary or Lions, may be able to provide varied means of local and national support to companies. The same may be said of religious social groups, such as Hadassah and the Knights of Columbus.

Stakeholder Nomenclature

Different commentators describe and divide the realm of stakeholders in divergent ways. Some are more expansive; some are less so. The Business Roundtable implicitly limits the universe of stakeholders to five categories: customers, employees, suppliers, communities, and shareholders.[3] One may also be familiar with a nascent lexicon of stakeholder terminology, with distinctions such as "internal" or "external," "primary" or "secondary," and "direct" or "indirect." Such a taxonomy has been intentionally avoided as there do not appear to be any universally accepted criteria for such classifications. Certain stakeholders could also conceivably morph from one variant to another based on industry and the question presented. Finally, any practical utility of such demarcations for matters of sustainability, if there is in fact any, is far outweighed by the strain imposed by the mental gymnastics and leaps of faith necessary to impose such categorization.

Conclusion

This is not meant to be an exclusive list of stakeholders. Notably, Larry Fink, Chairman and Chief Executive Officer of BlackRock, in his 2021 letter to CEOs, expands stakeholders to include *potential* customers and suppliers:

> It is clear that being connected to stakeholders – establishing trust with them and acting with purpose – enables a company to understand and respond to the changes happening in the world. Companies ignore stakeholders at their peril – companies that do not earn this trust will find it harder and harder to attract customers and talent, especially as young people increasingly expect companies to reflect their values.[4]

Nor is the intention to infer that all of the foregoing potential stakeholders will be stakeholders in every corporation or for every sustainability decision made by a corporation. Given the variables in every boardroom action, it is impossible to predict who the key stakeholders will be for a given decision by a particular company. It is the intent to provide a framework for the exploration of considerations beyond financial benefit to shareholders and the adoption of a more inclusive basis for decision-making. For it is the integration of shareholder reward with societal awareness that forms the basis of sustainability.

---

3. Business Roundtable, *Statement on the Purpose of a Corporation*, https://opportunity.businessroundtable.org /ourcommitment/ (last visited May 24, 2021).
4. Letter from Larry Fink, Chairman and Chief Executive Officer, BlackRock, Inc., to CEOs (2021), https://www .blackrock.com/corporate/investor-relations/larry-fink-ceo-letter (last visited May 24, 2021).

Take-Aways for Board Members

- Although some stakeholders will be stakeholders for the majority of board action, the identification of stakeholders in a particular decision should be made on a case-by-case basis.

- The identification of stakeholders in a board action should be made by the group analyzing the action, whether the entire board, a standing committee, or an ad hoc committee.

- Identify stakeholders at the onset of the deliberative process as that identification will help guide those reviewing the issue at hand.

- If identification of stakeholders becomes a stumbling block, consult with experts.

- Be expansive and thorough in identification of stakeholders. Inclusion is the future.

Chapter 10
Shareholder Proposals and Activism

Reuben Zaramian, Kai H.E. Liekefett, Derek Zaba, and Hana Lee

Changes in social norms and expectations in recent years have led business leaders and investors to reconsider shareholder primacy as the guiding principle for public companies. With this dominant theory of investment stewardship challenged, companies today are more seriously considering their responsibilities to their various stakeholders. In particular, many investors, who are typically the most influential stakeholder group, are holding companies accountable to higher standards of environmental, social, and governance concerns, potentially at the expense of maximizing investor returns. Environmental-, social-, and governance-related factors (typically referred to as *ESG*) serve as a reasonable metric for "sustainability" and help measure a company's impact on its various stakeholders. ESG constituents might include those that companies may not have considered until recently, such as diverse employee groups, the ecosystem surrounding production facilities, and intermediaries in a supply chain. As investor expectations broaden to encompass ESG concerns, companies will benefit from engaging stakeholders beyond their traditional spectrum to discuss responsibility for the stewardship and long-term viability of the enterprise.

This chapter focuses on shareholder behavior and what boards can expect when investors—historically the most important stakeholder group—take action based on their needs and changing expectations of a company.

Shareholder Behavior

A simple framework of shareholder behavior can help explain how most investors exercise control of their shares: they can (i) maintain or increase their shareholdings based on their expectations about the business and the associated preservation or growth in value; (ii) exit the investment, typically due to the achievement of predetermined targets or disappointing returns; or (iii) voice their perspectives by voting on and submitting proposals as well as directly engaging with the company in other ways. The first two behaviors describe the transfer and ownership of shares, which can *indirectly* impact a company's decisions and actions. The third behavior describes the mechanisms by which shareholders exert *direct* influence on the company with respect to important issues like sustainability issues. In particular, certain types of shareholder proposals inform a company about the views its investors have on the direction of the company and encourage (and sometimes compel) specific changes in its business, operations, and policies. In addition, shareholders are becoming increasingly comfortable directly engaging with companies in which they are invested through various actions that can be categorized as shareholder activism for the purpose of affecting business decisions and corporate policy. Sustainability-focused proposals and activism are essentially focused on creating greater value for companies over a longer time horizon rather than quarterly performance.

Shareholder Proposals

Shareholders can submit proposals for consideration at a company's annual meeting (a *Shareholder Meeting*) in one of two ways. First, a proposal can be submitted as a matter of state corporate law, typically pursuant to the "advance notice" provisions typically found in a company's bylaws (a *Business Proposal*). Business Proposals are binding and compel a company to act if approved at the Shareholder Meeting and are typically accompanied by a campaign to solicit support from other investors. Most companies have "advance notice" requirements that include submission deadlines, delivery procedures, and disclosure rules that require proponents to describe their ultimate purposes and derivative positions. Business Proposals may be excluded from the agenda of a Shareholder Meeting if the proponent does not comply with the specifications set forth in such rules. Given the import of these provisions and the increasing willingness of shareholders to submit Business Proposals, it is critical that boards review these requirements on a regular basis to ensure they reflect the latest developments.

The second way by which shareholders can submit proposals is under Rule 14a-8 (*Rule 14a-8 Proposals*) of the Securities Exchange Act of 1934 (the *Exchange Act*), which represents the vast majority of shareholder proposals received by public companies. These nonbinding (sometimes referred to as "precatory") proposals are included in the proxy materials of the company, but have certain eligibility requirements tied to ownership that are established by the U.S. Securities and Exchange Commission (the *SEC*) from time to time. Rule 14a-8 Proposals can be excluded from a company's proxy statement based on a number of grounds recognized under SEC rules that govern proxy materials, such as interference with the company's ordinary business operations or duplication of prior proposals. Nearly all shareholder proposals related to sustainability issues are submitted as Rule 14a-8

Proposals since companies are required to include these proposals in their own proxy materials (whereas for Business Proposals, the proponent must bear the expense of preparing proxy materials and running a campaign in compliance with the proxy solicitation regulations under Section 14(a) of the Exchange Act).

Notably, Rule 14a-8 Proposals must have a "proper purpose" in order to be included in a company's proxy materials. Among other things, this means that shareholders cannot submit proposals that would require a company to take actions that would affect the board's capacity to govern the company. For example, a shareholder cannot submit a proposal that, if passed, would require an oil and gas company to cease fossil fuel operations in favor of pursuing clean fuel initiatives. A shareholder can, however, indirectly affect a company's operations by voicing its concerns that would *lead to* a change in the composition of the company's board. The goal of such a change in the boardroom would be to remove directors perceived to be comfortable with the company's status quo to create vacancies for directors who are open to sustainability initiatives.

Although roughly half of all Rule 14a-8 Proposals end up withdrawn prior to the vote due to unilateral withdrawal by the proponent, rejection for inclusion in proxy materials by the company, or settlement between the parties, the remaining proposals that proceed to a shareholder vote receive a good amount of support. Between 2010 and 2020, nearly 5000 Rule 14a-8 Proposals that went to a shareholder vote received an average support level of around 20%. Historically, Rule 14a-8 Proposals focused on issues such as increasing shareholder rights under a company's organizational documents, including with respect to special meeting and written consent rights, board declassification, split chair/CEO, majority voting, proxy access proposals, and executive compensation. We distinguish such governance-related proposals from discussions on corporate sustainability as such traditional governance issues have been raised by shareholders for decades and are generally not the focus of discussions on corporate sustainability.

Unlike the most successful governance proposals, environmental and social proposals have not yet triggered pan-industry changes. However, environmental and social proposals have been increasing in both prevalence and support over time. Environmental and social proposals tend to address emerging issues and matters of regulatory concern. Environmental proposals focus on reporting related to climate change and environmental impact, waste and emission goals, renewable energy, recycling, and sustainable packaging. Recent environmental proposals that received majority support sought:

- A report on the company's plans for reducing its contribution to climate change and aligning its operations with Paris Agreement goals.
- A report on how the company is aligning its long-term business strategy with the projected long-term constraints posed by climate change.
- A review of the environmental impact of continued investment in petrochemical plants in a particular region.
- A report on ESG performance that focuses on wastewater reduction targets and product-specific environmental impacts.

Social proposals focus on a broader range of issues, including human capital (which is often an issue of employee diversity, but can also encompass issues of pay gaps, health, and safety), supply chains, data privacy, political lobbying, political contributions, and animal welfare. Recent social proposals have sought:

- The adoption of a policy requiring diverse candidates to be considered for management positions and board vacancies.
- A report on gender pay gaps.
- A report regarding human rights due diligence processes.
- A report on strengthening prevention of workplace sexual harassment.
- A report on measures related to the distribution of opioids.
- A report on pesticide use in the company's supply chain.
- The adoption of a policy regarding oversight on animal welfare in a company's supply chain.

One example of the evolution of investor perspectives on sustainability proposals is striking: In 2016, a sustainability-focused fund pressed a large multi-brand restaurant operator to eliminate the use of antibiotics in its livestock supply chain by submitting a Rule 14a-8 Proposal. The proposal achieved less than 10% support that year, but by the third time it was introduced in subsequent years, the proposal achieved nearly 40% support from investors, which was enough to pressure the company to implement a policy to phase out the use of antibiotics in its livestock supply chain within five years.

Despite the fact that Rule 14a-8 Proposals are precatory—meaning, a company is not required to act upon the resolution even if the proposal achieves the requisite number of shareholder votes to pass—boards must carefully consider the consequences of ignoring the concerns of proponents (typically socially responsible investment firms, pension funds, faith-based investors, special interest foundations, and concerned individuals), particularly if they receive a high percentage of support. In addition to the potentially negative publicity, proxy advisory firms like Institutional Shareholder Services Inc. and Glass, Lewis & Co. may issue negative voting recommendations for some or all of the company's directors at the company's next annual meeting, and institutional shareholders may use the company's inaction as a reason to vote against the board's recommendations in the future. Proxy advisory firms have even begun recommending that shareholders vote in favor of certain environmental and social proposals. Inaction by the board might also encourage shareholders to further escalate their engagement with the company.

Shareholder Activism

Public companies face shareholder activism at increasingly elevated levels—the question of an activist campaign is no longer "if" but, rather, "when." The term "shareholder activism" has evolved significantly in terms of what it encompasses. Shareholder activists are no longer viewed in the same light as the infamous corporate raiders, with activists now having longer investment horizons, broader support among both institutional investors and retail shareholders, and a much bigger toolkit comprising public pressure tactics and structural mechanisms in the form of shareholder rights. Importantly, activist investors and activist tactics no longer carry the stigmas they once did.

Whereas most investors diversify their investments across many companies and industries in order to manage risk and volatility, activists typically concentrate their investments in a smaller number of positions. Such narrow portfolios allow activists to devote a great amount of attention to each company's performance and direction within its industry against the backdrop of macroeconomic trends. When considering a company to invest in, activists assess two things: first, whether there is a meaningful opportunity to generate a return that is higher than similar or benchmark investments by creating or taking advantage of some value-enhancing event such as a divestiture, change in management or new cost-cutting initiative; second, whether the activist can make use of its rights under the company's organizational documents and applicable legal regime in order to accomplish its goals.

Generally, a key component of the second prong is whether the activist can obtain the support of institutional shareholders for the case for change. It is worth highlighting the impact of institutional investors during an activist campaign. Traditionally, institutional investors such as large index funds, pension funds, and sovereign wealth funds were considered "passive," meaning, their input was largely advisory in nature and they tended to support companies as the defenders of long-term value creation. In recent years, however, their role has changed, with many institutional investors now engaging in regular and deliberate dialogue with companies. Such engagement carries with it the expectation that companies will take the necessary steps to implement the investor's recommendations and guidelines in return for their support at the polls. Because such investors typically hold the largest positions in public companies and—unlike many retail and other investors—they tend to vote all of their shares, they have an outsized impact on the outcome of shareholder votes with the power to hold companies accountable for perceived failures. Without their support, companies and boards are significantly more vulnerable to losing key votes and director elections. Boards are strongly advised to align themselves with the sustainability and governance expectations of their largest institutional investors as a matter of maintaining good investor relations and a strong base of support.

Notably, increased institutional investor interest in ESG has set the stage for a wave of shareholder activism that will make sustainability criticism an integral component of traditional activism campaigns. In addition, a growing class of investors and specialized investment vehicles are becoming motivated by more than just risk-adjusted excess returns. Such "sustainability activists" and sustainability-focused funds are driven by the assumption that sustainable investments can generate high (if not higher) returns while addressing ESG issues particular to the company in question. Highlighted below are a few recent and high-profile situations where demands were made by activist funds to align a company's objectives with sustainability considerations or initiatives specific to its business:

- An activist fund launched a new impact fund and partnered with a large pension fund to pressure a large consumer technology company to address certain potential negative effects of its products on society as a whole. The campaign was largely focused on a single public letter to the board of directors of the company, which attracted significant media attention given the prominence of the target company and subject matter. The letter pointed out the detrimental mental health effects of overuse of the company's devices and led the company to change certain practices.

- An activist fund launched a new impact fund and targeted a regional electric utility company through a public letter addressed to the population of an entire U.S. state.

The letter highlighted concerns about the amount of oil the company imported in connection with its operations and the fact that the company would not meet the renewable energy goals it had established. The campaign was settled, resulting in the appointment of one of the fund's principals to the board of directors of the company.

- An activist fund sent a public letter to the board of directors of a large insurance company with global operations, urging it to split its businesses across geographic lines in order to create two standalone companies, each with its own long-term strategy, which would result in a greater realization of value and a significant reduction in the company's existing carbon footprint. The short-term result of the campaign was the initiation of a sales process for the company's business in the United States.

- An activist fund reached a settlement agreement with a regional electric utility company to, among other things, implement a five-year sustainability transformation plan to transition to the use of clean energy and develop a strategy to position the company to drive shareholder value creation.

- An impact-focused fund launched a campaign against a large oil and gas producer to develop a long-term strategic plan to enhance shareholder value in the face of industry changes and replace several directors with candidates with experience in the oil and gas industry and renewable energy. The campaign resulted in the company's disclosure of estimates of carbon emissions from the use of its products and the election of three of the fund's candidates at the annual meeting.

Activist investors perceive themselves as agents of corporate accountability who serve to convene a company's stakeholders on issues that may have previously been unseen or ignored by the board. However, public company directors must be alerted to the reality that activists may hide direct financial motivations within the ambit of sustainability concerns because of the strong support sustainability issues typically receive from institutional investors and the media. As has been the case with corporate governance criticism for decades, directors should seek to understand the motivations of an activist during an engagement in order to assess whether sustainability is being used simply as a means to a financial end or whether the suggestions identify a deficiency or blind spot in the company's operations or policies.

Sustainability-focused proposals and activism are essentially focused on creating greater value for companies over a longer time horizon rather than quarterly performance.

Unlike the most successful governance proposals, environmental and social proposals have not yet triggered pan-industry changes. However, environmental and social proposals have been increasing in both prevalence and support over time.

Activist investors perceive themselves as agents of corporate accountability who serve to convene a company's stakeholders on issues that may have previously been unseen or ignored by the board.

Sustainability issues continue to gain momentum in the hands of institutional investors and activist funds that are positioned to leverage these problems as value-enhancing propositions.

Take-Aways for Board Members

Sustainability issues continue to gain momentum in the hands of institutional investors and activist funds that are positioned to leverage these problems as value-enhancing propositions. Combined with the possibility that the future may continue to bring historic levels of sustainability-focused dialogue (and criticism), boards should be diligent in identifying areas in which the company can improve in order to preempt shareholder proposals and activism. In order to do so, directors should regularly consider the following:

- *Strategy*: Has the board developed a sustainable, long-term strategic plan with the input of directors that have the ESG competencies most relevant to the company?

- *Vulnerability*: How vulnerable is the company on the spectrum of sustainability concerns that exist in its business segments and at the organizational level?

- *Shareholders*: Who are the company's shareholders and what are their respective positions on sustainability issues? How well does the board understand the behavioral patterns of the company's shareholders?

- *Stakeholder Engagement*: Is the company proactively engaging with shareholders on sustainability issues? Can other stakeholders help the board identify blind spots?

- *Responsiveness*: Has the board been responsive to issues that have previously come up as proposals or through other engagements? Is the board working toward addressing issues raised by the company's business partners, customers, analysts, and proxy advisory firms?

- *Preparedness*: Does the board have the right to guide it in addressing ESG-related proposals and activism?

Chapter 11
Board Oversight of the Dynamic ESG Landscape

Beth-ann Roth

Introduction

The previous three chapters identified the drivers of sustainability (Chapter 8), the stakeholders who have an interest in or impact on a company's sustainability profile (Chapter 9), and how issues are raised and discussed with and/or by shareholders (Chapter 10). This chapter explores how boards incorporate those factors into the processes driven by the legal and fiduciary obligations they have to the company.

Members of a board of directors focus on their duties of loyalty and care in carrying out their responsibilities to the company they serve. For some boards (e.g., those overseeing mutual funds), these state-law duties are augmented by statutes specific to the industry in which the company operates. These duties form the framework for board service. Within the framework, there are hosts of considerations that go into the decisions that provide strategic direction for the company, such as those discussed in the previous three chapters. Boards need to establish how they will address those considerations.

From a procedural standpoint, the board typically demonstrates that it has taken into account the material information available to it through the board meeting process, which includes building a substantive board book. That manifestation of governance best practices protects the deliberative process in support of the "business judgment rule" presumption that directors have acted in the best interests of the company. From the perspective of evaluating whether the board has satisfied its duties, considering information arising from the various sources helps members identify factors to weigh that may impact their decision-making as it relates to the success of the company.

> Sustainability analysis is an essential component of the board's deliberative process.

It is this evaluative process into which the components of sustainability enter. Viewed through this lens, it becomes apparent that sustainability analysis is an essential component of the board's deliberative process. At times, some have found it difficult to envision principles of sustainability as factors relevant to the financial outcomes critical to a company's existence. However, anything that impacts a stakeholder's willingness to invest in, work for, do business with, or be a purchaser of the products of a company is likely to have an impact on the company's bottom line.

Incorporating the Drivers of Sustainability into Board Oversight

Environmental, social, and governance ("ESG") "drivers" will help the board determine policy priorities that are fundamental either to the company's product or to its existence as an employer or as a member of its community. If the product itself is "sustainable"—or it can be altered to be sustainable and there is a desire to make it so—that becomes a focus of importance in its production and marketing.

If the company's product cannot itself be sustainable, a company might choose to set itself apart and set an example by managing its manufacturing process in a way that goes above and beyond environmental regulatory requirements. This type of engagement can become critical when the company produces an essential product that is made using a process that is inherently polluting, such as is the case in the steel industry.

In yet other scenarios, the company may be an active participant in its community, making its relationship with its neighbors "sustainable." Or its supply-chain dealings, its energy choices, or its decisions to recycle its office supplies and move away from producing trash may make the office an environmentally friendly and "sustainable" workplace. The company may provide ESG funds as options for employees' retirement investments, demonstrating a respect for individual investment choices. The determination of which drivers are most relevant to the company is a policy matter to be determined by the board.

The board should make certain it is fully informed about the company's positions on matters relating to those aspects of sustainability that the company has identified as to its business and key relationships. A standing instruction for the Chief Sustainability Officer (or other management function assigned to oversee sustainability) to report on the company's positions helps the board evaluate whether the company is living up to its commitments in whatever areas it has deemed it important to be involved.

To the extent possible, the board should have management identify the metrics being used to measure success, and—in addition to the narrative accompanying presentations to the board—should establish some sort of standard reporting so that progress can be tracked. For aspects of sustainability that are not yet achievable but remain aspirational, the board should request regular updates from management so as to be able to track progress and evaluate whether the path, as then-configured, is appropriate.

Companies have limited resources, and both policy and business decisions require that choices be made. In this context, there will likely be "drivers" of sustainability that the board has not flagged as being of central importance to the company at a given time, at least as weighed against other pressing considerations. As such, the board may determine that these drivers cannot merit the dedication of scarce resources for immediate consideration. Nevertheless, it is critical that the board initially evaluate the potential public perception of what otherwise may appear to be the company's lack of engagement on an important issue. Proactive engagement, as discussed below, will be critical to the company's ability successfully to navigate the public response to its decisions. The narrative needs to be up-front and honest.

Early evaluation is more than theoretical, as shareholders may eventually raise the matters with management, or a topic may suddenly become a hot-button issue due to some large-scale event. If and when an issue does come to the fore, whether because the company itself deems it an appropriate time to address the issue or because of shareholder or outside forces, it is best that the company have as a record its prior reports to the board so that current management and board members can potentially act more quickly or at least understand the genesis of the company's emerging policy. Thus, even if a matter cannot realistically be implemented as an appropriate use of resources at the time the issue is raised, the memorialized discussions relating to the matter will help make future inquiries and decision-making much more fruitful.

The key will be to identify which "drivers" are both relevant to and important for the success of the company, and for the board to establish policies and priorities to respond to those needs. In this connection, the board should set up processes to demonstrate that it has its finger on the pulse on whatever sustainability factors will be deemed relevant drivers for the industry in which the business operates, and to be prepared with answers as to why others are not being addressed at any given time. Otherwise, the company may find itself the subject of challenges from stakeholders. As will be discussed below, the company should be proactive so as to avoid the risk of negative attention.

> Dedicated pre-meeting committee work and thoughtful board book preparation will go a long way toward making sure the board in fact has all it needs to make decisions, and that its decisions are less likely to become the subject of criticism.

The mechanics of how this is done is the same as for board consideration of any other issue. Board deliberations are not open to public review. Nevertheless, establishing good governance procedures serves as a board's best "insurance policy" should its decisions ever be questioned. Specifically, though the deliberative process is not subject to review and the minutes generally do not and should not memorialize the discussions leading up to how a decision was reached, the materials presented to the board in connection with its review of a decision item establish whether the board had sufficient information on which to base its conclusion. In this regard, dedicated pre-meeting committee work and thoughtful board book preparation will go a long way toward making sure the board in fact has all it needs to make decisions, and that its decisions are less likely to become the subject of criticism.

Take-Aways for Board Members

- Identify a baseline set of the sustainability "drivers" relative to your company, and agree which management team(s) will oversee their incorporation into operations.

- Request periodic reports from management (either directly or via a board committee established for that purpose) to report on the program that has been established.

- Establish a periodic review to determine whether any additional factors have become relevant.

Stakeholder Interests and Board Responses

In the chapter identifying stakeholders, we were introduced to a diverse array of voices that comprise a company's operations and, ultimately, its successes. As the list takes us past the first few categories that traditionally come to mind when considering who the stakeholders are, it becomes apparent that boards are faced with the challenge of taking into account a number of different constituencies. Sometimes, the interests of one group of stakeholders compete with those of another. So how does a board weigh the input of each while staying true to its obligation to make decisions in the best interests of the company while giving effect to each of its duties?

The board makes decisions based on what is in the best interests of the company, not what is best for others, whether those "others" be individual board members or any of the many stakeholders who are part of the company's landscape. However, that does not mean the board may exclude consideration of certain matters raised by stakeholders, even when those matters are not aligned with the company's current business plan.

Rather, the same deliberative process a board uses to evaluate whether a matter merits attention also contributes to decisions about issues raised by the range of stakeholders. In this regard—no different than with regard to other decisions—it is essential that a board have before it material information sufficient to support an analysis leading to a conclusion.

That being said, opinions from stakeholders are unlike other issues that can be considered and either adopted or rejected. The human element associated with those who can legitimately be deemed stakeholders strongly suggests that their interests, if not precisely aligned with those of the company, can potentially impact the business of the company. Accordingly, it makes sense to listen to the perspectives expressed by all stakeholders.

Beyond that, from a human relations standpoint, it is key for stakeholders to know that their voices have been heard and their concerns on the company's radar screen. This fact augurs in favor of a board's reaction to stakeholder expression being one of responsiveness and engagement. Vocal stakeholders provide a critical window on the world that enables the board to examine the company from different perspectives. That willingness to express views also creates a path for engagement that establishes the company as a trustworthy partner. Proactive engagement is always likely to be more productive than acting as a result of an adversarial challenge.

Take-Aways for Board Members

- Identify the company's "sustainability stakeholders."

- Request that management establish one or more channels of communication, make known the availability to communicate, and invite input. Engage thoughtfully and proactively.

- Request periodic reports from management on engagements and feedback so as to be able to take the pulse of stakeholder impressions as to the company's place on various sustainability scales.

ESG Activism and the Board: Best Practices for Successful Relationships

Shareholders are the owners of the companies in which they invest. They may take an active interest in the company, seeking information or demanding change. In the sustainability world, shareholder engagement will tend to focus on matters that can be characterized as relating broadly to ESG issues.

The history of shareholder activism on ESG issues includes successes that have resulted in companies acknowledging important issues raised by shareholders and taking appropriate action. Some, at the time the issues arose, seemed aspirational and not directly related to a company's business, and yet now are commonplace, even if not yet universal.

Many successes have been due to voluntary engagement between companies and their shareholders. Others have been brought about because of voting items proposed by shareholders and put forth for a vote in the company's proxy statement. (See subsection (b), below, entitled *The Annual Meeting and Shareholder Proposals*.) Finally, some shareholder successes have been the result of litigation to enforce shareholders' rights to exercise the corporate franchise when companies have refused to include a proposal in the company's annual meeting proxy statement.[1]

Regardless of the outcome of a vote, having the proposal appear in the proxy statement gets the issue circulated to the shareholder body, which is significant since the proxy statement is the sole formal vehicle for shareholders to disseminate matters of importance to them to the entire shareholder body. Giving the issue "air time" is critical even though companies are not bound by the results of the vote. Nevertheless, it behooves management and the board to pay attention, since when an issue garners support it is arguably a measure of materiality to the company's owners, and thus an issue to which management and the board should give due consideration.

Generally speaking, the decision whether a company chooses to act on a proposal garnering support has been deemed to be voluntary. However, the SEC has recently announced that it will step up its enforcement of material omissions, particularly as they relate to

---

1. See, e.g., Roosevelt v. Du Pont, 958 F.2d 416 (D.C. Cir. 1992) (appeal from action seeking injunction compelling Du Pont to include a shareholder proposal in annual meeting proxy materials relating to targeting a phase-out date for production of chlorofluorocarbons ("CFCs") consistent with an earlier date established by producers in other countries); and New York City Employees Retirement System v. Dole, 969 F.2d 1430 (2d Cir. 1992) (appeal from preliminary injunction requiring Dole to include a shareholder proposal in annual meeting proxy materials from the New York City Employees Retirement System relating to national health care).

climate change and other ESG issues,[2] so it makes sense to strengthen oversight in this area if for nothing other than establishing good compliance practices.

Those evaluations should not be left to chance. The board should direct management to establish a chain of responsibility and procedures to make sure the board is always aware of the issues being put forth, and the board should monitor the percentage of votes in favor of each resolution to get a sense of its importance to shareholders.[3]

Some companies—rather than being proactive and monitoring issues that may not have been in front of them but for shareholders having raised those issues—take advantage of the regulatory minimum requirements to keep shareholder voices at bay. That approach obviously creates strife, and is arguably not a "best practice" for a company seeking to hold itself out as embodying principles of sustainability. In the subsections below, we address what steps a board may choose to take in connection with its communications with stakeholders, and in particular shareholders.

Ongoing Engagement with Shareholders[4]

The issues on which shareholders seek to engage with the companies they own are wide-ranging. They touch on issues such as climate change, governance issues such as requiring an independent board chair, diversity and majority voting for directors, political contributions, lobbying spending, proxy access, ESG performance, and employee diversity. There tend to be trends over sets of years, and it is important for the board to be aware of them.

A proactive way for a company to engage stakeholders on issues of interest is in the context of sustainability reporting. (See Chapters 14 and 15 relating respectively to mandatory and voluntary reporting.) However, in addition to sustainability reports and the shareholder proposal process (see the discussion that follows in subsection (b) relating to *The Annual Meeting and Shareholder Proposals*), there are often ongoing efforts by shareholders to engage with management on issues of importance to them.

The communications landscape is virtually unregulated, except to the extent that the parties must take care not to be deemed to be soliciting votes, which triggers the requirement to file a proxy statement. Other than that, there are neither mechanisms to ensure shareholder access to management, nor are there mandates requiring that management engage with the very investors that provide the nonrevenue resources that permit the company to engage more fully in its operations.

> Some of the most successful corporate–shareholder collaborations have resulted in changes that the companies themselves ended up championing—even when they initially resisted—recognizing the ultimate benefits to the company, their shareholders, and their stakeholders.

---

2. *"SEC Announced Enforcement Task Force Focused on Climate the ESG Issues"* (March 4, 2021), https://www.sec.gov/news/press-release/2021-42.

3. The results of the vote may not present a full picture of shareholder support for a particular issue. The reason is that some broker-held shares may either not be voted or are voted in a manner that may not reflect an individual shareholder's position on an issue.

4. The relationship we address in this subsection relates primarily to shareholders. While other stakeholder voices are important, our focus on shareholders addresses the important relationships between the parties, and stresses the heightened duty corporations have to their shareholders versus other stakeholders.

For example, if a shareholder reaches out to management to engage in a dialogue, a company can choose to oppose the request and take an adversarial posture. For obvious reasons, that approach is not one that can be expected to yield a fruitful relationship. A better approach is for the company to choose to listen and engage. In this latter scenario, the company becomes a partner, and can even become an agent for change. Indeed, some of the most successful corporate–shareholder collaborations have resulted in changes that the companies themselves ended up championing—even when they initially resisted—recognizing the ultimate benefits to the company, their shareholders, and their stakeholders.[5]

Companies can be proactive and prepared for inquiries by establishing engagement systems for communicating with shareholders and—potentially—with other stakeholders. Dedicated personnel stays on top of the various issues of interest, and there is someone always in place proactively to engage in the event of a shareholder inquiry or demand. Having in place a coherent strategy to work with shareholders helps prevent the strained relationships that can otherwise take root.

The board should consider directing management to engage proactively with shareholder inquiries and to avoid confrontation. Indeed, if the company affirmatively establishes channels of communication, and assigns dedicated company personnel to receive and respond to inquiries, the relationship has the potential to be a level, two-party engagement as opposed to the company being a "target" awaiting a possible salvo. Depending on the issue, a well-thought-out engagement could potentially evolve into a multiparty initiative with other members of the sector, thereby showcasing the company's efforts as a leader for positive change. Under that construct, everyone wins. Such grandiose endings are not always possible (and they are rarely quick), but the public and the company's shareholders do take note of the company's efforts, and the impact on the company's image will tend to be positive.

Shareholders seeking to engage with a company may be individuals, or they may be "institutional investors" such as mutual fund companies or pension funds. Those reaching out may be loosely formed coalitions of investors with similar concerns. Proactive engagement will take planning and dedicated resources. But the potential successes from that approach could result in rewards for the company that go beyond the specific question at issue at any given time.

One challenge for the board will be to work with management to define how best to report on the substance of such engagements with shareholders. The company is not permitted to engage in selective disclosure. Accordingly, the company will need to establish internal controls and procedures to help decide when issues are ripe for public disclosure, and how best to accomplish that disclosure.

---

5. A number of years-long efforts among coalitions of some of the largest companies have yielded substantive positive changes due to shareholder-led initiatives. Some initial corporate responses were adversarial. Issues include the introduction of concepts that are recognized programs about which it is now surprising to recall that there was ever any resistance: recycling, label disclosures, discontinuing use of polystyrene foam, antibiotics in the food chain, mandatory arbitration, board diversity, disclosure of workforce composition, greenhouse gases, disclosure of political donations, and the adoption of human rights policies. See generally Paul Hodgson, *How Investor-Corporate Engagement Can Be Beneficial for All Concerned (With Examples!)*, Responsible Investor (Sept. 17, 2020), https://www.responsible-investor.com/articles/paul-hodgson-how-investor-corporate -engagement-can-be-beneficial-for-all-concerned-with-examples.

The Annual Meeting and Shareholder Proposals

An Overview of the Shareholder Proposal Process

The regulatory path via which shareholders are entitled to bring matters to management's attention is in connection with the company's annual meeting. In addition to the matters put forth by management which require shareholder approval under the federal securities laws—such as the election of directors and the selection of the company's auditors—the proxy rules contain provisions entitling shareholders to put forth proposals for a vote at the meeting.

That right, however, is not absolute. Rather, resolutions are subject to the company being able to exclude proposals for a limited number of reasons. If a company believes an exclusion applies, it seeks "no-action" relief from the SEC staff. If the SEC staff agrees with the company, it sends the company a letter stating that the staff will not recommend enforcement action as a result of the omission. The staff response does not opine on whether the decision to omit a proposal is legally sufficient, and typically does not provide an analysis to serve as a basis for its decision.

A decision in a no-action response not to recommend enforcement action applies only to the company that requested the relief; the letter may not be relied on as precedent by any other party, and even the Commission is free to disagree. However, as a practical matter, once the staff either concurs or declines to concur based on a specific set of facts, parties arguably know the position the staff will take in a similar inquiry, and companies regularly cite earlier decisions in their requests for no-action relief, though there are plenty of examples of similar facts yielding a different result. The staff does not typically provide an analysis to serve as a basis for its decision.

Since no-action concurrences by the staff only shield a company from regulatory enforcement action, they do not protect the company from being sued by the shareholders in court. Bringing suit is usually not practical for reasons of timing, cost, and shareholders not wanting to escalate an adversarial position out of fear of losing whatever chances for dialogue they have. Thus, as a practical matter, the SEC's informal process often effectively disenfranchises shareholders in connection with the sole formal mechanism that exists to give shareholders a voice.

Managing Shareholder Proposals

Many companies do respond to shareholders in an adversarial fashion rather than attempting to cultivate a collaborative relationship, and some appear to do so reflexively rather than engaging in careful thought as to why an adversarial approach makes sense. Boards should take into account that an adversarial posture is unlikely to put their company in a good light, and the results are not likely to be better than were the company to engage shareholders and other stakeholders in meaningful discussions about the issues being raised.

> The better way to build a relationship with shareholders is to be proactive and engage.

In the past, considerations for not wanting to include a proposal were the additional expense of printing the proxy statement, as well as the time involved for typesetting. With the prevalence of electronic dissemination of materials, and the advent of digital printing, those factors are less important. Accordingly, the company may decide simply to include the proposal, and let shareholders vote on it. Including the proposed resolution does not implicate acceptance by the company; the company typically indicates in the proxy statement whether it supports or opposes the proposed resolution. Since resolutions do not bind the company even if they pass, the risk to the company is minimal. If the proposal does receive significant support, it is a signal that the company might need to devote attention to its substance.

By the time shareholders reach the point of believing they need to submit a proposal in order to be heard, it often—but not always—suggests that communications have broken down. This, of course, assumes that the shareholder first attempted dialogue. While pre-submission dialogue is preferable, it does not always occur. The shareholder may believe an attempt at outreach will be futile, possibly based on past experience. Whatever the reason, it is not too late for the company to dial the situation back down and for the company to attempt a conversation.

The right to participate in the shareholder proposal process and having a private right of action to sue in court if a company omits a proposal from its proxy statement are both important safeguards for protecting shareholder rights. Arguably, many of the successful initiatives in which companies are now proud to have had a leadership role would not have come about had it not been for the shareholder proposal process forcing the company to pay attention. However, in the age of electronic communications, parties are often better served by communicating directly with one another to establish a thoughtful dialogue. Reactive management is not nearly as good as proactive engagement.

If communications do not succeed, then the shareholder proposal process is an efficient method of disseminating important information in connection with the voting of proxies. Ideally, shareholders should use the process to inform other shareholders of important policy issues. Management should view proposals as an opportunity to engage with those who support the existence of the business, rather than rushing to find a way to exclude a proposal.

Once a shareholder succeeds in having a proposal included in the annual meeting proxy statement, the company will typically include a recommendation as to whether shareholders should approve or vote against the proposal. In this connection, management follows the shareholder proposal with its own statement in support of its recommendation.

Given the often adversarial nature of this part of the annual meeting voting process, it is not difficult to guess that most companies recommend voting against shareholders' proposals. Were the shareholders and management of a particular company engaged in more productive communications, the outcome would likely be a negotiated one, or the company may already have implemented the shareholder's request to some degree, and there would either be no proposal put forth or it would often be withdrawn prior to the company filing its proxy statement with the SEC.

Partnering with Shareholders

The better way to build a relationship with shareholders is to be proactive and engage. With respect to those issues that make it to the proxy statement notwithstanding communications efforts, some companies go the extra mile and actually recommend that shareholders vote *in support of* a resolution. Following are some examples:

- In 2004, Coca-Cola recommended a vote in favor of a shareholder proposal requesting a report considering "the potential economic effects of the HIV/AIDS [and tuberculosis and malaria] on the Coca-Cola system's business and highlight Coca-Cola's initiatives in response to the issue."

- In 2011, Layne Christensen recommended a vote in favor of a resolution requesting publication of a sustainability report.

- In 2016, Kellogg recommended to shareholders a resolution recognizing its commitment to animal welfare.

- In 2021, IBM supported a resolution requesting an annual report "assessing IBM's diversity, equity and inclusion efforts."

- In 2021, GE supported the issuance of a report "evaluating and disclosing if and how the company has met the criteria of the Net Zero indicator or whether it intends to revise its policies to be fully responsive to such indicator." In its recommendation to support the proposal, GE stated affirmatively that it supports the goals of the Paris Agreement, that the company is taking action, and recognizing shareholder interest in issues relating to climate change.

Recommending a vote in favor of a shareholder resolution is relatively rare, but is beginning to occur with greater frequency and is worth considering. When management recommends an affirmative vote, the percent of votes in favor of a resolution tends to skyrocket. The benefits to the company when there is an alignment of shareholder interest and ability of the company to implement a resolution are obvious, and the company gets to tout its good corporate citizenship. It is not the norm, but certainly a concept of which the board and management should be aware and should consider as a matter of course whenever possible.

In sum, boards should encourage management to formalize an ongoing process for engaging shareholders, and establish a mechanism to facilitate communications. The system should be collaborative and provide shareholders with an opportunity to discuss concerns with management. The board should establish a regular reporting system for management to report to the board on shareholder engagement, including parameters for identifying when to inform the board outside the regular meeting cycle (e.g., if the company receives a shareholder proposal).

Take-Aways for Board Members

Goal: Non-adversarial relationships with shareholders, with maximum overall benefit to the company

- Establish a shareholder-specific channel to encourage proactive engagement with shareholders seeking responses on ESG issues.

- Require that management bring all shareholder proposals to the attention of the board. Ideally, with a shareholder-specific channel in place, there will be no shareholder proposals or a reduced number of them, signifying that communications are robust and meaningful.

- The board should meet with management and counsel to determine whether the company is amenable to corporate actions that may satisfy the shareholder's concerns.

  - Management should then reach out to the shareholder to engage in a dialogue. A mutual agreement as to a course of action may result in the shareholder withdrawing the proposal. Even if it is impractical for the company to undertake the action proposed by the shareholder, the shareholder may appreciate that the conversation has begun and still be willing to withdraw the proposal with an understanding that there is an open door for communications.
  - The dialogue should be undertaken from a perspective of understanding the shareholder's concerns.

- If the shareholder chooses to continue to want to include the shareholder proposal, it should engage counsel and management to discuss strategies.

  - The board has a choice *not* to seek no-action relief, but rather to include the proposal in its proxy statement without raising objections to which it believes it might be entitled.
    - Instead, the company has an opportunity to present its statement in the proxy statement, and take that opportunity to state the realities of its inability to implement the resolution.
    - In that connection, consider whether the company is in a position to recommend a vote in support of the proposal.
  - By including the proposal, the company demonstrates its appreciation for shareholders' concerns. Facilitating a vote on the matter also helps the company gauge its stakeholders' interest in the matter.
  - The company should monitor voting to determine whether the issue may be deemed importance to its shareholders, thereby requiring an evaluation of the company's disclosure on the matter.

Chapter 12

Sustainable Investing and Impact Investing

Beth-ann Roth

Introduction

As is evident from the preceding chapters, there is growing interest in viewing companies through a lens of sustainability. There is also a concurrent effort by companies to identify what sustainability means to them. According to the Forum for Sustainable and Responsible Investment (US SIF), U.S. professionally managed sustainable, responsible, and impact ("SRI") investments represented some $16.6 trillion by the beginning of 2020. That amount marked an increase of 42% over the preceding two-year period, and represented approximately 33% of all professionally managed assets.[1]

The demand for sustainable investment options has led to tremendous growth in businesses providing data to both companies and investors. What started as small research departments reviewing disclosure statements and communicating with management has grown into a range of sophisticated data and analysis providers collecting and distilling great amounts of information. These service providers produce robust assessments of business practices, provide data as to where companies stand on an ever-growing number of ESG issues, and help institutional investors evaluate to what extent shareholder proposals align with their own proprietary investment screens.

---

1. US SIF, *Report on Sustainable, Responsible and Impact Investing Trends* (2020). https://www.ussif.org/files/Trends%20Report%202020%20Executive%20Summary.pdf.

Over the same period, there has been an evolution in the phrases and acronyms used to identify this type of investing. Several decades ago, a common reference was to "socially responsible investing." Nowadays, the same acronym—SRI—has come to represent "sustainable, responsible, and impact" investing. Reference is also made to investing according to "ESG" (environmental, social, and governance) principles, and the focus on "impact" has become a moniker unto itself.

While the terminology varies, it is clear that movement is toward taking a holistic view of a business in assessing its overall value as an investment. The assessment goes beyond looking at profits alone—the financial bottom line based on revenue—recognizing that the way a company conducts business in fact contributes to its success and is an integral part of its financial bottom line. Overlaying profits with a consideration of ESG principles is often referred to as examining a company's double or triple bottom line.[2]

SRI Investing: The Corporate Nexus

The growth and expansion of SRI investing affects companies from a number of perspectives. The nexus of SRI to a company also reflects the classes of stakeholders described in Chapter 9:

The Company as a Potential Investment

> The company should evaluate itself from the perspective of the investor.

The company should evaluate itself from the perspective of the investor. The company itself is a potential investment, and it will be examined against the many types of both positive and negative "screens" investors may choose to ensure that their investments are consistent with the principles they choose to further.[3]

Investor considerations may be based on a whole host of considerations, including, but not limited to: the nature of a company's products; its supply chain; how the company permits its products to be used (e.g., whether the government purchases a company's software to use in weapons systems, or surveillance equipment is used in a manner that infringes on privacy rights or causes potential human rights abuses); the company's risk profile; and human capital management.

Boards—with the input of management—should work together to decide what aspects of sustainability are important to the company and its stakeholders based on its specific circumstances. The board may choose to evaluate what the company elects to highlight alongside its peer group, but the decisions made by the board as to the materiality of its ESG-related disclosures must be tailored to the company's individual profile, and not be based primarily on third-party lists or concerns.

---

2. The "double bottom line" assesses positive ESG impact beyond the basic measurement of performance. The "triple bottom line" concept encourages companies to work toward "profits" while also taking into account "people" and the "planet."
3. See *Investment Practices* section.

Materiality drives disclosure, and it is essential from a legal perspective that what gets highlighted is meaningful. The company's sustainability focus is detailed in its disclosure documents, and that information is then included in the evaluations undertaken by analytics service providers to determine where the company fits with respect to investors' ESG screens.

The investors in this category include individuals as well as institutional investors and their asset managers. Examples include mutual funds, private funds, pension funds, community development financial institutions, faith-based organizations, religious institutions, nonprofit organizations, and family offices.

• *Retirement Plans for the Company's Employees*

The company, as an employer, provides investment options for its employees' retirement plans. More and more companies are offering at least some screened portfolio choices from which employees may choose. Based on an analysis of the types of investment alternatives a company determines its employees would like to have as options, it will choose a plan sponsor that includes one or more screened portfolios.

• *The Company as an Impact Investor*

The company may elect to invest some of its assets in a manner that will "contribute to improvements in people's lives and the health of our planet."[4] The company may also choose to use assets set aside for special pools, such as a Community Reinvestment Act requirement if it has one, or a foundation that focuses on the community in which it is located or for some other specified purpose. Contrasted with a charitable giving program where the company donates assets—usually to a tax-exempt organization—the company would make an impact investment expecting a return on investment.

The Global Impact Investing Network ("GIIN") identifies the principal characteristics of impact investing: (1) the *intention* to have a positive social or environmental impact when making the investment; (2) the expectation that there will be a financial *return* on investment, or at least a return *of* the investment; (3) that financial returns—made across asset classes—will generally determine its target range of return from "concessionary" (i.e., below market rate) through market rate; and (4) "a commitment . . . to measure and report the social and environmental performance and progress of underlying investments . . . ."[5]

Some investors may include both sustainable and impact investments in the same portfolio. For example, a mutual fund portfolio applying screens to 75% of its portfolio holdings reserved 1% of its assets under management to invest in "high-social-impact" investments. In this case, the fund invested in a number of enterprises, including BancoSol in Bolivia, a nonprofit microfinance institution that ultimately succeeded in transforming into a commercial bank.[6]

---

4. GIIN, *Core Characteristics of Impact Investing* (Apr. 3, 2019), https://thegiin.org/characteristics.

5. GIIN, *What You Need to Know About Impact Investing*, https://thegiin.org/impact-investing/need-to-know/

6. Bonnie Brusky, *Linking FMIs to Commercial Financing in Latin America: Inter-American Development Bank Support of ProFund*, Case Studies in Donor Good Practices (May 2004), http://documents1.worldbank.org /curated/en/448541468300572922/pdf/342770cgap0donor0good0practice0cs112.pdf.

- *The Company's Customers and Vendors*

The company has both customers and vendors who may choose to do business with the company based on the company's product being sustainable, its operations being green, its workplace practices fair, its board independent and diverse, and because its business practices align with the customer's or vendor's own commitments to certain principles. This alignment can be due to formal adoption of criteria—such as for a B Corp or company that has registered in a state as a Public Benefit Corporation or something similar—or because it has committed to a certain set of standards for itself and its operations.

While this category does not involve a traditional use of investment dollars, customers and vendors may choose to rely on investment-related screening research groups and other resources for the information they need to choose their business partners.

The method each stakeholder uses to make an investment decision is becoming increasingly sophisticated and metrics-driven. Research has expanded over the years to such an extent that investors both demand and are increasingly able to focus on specific attributes—or ESG-related "screens"—to evaluate whether a particular investment meets the criteria the investor has chosen.

Investment Practices

> There is a misconception that SRI investing, by its nature, yields lower returns. To the contrary, the investor chooses among financially viable investments to narrow down the group that also reflects the investor's values.

"Screens" are filters used to determine whether an investment meets the criteria established by an investor. They are applied after an investment is deemed to be financially viable. There is a misconception that SRI investing, by its nature, yields lower returns. To the contrary, the investor chooses among financially viable investments to narrow down the group that also reflects the investor's values.[7] The screens themselves are often weighted in terms of the extent to which a factor impacts financial outcome within a particular industry. Many believe that ESG strategies tend toward being risk-averse.

Screens can be either "positive" or "negative." A positive screen looks for affirmative attributes, such as a company working to "[r]educe the negative impact of operations and practices on the environment, or [m]anage water scarcity and ensure efficient and equitable access to clear sources. A negative screen, on the other hand, would eliminate from a portfolio companies that, for example, [d]emonstrate poor management of environmental risks or contribute significantly to local or global environmental problems."[8]

---

7. See, e.g., Morgan Stanley Institute for Sustainable Investing, *Sustainable Reality: Analyzing Risks and Returns of Sustainable Funds* (2019), https://www.morganstanley.com/pub/content/dam/msdotcom/ideas/sustainable -investing-offers-financial-performance-lowered-risk/Sustainable_Reality_Analyzing_Risk_and_Returns_of _Sustainable_Funds.pdf.

8. Calvert Research and Management, *The Calvert Principles for Responsible Investment* (Jan. 30, 2020), https:// www.calvert.com/media/34498.pdf.

Screens are actively monitored, and can result in divestment of either an individual company—usually due to some action the company has taken in contravention of prior statements to the contrary—or a category of industry, resulting in removal from an investment portfolio. Divestment can occur as a matter of course to bring an investment portfolio into line with a stated strategy, or can be the result of a specific event, thereby bringing attention to a matter in a way that helps shape the dialogue surrounding an issue.

In addition to specific investment screens, investors often adopt guidelines or principles that help provide direction for their investment decisions. Guidelines and principles are often broadly categorized, and then fine-tuned to reflect the investor.

For example, the United States Conference of Catholic Bishops ("USCCB") has formulated its own guidelines for the Catholic Church as an investor.[9] Ceres is a nonprofit organization providing assistance to investors on issues relating to environmental stewardship with an eye toward influencing specific business sectors.[10] US SIF, as a trade association working to "shift investment practices toward sustainability," provides the following as examples of the types of categories on which sustainable investment analysis and screening is often based:[11]

Environmental	Social	Corporate Governance
• Water use and conservation • Sustainable natural resources/agriculture • Pollution/toxics • Clean technology • Climate change/carbon • Green building/smart growth	• Workplace safety • Labor relations • Workplace benefits • Diversity and antibias issues • Community development • Avoidance of tobacco or other harmful products • Human rights	• Board independence • Anti-corruption policies • Board diversity • Executive compensation • Corporate political contributions
Source: US SIF		

The United Nations ("UN") now oversees the Principles for Responsible Investment ("PRI"), which it terms a "blueprint" for responsible investment and application of ESG principles in investment.[12] The Principles largely incorporate the categories of responsible investing set forth above.

In building an ESG portfolio, the PRI proposes that investors use a combined approach of "integration, screening, and thematic" assessment. "Integration" is defined as "[e]xplicitly and systematically including ESG issues in investment analysis and decisions, to better manage risks and improve returns." The "thematic" approach involves "[s]eeking to combine

9. USCCB, *Socially Responsible Investment Guidelines* (Nov. 12, 2003), https://www.usccb.org/resources/socially-responsible-investment-guidelines-2003.

10. Ceres lists among its areas of focus: carbon asset risk, human rights, water, climate change governance, and deforestation. They work to influence the following sectors: banking and finance, food and agriculture, oil and gas, water infrastructure, electric power, insurance, and transportation. https://www.ceres.org/.

11. US SIF, *Examples of ESG Criteria Used by Sustainable Investors*, https://www.ussif.org/files/Examples%20of%20ESG%20Issues.png.

12. PRI, https://www.unpri.org/.

attractive risk return profiles with an intention to contribute to a specific environmental or social outcome. Includes impact investing."[13] The 17 "Sustainable Development Goals," by now well recognized by its pictograph representation of the aspirations it embodies, include the following categories:

The UN's involvement in the development of the SDGs represents a full-circle return to the roots of the responsible investing movement. When the Episcopal Church put forth a shareholder proposal to General Motors in 1971 regarding doing business in apartheid-era South Africa, Reverend Leon H. Sullivan—the first African-American to be on the board of a major U.S. corporation and then new to the board—broke with tradition by announcing to his fellow board members that he would support the resolution.

Though the shareholder proposal garnered little public support, Reverend Sullivan went on several years later to craft a set of seven principles for corporations to demand for their employees as a condition to doing business in South Africa.[14] Ten corporations, including IBM, signed on to the principles, representing "more than half of U.S. corporate investment in South Africa."[15] That number ultimately grew to over 100. The Sullivan Principles

---

13. PRI, *What is Responsible Investment?*, https://www.unpri.org/an-introduction-to-responsible-investment/what-is-responsible-investment/4780.article.

14. 1977: Non-segregation in all aspects of work life, equal employment practices, equal pay, development training, increasing non-whites in management, improving quality of life outside the workplace, and—added in 1984: work to eliminate laws impeding racial justice. These were aspirational, but had support from several large U.S. corporations.

15. Morton Mintz, *Activist Minister Took Bold Step at GM Annual Meeting in 1971*, Washington Post, June 3, 1987.

became an early screening tool in the nascent field of socially responsible investing, and an important catalyst in the public awareness of the concept of corporate social responsibility.

In early 1999, with apartheid having ended several years prior, Reverend Sullivan created the Global Sullivan Principles. The principles were designed to encourage corporations to support economic, social, and political justice wherever they have operations.[16] On November 2 of that year, Reverend Sullivan joined then Secretary-General of the UN Kofi Annan on a stage at the UN to announce the Global Sullivan Principles. Several months later, the UN launched its Millennium Development Goals dedicated to fighting poverty and disease, and to providing educational opportunities.[17] In 2012, the UN adopted the SDGs "to produce a set of universal goals that meet the urgent environmental, political and economic challenges facing our world."[18]

Corporate social responsibility and sustainable investing have continued to expand. Investment research now includes topics such as "gender lens" investing[19] and investments in private prisons.[20] The wealth of information available needs to be distilled and analyzed in order to be useful. Research and analytics firms fulfill that need.

Providers of Research and Analytics on Company Adherence to SRI/ESG Principles

The expansion of the topics being used to screen investments, coupled with the proliferation of disclosures relating to sustainability, has created the need for dedicated research resources on which investors and their advisers may rely. Firms provide data and analytics to help investors, and some also provide assistance with voting proxies consistent with the investment principles and strategies an investor has adopted. Some have divisions—walled off from the data analytics providers—designed to help companies with their own sustainability strategies.

> Investors and their advisers frequently seek information from more than one research and analytics provider, using the mix of information to suit their specific needs.

The sector is growing rapidly as the demand for information rises. However, it is important to recognize that the field is still emerging, and providers have their own proprietary standards. Since there are no uniform standards of measurement, and no single set of metrics, it can be difficult to compare assessments. The result is that investors and their advisers

---

16. Leon H. Sullivan, *Preamble to the Global Sullivan Principles* (Feb. 1, 1999). http://hrlibrary.umn.edu/links/sullivanprinciples.html#:~:text=The%20objectives%20of%20the%20Global,and%20boards%3B%20to%20train%20and.
17. PRI, *Background on the Goals*, https://www1.undp.org/content/sdg-accelerator/en/home/sdg-presa/SDGs2.html
18. *Id.*
19. See, e.g., US SIF, *Investing to Advance Women: A Guide for Investors* (2019), https://www.ussif.org/files/Publications/Investing%20to%20Advance%20Women_US%20SIF.pdf.
20. Worth Rises, *The Prison Industry: Mapping Private Sector Players* (Apr. 2020), https://static1.squarespace.com/static/58e127cb1b10e31ed45b20f4/t/5eb26cb17cc82c67c6254da6/1588751538880/The+Prison+Industry+-+2020.pdf.

frequently seek information from more than one research and analytics provider, using the mix of information to suit their specific needs.

Accordingly, unlike the concept of standardized performance results, which enables investors to compare the returns of various mutual funds, the determination of where a company fits on a sustainability scale tends to be subjective. Where a company fits on a scale will likely be driven by comparison of the company to others in the sector, based on its disclosure, which is why it is essential for each board to take a deep dive into determining the most important sustainability features of the company they serve.

ESG data providers also work with traditional rating companies to produce robust product offerings. Product offerings vary based on types of analysis and proprietary scoring models offered by the different service providers. A number of providers, for example, produce scores based on hundreds of different factors, though not all factors apply to every company they analyze. As a result, it is not unusual for investors to work with more than one provider.

Following are some of the business solutions offered by responsible investment service providers:

- ESG solutions: screening services, climate data, ESG risk ratings, analytics, research, and corporate ratings
- Market services: sizing, competitive benchmarking, product strategy, and opportunity identification across financial products (funds, annuities, insurance, mortgages)
- Retirement plan design and strategy
- Subscriptions to publications for investment officers of public and corporate entities, sovereign wealth funds, endowments, foundations, insurance funds, health care organizations, family offices, and defined contribution plans
- Economic profit measurement tools
- Assistance with the design and management of corporate governance, executive compensation, and sustainability programs

Some also provide proxy voting assistance and produce voting guidelines and benchmark policy recommendations for the growing number of issues facing both investors and companies. One company, for example, provides proxy analysis and voting recommendations that cover companies in the S&P 1500 plus Russell 3000, along with certain non-U.S. companies that list in the U.S. By way of example, some of the categories the service provider considers in evaluating the companies it reviews include the following, each of which are extensively broken down into subcategories:[21]

---

21. ISS, *United States Proxy Voting Guidelines Benchmark Policy Recommendations: Effective for Meetings on or after February 1, 2020* (Nov. 18, 2019), https://www.issgovernance.com/file/policy/active/americas/US-Voting -Guidelines.pdf.

Governance	Social and Environmental Issues
• Board of directors (e.g., diversity) • Audits • Shareholder rights and defenses • Poison pills (shareholder rights plans) • Capital/restructuring • Compensation Mutual Fund Proxies and Proposals	• Animal welfare • Consumer issues (including GMOs, pharmaceuticals, and tobacco) • Climate change • Diversity • Environment and sustainability • Human rights and labor issues • Political activities

Companies also provide proxy voting guidelines specific to SRI, sustainability, and climate, and for faith-based institutions and public funds. One such service provider—Institutional Shareholder Services ("ISS")—has researched and maintains voting guidelines for Canada, Latin America, Asia-Pacific, Europe, the Middle East, and Africa.[22]

Take-Aways for Board Members

SRI investing is rapidly growing, bringing in increasing amounts of investor dollars and creating the need for corporations to assess their place in these markets from a variety of perspectives. Given the in-depth scope of the analytics industry and its sophistication in terms of the many data points taken into account, boards need proactively to formulate their sustainability strategies.

Those strategies and actions should be set forth clearly in the company's disclosure documentation, working with counsel to take care not to be promissory in areas where performance is either aspirational or may not be under the company's control. In addition, given that ESG service providers also obtain information from the company itself, it is worthwhile to identify the company department that will manage and maintain those communications to help ensure an accurate flow of information to those who research and collect data. As in other areas, clear and effective communication is key.

---

22. ISS, *Voting Policies*, https://www.issgovernance.com/policy-gateway/voting-policies.

PART IV

Chapter 13
United States Federal, State, and Local Sustainability Legislation and Regulation

Kevin M. Coleman

Mandated Environmental, Social, and Governance (ESG) Disclosure

ESG-focused mandatory disclosure legislation at the federal level in the United States has been noticeably lacking, especially when compared to the European Union. As of the time of publication, there are no required ESG disclosures that companies must make or ESG frameworks to which companies must respond.[1] One obvious caveat is that public

---

1. Catherine M. Clarkin et al., *The Rise of Standardized ESG Disclosure Frameworks in the United States*, Sullivan & Cromwell (June 8, 2020), https://www.sullcrom.com/files/upload/SC-Publication-Rise-Standardized-ESG-Disclosure -Frameworks.pdf.

companies still must base their disclosure (or lack thereof in this case) on materiality.[2] There are, however, several bills introduced that would, if enacted, mandate ESG disclosure at the federal level.

In 2019, U.S. Representatives Juan Vargas and Jesús Garcia introduced the ESG Disclosure Simplification Act of 2019.[3] The bill definitively states that ESG metrics are "de facto material for the purposes of disclosures" under the Exchange Act."[4] Therefore, the bill would generally require publicly traded companies to disclose in their proxy statements: "(A) a clear description of the views of the issuer about the link between ESG metrics and the long-term business strategy of the issuer; and (B) a description of any process the issuer uses to determine the impact of ESG metrics on the long-term business strategy of the issuer."[5] The SEC would further be required to define "ESG metrics," which could include the incorporation of international standards.[6]

Additionally, also in 2019, Senator Elizabeth Warren and Representative Sean Casten introduced companion bills entitled "Climate Risk Disclosure Act of 2019."[7] Under these bills, companies would be required to make certain disclosures in their annual reports.[8] More specifically, such reports would include:

(A) the identification of, the evaluation of potential financial impacts of, and any risk-management strategies relating to—
(i) physical risks posed to the covered issuer by climate change; and
(ii) transition risks posed to the covered issuer by climate change;

(B) a description of any established corporate governance processes and structures to identify, assess, and manage climate-related risks; and

(C) a description of specific actions that the covered issuer is taking to mitigate identified risks.[9]

---

2. Jay Clayton, *Statement on Proposed Amendments to Modernize and Enhance Financial Disclosures; Other Ongoing Disclosure Modernization Initiatives; Impact of the Coronavirus; Environmental and Climate-Related Disclosure*, US Securities and Exchange Communication (Jan. 30, 2020), https://www.sec.gov/news/public-statement/clayton-mda-2020-01-30. In a January 2020 public statement, SEC Chairman Jay Clayton stated that the SEC's "commitment to ensur[ing] that our disclosure regime provides investors with a mix of information that facilitates well-informed capital allocation decisions" has been and should continue to be "disclosure-based and rooted in materiality, including providing investors with insight regarding the issuer's assessment of, and plans for addressing, material risks to its business and operations." *Id.*

3. ESG Disclosure Simplification Act of 2019, H.R. 4329, 116th Cong. (2019), https://congress.gov/116/bills/hr4329/BILLS-116hr4329rh.pdf; see Steven Lofchie, *Representatives Introduce Bill to Require ESG Disclosure by Issuers, Wickersham & Taft LLP,* Cadwalader Cabinet (Jan. 9, 2020), https://www.findknowdo.com/news/01/09/2020/representatives-introduce-bill-require-esg-disclosure-issuers.

4. H.R. 4329 at § 2(b)(3).

5. *Id.* at § 2(a).

6. *Id.* at § 2(b)(4).

7. Climate Risk Disclosure Act of 2019, H.R. 3623, 116th Cong. (2019), https://www.congress.gov/116/bills/hr3623/BILLS-116hr3623ih.pdf.

8. *Id.* at § 5(a).

9. *Id.* The rulemaking portion of the bill would require the SEC to promulgate disclosure rules-related "reporting standards for estimating and disclosing direct and indirect greenhouse gas emissions"; fossil fuels; and "establish[ing] a minimum social cost of carbon," among other matters. *Id.* at § 6(a).

Senator Brian Schatz and Representative Casten introduced companion bills entitled "Climate Change Financial Risk Act of 2019" in November of 2019,[10] which would require the Board of Governors of the Federal Reserve to establish a Climate Risk Scenario Technical Development Group that would aid in the development of three climate change risk scenarios under which financial institutions would be required to conduct stress testing that would be disclosed to the Federal Reserve.[11] The three scenarios would generally assume a 1.5-degree Celsius increase in global temperatures; a 2-degree Celsius increase in global temperatures; and "the likely and very likely average increase in global temperatures that can be expected, taking into consideration the extent to which national policies and actions relating to climate change have been implemented."[12]

It is worth noting that each of these three federal bills died in Congress with little or no chance of being revived.[13] The mere fact, however, that Congress is attempting to enact ESG-related legislation should cause companies and directors to take notice. Federal regulators and state legislatures are likely taking notice of congressional attempts to pass ESG legislation.

In addition to prompting from the above congressional action, the SEC could be spurred into action from a report issued by the U.S. Government Accountability Office (GAO) in July of 2020.[14] The report, which was commissioned in 2018,[15] primarily sought to determine "(1) why investors seek ESG disclosures, (2) public companies' disclosures of ESG factors, and (3) the advantages and disadvantages of ESG disclosure policy options."[16] The report found that investors want to use ESG data to, among other reasons, compare companies in which they invest; however, because there is no uniform, mandatory set of ESG disclosures, there were "substantial inconsistencies" among the disclosures.[17] Former SEC Chairman Jay Clayton responded to the GAO's report by reiterating the SEC's reliance on a principles-based and materiality approach to determine what companies should be required to disclose.[18]

Because of the GAO report, Clayton's response, shareholder urging, or the change in administration in Washington, the SEC appears to be paying more attention to ESG

---

10. Climate Change Financial Risk Act of 2019, S. 2903, 116th Cong. (2019), https://www.govinfo.gov/content/pkg/BILLS-116s2903is/pdf/BILLS-116s2903is.pdf.

11. *Id.* at § 4(a); Press Release, Rep. Sean Casten, Casten, *Schatz Introduce Legislation to Ensure U.S. Financial System Is Prepared for Climate Change* (Nov. 20, 2019), https://casten.house.gov/media/press-releases/casten-schatz-introduce-legislation-ensure-us-financial-system-prepared-climate.

12. S. 2903 at § 5(a).

13. See *H.R. 4329 (116th): ESG Disclosure Simplification Act of 2019*, GovTrack, https://www.govtrack.us/congress/bills/116/hr4329 (last visited May 11, 2021); *H.R. 3623 (116th): Climate Risk Disclosure Act of 2019*, GovTrack, https://www.govtrack.us/congress/bills/116/hr3623 (last visited May 11, 2021); and *S. 2903 (116th): Climate Change Financial Risk Act of 2019*, GovTrack, https://www.govtrack.us/congress/bills/116/s2903 (last visited May 11, 2021). The ESG Disclosure Simplification Act of 2019 died in Congress, but a committee voted in April 2021 to issue a report recommending the bill be considered further. See *H.R. 4329 (116th): ESG Disclosure Simplification Act of 2019*, GovTrack, https://www.govtrack.us/congress/bills/116/hr4329 (last visited May 11, 2021).

14. U.S. Gov't Accountability Office, *Disclosure of Environmental, Social, and Governance Factors and Options to Enhance Them* (2020), https://www.gao.gov/assets/710/707949.pdf [hereinafter GAO ESG Report].

15. Cydney Posner, *GAO Finds Lack of Consistency in ESG Disclosure—How Will the SEC Respond?*, Cooley PubCo (Aug. 10, 2020), https://cooleypubco.com/2020/08/10/gao-inconsistent-esg-disclosure/.

16. GAO ESG Report, *supra* note 14, at GAO Highlights.

17. Posner, *supra* note 15.

18. *Id.*

disclosure matters. For example, the SEC amended Regulation S-K in 2020 to require companies to describe their "human capital resources and any human capital measures or objectives that the company focuses on in managing its business."[19] For most companies, the first instance of such disclose appeared in their Form 10-K for 2020.

> The SEC also began turning its attention to climate change matters at the beginning of 2021.

In March of 2021, the SEC launched a Climate and ESG Task Force within its Division of Enforcement.[20] According to the SEC, "[t]he initial focus will be to identify any material gaps or misstatements in issuers' disclosure of climate risks under existing rules."[21] In the same month, the SEC staff was instructed to "evaluate our disclosure rules with an eye toward facilitating the disclosure of consistent, comparable, and reliable information on climate change."[22] The public was provided with the opportunity to comment on such disclosures.[23]

In September 2021, the SEC published a sample climate change comment letter demonstrating the various climate change matters the SEC may raise with companies.[24] It is expected the SEC will issue climate-related proposed rulemaking in early 2022.[25]

In the first quarter of 2021, the Federal Reserve Board (FRB) announced the creation of the Supervision Climate Committee (SCC) and the Financial Stability Climate Committee (FSCC).[26] The SCC is meant to "strengthen the FRB's capacity to identify and assess financial risks from climate change and to develop a program to ensure the resilience of supervised financial institutions to those risks," while the FSCC is tasked with "examin[ing] the macroprudential aspects of climate change."[27] As with the SEC, these groups may propose regulations in the future designed to reduce the effects of climate change.

---

19. Jonathan M. Ocker et al., *Maximizing Human Capital Disclosure Under New Guidance*, PILLSBURY WINTHROP SHAW PITTMAN LLP (Nov. 12, 2020), https://www.pillsburylaw.com/en/news-and-insights/human-capital-disclosure -guidance.html.

20. Press Release, *SEC Announces Enforcement Task Force Focused on Climate and ESG Issues*, US SECURITIES AND EXCHANGE COMMUNICATION (Mar. 4, 2021), https://www.sec.gov/news/press-release/2021-42.

21. *Id.*

22. Public Statement from Acting Chair Allison Herren Lee, *Public Input Welcomed on Climate Change Disclosures*, US SECURITIES AND EXCHANGE COMMUNICATION (Mar. 15, 2021), https://www.sec.gov/news/public-statement/lee-climate -change-disclosures.

23. *Id.*

24. SEC Climate Change Comment Letters Signal Early Action on Environmental, Social, and Governmental Disclosures, SIDLEY AUSTIN LLP (Oct. 7, 2021), https://www.sidley.com/en/insights/newsupdates/2021/10/ secclimate-change-comment-letters-signal-early-action.

25. The SEC's Recent and Planned Activity on Climate Change Disclosures: What Companies Can Do To Prepare, KIRKLAND & ELLIS LLP (Oct. 1, 2021), https://www.kirkland.com/publications/kirkland-alert/2021/09/ sec-climatechange-disclosures.

26. See J. Paul Forrester et al., *US Federal Reserve Announces New Climate Committee and Provides More Guidance on Its Approach to Addressing Climate Change Risks*, MAYER BROWN (Mar. 26, 2021), https://www .mayerbrown.com/en/perspectives-events/publications/2021/03/us-federal-reserve-announces-new-climate -committee-and-provides-more-guidance-on-its-approach-to-addressing-climate-change-risks#:~:text=On%20 March%2023%2C%202021%2C%20Federal,related%20risks%20to%20financial%20stability.

27. *Id.*

Though not required, many companies are making voluntary ESG-based disclosures under one or a combination of disclosure frameworks. The most prolific of such frameworks are those promulgated by the Sustainable Accounting Standard Board, Task Force on Climate-Related Financial Disclosures, and Global Reporting Initiative.

State-Mandated Diversity Board Requirements and Related Disclosure

Beginning with California in 2018,[28] some states have started instituting board diversity requirements for publicly held companies headquartered within their borders. Under California's groundbreaking legislation,[29] "each company with four or fewer directors must have at least one female Director, those with five directors must have at least two females on their boards, while boards with six or more members must have at least three female directors" by the end of 2021.[30]

Since then, other states have followed California's lead with their own board diversity requirements. In August of 2019, Illinois passed a similar law to that of California.[31] Unlike California's law, however, the Illinois statute incorporated racial and ethnic diversity in addition to gender diversity.[32]

Maryland, in October of 2019, passed legislation requiring all business entities headquartered in the state to make annual disclosures as to the total number of overall and female directors on their boards.[33] New York took a similar, but expanded approach, at the end of 2019 by requiring all corporations that are simply *authorized to do business in New York*, to report the total number of overall and female directors on their boards.[34]

As of August 2020, other states considering mandatory board diversity legislation include Hawaii, Massachusetts, Michigan, New Jersey, and Washington.[35]

---

28. Casey Leins, *Report: Some California Corporations Ignore Law Requiring Females on Boards*, U.S. NEWS (Mar. 4, 2020), https://www.usnews.com/news/best-states/articles/2020-03-04/many-california-corporations -refuse-to-follow-gender-diversity-law-report-finds. Note that California's law does not consider where a company is *incorporated*, only whether it is *headquartered* in California. Cydney Posner, *New Report on California Board Gender Diversity Mandate*, COOLEY PUBCO (Mar. 6, 2020), https://cooleypubco.com/2020/03/06/california -board-gender-diversity-report/.

29. S.B. 826, 2018 Leg. (Cali. 2018) (enacted), https://leginfo.legislature.ca.gov/faces/billPdf.xhtml?bill_id =201720180SB826&version=20170SB82694CHP.

30. Michael Hatcher & Weldon Latham, *States Are Leading the Charge to Corporate Boards: Diversify!*, JACKSON LEWIS P.C. (May 12, 2020), https://corpgov.law.harvard.edu/2020/05/12/states-are-leading-the-charge-to-corporate -boards-diversify/.

31. *Id.*

32. *Id.*

33. *Id.*

34. Anna Broccolo & Teri Wilford Wood, *New York Enacts Legislation Related to Board Diversity*, 10 NAT'L L. REV. 17 (2020), https://www.natlawreview.com/article/new-york-enacts-legislation-related-to-board-diversity.

35. Hatcher & Latham, *supra* note 28.

At the end of September 2020, California followed up its 2018 legislation by passing a new bill requiring public corporations headquartered in the state to have a specified number of directors (based on overall board size) from "underrepresented communities."[36]

State ESG Legislation

> To compensate for a lack of ESG legislation at the federal level, states are beginning to institute their own ESG investing legislation.

For example, Delaware, which boasts as being the state of incorporation for over 66 percent of Fortune 500 companies,[37] passed legislation in 2018 holding that

> when considering the needs of the beneficiaries, the fiduciary may take into account the financial needs of the beneficiaries as well as the beneficiaries' personal values, including the beneficiaries' desire to engage in sustainable investing strategies that align with the beneficiaries' social, environmental, governance or other values or beliefs of the beneficiaries.[38]

In August of 2019, Illinois passed the Sustainable Investing Act, mandating that all Illinois government entities, which include pension funds, and holding and managing public funds, "should integrate material, relevant, useful sustainability factors into their policies, processes, and decision-making."[39] In doing so, the law "requires all public or government agencies involved in managing public funds to 'develop, publish, and implement sustainable investment policies applicable to the management of all public funds under its control.'"[40] According to Illinois State Treasurer Michael Frerichs,

36. AB-979, 2020 Leg. (Cali. 2020) (enacted), http://leginfo.legislature.ca.gov/faces/billPdf.xhtml?bill
_id=201920200AB979&version=20190AB97993ENR; Cydney Posner, *California Mandates Board Diversity for "Underrepresented Communities,"* Cooley PubCo (Oct. 1, 2020), https://cooleypubco.com/2020/10/01/california-mandates-board-diversity-underrepresented-communities/. A "director from an underrepresented community" is defined as someone identifying as "Black, African American, Hispanic, Latino, Asian, Pacific Islander, Native American, Native Hawaiian, or Alaska Native, or who self-identifies as gay, lesbian, bisexual, or transgender." AB-979, 2020 Leg. (Cali. 2020) (enacted) at § 301.4(e)(1).
37. Delaware Division of Corporations, *About the Division of Corporations*, https://corp.delaware.gov/aboutagency/ (last visited Aug. 14, 2020).
38. S.B. 195, 149th Gen. Assem. (Del. 2018), https://legis.delaware.gov/json/BillDetail/GeneratePdfDocument?legislationId=26606&legislationTypeId=1&docTypeId=2&legislationName=SB195.
39. Illinois Sustainable Investing Act, H.B. 2460 (Pub. Act 101-0473) (Ill. 2019), https://www.ilga.gov/legislation/publicacts/fulltext.asp?Name=101-0473&GA=101; see Tom Croft, *Illinois Treasurer Michael Frerichs Wins Sustainable Investing Act, First State ESG Bill in U.S.!,* Heartland Capital Strategies (Oct. 3, 2019), https://www.heartlandnetwork.org/single-post/2019/10/03/Illinois-Treasurer-Michael-Frerichs-Wins-Sustainable-Investing-Act-First-State-ESG-Bill-in-US#:~:text=Public%20Act%20101%2D473%2C%20the,processes%2C%20and%20decision%2Dmaking.
40. Ali Zaidi, *States Take Lead on ESG Investment Regulations While Feds Stand Still*, Kirkland & Ellis (Oct. 4, 2020), https://www.kirkland.com/publications/article/2019/10/states-take-lead-on-esg-investment-regulations-whi.

additional risk and value-added factors need to be integrated into the decision-making process. These sustainability factors do not replace traditional financial and technical indicators. They serve as a complement to traditional analysis, providing an additional layer of data that our analysts and fund managers can use to better assess the risk profile and return potential of individual investments.[41]

More specifically, the Illinois statute holds that each "sustainable investment policy should include material, relevant, and decision-useful sustainability factors [and such] factors may include, but are not [to] be limited to: (1) corporate governance and leadership factors; (2) environmental factors; (3) social capital factors; (4) human capital factors; and (5) business model and innovation factors."[42]

Federal ESG Legislation

In June of 2020, the Department of Labor (DOL) published a proposed rule for comment[43] "that would further burden the ability of fiduciaries of private-sector retirement plans to select investments based on ESG factors and would bar 401(k) plans from using a fund with any ESG mandate as the default investment alternative for non-electing participants."[44] According to the proposal, the DOL "is concerned . . . that the growing emphasis on ESG investing may be prompting ERISA plan fiduciaries to make investment decisions for purposes distinct from providing benefits to participants and beneficiaries and defraying reasonable expenses of administering the plan" rather than "maximizing the funds available to pay retirement benefits" as required by statute.[45] The proposal sought to "make clear that ERISA plan fiduciaries may not invest in ESG vehicles when they understand an underlying investment strategy of the vehicle is to subordinate return or increase risk for the purpose of non-pecuniary objectives."[46] Put another way, the DOL's proposed rule "would prohibit a retirement plan fiduciary from making any investment, or choosing an investment fund, based on the consideration of an [ESG] factor unless that factor independently represents a material economic investment consideration under generally accepted investment theories."[47] Interestingly, the DOL's final rule,[48] issued on October 30, 2020, pulled back from the proposed rule by omitting references to "ESG," but only permits the consideration of "non-pecuniary factors as a deciding factor in making an investment decision where the plan fiduciary is considering several investment opportunities and is unable to

---

41. Croft, *supra* note 37.

42. Zaidi, *supra* note 38.

43. Financial Factors in Selecting Plan Investments, 85 Fed. Reg. 39,113 (proposed June 30, 2020) (to be codified at 29 C.F.R. pt. 2550), https://www.govinfo.gov/content/pkg/FR-2020-06-30/pdf/2020-13705.pdf.

44. Martin Lipton, *DOL Proposes New Rules Regulating ESG Investments*, WACHTELL, LIPTON, ROSEN & KATZ (July 7, 2020), https://corpgov.law.harvard.edu/2020/07/07/dol-proposes-new-rules-regulating-esg-investments/.

45. Financing Factors in Selecting Plan Investments, 85 Fed. Reg. at 39,115.

46. *Id.* at 39,116.

47. Lipton, *supra* note 42.

48. Financial Factors in Selecting Plan Investments (to be codified at 29 C.F.R. pt. 2550), https://www.dol.gov/sites/dolgov/files/EBSA/temporary-postings/financial-factors-in-selecting-plan-investments-final-rule.pdf.

distinguish these alternatives solely on the basis of pecuniary factors."[49] Following change in administration from the 2020 election, the DOL announced that "[u]ntil the publication of further guidance, the department will not enforce either final rule or otherwise pursue enforcement actions against any plan fiduciary based on a failure to comply with those final rules with respect to an investment."[50] In October 2021, the DOL announced a proposed rulemaking "intended to remove barriers implemented by the prior administration that the DOL believes limited fiduciaries' ability to consider climate change and other ESG matters as factors when selecting investments and exercising shareholder rights."[51]

The Dodd-Frank Act of 2010 (Dodd-Frank) also contains a sustainability provision related to "conflict mineral supply chain optimization."[52] Pursuant to Section 1502 of Dodd-Frank, impacted companies must "conduct due diligence into the source and chain of custody of specified minerals"[53] and make related disclosures, which should "give their supply chains more transparency, thus improving sustainability. All of this will, in theory, create supply chain optimization."[54] This has both environmental and social implications for companies required to make such disclosures.

State Climate Change Legislation

> In addition to leading the way on ESG legislation, states appear to also be taking charge with respect to climate change legislation.

As of April 2020, "15 states and territories have taken legislative or executive action to move toward a 100 percent clean energy future."[55] Further, some of these states' goals are "more ambitious than those laid out by the Paris Agreement."[56]

---

49. *Department of Labor Swiftly Finalizes Rule on Consideration of Only Pecuniary (Not ESG) Factors in Investment Decisions*, SIDLEY AUSTIN LLP (Nov. 2, 2020), https://www.sidley.com/en/insights/newsupdates /2020/11/department-of-labor-swiftly-finalizes-rule-on-consideration-of-only-pecuniary-factors.

50. News Release, *US Department of Labor Releases Statement on Enforcement of Its Final Rules on ESG Investments, Proxy Voting by Employee Benefit Plans*, DEP'T OF LABOR (Mar. 10, 2021), https://www.dol.gov /newsroom/releases/ebsa/ebsa20210310.

51. U.S. Department of Labor Proposes ESG-Related Updates to the ERISA Investment Duties Regulation, SULLIVAN & CROMWELL (Oct. 19, 2021), https://www.sullcrom.com/files/upload/sc-publication-US-Department-of-Labor-Proposes-ESG-Updates-ERISA-Investment-Duties.pdf.

52. Paul Ellis, *What Does Dodd-Frank Have to Do with ESG?*, PAUL ELLIS CONSULTING (June 14, 2015), http://www .paulellisconsulting.com/what-does-dodd-frank-have-to-do-with-esg/.

53. Sara K. Orr et al., *Companies Should Consider ESG Supply Chain Issues*, LATHAM & WATKINS LLP (Sept. 10, 2019), https://www.globalelr.com/2019/09/companies-should-consider-esg-supply-chain-issues/.

54. Ellis, *supra* note 49.

55. Rita Cliffton et al., *States Are Laying a Road Map for Climate Leadership*, CTR. FOR AM. PROGRESS (Apr. 30, 2020), https://www.americanprogress.org/issues/green/reports/2020/04/30/484163/states-laying -road-map-climate-leadership/.

56. Rebecca Cooper, *States Take the Lead to Address Climate Change*, NAT'L ACAD. FOR STATE HEALTH POLICY (Dec. 2, 2019), https://www.nashp.org/states-take-the-lead-to-address-climate-change/; see also Hillary Rosner, *How State and Local Governments Are Leading the Way on Climate Policy*, NAT'L AUDUBON SOC'Y (Fall 2019), https:// www.audubon.org/magazine/fall-2019/how-state-and-local-governments-are-leading-way.

Several states are also under growing pressure to divest state-managed funds from fossil fuel investments. For example, California,[57] Massachusetts,[58] New Jersey,[59] and New York[60] are under pressure from public sources to place a moratorium on new fossil fuel investments and/or divest from current investments.

Take-Aways for Board Members

- ESG legislation and regulation is a growing and dynamic area of the law, and changes in requirements can impact companies' practices and disclosures.
- Directors should receive periodic updates from management on how the company is tackling new or revised ESG requirements.
- Directors should ensure management is monitoring and preparing for potential future changes in ESG legislation and regulations.

---

57. Heath Madom, *California Teachers Should Tell CalSTRS to Divest from Fossil Fuels*, EdSource (July 14, 2020), https://edsource.org/2020/california-teachers-should-tell-calstrs-to-divest-from-fossil-fuels/636066.

58. Sarah Shemkus, *Massachusetts Divestment Movement Seeks to Capitalize on Fossil Fuels' Decline*, Energy News Network (Dec. 3, 2019), https://energynews.us/2019/12/03/northeast/massachusetts-divestment-movement-seeks-to-capitalize-on-fossil-fuels-decline/.

59. John Reitmeyer, *Campaign Continues Against State Pension Investment in Fossil Fuels*, NJSpotlight (Sept. 20, 2019), https://www.njspotlight.com/2019/09/19-09-19-environmentalists-continue-push-against-investing-state-pension-funds-in-fossil-fuels/.

60. Kristoffer Tigue, *Could New York's Youth Finally Convince the State to Divest Its Pension of Fossil Fuels?*, Inside Climate News (May 15, 2020), https://insideclimatenews.org/news/14052020/divestment-new-york-pension-plans-fossil-fuels.

Chapter 14
Public Company Mandatory Reporting on ESG Matters

Sonia G. Barros, Rebecca Grapsas, and Claire H. Holland

Mandatory disclosure of sustainability matters by U.S. public companies is currently grounded in materiality considerations and specific line-item disclosure requirements. The federal securities laws do not currently require disclosure of sustainability matters in Securities and Exchange Commission (SEC) filings pursuant to a detailed and uniform mandatory framework. To date, the SEC has resisted pressure to adopt such a framework, although it significantly increased its focus on environmental, social, and governance (ESG) topics in 2021. Ongoing rapid development of requirements and guidance around ESG reporting requirements and voluntary standards is expected for the foreseeable future.

While a broad framework for mandatory public company reporting of sustainability matters does not exist at this time, disclosure on sustainability topics may be required to the extent material to a company, even in the absence of a specific line-item requirement identifying a particular ESG-related risk. The SEC considers information material if there is a substantial likelihood that a reasonable investor would consider it important in making an investment decision in the context of the total mix of available information. While there is no duty to disclose all material information, many of the SEC's disclosure requirements are principles-based, requiring disclosure of information to the extent material to an understanding of the company's business, and where "necessary in order to make the statements made, in the light of the circumstances under which they are made, not misleading."[1] Using these standards, public companies must consider whether and the extent to which disclosure of sustainability-related risks and effects may be necessary in their annual and quarterly reports, proxy statements, and other SEC filings.

Many companies are also voluntarily disclosing ESG information pursuant to their chosen standards as set by nongovernmental standard setters; this type of "private ordering" disclosure is discussed in Chapter 15.

This chapter discusses existing SEC requirements and guidance underpinning sustainability disclosures, as well as relevant rulemaking and other developments. The term "sustainability" as used herein refers to topics bearing on corporate responsibility and citizenship including environmental matters such as climate change, waste, water and natural resources, and social and employee-related matters such as respect for human rights, workforce diversity, equity and inclusion, and board diversity. See also Chapter 1. Discussion of long-standing disclosure requirements relating to corporate governance matters (such as director independence and qualifications, key board committees, board leadership, director nominations, executive and director compensation, related person transactions, and the code of conduct) is beyond the scope of this chapter.

> While a broad framework for mandatory public company reporting of sustainability matters does not exist at this time, disclosure on sustainability topics may be required to the extent material to a company, even in the absence of a specific line-item requirement identifying a particular ESG-related risk.

SEC Requirements Most Likely to Trigger Disclosure of Sustainability Matters

Business Description

Regulation S-K Item 101 requires companies to disclose various information about their business. This includes providing disclosure of the material effects that compliance with governmental regulations, including environmental regulations, may have on the company's capital expenditures, earnings, and competitive position to the extent material to an understanding of the company's business taken as a whole. A company must disclose material estimated capital expenditures for "environmental control facilities" for the current fiscal year and any other material subsequent period.

A new provision added to Regulation S-K Item 101 in August 2020 requires a public company to describe its human capital resources, including any human capital measures or objectives that the company focuses on in managing the business, to the extent material to an understanding of the company's business taken as a whole. The SEC acknowledges that the exact measures or objectives will depend on the nature of the company's business and workforce but identifies as nonexclusive examples measures and objectives that address the development, attraction, and retention of personnel. Disclosure must be tailored to a

---

1. See 17 CFR § 240.12b-20.

company's particular business, workforce, and facts and circumstances, which will evolve over time.

If the information elicited about the material effects of compliance with government regulations or human capital resources is material to a particular segment of the company's business, the company must also identify the segment.

Legal Proceedings

Regulation S-K Item 103 requires companies to disclose information relating to material pending legal proceedings to which they or their subsidiaries are a party, including proceedings in which their property is the subject of the litigation. Similar actions that, to the company's knowledge, are contemplated by governmental authorities must be disclosed. Disclosure is required even if the proceeding was initiated by the company. Item 103 includes specific disclosure requirements for certain types of environmental proceedings. Administrative or judicial proceedings arising under environmental laws must be disclosed if: (1) the proceeding is material to the business or financial condition of the company; (2) the proceeding involves a claim for damages, or involves potential monetary sanctions, capital expenditures, deferred charges or charges to income and the amount involved exceeds 10% of the current assets of the company and its subsidiaries on a consolidated basis; or (3) a governmental authority is a party and the proceeding involves potential monetary sanctions, unless the company reasonably believes the proceeding will result in no sanctions or sanctions of less than $300,000 or, at the election of the company, such other threshold that it determines is reasonably designed to result in disclosure of material environmental proceedings so long as this company-specific threshold does not exceed the lesser of $1 million or 1% of the current assets of the company and its subsidiaries on a consolidated basis.

Risk Factors

Regulation S-K Item 105 requires a company to disclose, "where appropriate," the material factors that make an investment in the company's securities speculative or risky. Risks that the company does not deem material are not required to be disclosed. The SEC discourages disclosure of boilerplate risk factors that could apply to any company (e.g., climate change, acts of terrorism/war), unless the company explains how each disclosed risk would specifically impact the company's operations and financial condition. If a risk has started to materialize and the previous disclosure had characterized it as only a theoretical risk, the disclosure should describe specifically what has occurred and the risks going forward.

Management's Discussion & Analysis of Financial Condition and Results of Operations (MD&A)

Regulation S-K Item 303 requires companies to disclose information relevant to assessing their financial condition, changes in financial condition, and results of operations. In addition, if the company knows of events that are reasonably likely to cause a material change in the relationship between costs and revenues, such as known or reasonably likely future increases in costs of labor or materials or price increases or inventory adjustments, disclosure is required of the reasonably likely change in the relationship.

As discussed in the final rule release of Item 303 amendments adopted in November 2020, the "reasonably likely" threshold requires a thoughtful analysis that applies an objective assessment of the likelihood that an event will occur balanced with a materiality analysis regarding the need for disclosure about the event. Management should make this determination objectively with the goal of helping investors clearly understand the potential material consequences of the known forward-looking statements or uncertainties. Companies should disclose known trends, demands, commitments, events, or uncertainties that are not remote, or where management cannot make an assessment as to the likelihood that they will come to fruition, and that would be reasonably likely to have a material effect on the company's future results or financial condition were they to come to fruition, if a reasonable investor would consider omission of the information as significantly altering the mix of information made available in the company's disclosures.[2]

This rule can drive disclosure of sustainability matters that are known trends, demands, commitments, events, or uncertainties that are not remote. Companies should quantify the relevant impact to the extent feasible (this may not be required if the potential impact is not estimable with any degree of certainty).

Financial Statements

Regulation S-X requires U.S. public companies to issue financial statements that comply with U.S. generally accepted accounting standards issued by the Financial Accounting Standards Board (FASB). The SEC's Acting Chief Accountant recently advised companies that they should review FASB guidance that discusses the intersection of ESG matters with financial accounting standards, including topics such as risks and uncertainties, inventory, impairments, loss contingencies, environmental obligations, asset retirement obligations, and tax.[3]

SEC Guidance on Climate Change Disclosure (2010)

In 2010, the SEC issued an interpretive release (the Climate Change Release) indicating that disclosure about the potential impact of global climate change may be required in SEC filings if a company's business is likely to be materially affected by global climate change.[4]

The SEC asserts in the Climate Change Release that its existing disclosure requirements, specifically the disclosure items discussed above relating to Business Description, Legal Proceedings, Risk Factors, and MD&A, may apply to climate change-related information. The release also specifies four examples of climate-change-related issues that a company

---

2. SEC Release No. 33-10890, *Management's Discussion and Analysis, Selected Financial Data, and Supplementary Financial Information* (Nov. 19, 2020), https://www.sec.gov/rules/final/2020/33-10890.pdf (November 2020 MD&A Release).

3. Accounting Today, *SASB Moves Forward on ESG Standards* (May 6, 2021), https://www.accountingtoday.com/news/sasb-develops-new-esg-standards-as-the-sec-calls-for-better-disclosure; FASB, *Staff Educational Paper – Intersection of Environmental, Social, and Governance Matters with Financial Accounting Standards* (Mar. 19, 2021), https://fasb.org/cs/ContentServer?c=Document_C&cid=1176176379917&d=&pagename=FASB%2FDocument_C%2FDocumentPage.

4. SEC, *Commission Guidance Regarding Disclosure Related to Climate Change,* Release No. 33-9106 and 34-61469 (Feb. 2, 2010), https://www.sec.gov/rules/interp/2010/33-9106.pdf.

should consider when determining whether disclosure is required under one or more of those items.

Legislation and Regulation

The Climate Change Release states that legislative and regulatory developments may trigger disclosure. The SEC reminds companies to consider whether international, state, or local climate change requirements impose an obligation on them to disclose the material costs of complying with environmental regulations under Regulation S-K Item 101.

Depending on a company's particular circumstances (e.g., an energy company that is particularly sensitive to greenhouse gas (GHG) legislation), risk factor disclosure may be required regarding existing or pending legislation or regulation that relates to climate change. The SEC advises companies to consider the specific risks they face and avoid generic disclosure.

The SEC argues that Item 303 requires companies to evaluate whether climate change statutes or regulations are reasonably likely to have a material effect on their financial condition or results of operations. With regard to a known climate change uncertainty, such as pending legislation or regulation, the SEC advises companies to engage in a two-step analysis. The first step is to determine whether the pending legislation or regulation is reasonably likely to be enacted. Unless management can make that negative determination, it must assume the legislation or regulation will be enacted. If management must assume enactment, it proceeds with the second step of the analysis. In that step, unless management can determine that enacted legislation or regulation is not reasonably likely to have a material effect on it, its financial condition or results of operations, disclosure is required.[5] The Climate Change Release does not demand disclosure of the amount of GHG emissions, but it indicates that a company should have enough information about them to assist it in making judgments about disclosure. The Climate Change Release also states that the company needs to consider disclosure, if material, of the difficulties of assessing the timing and effect of the pending legislation or regulation.

Examples of the financial consequences of pending climate change legislation and regulation identified by the SEC include possible costs to upgrade facilities and equipment to reduce emissions to meet regulatory limits or to reduce the costs of acquiring allowances or offset credits in a cap-and-trade program. Changes to profit or loss might also result from a change in demand for goods or services arising from legislation or regulation.

Because climate change legislation and regulation are evolving quickly, the SEC advises companies to regularly evaluate their potential disclosure obligations in light of new developments.

International Accords

The Climate Change Release advises companies to evaluate the impact of proposed and existing treaties and other international accords concerning climate change, and to consider whether those impacts should be disclosed under existing SEC requirements, especially Item 303. For companies that are reasonably likely to be affected by potential international

---

5. This two-step test should be evaluated in light of the clarification the SEC provided in the November 2020 MD&A Release.

climate change agreements, the SEC advises them to monitor the progress of the agreements when making disclosure decisions.

Indirect Consequences of Regulation or Business Trends

The Climate Change Release states that "[l]egal, technological, political and scientific developments regarding climate change may create new opportunities or risks for registrants." They may create new or increased demand for some products or services, such as for energy-efficient products that result in lower emissions than competing products and for electricity generated from alternative energy sources. Similarly, they may create decreased demand for goods that cause significant GHG emissions or services related to carbon-based energy, such as drilling or equipment maintenance services. According to the Climate Change Release, those business trends or risks may need to be disclosed as risk factors or in the MD&A. In some cases, the developments may have a sufficiently significant impact on a company's business that disclosure would be required under Item 101, as might be the case if a company decided to change its plan of operation to benefit from potential opportunities.

A novel perspective suggested by the Climate Change Release is the possible need to disclose reputational risk resulting from climate change developments. "Depending on the nature of a registrant's business and its sensitivity to public opinion," the SEC asserts, "a registrant may have to consider whether the public's perception of any publicly available data relating to its GHG emissions could expose it to potential adverse consequences to its business operations or financial condition resulting from reputational damage."

Physical Impacts of Climate Change

The Climate Change Release contends that "[s]ignificant physical effects of climate change, such as effects on the severity of weather (for example, floods or hurricanes), sea levels, the arability of farmland, and water availability and quality, have the potential to affect a registrant's operations and results." The Climate Change Release relies on a 2007 Government Accountability Office report and the sources it cites for the proposition that elevated levels of GHGs can cause severe weather. The Climate Change Release identifies examples of the possible consequences of severe weather as including: (1) property damage and disrupted operations for businesses on coastlines; (2) indirect financial and operational impacts if the operations of major customers or suppliers are disrupted by hurricanes or floods; (3) increased claims for insurers and reinsurers; (4) decreased agricultural output in areas impacted by drought; and (5) increased premiums and deductibles, or decreased insurance coverage availability, for facilities and operations in areas prone to severe weather. The Climate Change Release advises companies with businesses that may be harmed by severe weather or other climate-related events to consider disclosing "material risks of, or consequences from, such events in their publicly filed documents."

Conflict Minerals Disclosure

As mandated by the Dodd-Frank Wall Street Reform and Consumer Protection Act, SEC rules require companies that use certain minerals to disclose whether the minerals financed or benefitted armed groups in the Democratic Republic of Congo or an adjoining country.[6] The specified "conflict minerals" are cassiterite, columbite-tantalite, gold, and wolframite. If these conflict minerals are "necessary to the functionality or production of a product manufactured or contracted . . . to be manufactured," the company must determine whether the minerals originated in the covered countries. If so, the company must conduct due diligence on the source and supply chain. The specific disclosure requirements vary depending on the origination of the minerals and results of due diligence. A company must make any required disclosures annually on a Form SD (Specialized Disclosure Report) filed with the SEC no later than May 31 after the end of the company's most recent calendar year.

Activities Involving Iran, Specially Designated Nationals, and Blocked Persons

The Iran Threat Reduction and Syria Human Rights Act of 2012 requires disclosure in annual and quarterly reports if, during the reporting period, the company or an affiliate knowingly engaged in a wide range of proscribed activities, including violations of the Iran Sanctions Act of 1996 or the Comprehensive Iran Sanctions, Accountability and Divestment Act of 2010, transactions with persons or entities listed on the U.S. Department of the Treasury's Office of Foreign Assets Control's Specially Designated Nationals and Blocked Persons List, and transactions with the government of Iran or any entity that is owned or controlled, directly or indirectly, by the government of Iran. Companies subject to this requirement are required to disclose each activity in detail, including the nature and extent of the activity, the gross revenues and net profits, if any, attributable to the activity, and whether the company or its affiliate intends to continue the activity. In addition, the issuer must file a separate "IRANNOTICE" with the SEC, a copy of which is forwarded to the President of the United States for investigation. This requirement does not include a materiality threshold or de minimis exception, and thus even minor violations must be identified and reported.[7]

Director Diversity Characteristics

In recent years, institutional investors, members of Congress, proxy advisory firms, and others have been pressing public companies to improve their board diversity and related disclosures.

Regulation S-K Item 401(e) requires a company to briefly discuss the specific experience, qualifications, attributes, or skills that led to the conclusion that a person should serve as a director. Regulation S-K Item 407(c)(2)(vi) requires disclosure of whether, and if so how, the nominating committee (or the board) considers diversity in identifying nominees for

---

6. Section 1502 of the Dodd-Frank Wall Street Reform and Consumer Protection Act added Section 13(p) to the Exchange Act. In August 2012, the SEC promulgated a final rule relating to conflict minerals as new Rule 13p-1 under the Exchange Act: SEC Release No. 34-67716, *Conflict Minerals* (Aug. 22, 2012), https://www.sec.gov/rules /final/2012/34-67716.pdf. The first reporting period for all companies was the 2013 calendar year with the first Form SD filings due by May 31, 2014. In 2017, following legal challenges to the rule and a remand to the SEC for further action, the SEC's Division of Corporation Finance issued a statement indicating that it will not recommend enforcement action to the SEC if a company discloses on a Form SD that it has conducted a reasonable country-of-origin inquiry but does not provide disclosure about the due diligence inquiry into any conflict minerals in its supply chain or obtain an independent private sector audit of its conflict minerals report. The SEC's no-action position is available at https://www.sec.gov/news/public-statement/corpfin-updated-statement-court-decision-conflict-minerals-rule.
7. Securities Exchange Act of 1934, as amended, Section 13(r).

director. If the nominating committee (or the board) has a diversity policy related to identifying director nominees, the company should describe how this policy is implemented and how the nominating committee (or the board) assesses the effectiveness of the policy. If the nominating committee (or the board) considered "certain self-identified diversity characteristics" (e.g., race, gender, ethnicity, religion, nationality, disability, sexual orientation, or cultural background) when determining an individual's specific experience, qualifications, attributes, or skills for board membership, then the SEC expects the company to disclose those characteristics and how they were considered in the nomination process. This disclosure would only be required if a director or nominee self-identified with a particular characteristic and consented to the company's disclosure of that characteristic. The guidance also requires a company to disclose how its diversity policy, if any, takes into account nominees' self-identified diversity attributes and any other qualifications (e.g., diverse work experiences, military service, or socioeconomic or demographic characteristics).[8]

In August 2021, the SEC approved rule amendments proposed by NASDAQ in December 2020 and modified in February 2021.[9] Once effective, new Nasdaq Rules 5605(f) and 5606 will require Nasdaq-listed companies, subject to certain exceptions and transition periods, to:

- publicly disclose in an aggregated form using a uniform format, to the extent permitted by applicable law, information on the voluntary self-identified gender, race, and LGBTQ+ status of the company's board of directors (Nasdaq Rule 5606);[10] and

- have, or explain why it does not have, at least two "diverse" directors (meaning a director who self-identifies as a female, an underrepresented minority and/or LGBTQ+) including at least one director who self-identifies as a female, and at least one director who self-identifies as either an "underrepresented minority" (Black

---

8. SEC Division of Corporation Finance, *Compliance & Disclosure Interpretations of Regulation S-K, Questions No. 133.13 and 116.11* (Feb. 6, 2019), https://www.sec.gov/divisions/corpfin/guidance/regs-kinterp.htm.

9. SEC Release No. 34-92590; File No. SR-NASDAQ-2020-081; File No. SR-NASDAQ-2020-082, *Order Approving Proposed Rule Changes, as Modified by Amendments No. 1, to Adopt Listing Rules Related to Board Diversity and to Offer Certain Listed Companies Access to a Complimentary Board Recruiting Service* (Aug. 6, 2021), https://www.sec.gov/rules/sro/nasdaq/2021/34-92590.pdf. See also SEC Release No. 34-90574; File No. SR-NASDAQ-2020-081, *Notice of Filing of Proposed Rule Change to Adopt Listing Rules Related to Board Diversity* (Dec. 4, 2020), https://www.sec.gov/rules/sro/nasdaq/2020/34-90574.pdf; SEC Release No. 34-91286; File No. SR-NASDAQ-2020-081, *Notice of Filing of Amendments No. 1 and Order Instituting Proceedings to Determine Whether to Approve or Disapprove Proposed Rule Changes, as Modified by Amendments No. 1, to Adopt Listing Rules Related to Board Diversity and to Offer Certain Listed Companies Access to a Complimentary Board Recruiting Solution to Help Advance Diversity on Company Boards* (Mar. 10, 2021), https://www.sec.gov/rules/sro/nasdaq/2021/34-91286.pdf. The full text of Amendment No. 1 (Feb. 26, 2021) is available at https://www.sec.gov/comments/sr-nasdaq-2020-081/srnasdaq2020081-8425992-229601.pdf.

10. All Nasdaq-listed U.S. companies are required to publicly disclose director self-identified board-level diversity statistics using a standardized disclosure matrix template by the later of: (1) August 8, 2022; or (2) the date the company files its proxy statement or its information statement for its annual meeting of shareholders (or, if the company does not file a proxy or information statement, the date it files its Form 10-K) during the 2022 calendar year. If a company files its 2022 proxy or information statement (or its Form 10-K) before August 8, 2022 and does not include the matrix, the company will have until August 8, 2022 to disclose its matrix. Such disclosure can either be made on the company's website or provided in an amended annual report, such as on Form 10-K. If a company files its 2022 proxy or information statement (or its Form 10-K) on or after August 8, 2022, then the company must either include the matrix in its proxy or information statement (or its Form 10-K), or post the matrix on its website within one business day of filing its proxy or information statement (or its Form 10-K) (Nasdaq Rule 5606; Nasdaq FAQ No. 1796).

or African American, Hispanic or Latinx, Asian, Native American or Alaska Native, Native Hawaiian or Pacific Islander, or two or more races or ethnicities) or as LGBTQ+ (lesbian, gay, bisexual, transgender, or a member of the queer community) (Nasdaq Rule 5605(f)).[11]

Board Oversight

Regulation S-K Item 407(h) and Item 7 of Schedule 14A require a company to disclose the extent of the board's role in the risk oversight of the company, including a description of how the board administers its risk oversight function. To the extent sustainability-related risks are material to a company's business, the discussion should include the nature of the board's role in overseeing the management of those risks. The SEC believes this disclosure should provide important information to investors about how a company perceives the role of its board and the relationship between the board and senior management in managing the material risks facing the company. Companies are increasingly discussing in their proxy statements whether the full board of directors or a board committee has responsibility for oversight of sustainability-related matters.

Other Sources of Sustainability Disclosure Obligations

Disclosure about sustainability matters may also be required by other applicable laws. For example:

- The Greenhouse Gas Reporting Program requires reporting of GHG data and other relevant information from large GHG emission sources, fuel and industrial gas suppliers, and CO_2 injection sites in the United States. Emissions are reported annually, and the reported data are made available to the public.[12]

- Certain companies doing business in California must disclose their efforts to eradicate human trafficking in their supply chains.[13]

- State laws may require disclosure of board and/or executive officer diversity statistics and other diversity-related information. For example, public companies with principal executive offices located in Illinois must disclose annually in state filings the diversity of their boards, how demographic diversity is considered in their processes for identifying and appointing director nominees and executive officers, and plans to

---

11. A transition period will apply, based on a company's listing tier and/or board size:
   - Companies listed on Nasdaq Global Select Market or Nasdaq Global Market are required to have, or explain why they do not have, one diverse director by August 7, 2023, and two diverse directors by August 6, 2025;
   - Companies listed on the Nasdaq Capital Market are required to have, or explain why they do not have, one diverse director by August 7, 2023, and two diverse directors by August 6, 2026; and
   - Companies with boards that have five or fewer directors, regardless of listing tier, are required to have, or explain why they do not have, one diverse director by August 7, 2023.
   - (Nasdaq Rule 5605(f)(5); Nasdaq FAQ No. 1748).
12. See Environmental Protection Agency, *Greenhouse Gas Reporting Program*, https://www.epa.gov/ghgreporting.
13. The *California Transparency in Supply Chains Act of 2010*, which took effect on January 1, 2012, requires certain retailers and manufacturers to provide website disclosure detailing whether, and to what extent, they investigate or monitor slavery or human trafficking in their direct product supply chains.

promote director and officer diversity.[14] New York and Maryland have similar statutes that require disclosure to the state of the number of female directors.[15]

Recent SEC Efforts to Tackle Climate and ESG Disclosures

In 2021, several important developments signaled heightened SEC focus on ESG disclosures, particularly those relating to climate. At the time of writing, these include:

- The formation by the SEC Division of Enforcement of a new 22-member Climate and ESG Task Force in March 2021, to target ESG-related misconduct and potential violations.[16]

- The opening of a comment period (that closed in June 2021) by then-Acting SEC Chair Allison Herren Lee on climate change disclosure, including 15 sets of questions intended to assist the SEC Staff as it considers climate change disclosure rule amendments.[17]

- Statements by then-Acting SEC Chair Lee directing enhanced regulatory scrutiny of climate-related disclosure in public company filings,[18] then-Acting Director of the Division of Corporation Finance expressing support for developing an ESG disclosure system,[19] and the SEC Division of Corporation Finance's Chief Accountant about increased scrutiny of company disclosures relating to climate, including accounting for climate-related risks and impacts.[20]

- The inclusion on the SEC's Spring 2021 regulatory agenda of proposed new rules requiring disclosure relating to climate risk and human capital including workforce diversity and board diversity.[21]

- The release of a sample letter illustrating the type of comments the SEC's Division of Corporation Finance has been issuing to companies regarding their climate-related discourse or lack thereof.[22]

---

14. Public Act 101-0589 took effect when signed by the Illinois Governor on August 27, 2019, and required Illinois-headquartered corporations to report the newly required information as soon as practicable but no later than January 1, 2021.

15. New York Business Corporation Law, Section 408(1) as amended by A6330, 2019 Leg., Reg. Sess. (N. Y. 2019); S4278, 2019 Leg., Reg. Sess. (N. Y. 2019); Maryland Code, Tax-General Section 11-101(c)(2) as amended by HB1116, 2019 Leg., 440th Sess. (Md. 2019); SB 911, 2019 Leg., 440th Sess. (Md. 2019).

16. Press Release, *SEC Announces Enforcement Task Force Focused on Climate and ESG Issues* (Mar. 4, 2021), https://www.sec.gov/news/press-release/2021-42.

17. Public Statement, Acting Chair Allison Herren Lee, *Public Input Welcomed on Climate Change Disclosures* (Mar. 15, 2021), https://www.sec.gov/news/public-statement/lee-climate-change-disclosures.

18. Public Statement, Acting Chair Allison Herren Lee, *Statement on the Review of Climate-Related Disclosure* (Feb. 24, 2021), https://www.sec.gov/news/public-statement/lee-statement-review-climate-related-disclosure.

19. Public Statement, John Coates, Acting Director, Division of Corporation Finance, *ESG Disclosure – Keeping Pace with Developments Affecting Investors, Public Companies and the Capital Markets* (Mar. 11, 2021), https://www.sec.gov/news/public-statement/coates-esg-disclosure-keeping-pace-031121.

20. Bloomberg Tax, *SEC to Review Existing Accounting Related to ESG Factors* (May 5, 2021).

21. Press Release, *SEC Announces Annual Regulatory Agenda* (June 11, 2021), https://www.sec.gov/news/press-release/2021-99.

22. Sample Letter to Companies Regarding Climate Change Disclosures (Sep. 22, 2021), https://www.sec.gov/corpfin/sample-letter-climate-change-disclosures.

The SEC has also developed a new ESG landing page at www.sec.gov, which tracks various SEC developments in the ESG area pursuant to its "all-agency" approach.

> In 2021, several important developments signaled heightened SEC focus on ESG disclosures, particularly those relating to climate.

> Require board-level review of key sustainability disclosures and work with senior management (including legal) to confirm that required sustainability disclosures made in SEC filings are accurate and consistent with the company's voluntary disclosures.

Take-Aways for Board Members

- Decide on a disclosure philosophy with respect to sustainability matters—whether to disclose only what is technically required to be disclosed or to provide voluntary disclosure to position itself as a sustainability leader. This decision may depend on the company's industry, strategy, shareholder base, and other factors. Periodically review this decision in light of how the company's disclosures compare to those of its peers and priorities of its major shareholders.

- Ensure that a comprehensive internal reporting process is in place relating to sustainability disclosures. Sustainability risks should be considered as part of company's overall risk profile and integrated into its existing risk management and financial reporting processes, including proper documentation of the company's internal analyses of such risks. A company should make and document materiality determinations with respect to sustainability risk just as it would for any other business risk even though many sustainability-related risks may be longer term in nature.

- Require board-level review of key sustainability disclosures and work with senior management (including legal) to confirm that required sustainability disclosures made in SEC filings are accurate and consistent with the company's voluntary disclosures. The SEC Staff is increasingly commenting on inconsistencies between disclosures in filed versus non-filed communications.

- Stay informed of pending legislation, SEC rulemaking and guidance, and other developments that may impact sustainability disclosures through periodic briefings to the board (or relevant committee).

Chapter 15
Voluntary Reporting on ESG Matters

Rebecca Grapsas and Claire H. Holland

In response to pressure from investors, employees, and the community, many U.S. companies are voluntarily disclosing sustainability information pursuant to disclosure standards set by nongovernmental standard setters. Standard setters have developed voluntary standards to address this increased interest in sustainability reporting in the absence of a broad framework for mandatory public company reporting of sustainability information, which is currently materiality-based with some specific line-item requirements.

Voluntary disclosure by U.S. companies of environmental, social, and governance (ESG) information has become far more prevalent in the last several years as pressure from investors and others to make such disclosure has accelerated. The voluntary reporting on sustainability landscape is rapidly evolving, with recent changes in the bodies that set the standards as well as changes to disclosure requirements and recommendations as set forth in the various standards.

The multitude of sustainability disclosure frameworks and standards that currently exists has made it challenging for companies to navigate and respond to overlapping and sometimes conflicting standards, and for investors to compare sustainability information across companies. These challenges are compounded by the voluntary nature of the standards—companies can decide which standards to comply with and to what extent—and the fact that third-party assurance of the accuracy of the information is not required and often not provided in any meaningful way or at all. To help companies provide more reliable, standardized, and comparable sustainability information, global efforts are underway to develop a coherent and comprehensive sustainability reporting system, as discussed below. Note that while U.S. companies may look to sustainability disclosure requirements in place in the European Union and/or the United Kingdom, those requirements are outside the scope of this chapter.

This chapter discusses existing voluntary reporting standards bearing on sustainability disclosures by U.S. companies, as well as relevant developments. The term "sustainability" as used herein refers to topics bearing on corporate responsibility and citizenship including environmental matters such as climate change, waste, water and natural resources, and social and employee-related matters such as respect for human rights, workforce diversity, equity and inclusion, and board diversity. See also Chapter 1.

Chapter 14 discusses mandatory disclosure requirements that apply to U.S. public companies, as well as significant recent developments in that area.

> In response to pressure from investors, employees, and the community, many U.S. companies are voluntarily disclosing sustainability information pursuant to disclosure standards set by nongovernmental standard setters.

Voluntary Sustainability Reporting Standard Setters

Several organizations have issued standards for voluntary reporting of sustainability information, including the following of particular relevance to U.S. companies:

- *Carbon Disclosure Standards Board (CDSB)*. CDSB is an international consortium of business and environmental nongovernmental organizations established at the World Economic Forum (WEF) meeting in Davos in 2007.[1] CDSB issued its first framework in 2010 focused on climate change and, in 2015, published the CDSB Framework as expanded to cover reporting of environmental and climate change information in mainstream reports such as annual reports. The CDSB Framework was updated in April 2018 to align with Task Force on Climate-related Financial Disclosures (TCFD) recommendations (discussed below) and includes seven Guiding Principles and 12 Reporting Requirements.[2]

- *CDP (formerly Carbon Disclosure Project)*. CDP is an international nonprofit organization established in 2000 that scores corporations on environmental risks and opportunities related to climate change, water security, and deforestation based on information obtained through annual questionnaires.[3] The questionnaires include questions that can differ depending on the company's industry; for example, the 2021 climate change questionnaire for oil and gas companies includes over 140 questions.[4] CDP provides the Secretariat for CDSB (discussed above).

---

1. See CDSB, *About CDSB*, https://www.cdsb.net/our-story.
2. CDSB, *CDSB Framework for Reporting Environmental Information & Climate Change Information* (Dec. 2019), https://www.cdsb.net/sites/default/files/cdsb_framework_2019_v2.2.pdf.
3. See CDP, *About Us*, https://www.cdp.net/en/info/about-us.
4. See CDP, *Guidance for Companies: CDP Questionnaires 2021*, https://www.cdp.net/en/guidance/guidance-for-companies#6c84d1acb017e380e18853ad8966994a.

- *Global Reporting Initiative (GRI)*. GRI is an international organization that issued international guidelines for sustainability reporting in 2000 and sustainability reporting standards in 2016.[5] The GRI Standards are a modular set, starting with the universal Standards, as well as the Topic Standards which are based on the organization's material topics (economic, environmental, or social). The Topic Standards cover matters such as energy, emissions, water, waste, diversity, child labor, customer privacy, suppliers, anti-corruption, tax, and procurement practices.[6]

- *Task Force on Climate-related Financial Disclosures (TCFD)*. TCFD was established by the Financial Stability Board in December 2015 to help identify the information needed by investors, lenders, and insurance underwriters to appropriately assess and price climate-related risks and opportunities.[7] In 2017, TCFD released a framework to help companies evaluate and disclose financial risks posed to their business by climate change. The framework's recommendations for climate-related financial disclosures are structured around four thematic areas that represent core elements of how organizations operate: governance (such as board oversight of climate-related risks and opportunities), strategy (such as organizational resilience under different climate-related scenarios), risk management (such as processes for identifying, assessing, and managing climate-related risks), and metrics and targets (such as Scope 1, Scope 2, and Scope 3 greenhouse gas (GHG) emissions).[8]

- *Value Reporting Foundation (VRF)*. VRF was formed in June 2021 following the merger of the Sustainability Accounting Standards Board (SASB) and the International Integrated Reporting Council (IIRC).[9] In 2018, SASB developed the SASB framework with industry-specific sustainability accounting standards for 77 industries. Each Industry Standard sets forth disclosure topics and related accounting and activity metrics which according to VRF would be reasonably likely to be material to a company in that industry. For example, for a company in the Industrial Machinery and Goods industry, disclosure topics include energy management, employee health and safety, and fuel economy and emissions in use-phase, accounting metrics include total energy consumed, total recordable incident rate and sales-weighted fuel efficiency for non-road equipment, and activity metrics include number of units produced by product category.[10] IIRC issued its International Integrated Reporting Framework in 2013 and updated it in January 2021, to facilitate integrated reporting of sustainability information together with financial information.[11]

---

5. See GRI, *About GRI*, https://www.globalreporting.org/about-gri/.

6. GRI, *GRI Standards by Language: English* (last updated May 2020), https://www.globalreporting.org/standards/download-the-standards/.

7. See TCFD, *About*, https://www.fsb-tcfd.org/about/.

8. TCFD, *Final Report: Recommendations of the Task Force on Climate-related Financial Disclosures* (June 2017), https://assets.bbhub.io/company/sites/60/2020/10/FINAL-2017-TCFD-Report-11052018.pdf.

9. See VRF, *About Us*, https://www.sasb.org/about/.

10. VRF, *Download SASB Standards*, https://www.sasb.org/standards/download/. VRF is also developing a SASB XBRL taxonomy; see *SASB XBRL Taxonomy Available for Comment* (Mar. 1, 2021), https://www.sasb.org/blog/taxonomy-available-for-public-comment/.

11. IIRC, *International <IR> Framework* (last updated Jan. 2021), https://integratedreporting.org/wp-content/uploads/2021/01/InternationalIntegratedReportingFramework.pdf.

- *World Economic Forum (WEF).* In September 2020, the WEF, together with Deloitte, EY, KPMG, and PwC, issued a set of 21 core and 34 expanded metrics and disclosures for sustainability reporting.[12] "Core" metrics and disclosures are more well-established or critically important metrics and disclosures, which are primarily quantitative, are already being reported by many firms (albeit often in different formats), and/or can be obtained with reasonable effort. "Expanded" metrics and disclosures tend to be less well-established in existing practice and standards and have a wider value chain scope or convey impact in a more sophisticated or tangible way, such as in monetary terms. The recommended metrics are organized under four pillars that are aligned with the United Nations Sustainable Development Goals and principal ESG domains: Principles of Governance, Planet, People, and Prosperity.

In addition, two new standard-setting bodies have been formed or are proposed that are relevant to U.S. companies:

- *International Sustainability Standards Board (ISSB).*[13] In September 2020, the International Financial Reporting Standards Foundation (IFRSF) issued a Consultation Paper on Sustainability Reporting including a proposal to create an ISSB that would issue global sustainability standards.[14] The IFRSF is responsible for developing through the International Accounting Standards Board (IASB) as the IFRSF's standard-setting body, a set of global accounting standards (IFRS) which are mandated in more than 140 jurisdictions (and permitted in many others). In April 2021, the IFRSF published an exposure draft proposing amendments to the IFRSF Constitution to accommodate an ISSB.[15] In June 2021, the International Organisation of Securities Commissions (IOSCO) elaborated on its vision and expectations for the IFRSF's work toward establishing global baseline sustainability standards,[16] following its February 2021 announcement of its intention to work with the IFRSF in developing a plan to establish a new ISSB.[17] At the United Nations COP26 summit in November 2021, the IFRSF officially announced the

12. WEF, *Measuring Stakeholder Capitalism: Towards Common Metrics and Consistent Reporting of Sustainable Value Creation* (Sept. 22, 2020), https://www.weforum.org/reports/measuring-stakeholder-capitalism-towards -common-metrics-and-consistent-reporting-of-sustainable-value-creation.

13. IFRSF, *Sustainability Reporting Work Plan*, https://www.ifrs.org/projects/work-plan/sustainability-reporting/.

14. IFRSF, *IFRS Foundation Trustees Consult on Global Approach to Sustainability Reporting and on Possible Foundation Role* (Sept. 30, 2020), https://www.ifrs.org/news-and-events/news/2020/09/ifrs-foundation-trustees -consult-on-global-approach-to-sustainability-reporting/; IFRSF, *Consultation Paper on Sustainability Reporting* (Sept. 2020), https://www.ifrs.org/content/dam/ifrs/project/sustainability-reporting/consultation-paper-on -sustainability-reporting.pdf.

15. IFRSF, *IFRS Foundation Trustees Publish Institutional Arrangements for Proposed New Sustainability Standards Board* (Apr. 30, 2021), https://www.ifrs.org/news-and-events/news/2021/04/ifrs-trustees-publish-institutional- arrangements-for-proposed-new-sustainability-standards-board/; IFRSF, *Exposure Draft and Comment Letters: Proposed Targeted Amendments to the IFRS Foundation Constitution to Accommodate an International Sustainability Standards Board to Set IFRS Sustainability Standards* (Apr. 2021; comment period ends July 29, 2021), https://www.ifrs.org/projects/work-plan/sustainability-reporting/exposure-draft-and-comment-letters/.

16. IOSCO, *IOSCO Elaborates on Its Vision and Expectations for the IFRS Foundation's Work Towards a Global Baseline of Investor-Focussed Sustainability Standards to Improve the Global Consistency, Comparability and Reliability of Sustainability Reporting* (June 28, 2021), https://www.iosco.org/news/pdf/IOSCONEWS608.pdf.

17. IOSCO, *IOSCO Sees an Urgent Need for Globally Consistent, Comparable, and Reliable Sustainability Disclosure Standards and Announces Its Priorities and Vision for a Sustainability Standards Board Under the IFRS Foundation* (Feb. 24, 2021), https://www.iosco.org/news/pdf/IOSCONEWS594.pdf.

formation of a new ISSB to develop a comprehensive global baseline of sustainability disclosure standards.[18]

- *Taskforce on Nature-related Financial Disclosures (TNFD).* In July 2021, the TNFD was launched, with the aim of disseminating in 2023 a reporting framework focused on nature-related information such as living (biotic) nature, water, soil and air, and mineral depletion.[19]

Work on convergence toward global sustainability reporting standards has accelerated in recent months, particularly the efforts of the IFRSF to establish a new ISSB. The IFRSF's efforts are supported by the G7 Finance Ministers, global regulators in the form of IOSCO,[20] and key institutional investors such as BlackRock, which has described a new ISSB as "the optimal outcome."[21] In March 2021, the IFRSF announced the formation of a working group including CDSB, TCFD, VRF, and WEF. The working group is focused on accelerating the convergence of global sustainability reporting standards, including by contributing to preparations for a potential new ISSB. The working group will also engage closely with CDP and GRI, and IOSCO will participate as an observer.[22] IOSCO has issued several recent reports that are relevant to the IFRSF's work in establishing an ISSB[23] and has formed a new Technical Expert Group to work closely with the IFRSF working group.[24]

Concurrent with the November 2021 announcement of the formation of the ISSB, the IFRSF declared that it would complete consolidation of CDSB and VRF into the new board by June 2022. The IFRSF also announced the publication of two prototype documents developed by the IFRSF working group for consideration by the new ISSB when it commences work early in 2022. One prototype sets out general sustainability disclosures and the other focuses on climate-related disclosures that build on the TCFD's recommendations and includes industry-specific disclosures.[25]

---

18. IFRSF, *IFRSF Foundation Announces International Sustainability Standards Board, Consolidation with CDSB and VRF, and Publication of Prototype Disclosure Requirements* (Nov. 3, 2021), https://www.ifrsf.org/news-and-events/news/2021/11/ifrs-foundation-announces-issb-consolidation-with-cdsb-vrf-publication-of-prototypes/.

19. See TNFD, *How It Works*, https://tnfd.info/how-it-works/; TNFD, *Proposed Technical Scope, Recommendations for the TNFD* (June 4, 2021), https://tnfd.info/wp-content/uploads/2021/06/TNFD-%E2%80%93-Technical -Scope-2.pdf.

20. Public Statement, Erkki Liikanen, Chair of the IFRSF Trustees, *Is There a Path to Global Sustainability Standards?*, CFA Inst. Glob. Financ. Regul. Symp. (June 29, 2021), https://www.ifrs.org/news-and-events/news /2021/06/is-there-a-path-to-global-sustainability-standards/.

21. BlackRock, Inc., *Sustainability Reporting: Convergence to Accelerate Progress* (Oct. 2020), https://www. blackrock.com/corporate/literature/publication/blk-commentary-sustainability-reporting-convergence.pdf.

22. IFRSF, *IFRS Foundation Trustees Announce Working Group to Accelerate Convergence in Global Sustainability Reporting Standards Focused on Enterprise Value* (Mar. 22, 2021), https://www.ifrs.org/news-and-events/news/2021 /03/trustees-announce-working-group/.

23. See, e.g., IOSCO, *Environmental, Social and Governance (ESG) Ratings and Data Products Providers, Consultation Report* (July 2021), https://www.iosco.org/library/pubdocs/pdf/IOSCOPD681.pdf; IOSCO, *Report on Sustainability-Related Issuer Disclosures* (June 2021), https://www.iosco.org/library/pubdocs/pdf/IOSCOPD678. pdf; IOSCO, *Recommendations on Sustainability-Related Practices, Policies and Procedures and Disclosure in Asset Management* (June 30, 2021; comment period ends Aug. 15, 2021), https://www.iosco.org/library/pubdocs/pdf /IOSCOPD679.pdf.

24. IOSCO, *IOSCO Technical Expert Group to Undertake an Assessment of the Technical Recommendations to Be Developed as Part of the IFRS Foundation's Sustainability Project* (Mar. 30, 2021), https://www.iosco.org/news /pdf/IOSCONEWS599.pdf.

25. IFRSF, *IFRSF Foundation Announces International Sustainability Standards Board, Consolidation with CDSB and VRF, and Publication of Prototype Disclosure Requirements* (Nov. 3, 2021), https://www.ifrs.org/news-and-events/ news/2021/11/ifrs-foundation-announces-issb-consolidation-with-cdsb-vrf-publication-of-prototypes/.

The newly established TNFD has also stated that it intends for its outputs to be integrated into existing frameworks, including those published by CDSB, GRI, SASB/VRF, and the new ISSB.[26]

Other key developments involving IFRSF working group members and collaborators include:

- In July 2020, GRI and SASB announced a collaborative workplan to provide materials to help stakeholders better understand how GRI and SASB standards can be used concurrently.[27] In April 2021, GRI and SASB published a "practical guide" that explores the experiences of four global companies (including General Motors) that use the two sets of standards together.[28]

- In September 2020, GRI, SASB, IIRC, CDP, and CDSB published a joint statement outlining their plans to collaborate to develop a comprehensive, globally accepted sustainability reporting framework.[29] The group aims to agree, whenever possible, on a common set of sustainability topics and related disclosure requirements that can serve distinct materiality concepts. That way, a company that chooses to make disclosure about a particular sustainability topic will need to gather information about performance on that topic only once—which can then be communicated to users by various means (e.g., sustainability reports, SEC filings, corporate websites) depending on their needs and objectives. Users of sustainability data should benefit from the combined standards in that they should produce more complete, consistent, and comparable information for decision-making. In December 2020, this group issued a prototype climate-related financial disclosure standard.[30]

It remains to be seen the degree to which global regulatory convergence will occur and the role that regulators will play in aligning on standards for measurement, management, and reporting of sustainability matters.

> Work on convergence toward global sustainability reporting standards has accelerated in recent months, particularly the efforts of the International Financial Reporting Standards Foundation to establish a new International Sustainability Standards Board.

---

26. See TNFD, *How It Works*, https://tnfd.info/how-it-works/.

27. GRI & SASB, *Promoting Clarity and Compatibility in the Sustainability Landscape* (July 13, 2020), https://www.globalreporting.org/about-gri/news-center/2020-07-13-promoting-clarity-and-compatibility-in-the-sustainability-landscape/.

28. GRI & SASB, *A Practical Guide to Sustainability Reporting Using GRI and SASB Standards* (Apr. 8, 2021), https://www.globalreporting.org/media/mlkjpn1i/gri-sasb-joint-publication-april-2021.pdf.

29. CDSB, CDP, GRI, IIRC and SASB, *Statement of Intent to Work Together Towards Comprehensive Corporate Reporting* (Sept. 11, 2020), https://29kjwb3armds2g3gi4lq2sx1-wpengine.netdna-ssl.com/wp-content/uploads/Statement-of-Intent-to-Work-Together-Towards-Comprehensive-Corporate-Reporting.pdf.

30. CDSB, CDP, GRI, IIRC and SASB, *Reporting on Enterprise Value: Illustrated with a Prototype Climate-Related Financial Disclosure Standard* (Dec. 18, 2020), https://29kjwb3armds2g3gi4lq2sx1-wpengine.netdna-ssl.com/wp-content/uploads/Reporting-on-enterprise-value_climate-prototype_Dec20.pdf.

> It remains to be seen the degree to which global regulatory convergence will occur and the role that regulators will play in aligning on standards for measurement, management, and reporting of sustainability matters.

Prevalence of Usage of Voluntary Standards

Most U.S. companies that voluntarily disclose aspects of their ESG programs do so by disclosure in a sustainability or ESG report. The number of companies issuing such reports has rapidly increased in recent years. In 2019, 90% of S&P 500 companies published a sustainability report (compared to 86% in 2018 and 20% in 2011).[31] In 2019, 65% of Russell 1000 companies published a sustainability report.[32]

The Center for Audit Quality (CAQ) issued reports in April 2021 (CAQ S&P 100 Report) and in August 2021 (CAQ S&P 500 Report) that found that while all S&P 100 companies and 95% of S&P 500 companies had some ESG information available, the vast majority reported ESG information outside of an SEC filing, typically in a standalone ESG report.[33]

The increase in voluntary sustainability reporting has been driven by various factors including:

- Accelerating interest in ESG matters by employees and the community more broadly, with a focus on the corporation's role in addressing environmental and social issues, including issues of racial and gender equality, employee health and safety (particularly during the COVID-19 pandemic) and social justice, and expanding expectations around transparency in these areas.

- Investor pressure through engagement with companies and votes in support of shareholder proposals calling for sustainability reports and other ESG disclosures. Increasingly, investors view ESG as fundamental to corporate performance and believe that companies with strong ESG profiles are more likely to successfully navigate adverse conditions than peers with weaker ESG profiles.[34]

---

31. Governance & Accountability Institute, Inc. (G&A), *Flash Report 2020 S&P 500, 90% of S&P 500 Index Companies Publish Sustainability/Responsibility Reports in 2019* (July 16, 2020), https://www.ga-institute.com/research-reports/flash-reports/2020-sp-500-flash-report.html.
32. G&A, *Flash Report 2020 Russell 1000, 65% of Russell 1000 Index Published Sustainability/Responsibility Reports in 2019* (Oct. 26, 2020), https://www.ga-institute.com/research-reports/flash-reports/2020-russell-1000-flash-report.html. 2020 was the first year that G&A issued a report covering the Russell 1000.
33. Center for Audit Quality, *S&P 100 and ESG Reporting* (Apr. 29, 2021; data as of Mar. 12, 2021), https://www.thecaq.org/sp-100-and-esg-reporting/; Center for Audit Quality, S&P 500 and ESG Reporting (Aug. 9, 2021), https://www.thecaq.org/sp-500-and-esg-reporting/. Note that SASB has initially anticipated that companies would use its standards to disclose information in the annual report on Form 10-K, but it has since moved away from this position; see SASB, *Sustainability Accounting Standards and SEC Filings* (June 5, 2019), https://corpgov.law.harvard.edu/2019/06/05/sustainability-accounting-standards-and-sec-filings/.
34. See, e.g., BlackRock, Inc., *Sustainable Investing: Resilience Amid Uncertainty* (May 2020), https://www.blackrock.com/corporate/literature/investor-education/sustainable-investing-resilience.pdf; McKinsey Quarterly, *Five Ways That ESG Creates Value* (Nov. 14, 2019), https://www.mckinsey.com/business-functions/strategy-and-corporate-finance/our-insights/five-ways-that-esg-creates-value.

- Increased corporate commitments to ESG-focused goals such as emissions reduction, diversity, equity, and inclusion, and the United Nations Sustainable Development Goals.[35]

- A desire by companies to improve ESG-focused ratings issued by organizations such as Institutional Shareholder Services, Sustainalytics, Bloomberg, and MSCI, which compile ESG ratings based on publicly available information.

- Requirements to disclose particular information as a condition of inclusion in certain ESG-focused stock exchange indices or funds.

As sustainability reporting has increased, so too has usage of the various voluntary sustainability disclosure standards discussed above. In particular, disclosing sustainability information in line with the SASB and TCFD frameworks is strongly encouraged by major institutional investors BlackRock, State Street, and Vanguard.[36] For example, in his letter to portfolio company CEOs in 2020, BlackRock's Chairman and CEO Larry Fink stated that BlackRock would vote against board members when companies have not made sufficient progress on sustainability and disclosing sustainability-related information in line with SASB and TCFD by the end of 2020.[37]

Usage data relevant to U.S. companies is available regarding the following major voluntary standards, although wide variations exist between companies as to the extent of alignment with the various standards:[38]

- *CDP*: CDP questionnaires are completed by more than 9,600 companies globally in 2020, 2,500 of which are based in North America, and including 87% of S&P 100 and 74% of S&P 500 companies. Many companies post the completed questionnaires on their corporate websites.

- *GRI*: Over 15,000 organizations register reports with GRI; 9% are U.S.-based. GRI standards are used by 76% of S&P 100 and 66% of S&P 500 companies.

- *TCFD*: 41% of public companies overall (50% U.S.) disclose some TCFD-aligned information. The TCFD framework is used by 65% of S&P 100 and 48% of S&P 500 companies.

- *VRF*: 1211 SASB reporters (2019 onward), 49% of which are U.S.-based. The SASB framework is used by 67% of S&P 100 and 72% of S&P 500 companies.

35. See, e.g., GRI, *Linking the SDGs and the GRI Standards* (last updated Mar. 2021), https://www.globalreporting .org/search/?query=Linking+the+SDGs+and+the+GRI+Standards; VRF, *What Is the Connection Between SASB and the SDGs?* (June 18, 2020), https://www.sasb.org/blog/what-is-the-connection-between-sasb-and-the-sdgs/.

36. See, e.g., BlackRock, Inc., *Larry Fink's 2021 Letter to CEOs* (Jan. 26, 2021), https://www.blackrock.com /corporate/investor-relations/larry-fink-ceo-letter; State Street Global Advisors, *CEO's Letter on Our 2021 Proxy Voting Agenda* (Jan. 11, 2021), https://www.ssga.com/us/en/institutional/ic/insights/ceo-letter-2021-proxy-voting -agenda; Vanguard, *Investment Stewardship 2020 Annual Report* (Sept. 15, 2020), https://global.vanguard.com /documents/vanguard-investment-stewardship-2020-annual-report.pdf.

37. BlackRock, Inc., *Larry Fink's 2020 Letter to CEOs: A Fundamental Reshaping of Finance* (Jan. 14, 2020), https://www.blackrock.com/corporate/investor-relations/2020-larry-fink-ceo-letter.

38. CAQ S&P 100 Report; CAQ S&P 500 Report; other data from CDP, GRI, TCFD, and VRF websites.

Compliance with more than one set of voluntary disclosure standards is typical for large U.S. companies. Per the CAQ S&P 100 Report (which was issued before the IIRC and SASB merger) and the CAQ S&P 500 Report, 88 companies in the S&P 100 and 92 in the S&P 500 comply with at least two of the sets of standards issued by CDP, GRI, IIRC, SASB, and TCFD, and 44 S&P 100 and 146 S&P 500 companies comply with four of those five sets of standards.

Compliance with multiple sets of standards can be particularly beneficial where different reporting standards recommend different disclosures on the same topic. [See, for example, a summary of disclosure standards regarding workforce diversity, equity, and inclusion under selected voluntary disclosure regimes as compared to Equal Employment Opportunity Commission data (EEO-1) that U.S. companies are required to collect.] [Note to Rick: If space limitations require, could delete this bracketed text and the Appendix]

Third-Party Assurance

Reliance on voluntary standards in the absence of mandatory disclosure requirements has led to wide variations in the accuracy and reliability of disclosure. Information quality can be improved by disclosure requirement standardization, as well as third-party assurance. Per the CAQ S&P 100 Report and CAQ S&P 500 Report:

- 70% of S&P 100 and 47% of S&P 500 companies received assurance over at least some of their ESG information from an engineering or consulting firm that was not a public company auditing firm. At 58 of these S&P 100 companies and 123 of these S&P 500 companies, assurance covered only select metrics related to GHG emissions. At the other 12 S&P 100 companies and 106 S&P 500 companies, assurance covered a wider range of ESG metrics.

- 11% of S&P 100 and 6% of S&P 500 companies received assurance from a public company auditing firm over at least some of their ESG information. At six of these S&P 100 companies and nine of these S&P 500 companies, assurance covered only select metrics related to GHG emissions. At the other five S&P 100 companies and 22 S&P 500 companies, assurance covered a wider range of ESG metrics.

Requiring third-party assurance of sustainability disclosures is a focus of various accounting and auditing professional bodies, including the Association of International Certified Professional Accountants, CAQ,[39] and the International Federation of Accountants.[40]

---

39. CAQ, *ESG Reporting and Attestation: A Roadmap for Audit Practitioners* (Feb. 2021), https://www.thecaq .org/wp-content/uploads/2021/02/caq-esg-reporting-and-attestation-roadmap-2021-Feb_v2.pdf.
40. International Federation of Accountants and IIRC, *Accelerating Integrated Reporting Assurance in the Public Interest* (Feb. 26, 2021), https://www.ifac.org/knowledge-gateway/preparing-future-ready-professionals /publications/accelerating-integrated-reporting-assurance-public-interest.

Take-Aways for Board Members

- Work with management to determine the content and scope of specific ESG voluntary disclosures including what and where to report, which framework and metrics to use, and whether to publicly disclose ESG goals for the company, and how frequently to report on progress toward goals. When making these decisions, bear in mind the company's industry, strategy, shareholder base, and risk of activism and litigation (for example, shareholder derivative lawsuits have been brought against companies that touted their diversity and inclusion efforts), peer company disclosure practices, and other relevant factors.

- Review the extent to which ESG considerations and related disclosures are integrated into business decisions, including strategic decisions and risk assessments. To this end, ensure that sustainability risks are factored into the enterprise risk management system and review how ESG-related risks are identified and how materiality of those risks is assessed.

- Ensure that key sustainability disclosures are reviewed at the board level, and work with management to confirm that disclosures in sustainability reports and other website disclosure are accurate (thereby avoiding "greenwashing") and consistent with SEC filings. As with financial reporting, ensure that internal controls and disclosure controls and procedures capture sustainability disclosures. Determine whether voluntary reporting should occur through a disclosure committee.

- Keep abreast of developments relating to key voluntary disclosure standards, including the new ISSB, and other developments that may impact sustainability disclosures through periodic briefings to the board (or relevant committee). Also consider whether to be an early adopter of forthcoming mandatory ESG disclosure standards.

- Be prepared to engage with key institutional investors and other stakeholders on ESG issues including voluntary disclosures. Be aware of trends regarding support for ESG-focused shareholder proposals, including the record number of environmental and social proposals that achieved majority support in 2021 (34 as of July 2021, up from last year's record of 21), in large part due to increased willingness by BlackRock to vote in favor of such proposals.[41]

---

41. See Alliance Advisors, *2021 Proxy Season Review* (July 2021), https://www.allianceadvisors.com/newsletters/2021-proxy-season-review; Nasdaq, *A Record Year for ESG Shareholder Resolutions* (Jun. 28, 2021), https://www.nasdaq.com/articles/a-record-year-for-esg-shareholder-resolutions-2021-06-28; B. Mirchandani, *What You Need to Know About the 2021 Proxy Season*, FORBES (Jun. 28, 2021), https://www.forbes.com/sites/bhaktimirchandani/2021/06/28/what-you-need-to-know-about-the-2021-proxy-season/?sh=368a27347f5e.

Comparison of Voluntary Standards—Workforce Diversity[42]

Summary of Disclosure Standards Regarding Workforce DEI Under the EEO-1 Survey and Selected Voluntary Disclosure Regimes[43]	
Employer Information Report EEO-1 Section D— Employment Data	Disclosure in tabular format of the number of employees that fall within specified racial/ethnic, gender, and job categories: • Racial/ethnic categories are (1) Hispanic or Latino, (2) White, (3) Black or African American, (4) Native Hawaiian or other Pacific Islander, (4) Asian, (5) American Indian or Alaska native, and (6) "two or more races." • Gender categories are (1) male and (2) female. • Job categories are (1) executives/senior-level officials and managers, (2) first-/midlevel officials and managers, (3) professional, (4) technicians, (5) sales workers, (6) administrative support workers, (7) craft workers, (8) operatives, (9) laborers and helpers, and (10) service workers.
Sustainability Accounting Standards Board (SASB) Workforce Diversity, & Inclusion— Example[44]	*A reporting company determines which SASB-recommended disclosure topics are material and which associated metrics to report.*[45] The following example illustrates the SASB-recommended disclosures for companies in the Internet Media & Services industry. **Disclose percentage of employees that are foreign nationals.** Foreign nationals are defined as anyone requiring a visa for work in the country in which he or she is employed. The percentage shall be calculated as the number of employees that are foreign nationals divided by the total number of the entity's employees. Note to standards: The entity shall describe potential risks from recruiting foreign nationals, which may arise from immigration, naturalization, or visa regulations. The entity shall describe management's approach to addressing the risks it has identified related to recruiting foreign nationals, which may include developing local talent pools, political lobbying for immigration reform, outsourcing of operations, or joining or forming industry partnerships.

continued

---

42. For a discussion of voluntary standards that bear on the oil and gas industry, see M. Crough & S. Bharmal, *Statutory and Voluntary Programs and Regimes in the United States Focusing on the E in ESG*, Oil, Gas & Energy Law (2020), https://www.sidley.com/-/media/publications/ov185article04.pdf?la=en.

43. This summary presents abridged versions of standards and is not a complete representation of all text and standards that may be applicable to workforce diversity within each disclosure regime.

44. The example provided is a redacted version of standard TC-IM-330a.3 contained in SASB, Internet Media & Services Industry Standard, Version 2018-10 (October 2018). SASB does not include Workforce Diversity & Inclusion standards in all of its separate industry standards manuals for 77 industries across 11 sectors. The Workforce Diversity & Inclusion standards may also vary across the industry standards manuals in which they appear. According to the SASB Materiality Map as of July 2021 (https://materiality.sasb.org/), SASB considers employee engagement, diversity, and inclusion "to likely be a material issue for companies" in 12 of the 77 industries for which SASB has published standards manuals. In September 2019, SASB initiated the Human Capital Research Project, to assess the scope and prevalence of various human capital management themes across SASB's sectors and within its 77 industries. As of July 2021, this project is at the post-consultation analysis phase, with preliminary insights from its recent public consultation presented in March 2021; see *SASB Presents Preliminary Insights on Human Capital Project* (Mar. 3, 2021), https://www.sasb.org/wp-content/uploads/2021/03/2021_02-Standards-Board-Meeting-Outcomes-Final.pdf.

45. SASB states that it "recognizes that each company is responsible for determining what information is material and . . . should be included in its SEC filings." In identifying from its perspective "sustainability topics that are reasonably likely to have material impacts," SASB "applies the definition of 'materiality' established under the U.S. securities laws." SASB, *SASB Conceptual Framework* (Feb. 2017; currently under revision), https://www.sasb.org/wp-content/uploads/2020/02/SASB_Conceptual-Framework_WATERMARK.pdf.

	Disclose percentage of gender and racial/ethnic group representation for (1) management, (2) technical staff, and (3) all other employees.
	1. The entity shall disclose gender representation for all employees and racial/ethnic group representation for its US employees by employee category. The following employee categories shall be used: (1) management, (2) technical staff, and (3) all other employees.
	2. Gender and racial/ethnic group representation shall be disclosed in percentages, where the percentage shall be calculated as the number of employees in each gender or racial/ethnic group in each employee category divided by the total number of employees in the respective employee category.
	3. For US employees, the entity shall categorize the employees in accordance with the EEO-1 Survey Instruction Booklet.
	4. For non-US employees, the entity shall categorize the employees in a manner generally consistent with the definitions provided above, though in accordance with, and further facilitated by, any applicable local regulations, guidance, or generally accepted definitions.
	5. The entity shall categorize the gender of its employees as female, male, or not disclosed/available.
	6. The entity shall categorize the racial/ethnic group of its US employees in accordance with the EEO-1 Survey Instruction Booklet and use the following categories: Asian, Black or African American, Hispanic or Latino, White, Other (which includes Native American or Alaska native, native Hawaiian or Pacific Islander, and "Two or More Races" classifications), or not disclosed/available.
	7. The entity may provide supplemental disclosures on gender and/or racial/ethnic group representation by country or region.
	8. The entity may provide supplemental contextual disclosures on factors that significantly influence gender and/or racial/ethnic group representation, such as the country or region where employees are located.
	9. The entity may disclose gender and/or racial/ethnic group representation by employee category in [specified] table formats.
	Note to standards:
	The entity shall describe its policies and programs for fostering equitable employee representation across its global operations. . . . Relevant aspects of employee representation include, at a minimum, gender and race/ethnicity. The entity may disclose other aspects of its workforce, such as age, physical abilities/qualities, sexual orientation, and religious beliefs as relevant to local jurisdiction.
Global Reporting Initiative (GRI)	*Companies are asked to cover material topics as defined by GRI.[46] All reporting companies must comply with certain "General Disclosures" (GRI 102). Beyond this, "Core" reporters comply with all "Management Approach" disclosures (GRI 103) and at least one "Topic-Specific" disclosure from among several recommendations (GRI series 200, 300, 400), and "Comprehensive" reporters comply with all Management Approach disclosures and all "Topic-Specific" disclosures.*

---

46. GRI defines a "material topic" as a "topic that reflects a reporting organization's significant economic, environmental and social impacts; or that substantively influences the assessments and decisions of stakeholders." GRI, *Consolidated Set of GRI Sustainability Reporting Standards 2020*, GRI 101 (May 2020) at 27.

General Disclosures (GRI 102)

- Disclosure of the total number of employees by employment contract (permanent and temporary), by gender and by region, and the total number of employees by employment type (full-time and part time), by gender (102-8)

Management Approach (GRI 103)

- Disclosure, for each material topic covered, regarding how the organization manages the topic, including a description of related policies, commitments, and goals and targets (103-2)
- Disclosure, for each material topic covered, regarding the effectiveness of the management approach (103-3)

Pursuant to GRI 103, see

- Disclosure of management approach for employment, including policies and practices with respect to discrimination, compensation, promotion, privacy, human resource development, and industrial relations (GRI 401)
- Disclosure of management approach for diversity and equal opportunity (GRI 405)
- Disclosure of management approach for nondiscrimination (GRI 406)

Topic-Specific (GRI series 200, 300, 400)

Series 200 (Economic Topics)

- Disclosure of the relevant ratio of the entry-level wage by gender at significant locations of operation to the minimum wage, applicable when a significant proportion of employees is compensated based on wages subject to minimum wage rules (202-1)

Series 400 (Social Topics)

- Disclosure by age group, gender, and region of the total number and rate of (a) new employee hires and (b) employee turnover (401-1)
- Disclosure by gender of (a) the total number of employees who (i) were entitled to parental leave, (ii) took parental leave, (iii) returned to work after parental leave ended, and (iv) returned to work after parental leave ended and still employed 12 months after returning to work and (b) return to work and retention rates of employees who took parental leave (401-3)
- Disclosure of numbers and rates of work-related fatalities, injuries, and/or ill health if they are significantly higher for certain types of worker demographics (e.g., sex, gender, migrant status, age, or worker type) (403-10, Reporting Recommendations 2.2.1 and 2.4.1)
- Disclosure of average hours of training that employees have undertaken by gender and employee category (404-1)
- Disclosure of the percentage of total employees by gender and by employee category who received a regular performance and career development review (404-3)
- Disclosure of the percentage of employees per employee category in each of the following diversity categories: (a) gender; (b) age group: under 30 years old, 30–50 years old, over 50 years old; (c) other indicators of diversity such as where relevant (such as minority based on ancestry or ethnic origin, citizenship, creed, or disability or other vulnerable groups such as ex-combatants, the internally displaced, refugees or returning refugees, and HIV/AIDS-affected households) (405-1)
- Disclosure of the ratio of the basic salary and remuneration of women to men for each employee category by level (such as senior management and middle management) and function (such as technical, administrative, production) and by significant locations of operation (and defining "significant locations of operation") (405-2)

continued

	• Disclosure of the total number of incidents of discrimination, status of the incidents, and actions taken with reference to (a) incident reviewed by the organization; (b) remediation plans being implemented; (c) remediation plans that have been implemented, with results reviewed through routine internal management review processes; and (d) incident no longer subject to action (406-1)
World Economic Forum (WEF) Measuring Stakeholder Capitalism: Towards Common Metrics and Consistent Reporting of Sustainable Value Creation (Sept. 2020)	Companies are expected to provide annual report disclosure on metrics that are material or relevant to the organization. "Core metrics and disclosures" are listed below. The WEF paper also describes "expanded metrics and disclosure"; these are not listed below. *Dignity and Equality* • Diversity and inclusion (%)—percentage of employees per employee category, by age group, gender, and other indicators of diversity (e.g., ethnicity) (see GRI 406-1b) • Pay equality (%)—ratio of the basic salary and remuneration for each employee category, by significant locations of operation for priority areas of equality: women to men, "minor to major" ethnic groups, and other relevant equality areas (see GRI 405-2) • Wage level (%)—ratios of standard entry-level wage by gender, compared to local minimum wage for specific categories of workers, and ratio of annual CEO compensation to median of annual total employee compensation (excluding the CEO) (see GRI 202-1) • Risk of incidents of child, forced, or compulsory labor—explanation of operations and suppliers considered to have significant risk for incidents of child labor, forced, or compulsory labor. Such risks could emerge in relation to: (a) type of operation (such as manufacturing plant) and type of supplier; and (b) countries or geographic areas with operations and suppliers considered at risk (see GRI 408-1b, GRI 409-1) *Health and Well-Being* • Health and safety (%)—number and rate of fatalities as a result of work-related injury; high-consequence work-related injuries (excluding fatalities); recordable work-related injuries; main types of work-related injury; and the number of hours worked. An explanation of how the organization facilitates workers' access to nonoccupational medical and healthcare services, and the scope of access provided for employees and workers (see GRI 403-9a&b, GRI 403-6a) *Skills for the Future* • Training provided (#, $)—average hours of training per person that the organization's employees have undertaken during the reporting period, by gender and employee category (total number of trainings provided to employees divided by the number of employees), and average training and development expenditure per full time employee (total cost of training provided to employees divided by the number of employees) (see GRI 404-1, SASB HC 101-15)

Chapter 16
Sustainability Ratings

Marie Elena Angulo and Jessica Mendoza

Introduction

Environmental, social, and governance (ESG) rating providers typically assign ratings by scoring a company's performance in the three ESG categories (environmental, social, and governance). The ratings are based primarily on nonfinancial metrics derived from publicly available information. Although not all ESG rating providers give companies being rated the chance to interact with their research teams, some offer companies the opportunity to review their rating before it is published, while others have procedures for companies to address errors after publication.

According to SustainAbility's *2020 Rate the Raters*, over 600 ESG ratings and rankings existed globally as of 2018.[1] Customarily, ESG rating providers sell their products to multiples parties, including institutional investor clients, trading terminals (like Bloomberg), proxy advisory firms, and mass media outlets (like Yahoo Finance). Moreover, the recent availability of summary ESG rating information on media outlets like Yahoo Finance has made ESG ratings available to a wider audience.

> ESG ratings impact financial decisions. They can play a role in determining whether an investor buys a company's stock, whether a stock is included in an exchange-traded fund, and even whether a supplier bids for a contract or a consumer buys a company's services or products.

---

1. Christina Wong & Erika Petroy, *Rate the Raters 2020: Investor Survey and Interview Results*, SustainAbility (2020).

ESG ratings impact financial decisions. They can play a role in determining whether an investor buys a company's stock, whether a stock is included in an exchange-traded fund, and even whether a supplier bids for a contract or a consumer buys a company's services or products. Ratings are also used to determine if bonds or loans qualify as sustainable, which could lead to lower interest rates.

But ESG ratings are not perfect. They are criticized for being overly dependent on information published publicly or provided directly by the company being assessed. This is problematic because companies with challenging ESG issues are more likely to make their ESG efforts known publicly (and are more likely to describe such efforts in a positive light) than companies with minimal ESG issues. Further, companies with the resources to produce better ESG disclosures, or located in jurisdictions with more stringent ESG disclosure requirements like the European Union, may receive higher ratings than peer companies with fewer resources or those that are located in countries without stringent requirements like the United States. For example, in 2018, Sustainalytics, a Morningstar, Inc Company and one of the best-known rating companies, rated Germany's BMW better than the electric car company Tesla.[2] This was not because of how Tesla was conducting its business but because its disclosures were not viewed by Sustainalytics as sufficiently robust.[3]

Moreover, the use of diverse methodologies means that a company may get a high ESG rating from one rater and a low ESG rating from another. In 2018, Bank of America was rated "below average" by RepRisk AG (RepRisk), but "well above average" by Sustainalytics.[4] In addition, what may be considered a mistake in the analysis of the data could result in a low ESG rating. In 2018, Barrick Gold was so dissatisfied with the rating it obtained from MSCI Inc. (MSCI) that it issued a statement challenging the score. Barrick outlined five concerns with MSCI's analysis and methodology. In the company's view, the report presented a retrospective view of the company that overemphasized perceived public controversies and resulted in a distorted and misleading assessment of Barrick's ESG performance.[5] In particular, Barrick challenged MSCI's conclusion that "no areas of substantial strengths in managing material risks or capitalizing on growth opportunities are identified for this company," a statement Barrick contends is objectively false, misleading, and contradictory to the strengths MSCI itself identified in the report.

Types of ESG Rating Providers

One way to categorize ESG rating providers is by their objectives, data sources, and coverage. Based on this categorization, there are three types of ESG rating providers: (i) fundamental or market, (ii) comprehensive or ESG exclusive, and (iii) specialists.[6]

---

2. Timothy Doyle, *The Big Problem with "Environmental, Social And Governance" Investment Ratings? They are Subjective*, Invest. Bus. Daily, Aug. 9, 2018.

3. James Mackintosh, *Is Tesla or Exxon More Sustainable? It Depends Whom You Ask,* Wall Street J., Sept. 2019; Kate Allen, *Lies, Damned Lies and ESG Rating Methodologies*, Financ. Times, Dec. 6, 2018.

4. Doyle, *supra* note 2.

5. Barrick Gold, *Response to MSCI ESG Rating Report* (Sept. 2018).

6. Elise Douglas et al., *Responsible Investing: Guide to ESG Data Providers and Relevant Trends*, 8 J. Environ. Invest. 95 (2017).

Fundamental or market data providers collect publicly available data to characterize market trends and circulate information to users in a systematic way.[7] These providers offer analytical tools to investors to understand better trends and investment performance of covered companies.[8] All market data providers now offer some sort of ESG data as a subset of their products and services. Examples of market providers and their products include Bloomberg's ESG Disclosure Score, MSCI's ESG Rating and FTSE Russell's ESG Rating. Institutional investors, portfolio managers, and analysts are the target audience and are typically available for a hefty price through each provider's research portal or terminal.[9]

Comprehensive or ESG-exclusive providers focus solely on ESG matters. Each comprehensive provider uses its own research methodology and a combination of objective and subjective data covering all ESG market segments to analyze and assess corporate sustainability performance.[10] Examples of comprehensive providers include Corporate Knights, EcoVadis, Institutional Shareholder Services Corporate Rating, Refinitiv, RobecoSAM, Sustainalytics, and TruValue Labs. The principal users of the ratings provided by these providers are investors, companies, and the general public. Of these providers, the general public has the easiest access to scores provided by Sustainalytics, which are available on Yahoo Finance. Corporate Knight's Global 100, an annual ranking of the 100 most sustainable publicly listed companies in the world based on publicly disclosed data, is also available for free online.[11]

Specialist providers specialize in a particular ESG issue, such as carbon scores, gender diversity, or human rights.[12] For example, Equileap scores companies on gender equality, whereas the Carbon Disclosure Project produces the Climate Performance Score and the Climate Disclosure score, which focuses on climate issues. A wide range of investors (i.e., pension funds, investment banks, asset managers, etc.) use specialty ESG providers to overcome a particular issue facing a company. For example, to address concerns raised by the #MeToo movement, investors can use Equileap to distinguish top-performing companies on gender diversity from companies that scored poorly on sexism and harassment.

Due to the quickly developing ESG space, the line between provider types is constantly changing and even blurring. Alliances continue to be struck between market providers and ESG raters.[13] Over the past decade, the ESG rating agency market has undergone a phase of significant growth as well as consolidation. Not only have new financial rating and information providers entered the market, but established financial providers have acquired

---

7. Feifei Li & Ari Polychronopoulos, *What a Difference an ESG Ratings Provider Makes!*, Research Affiliates (Jan. 2020).

8. Douglas et al., *supra* note 6.

9. MSCI is one of the few market providers that publish its rating of 2,800+ companies on its website, which can be accessed for free.

10. Elena Escrig-Olmedo et al., *Rating the Raters: Evaluating How ESG Rating Agencies Integrate Sustainability Principles*, Sustainability, Feb. 2019, at 3, 915.

11. Corporate Knights, *The 2020 Global 100: Overview of Corporate Knights Rating Methodology* (Oct. 7, 2019).

12. Li & Polychronopoulos, *supra* note 7.

13. RepRisk is integrated with FTSE Russell and RobecoSAM's ratings. ISS partnered with RepRisk to incorporate additional governance issues in their analysis. Douglas et al., *supra* note 6, at 99. BNY Mellon Investment Management partnered with Sustainalytics to offer ESG data to issuers. Betty Moy Huber & Michael Comstock, *ESG Reports and Ratings: What They Are, Why They Matter*, Harvard Law School Forum on Corporate Governance (July 27, 2017).

many of the early ESG raters.[14] Even traditional credit rating agencies have gotten on board. Standard and Poor (S&P), Fitch, and Moody's now offer some form of ESG research, ratings, or indices.[15]

The tables below summarize nine ESG ratings from fundamental or comprehensive providers.

Fundamental Providers

Bloomberg ESG Disclosure Score[16]	
Audience	Institutional investors, portfolio managers, and financial analysts
Sources	Direct sources only (i.e., annual reports, sustainability reports, company websites, and third-party research)
Description	Bloomberg rates companies annually based on their public disclosure of quantitative and policy-related ESG data. The score measures transparency instead of performance (i.e., the more information disclosed, the higher the disclosure score)
Scale	0.1–100
Scope	11,700+ publicly listed companies in 102 countries (84% of global market cap)
Methodology	The score covers 120 indicators, seven of which are considered essential (payroll, energy, greenhouse gasses, water, waste, employee turnover, and injury rate). At the time of this writing, Bloomberg has not made its full methodology publicly available online
Availability	Available to paying clients on the Bloomberg Terminal and as an enterprise data feed via Bloomberg Data License

FTSE Russell ESG Ratings[17]	
Audience	Investors, portfolio managers, and financial analysts
Sources	Company public disclosure is the singular data source
Description	This rating seeks to measure a company's exposure to and management of ESG issues
Scale	Absolute ESG Rating: 0.5–1 ESG Supersector ESG Rating: 1–100
Scope	7,200+ securities in 47 developed and emerging markets
Methodology	300+ indicators across 14 themes. Points are assigned per indicator met. The data is then grouped into the three ESG categories. A risk relative scoring method is used, where a company's exposure to each theme influences indicator applicability and weighting rather than taking a sector-only approach
Availability	Available to paying clients through the FTSE Russell Research Portal

---

14. Acquisitions include Thomson Reuters' 2009 acquisition of Asset4, the first provider of ESG data to investors; Bloomberg's 2009 acquisition of New Energy Finance, a news and data provider focused on carbon and clean energy; and ISS's 2015 acquisition of Ethix SRI Advisors, a socially responsible investing research firm. Huber & Comstock, *supra* note 13.

15. In 2019, S&P Global acquired RobecoSAM's ESG rating business, and Moody's acquired a majority stake in Vigeo Eiris, a specialty rater focused on environmental issues. Caleb Mutua & Jacqueline Poh, *Moody's, S&P Race Into ESG Ratings Space with Acquisitions*, Bloomberg News, Nov. 22, 2019.

16. Bloomberg Professional Services, *ESG Data Coverage*; Huber & Comstock, *supra* note 13.

17. FTSE Russell, *ESG Ratings and Data Model: Integrating ESG into Investments* (2020).

MSCI ESG Ratings[18]	
Audience	Institutional investors, portfolio managers, and financial analysts
Sources	Publicly available government, regulatory and nongovernmental organization (NGO) data sets, company disclosure, and 2,100 media sources
Description	This rating aims to identify ESG risks or opportunities facing a company and its industry. The overall ESG rating relative to industry peers consists of issue scores and weights
Scale	CCC to AAA
Scope	7,500+ companies and 650,000+ equity and fixed-income securities
Methodology	MSCI analyzes 1000+ data points on ESG policies, programs, and performance, on both exposure and management metrics. Each year, 37 key issues are selected for each industry and weighted using MSCI's framework
Availability	• Used to construct the 1,500+ MSCI ESG Indexes, making MSCI the largest provider of ESG ratings[19] • Ratings for 2,800 companies are available for free at MSCI.com

Fundamental/ESG-Exclusive

Refinitiv ESG Scores[20]	
Audience	Institutional investors, portfolio managers, and financial analysts
Sources	Verifiable reported data from the public domain (e.g., annual reports, NGO websites, corporate social responsibility (CSR) reports, company websites, SEC filings, news sources)
Description	Refinitiv's ESG score is a reflection of a company's sustainability performance, commitment, and effectiveness, and its ESG Combined score overlays the ESG score with ESG controversies to track a company's sustainability impact and conduct over time
Scale	Percentages and letter grades (D– to A+)
Scope	Nearly 9,000 companies since 2002 across 87 countries
Methodology	Analysts manually process 450+ ESG data points, of which 186 are considered material and comparable per industry. These are then grouped into ten themes (resource use, emissions, innovation, workforce, human rights, community, product responsibility, management, shareholders, and CSR strategy), producing three pillar ESG categories and an overall score. For E and S, the scores are based on relative performance of ESG factors within the company's sector. For G, the scores are based on relative performance in the country of incorporation
Availability	Available for purchase on Eikon, Microsoft Excel add-in, Datastream, and via Datastream Data Loader QA Direct and QA Point

18. MSCI ESG Research, *MSCI ESG Ratings Methodology* (Sept. 2019).
19. Kelly Mumford, *Reporting and Disclosing Corporate ESG & Sustainability Result-Key Resources Roundup,* G&A Institute (June 16, 2020).
20. Refinitiv, *Environmental, Social and Governance (ESG) Scores from Refinitiv* (Apr. 2020).

ESG-Exclusive

EcoVadis CSR Rating[21]	
Audience	Companies wishing to take sustainability into account in purchasing decisions and/or leverage their ESG rating over industry peers
Sources	Online questionnaire, company-provided supporting documentation, third-party endorsements, training materials, and external sources (NGOs, local authorities, regulatory bodies, auditors, trade unions, etc.). Also offers site audits performed by third-party organizations
Description	This rating measures the quality of a company's CSR management system by evaluating the company's policies, actions, and results
Scale	0–100
Scope	65,000 companies in 160 countries across 200 industries[22]
Methodology	Bases its methodology on seven principles. It considers 21 CSR criteria that are grouped into four themes (environment, labor & human rights, ethics, and sustainable procurement). Each of the three management layers carries a particular weight (25%—policies, 40%—actions, and 35%—reporting) and is separated into seven management indicators. Each indicator is assigned a score between 0 and 100. A theme score is based on the scores of each indicator and their relative weight. The overall score is a weighted average of the four theme scores
Availability	Companies can subscribe for a period of one or three years across various price points. Each company receives a scorecard that it can share with multiple customers at their discretion, but scores are not available publicly

ISS-Oekem Corporate Rating[23]	
Audience	Institutional investors, portfolio managers, and financial analysts
Sources	Analyst collects information from media and other public sources, the companies being rated, interviews with stakeholders, and from third-party experts
Description	The ESG rating assesses a company's sustainability performance on best-in-class basis. Each rating is accompanied by an analyst's opinion on key results across three dimensions of sustainability opportunities, sustainability risks, and governance
Scale	D– to A+
Scope	6,300 issuers
Methodology	The performance assessment draws from a pool of 800+ indicators, 90% of which are sector-specific. The rating structure provides different weights at the topic level and for each pillar (environment, social, and governance) depending on the industry. For each industry, four to five key issues, representing more than 50% of the overall weight in any rating, are identified. Also carries out negative screening in controversial business fields and practices
Availability	Available via the ISS DataDesk and FactSet for a fee

---

21. EcoVadis, *EcoVadis CSR Methodology Overview and Principles* (Aug. 3, 2020).

22. https://www.EcoVadis.com.

23. ISS-Oekom, *Methodology: ISS-Oekom Corporate Rating* (2018).

RobecoSAM Corporate Sustainability Assessment (CSA)[24]	
Audience	Institutional asset owners and financial intermediaries
Sources	Information is provided by each company directly through the annual CSA, an online industry-specific questionnaire. Also uses third-party sources such as news articles and stakeholder commentaries from NGOs
Description	The RobecoSAM CSA, now issued by S&P Global, identifies companies more likely to outperform their industry peers due to their ESG best practices
Scale	0–100
Scope	The largest 3,500 publicly traded companies are invited to complete a CSA. 3,400+ other companies are invited to participate for inclusion in regional and country-specific ESG indices
Methodology	Each question receives a score from 0 to 100, which is weighted and grouped into broader areas called criteria. For some criteria, a Media & Stakeholder Analysis is applied to adjust scores downward based on the scope of negative impact stemming from a controversial event. Criteria scores are weighted, summed, and grouped into dimensions (economic, environmental, and social). Dimension values are weighted and summed to find the overall sustainability score
Availability	This rating serves as the research backbone of the Dow Jones Sustainability Indices (DJSI). The top 10% of companies in each industry are included in the DJSI World. The top 15% of companies are included in RobecoSAM's annual Sustainability Yearbook, available for free.
Sustainalytics Company ESG Risk Ratings[25]	
Audience	Investors, credit providers, pension funds, and asset managers
Sources	Publicly available information and direct engagement with companies
Description	Measures a company's unmanaged risks (i.e., material ESG risks that have not been managed by the company) and comprises a quantitative score and a risk category.
Scale	100–0 (100 being the *highest risk*)
Scope	12,000+ companies across 138 subindustries
Methodology	Sustainalytics uses 450 fields and 220+ indicators divided into three themes: environmental, social, and governance. Three building blocks inform a company's overall risk rating: corporate governance, material ESG issues, and idiosyncratic issues. The rating is composed of two scores: exposure and management. The exposure score measures vulnerability to risks, whereas the management score reflects a company's ability to manage such risks
Availability	A snapshot is available for free on Sustainalytics' website and Yahoo Finance. Can also be accessed through Global Access, Datafeeds for a fee.

24. RobecoSAM, *Measuring Intangibles: RobecoSAM's Corporate Sustainability Assessment Methodology* (Sept. 2018).
25. Sustainalytics, *The ESG Risk Ratings: Methodology-Abstract Version* 2.0 (Nov. 2019).

TruValue Labs Insight360 Scores[26]	
Audience	Asset owners, portfolio managers, analysts, financial advisors, consultants, and quants
Sources	100,000+ online sources of publicly available information
Description	Provides an overall score and sustainability trends over time, as well as specific performance for individual categories. Includes positive and negative events. Claims to be the first company to use artificial intelligence to gather ESG data
Scale	0–100
Scope	16,000+ companies
Methodology	Uses artificial intelligence to "read" articles and categorize items. The Standard Edition has 14 categories (anticompetitive behavior, business model, corporate governance, data security & privacy, atmosphere, land, water, human capital, marketing practices, political influence, product integrity & innovation, social impact, supply chain, and sustainable energy use & production), and the Sustainability Accounting Standards Board (SASB) Edition uses SASB standards. Positive stories receive a score above 50 and negatives stories score below 50
Availability	Only available to customers of TruValue Labs

The Divergence of ESG Ratings

Due to the high number and variety of rating providers, and the difference in number of indicators used and sources of data, there is a lack of correlation and consistency in ratings from different providers. This lack of correlation and inconsistency can lead to one company being given a top rating by one provider and a below-average rating by another as described above.[27] For example, in 2017, one provider gave Wells Fargo a 0.84 (a good score), while another gave it a 0.31 (an abysmal score).[28]

In May 2020, researchers at MIT Sloan School of Management published the results of an investigation into the divergence of sustainability ratings based on data from six raters. The authors identified three principal reasons why ratings from different providers disagree: scope divergence, measurement divergence, and weight divergence.[29]

Scope divergence occurs when ratings are based on different attributes. One provider may include clean energy while another might not, causing the ratings to diverge. Divergence in measurement occurs when different indicators are used to measure the same attribute. For example, a company's clean energy practices could be evaluated on the basis of "minimizing environmental impacts from energy use" or by "carbon intensity." Both capture aspects of the attribute of clean energy, but not in the same way. Divergence in weight occurs where raters define the relative importance of attributes differently. For example, for one provider, the score for "business ethics incidents" could make up 20% of the aggregate governance score calculation, while another provider assigns it minimal

---

26. TruValue Labs, *The New Fundamentals* (Nov. 2018).
27. Jacqueline Poh, *Conflicting ESG Ratings Are Confusing Sustainable Investors*, BLOOMBERG NEWS, Dec. 11, 2019.
28. Li & Polychronopoulos, *supra* note 7.
29. Florian Berg et al., *Aggregate Confusion: The Divergence of ESG Ratings*, MIT – SLOAN SCHOOL OF MANAGEMENT (May 17, 2020).

weight. Wells Fargo's score of zero in 2017 from one provider for too many "business ethics incidents" helped lower their overall governance score from that provider for that year.

Users of rating data, particularly directors and managers, should pay close attention to the underlying data (i.e., attributes and indicators) behind a rating and how this underlying data is weighted. Without a comprehensive understanding of these different biases, directors and managers will have a difficult time determining which ratings best align with their company's investment objectives.

ESG Disclosure and How ESG Ratings Are Used

Rating providers argue that their main challenge is the lack of consistency in ESG disclosure by the companies and that their systems will improve significantly if companies worldwide are forced to report ESG data under specified frameworks.[30] Corporate disclosure is important because ESG raters create their ratings based primarily on publicly available information. The terms used in a company's ESG disclosure can affect how the information is scored. If a term is missing, it will not be scored well or at all. If a company describes an activity as a practice, versus a policy, the analyst, depending on which one, may give it a lower score. Companies that include the "right" terms may end up scoring higher based on the quality of their disclosure, not what they are doing to address ESG issues.

Stakeholders look for ESG rating providers that can aggregate a company's nonfinancial ESG disclosure, published at different times and on different platforms, and present such disclosure in a comparable and standardized format. These stakeholders, however, use ESG ratings differently. ESG ratings may not reflect a stakeholder's priorities or areas of focus at a particular time.

For investors, ratings are a quick way to assess how sustainably a company operates, the robustness of its disclosure, and how it compares to its peers. According to SustainAbility,[31] investors that do not have the capability to do research internally or lack ESG expertise tend to rely more on ratings, and many investors use ratings to complement their internal research. Ratings can identify risks or untapped opportunities. For example, in its rating of Volkswagen and Fiat, Sustainalytics flagged governance issues prior to the diesel emission scandal.[32] Asset managers include ratings in their valuations models and can use ratings to build investment products or to show that their existing products are sustainable. Finally, ESG ratings can be used by investors to make voting decisions. Proxy advisory firms increasingly incorporate ESG factors in their voting recommendations.

Investors in the debt capital markets also use ESG ratings when investing in sustainability bonds. According to Moody's, global issuances of sustainable bonds totaled $99.9 billion in the second quarter of 2020, a 65% increase from the first three months of 2020.[33] Credit rating agencies and accounting firms are among the list of verifiers for institutions involved

---

30. Poh, *supra* note 27.

31. Wong & Petroy, *supra* note 1, at 17.

32. Silda Wall Spitzer & John Mandyck, *What Boards Need to Know About Sustainability Ratings*, HARV. BUS. REV., May 2019.

33. Moody's Investor Service, *Research–Sustainable Bond Issuance Hits Record High in Q2 as Social Bonds Surge* (Aug. 17, 2020). In its report, Moody's forecasted that total sustainable bond issuance in 2020 could reach $325 billion to $375 billion.

in sustainability bond financings, but environmental consultancies and research institutes are increasingly becoming involved as well.[34]

ESG ratings are also used by lenders to incentivize borrowers to perform more sustainably. As ESG ratings are integrated into the credit analysis, companies with higher ESG ratings may be able to borrow at lower interest rates. In cases where borrowers demonstrate their internal capability to support their performance as measured against agreed sustainability performance targets, engagement of an independent rating provider may not be necessary. However, in cases where an external rater is required, engagement of the rater is agreed by the institutions participating in the loan and such rater reviews the borrower's performance at least once a year. According to Bloomberg Law, as of June 2019, ESG ratings affected the price borrowers paid on approximately US$32 billion of loans worldwide, up from US$3 billion in 2017.[35] In 2019, Moody's, S&P, and Fitch announced initiatives to add an ESG score to their traditional assessments of creditworthiness.

Finally, good ESG ratings could encourage consumers that are sustainability-minded to purchase a company's products or services. They can be a factor in a company's supply chain if manufacturers and other supply-chain parties impose sustainable practices for suppliers. For employees, a high ESG rating may be a source of pride and engagement.[36]

Take-Aways for Board Members

- Ensure that your company's ESG disclosure is clear and comprehensive, and reflects how ESG risks are being managed. Good disclosure equals better ratings.

- Know which ESG rating providers are rating your company. Work with management to ensure that the ratings reflect your company's ESG performance.

- Engage with management and the relevant ESG rating provider to correct any material mistakes in the ESG rating.

- Understand how your corporate stakeholders use ESG ratings, and prepare to engage directly with large institutional investors wishing to discuss your company's ESG ratings.

- Develop internal expertise to validate your company's performance in financing transactions, and disclosure of such expertise to institutions involved can reduce costs of engaging an external reviewer.

---

34. Kate Allen, *Boom in Green Bonds Attracts Green Rating Agencies*, FINANC. TIMES, May 13, 2018.
35. Jacqueline Poh, *ESG Ratings Face Skepticism Even as Loan-Market Importance Grows*, BLOOMBERG NEWS, June 4, 2019.
36. Spitzer & Mandyck, *supra* note 32.

Chapter 17
Litigation and Risk Management

Peter P. Tomczak

Lawsuits about sustainability and environmental, social, and governance (ESG) issues—collectively referred to here as "ESG litigation"—both directly and indirectly influence companies' abilities and incentives to offer particular products and services, or even adopt certain business models. This is unsurprising, as all forms of litigation influence corporate conduct to a certain extent. But as explained below, ESG litigation presents unique, significant challenges for directors tasked with setting corporate strategy and creating long-term value for corporate stakeholders. Directors therefore must recognize and oversee the management of heightened legal risks arising from ESG litigation.

This chapter highlights how ESG litigation impacts the core missions and models of corporations. The current, rapid evolution of an exponentially increasing amount of ESG litigation has been caused in part by the changing legal landscape and sheer diversity and number of newly adopted ESG laws and regulations, both in the United States and internationally (see Chapters 8 and 13). Private plaintiffs are targeting what they assert are corporate failures to meet corporations' own policies and pronouncements and specific substantive legal standards that are addressed in greater detail in later chapters of this book, such as climate change (see Chapters 8, 15, and 20), energy and water use (see Chapter 20), and human rights and capital in the global supply chain (see Chapter 19). Equally important as the volume and variety of ESG litigation is how novel legal theories are being used to pursue sustainability and ESG goals. Plaintiffs are grounding their claims in legal obligations explored in earlier chapters of this book, such as directors' duties for sustainability (see Chapter 4) and securities disclosure laws (see Chapters 14–15), in addition to bringing consumer fraud and common law claims, among other causes of action.

The specific legal risks from ESG litigation vary greatly across industries, companies, company cultures, and business models. However, directors will enhance their ability to oversee ESG litigation by applying a general framework that examines each of the multiple forms of ESG litigation. Directors then may better identify, scope, and evaluate their corporations' respective legal risk profiles and, exercising their business judgment, implement certain practices to oversee more effectively legal risk from ESG litigation. By doing so, conscientious and talented directors will continue to create long-term value for all stakeholders.

The Unique Challenges of ESG Litigation

Litigation affects directors' decisions regarding what business strategies can and should be pursued. At a basic level, litigation alters the expected and actual benefits of engaging in certain commercial activities. All forms of litigation cause defendant corporations to incur costs, in the form of legal expenses plus any monetary and nonmonetary consequences of a judgment or settlement. This internalization of costs associated with the business conduct at issue in the litigation makes engaging in that conduct more expensive and, all else being equal, less appealing.

Beyond merely altering the benefits of engaging in certain economic activities, litigation may preclude a corporation from offering certain products and services. There are many different ways for corporations to make a profit, but they must result from "lawful business" conducted through "lawful acts." As ESG principles increasingly evolve from aspirational goals to legal requirements, they may create a basis to restrict corporate conduct, including ultimately through litigation by private parties or enforcement by governmental authorities.

ESG litigation presents several distinct challenges for corporations and their leadership. As an initial matter, within the basic framework described above, ESG litigation may substantially increase the costs associated with certain activities and products. As is apparent from the summary set out in this book (see *infra*, Chapter 13), the sheer volume and complexity of newly adopted legislation and regulation targeting sustainability and ESG issues, and intense focus on them by consumers and society (and the plaintiffs' bar, prosecutors, and regulators), has resulted in more ESG litigation. Recent waves of ESG litigation have targeted corporations' alleged contributions to anthropomorphic climate change, use of non-recyclable plastic materials, lack of diversity in their director and officer ranks, and complicity in human trafficking and slavery. Creative plaintiffs' lawyers have repurposed traditional claims, such as consumer fraud, to challenge business both in parallel with or in lieu of substantive ESG regulation of such conduct. Moreover, as sustainability and ESG principles become implemented in laws and regulation, directors increasingly have become the target of fiduciary duty claims alleging that they failed to exercise adequate oversight in light of their corporations' failures to comply with such legal requirements.[1]

ESG litigation also may entail complexities in measuring damages and awarding monetary relief. Many sustainability and ESG laws and regulations, and ensuing ESG litigation, seek to force defendant corporations to recognize and pay for costs experienced by

---

1. See *supra* Ch. 4(I)(B) (discussing directors' fiduciary duties of oversight and the interplay between those duties and sustainability and principles) and *infra* §II(C) (discussing governance-based ESG litigation).

uninvolved third parties (negative externalities), many of which previously may not have been captured and allocated by the legal system. Plaintiffs in ESG litigation also increasingly seek to hold corporations liable for their public statements about ESG or their global supply chain business partners' conduct. Traditional strategies to mitigate risk and cost may be ineffective. For example, insurance may not yet be available to mitigate the costs of nascent sustainability and ESG claims. Business combinations and acquisitions also may not reduce exposure to an industry-wide or worldwide problem.

The real importance of ESG litigation transcends such simple cost–benefit analysis. ESG laws and litigation may directly prohibit previously legal activities that form the basis of a corporation's core business strategy, competitive advantage or global reputation. One of the most visible examples of this is climate change regulation and litigation. As BlackRock CEO Larry Fink presaged in his 2021 letter to CEOs, "There is no company whose business model won't be profoundly affected by the transition to a net zero economy...." More than 1,000 lawsuits involving the alleged consequences of climate change had already been filed in the United States by 2019,[2] and one report tallied 1,587 climate change litigation cases having been filed globally (76% of which were filed in the United States) between 1986 and July 2020.[3] Notably, on May 26, 2021, the District Court of The Hague rendered a groundbreaking judgment that ordered a company to change its corporate policies to comply with "universally accepted" carbon dioxide emission reduction targets and, for the corporate defendant in that case, reduce its various types of carbon dioxide emissions by net 45% (compared to 2019 levels) by 2030.[4] That judgment is subject to appeal but, regardless of its ultimate outcome, it makes clear the profound risks arising from ESG litigation. Directors now must consider how anticipated regulation and litigation of their contribution to climate change will increase the costs of their corporations' business models or outright prohibit existing commercial operations. In this and other areas, however, directors may be unsure how to reconcile potentially competing mandates, especially when seeking to comply with sustainability and ESG legal rules adopted by multiple international jurisdictions.

Nor is ESG litigation simply about maximizing monetary recoveries. A plaintiff's goal in filing a lawsuit may be to stop the underlying conduct, either by rendering the activity economically unfeasible or by having a court enjoin its continuation. Indeed, the plaintiff in the case that resulted in the May 26, 2021 decision by the District Court of The Hague noted above has publicly announced its intention to commence conversations with other companies toward having them reduce their carbon dioxide emissions. Alternatively, a plaintiff may be motivated to expose publicly the true nature of or costs associated with a corporation's business operations. ESG litigation may also support other legal and business strategies such as waging a proxy fight to remove directors, passing shareholder resolutions, convincing regulators and legislators to enact legal rules, damaging a corporation's

2. See Veena Ramani & Hannah Saltman, *Running the Risks: How Corporate Boards Can Oversee Environmental, Social and Governance Issues* (Nov. 25, 2019), https://corpgov.law.harvard.edu/2019/11/25/running-the-risks-how -corporate-boards-can-oversee-environmental-social-and-governance-issues/.
3. See Joana Setzer & Rebecca Byrnes, *Global Trends in Climate Change Litigation: 2020 Snapshot* (July 2020), https://www.lse.ac.uk/granthaminstitute/wp-content/uploads/2020/07/Global-trends-in-climate-change -litigation_2020-snapshot.pdf.
4. Milieudefensie a.o. v. Royal Dutch Shell plc, C/09/571932/HA ZA 19-379 (engelse versie) (Rechtbank Den Haag 2021).

global brand, or convincing consumers to boycott products, until the corporation changes its behavior.

By its frequency, complexity, direct relevance to fundamental business strategy, and underlying motivations, ESG litigation presents heightened legal risks to corporations. Directors should consider the potential risks and costs created by ESG litigation in devising corporate strategies and managing the business and affairs of the corporations they serve. That task is more easily advised than accomplished. The true legal risk from ESG litigation will depend on many factors and is unique to the corporation, its industry, business model, products, services, and culture. As with other complex decisions made by boards of directors, directors should first gather and consider all reasonably available facts, relying on the opinions and reports of both the corporation's management and outside expert advisers, about the corporation's particular exposure to ESG litigation.

> ESG litigation presents heightened risks to corporation by its frequency, complexity, direct relevance to fundamental business strategy, and underlying motivations of plaintiffs.

Categories of ESG Litigation, and a Framework for Assessing Legal Risk from ESG Litigation

Businesses are beset with an ever-increasing amount and variety of ESG litigation. Undoubtedly, sustainability or ESG issues are themselves expansively defined and understood to include, among other things, climate change, pollution, environmental degradation, racism, food safety, support for authoritarian states' monitoring of their citizens, sustainable farming, animal husbandry, human slavery and trafficking, human capital management, and diversity in board and senior management ranks (and some commentators would also add technology, cybersecurity, and employee and labor relations). But the increase in ESG litigation is not driven only by semantics. Market forces from consumer preferences to institutional investor expectations are causing companies to design and adopt sustainability and ESG principles as part of their corporate strategy, and communicate about them to all stakeholders. Simultaneously, ESG issues are more frequently being addressed by new laws and regulations. This confluence of market and legal trends means more activities subject to more legal regulation, which in the United States and many other jurisdictions is a recipe for more litigation.

The upsurge in ESG litigation is also attributable to the resourcefulness of the plaintiffs' bar to use new causes of action and repurpose existing theories of liability. Currently, ESG litigation predominantly comes in three forms:

- *Disclosure-based ESG litigation*—a company's statements about an ESG issue are challenged for allegedly being misleading or deceptive.
- *Conduct-based ESG litigation*—a company's underlying activities are directly challenged for allegedly violating a law addressing an ESG issue.
- *Governance-based ESG litigation*—a company's leadership is challenged for allegedly failing to satisfy fiduciary duties and other obligations attendant to its role

in managing the business and affairs of the business enterprise with respect to an ESG issue.

Any of these forms of litigation may entail "bet the company" monetary and nonmonetary relief, including large damage awards, injunctive relief to cease business practices or conform economic activities to legal standards, reputational damage to relationships with various corporate stakeholders, and significant managerial distraction. The prevalence and importance of ESG litigation is further magnified by the availability of class action procedural devices.

> Directors should ask corporate management to evaluate and report on the corporation's exposure to disclosure-based, conduct-based, and governance-based ESG litigation, as well as related litigation risks.

Each company's exposure to risks arising from ESG litigation is contextual. Nevertheless, the categories above provide a framework for directors to oversee their corporations' risk management with respect to, and evaluate the various legal risks arising from, ESG litigation. As shown below, plaintiffs have filed lawsuits in every one of these categories to address what they believe are the failures of corporations to adhere to sustainability and ESG principles. Directors thus should ask responsible corporate management to evaluate and report on the corporation's exposure to ESG litigation in each of these three dimensions.

Disclosure-Based ESG Litigation

Disclosure-based ESG litigation represents an already significant and still growing legal risk to both public and private companies. Because of the importance of sustainability and ESG principles to all corporate stakeholders, many companies voluntarily publicize statements and information about their commitment to tackle sustainability and ESG issues in their business through a variety of channels, including in SEC filings, glossy sheet CSR reports, websites, product labels, and marketing campaigns. Corporate goals and policies have become more ambitious with respect to ESG issues. Disclosure-based ESG litigation generally makes these crucial communications riskier.

In the United States, disclosure-based ESG litigation to date has been pursued primarily under federal and state securities laws, and state consumer protection and consumer fraud laws. The essence of these claims is that the company misstated or misled the relevant audience on its sustainability and ESG strategy or activities; as such, plaintiffs may pursue disclosure-based claims without showing a violation or even the existence of laws directly regulating the underlying conduct at issue. Unsurprisingly, disclosure-based ESG litigation is often an initial litigation battleground for the imposition of liability relating to sustainability and ESG issues.

Securities Law Disclosure Claims

Companies whose securities trade publicly in the United States have experienced a significant rise in the number of claims asserting that statements by those companies about their sustainability and ESG efforts violated U.S. federal and state securities laws. The legal landscape for sustainability and ESG disclosures was discussed at length in Chapters 14 (public company mandatory reporting) and 15 (voluntary reporting). Laws and rules have been sporadically passed requiring disclosure of specific ESG issues, such as conflict minerals and select climate change disclosures. In the first six months of 2021, contemplated legislation and rulemaking by the U.S. Congress and U.S. Securities and Exchange Commission, respectively, would seek to establish more standardized disclosure of sustainability and ESG information. Suffice to say, in the first half of 2021 in the United States, there is no mandatory comprehensive disclosure regime under U.S. securities laws pursuant to which public companies must report sustainability and ESG information. Nevertheless, because of the commercial importance of communicating its ESG strategy to stakeholders, businesses choose to disclose sustainability and ESG information in published reports, media releases, and on company websites. These statements and omissions by public companies both in and outside of public securities filings may give rise to liability under U.S. federal and state securities laws.

Plaintiffs often file disclosure-based claims under U.S. federal securities laws in the wake of catastrophes or scandals and resulting substantial drops in a company's stock price. Many ESG litigation securities fraud claims allege violations of the antifraud provisions of the U.S. federal securities laws, in particular Section 10(b) of the Securities Exchange Act of 1934, as amended, and Rule 10b-5 promulgated thereunder. Under the SEC's Rule 10b-5, it is unlawful, in connection with the purchase and sale of a security, to make any untrue statement of material fact or to omit to state a material fact necessary in order to render statements made not misleading. Private plaintiffs seeking to establish liability generally must prove that: the defendant made a material misstatement or omission; the defendant did so with an intent to deceive, manipulate, or defraud; there is a connection between that misstatement or omission and the purchase or sale of a security; they relied on the misstatement (which is presumed with omissions); and there was reliance, causation, and economic loss.

> Many cases deciding whether an ESG disclosure is actionable under the federal securities laws have hinged on whether the alleged misstatement was sufficiently factual and measurable, as opposed to being generalized and aspirational.

A key element of any securities law claim challenging the accuracy of a disclosure is materiality. A stated or omitted fact is "material" if there is a substantial likelihood that a "reasonable investor" would view that fact as important in the decision to buy or sell the security, or the total mix of information as having been significantly altered if that fact were to be disclosed. Significant in the context of ESG litigation, sufficiently vague and aspirational statements by reporting companies are often deemed to be incapable of being relied on by a reasonable investor. Indeed, many cases deciding whether a statement or disclosure about sustainability or ESG is actionable have hinged on whether the alleged misstatement was sufficiently factual and measurable as opposed to generalized and aspirational.

The difference between actionable concrete disclosures and non-actionable puffery is a close call, which may be influenced by where the alleged misstatement occurred. A brief review of case law demonstrates just how narrow is this distinction. Courts have held that alleged misstatements about sustainability or ESG were merely aspirational, and have dismissed plaintiffs' claims. For example, a U.S. federal district court dismissed securities fraud claims challenging statements by YUM! Brands, Inc., in its Code of Conduct and during earnings calls about its commitment to food safety in light of reports that the company knew of the presence of drug and antibiotic residue in its chicken, which allegedly caused a 17% drop in the company's stock price. As the court explained, "[t]o treat a corporate code of conduct as a statement of what a corporation will do, rather than what a corporation aspires to do, would turn the purpose of a code of conduct on its head."[5] Following the revelation of a widespread bribery scheme involving the former senior corporate officers of Braskem S.A., plaintiffs filed securities fraud claims based on statements in the company's Code of Conduct, press releases, and sustainability reports about the company's ethics and values. The court dismissed those claims because the alleged misstatements were immaterial puffery, also with the Code of Conduct being a "particularly inapt candidate" to serve as a source of misstatements as "statements within such codes tend to be 'explicitly aspirational,'" with qualifying language reflecting this nature.[6] In a similar decision, a court held that alleged misstatements by Sanofi about the effectiveness of its corporate compliance program in the company's CSR report amounted to mere puffery, and dismissed the disclosure claims there.[7]

More recently, courts have dismissed a rash of lawsuits brought against companies and their boards of directors for alleged misstatements about their commitment to diversity. The complaints contained photos of directors and senior executives in an attempt to undermine visually the veracity of aspirational statements regarding diversity, equity, and inclusion. Many of these lawsuits were filed in California, whose Governor on September 30, 2020, signed into law a bill requiring publicly held companies headquartered in that state to have a minimum number of board members from underrepresented communities. A U.S. federal court on the opposite coast also dismissed claims asserting that statements by CBS Corp. about its commitment to a harassment-free workplace and the highest ethical standards were misleading in light of reported sexual misconduct and harassment by its CEO, finding that the statements at issue were too general and aspirational to justify reasonable reliance, and were otherwise not material.[8]

But in other cases, courts have agreed with plaintiffs in early procedural stages that their complaints sufficiently pleaded claims for violations of securities laws. A U.S. federal district court allowed certain claims brought against energy giant BP PLC in the wake of the 2010 Deepwater Horizon disaster to proceed beyond the motion to dismiss stage. The plaintiffs in that case challenged the accuracy of statements by BP in its annual reports, press releases, and sustainability reports concerning the efficacy and operation of its safety

---

5. Bondali v. Yum! Brands, Inc., 620 F. App'x 483, 490 (6th Cir. 2015).
6. *In re* Braskem S.A. Sec. Litig., 246 F. Supp. 3d 731, 755 (S.D.N.Y. 2017). (quoting City of Pontiac Policemen's & Firemen's Ret. Sys. v. UBS AG, 752 F.3d 173, 183 (2d Cir. 2014)).
7. *In re* Sanofi Sec. Litig., 155 F. Supp. 3d 386 (S.D.N.Y. 2016).
8. Construction Laborers Pension Tr. for S. Cal. v. CBS Corp., 433 F. Supp. 3d 515 (S.D.N.Y. 2020).

program, including statements by its CEO about the company's process safety program made after a previous refinery explosion. According to the plaintiffs, statements about the company's safety program were misleading because they emphasized the comprehensive nature of that program but failed to disclose it did not encompass sites owned by third parties, which included the Transocean-owned drilling unit at issue.[9] In another case that followed the deaths of 29 miners in a 2010 explosion, a court refused to dismiss securities fraud claims against Massey Energy Co. that focused on the company's pronouncements of its commitment to safety, which it made in part to restore its reputation with corporate stakeholders and regulators following another fatal mine accident 4 years earlier. That case settled with a payout to the plaintiff class of USD 265 million, plus more than USD 30 million in legal fees and costs. In May 2020, a U.S. federal district court declined to dismiss securities fraud claims brought by a class of investors against Vale SA that challenged the accuracy of statements by the company in its SEC filings and sustainability reports about the company's commitment to environmental, health, and safety issues after a 2019 dam failure resulted in the deaths of 259 people, with a substantial decline in the value of the company's American Depository Shares.[10] Significantly, liability for disclosure claims may extend to the directors and officers of the corporation, as shown by the court's denial of motions to dismiss plaintiffs' complaint challenging the accuracy of disclosures made by ExxonMobil Corp. about carbon proxy cost business strategy relating to climate change, noting the ExxonMobil directors' and officers' involvement in deliberations and discussions about those topics.[11]

The legal risk arising from securities fraud claims targeting similar alleged misstatements may be influenced going forward by a recent U.S. Supreme Court decision and further litigation of that case. On June 21, 2021, the Supreme Court issued its opinion in *Goldman Sachs Group v. Arkansas Teacher Retirement System*.[12] The plaintiff class of Goldman Sachs shareholders asserted that broad statements by Goldman Sachs—such as "Our clients' interests always come first"; "We are dedicated to complying fully with the letter and spirit of the laws, rules, and ethical principles that govern us"; and "Integrity and honesty are at the heart of our business"—were misleading in light of alleged conflicts of interest in certain transactions. The parties' dispute had "largely evaporated" by the time of the appeal to the Supreme Court as the plaintiffs conceded that more generic statements are less likely to affect a security's price. The Supreme Court ruling confirmed that, as such, the generic nature of an alleged misstatement may be considered as evidence in assessing any potential impact on share price at the critical class certification phase. The court remanded the case for further consideration of the generic nature of the statements at issue. The decision and ensuing litigation of the case on remand may make it more difficult for plaintiffs to bring federal securities claims for aspirational and generic statements—ones that public companies frequently make on a variety of sustainability and ESG topics.

The importance for companies to convey how their strategies and operations embrace sustainability and ESG issues has never been greater. The intense focus of multiple corporate stakeholders on these topics demands a proactive communication strategy. Yet, against this backdrop and as shown by the cases noted above and others, without adequate oversight

---

9. *In re* BP plc, 2013 U.S. Dist. LEXIS 17149 (S.D. Tex. 2013).

10. *In re* Vale S.A. Sec. Litig., 2020 U.S. Dist. LEXIS 91150 (S.D.N.Y. 2017).

11. Ramirez v. Exxon Mobil Corp., 334 F. Supp. 832 (N.D. Tex. 2018).

12. 141 S. Ct. 1951 (2021).

over ESG disclosures, sustainability and ESG failures may lead to being sued for securities fraud. Securities law disclosure claims continue to evolve. Potential seismic shifts, such as the anticipated establishment of a more comprehensive disclosure regime on sustainability and ESG issues and potential revisiting of the concepts of materiality and the "reasonable investor" that are the lynchpins of U.S. securities litigation, will only increase the risk of ESG litigation based on securities fraud claims. Finally, while the above discussion has focused on private securities fraud litigation, statements made throughout the initial months of 2021 by newly appointed SEC officials signal greater SEC enforcement targeting material misstatements and omissions on ESG issues.

Consumer Law Disclosure Claims

Plaintiffs in disclosure-based ESG litigation also have resorted to consumer protection and consumer fraud statutes, in particular those of California (e.g., the California Consumer Legal Remedies Act, the Unfair Competition Law, and the California Truth in Environmental Advertising Law), to assert that a company is liable for misleading consumers about sustainability and ESG issues. In consumer law disclosure claims, concepts of materiality and reliance remain important, even if they are not expressly identified as a specific element in a formal legal test.

Traditionally, plaintiff consumers focused on warranties and product labels, specifically whether representations thereon were deceptive by omission or affirmative inaccuracy. Claims that product labels were deceptive for omitting key facts have been more readily rejected by courts because, to be actionable, alleged omissions must be contrary to regulations or representations made or required to be made by companies. An underlying obligation to disclose sustainability and ESG information to consumers often does not exist, thereby precluding many consumer law disclosure claims in ESG litigation that are based on purported omissions.

In contrast, consumers have had greater success in attacking the accuracy of representations made on labels. An initial wave of litigation challenged labels that described products as "organic," "natural," "healthy," or similar characterizations. Plaintiffs also achieved mixed results in claiming that a label erroneously imparted a third party's approval or endorsement of a product. A U.S. federal district court in California held that references to "Greenlist Ingredients," which was actually a defendant-created index, were misleading, while a California state court held that a green-colored water drop on water bottles was not tantamount to a misrepresented seal of approval. More recently, courts have declined to dismiss claims by consumers that labels of "dolphin safe" tuna and "recyclable" plastic coffee pods were misleading. In a closely watched case, a California state court is evaluating whether a recycling symbol on plastic packaging is misleading in light of the significant, practical difficulties in recycling such plastic products and attendant harm to the environment.

> Plaintiffs now are looking beyond what is or is not on the product's label to general public statements, such as those in sustainability reports and on company websites, to assert consumer fraud and consumer protection claims. An important inquiry remains whether the alleged misstatements are sufficiently definite and factual as to be actionable.

Plaintiffs now are looking beyond what is or is not on the product's label, and drawing upon general public statements, such as those in sustainability reports and on company websites, as bases to assert consumer fraud and consumer protection claims. Highlighting this trend, a June 16, 2021 complaint filed in a California U.S. federal district court by the Sierra Club against multiple bottled water manufacturers alleged unlawful, unfair, and deceptive business practices amounting to "greenwashing" arising from the "100% Recyclable" representation affixed to single-use plastic bottles, as well as similar statements made on websites as part of defendants' national marketing campaigns on websites. An important issue still is whether the alleged misstatements are sufficiently definite and factual as to be actionable, or if they are aspirational and not likely to deceive or be relied on by a reasonable consumer. For example, plaintiffs claimed that the sustainability report (CSR) of dairy agricultural marketing cooperative Darigold, Inc., contained misstatements about, among other things, animal welfare, sustainable farming, and treatment of its workforce. The court in that case rejected the plaintiffs' claims, characterizing the company's statements as "aspirational" and "hav[ing] not been shown to be false in any material respect," such that they were not likely to deceive a reasonable consumer.[13] A U.S. federal district court in California dismissed consumer fraud and consumer protection claims against Nestlé USA, Inc., alleging that statements on its website were deceptively inaccurate because they failed to disclose that seafood in cat food was caught by small fishing boats that used forced labor. The court held that the statements at issue were aspirational and could not be reasonably relied on by consumers, even while acknowledging that other publicly available documents "set forth [Nestlé's] firm requirements for suppliers."[14]

In contrast, courts have allowed consumer fraud claims to proceed when the allegedly deceptive statement related to a verifiable fact. While dismissing certain claims based on statements by defendant retailers about labor performance which were determined to be aspirational in nature, the court in the same case allowed other claims based on those defendants' more detailed statements and statistics about auditing programs and their process could have influenced a reasonable consumer's decision and were actionable.[15] In light of a supplier's purported contamination of drinking water for a local community, plaintiffs challenged the accuracy of specific factual statements made by Chiquita Brands International, Inc., on its website about its environmentally friendly practices, which included descriptions of how the company reforested natural watercourses impacted by its operations, used solid waste traps at stations to avoid water pollution, and used natural plants instead of chemicals to control weeds. The court rejected Chiquita's motion to dismiss.[16] In another example, a court refused to dismiss a plaintiff's claim that Mary Kay cosmetics were, in fact, tested on animals to comply with Chinese market rules, thereby contravening the company's statements that it did not engage in animal testing.[17] The court's reasoning highlighted the reasons why consumer fraud claims are increasingly used to challenge company's representations about ESG:

---

13. Ruiz v. Darigold, Inc./Nw. Dairy Ass'n, 2014 U.S. Dist. LEXIS 155384, *10 (W.D. Wash. 2014).

14. Barber v. Nestlé USA, Inc., 154 F. Supp. 3d 954, 963–64 (C.D. Cal. 2015).

15. Nat'l Consumers League v. Wal-Mart Stores, Inc., 2016 WL 4080541 (D.C. Super. 2016).

16. Water & Sanitation Health, Inc. v. Chiquita Brands Int'l, Inc., 2014 U.S. Dist. LEXIS 70673 (W.D. Wash. 2014).

17. Stanwood v. Mary Kay, Inc., 941 F. Supp. 2d 1212 (C.D. Cal. 2012).

As consumers have grown more aware of the social, environmental, and political impact of their purchasing decisions, they have tended to look to more factors, including company-wide operations, to inform their consumption choices. Consumers receive this information from a variety of sources, but one of the most direct and important remains the company itself. Companies, realizing this, have tailored their marketing to such consumers. It should not be unexpected then, that when companies make misrepresentations about their company-wide operations, they face potential liability in court to consumers who relied on those representations in purchasing their products.[18]

The above cases and other lawsuits that continue to be filed demonstrate how private plaintiffs have creatively harnessed consumer protection and consumer fraud laws to address a wide variety of sustainability and ESG issues. The U.S. Federal Trade Commission (FTC) has also used U.S. federal consumer protection laws to remedy alleged misconduct involving sustainability and ESG issues. By way of example, in 2016, the FTC sued Volkswagen Group of America asserting that the automobile manufacturer deceived consumers in selling or leasing vehicles the company falsely represented as low emission or compliant with emission standards when, in fact, they were not. The FTC's claims were part of a USD 14.7 billion settlement that resolved similar claims by multiple government and state agencies and Attorneys General. The FTC also publishes its Green Guides, which provide general principles on environmental marketing claims towards helping companies ensure their product claims are truthful and non-deceptive. Though the number of claims brought by the FTC under its Green Guides have decreased over the past decade, private plaintiffs are now using alleged violations of the Green Guides as the basis for claims of deceptive practices and misleading disclosures.

Conduct-Based ESG Litigation

Laws enacted in both the United States and other international jurisdictions increasingly aim to regulate directly conduct that violates sustainability and ESG principles. From climate change to human rights violations, to bribery and corruption, these laws seek to prohibit practices and conduct that contribute to sustainability and ESG problems. Such conduct-based ESG litigation is linked to disclosure regimes, as laws mandating disclosure of sustainability and ESG information (such as the California Transparency in Supply Chains Act) reveal the factual basis for complaints in conduct-based ESG litigation. Significantly, in this evolving area, companies are more frequently finding themselves being sued and held liable for the actions of their suppliers and third-party intermediaries, such as sales channel partners.

A key legal basis for conduct-based ESG litigation in the United States is the Alien Tort Statute.[19] Passed in 1789 for reasons that are not entirely clear, the single-sentence Alien Tort Statute establishes the jurisdiction of U.S. federal courts to adjudicate claims filed by non-U.S. citizens alleging torts that violate international law or U.S. treaties. The statute was dormant for almost 200 years, but was revived in a 1980 lawsuit by Paraguayan

---

18. *Id.* at 1218.
19. 28 U.S.C. § 1350.

citizens for the torture and murder of a family member. After clarifying and limiting the types of international obligations and law that may serve as the basis for a plaintiff's claim under the Alien Tort Statute in 2004, the U.S. Supreme Court ruled that the Alien Tort Statute did not apply to purely extraterritorial conduct, and to be actionable, conduct must "touch and concern" U.S. territory in 2013.

Slavery, Forced Labor, and Human Trafficking

Victims of human rights abuses have pursued conduct-based ESG litigation in the United States. For example, in ongoing litigation against Nestle USA, Inc., and Cargill, Inc., that started more than a decade ago, the plaintiffs seek redress for alleged child slavery and forced child labor practices by farmers in Cote d'Ivoire who supplied cocoa to these companies. For the requisite territorial nexus, the plaintiffs alleged that from and in the United States, the companies made financing decisions, provided funding and support to farmers and cooperatives in Cote d'Ivoire that used forced child labor, and oversaw the inspection of those facilities and farms in Cote d'Ivoire. The defendant companies argued these allegations were insufficient under the Alien Tort Statute and, having lost their argument in the Court of Appeals, they appealed to the U.S. Supreme Court. In its June 17, 2021 opinion, the Supreme Court reversed the Court of Appeals, holding that the plaintiffs must show that the conduct relevant to the statute's focus occurred in the United States.[20] The various opinions authored and joined in by different Supreme Court Justices may have further complicated the law on other issues relating to the Alien Tort Statute. Moreover, the decision prompted renewed calls for the U.S. Congress to legislate more comprehensively on human rights, with some commentators advocating for legislation similar to recently enacted laws in the U.K., France, Australia, and other nations, addressing forced labor and human rights due diligence throughout global supply chains.

Claims for human trafficking have also been filed against companies that purportedly benefitted from such practices, with plaintiffs more recently focusing on alleged human trafficking and slavery by third parties in supply chains. Several such lawsuits have been brought under the U.S. Trafficking Victims Protection Act (TVPA).[21] Initially enacted in 2000, and reauthorized multiple times, the TVPA imposes criminal and civil penalties on those who knowingly benefit from participating in a venture involving labor or services provided or obtained by means of force, threats, or abuse, when the person knew or recklessly disregarded how such labor or services were obtained. In 2019, more than 100 hotel and motel businesses were sued under the TVPA, for having allegedly improperly benefited from sex trafficking on their premises. Several of these lawsuits have survived motions to dismiss. A 2020 study reported that plaintiffs have filed 458 cases in U.S. federal courts under the TVPA, with approximately $255 million in civic damages having been paid or awarded to trafficking victim plaintiffs.[22]

Notably, acts by business partners and suppliers can serve as a basis for liability under the TVPA. For example, a class action lawsuit filed in 2019 sought to hold multiple large

---

20. Nestlé USA, Inc. v. Doe, 141 S. Ct. 1931 (2021).

21. 18 U.S.C. §§1591 et seq.

22. The Human Trafficking Legal Center, Federal Human Trafficking Civil Litigation: 2020 Data Update (2021), at 5, http://www.htlegalcenter.org/wp-content/uploads/Federal-Human-Trafficking-Civil-Litigation-Data-Update-2020 FINAL.pdf.

multinational companies liable for forced and child labor in cobalt mines in the Democratic Republic of Congo. In February 2021, a class action lawsuit was filed on behalf of eight Malian men who alleged that they were trafficked as children and forced to harvest cocoa in Cote d'Ivoire that was ultimately supplied to food and agribusiness companies for use in their products. The plaintiffs assert that the defendants were sufficiently knowledgeable of the plaintiffs' plight to be held liable under the TVPA. More detailed information on human rights and human capital issues in the supply chain is provided in Chapter 19.

Climate Change

Another issue for which plaintiffs have pursued ESG litigation in an attempt to directly curtail commercial activity is climate change. Plaintiffs have often sued state and local governments in the United States. For more than a decade, private litigants also have sued energy and extractive resource companies in an effort to cause them to alter their operations and, more fundamentally, their business models to reduce their contributions to anthropomorphic climate change. The U.S. Supreme Court has significantly limited plaintiffs' ability to sue companies under federal common law claims for alleged injuries and damages resulting from climate change. Courts have also rejected climate change claims for asserted violations of the U.S. Constitution and the public trust doctrine.

More recently, state and local governments, sometimes joined by private litigants, have pursued claims against companies under state tort laws as well as trespass, negligence, and public nuisance theories. Climate change lawsuits have also been filed by U.S. states' Attorneys General under disclosure theories, such as the New York Attorney General's claims against ExxonMobil Corporation for alleged violations of New York's state securities law (the Martin Act), which the defendant corporation recently defeated at trial. Another lawsuit against ExxonMobil, this one by the Massachusetts Attorney General for alleged violations of Massachusetts state securities and consumer protection laws, is currently ongoing. Outside of the United States, on May 26, 2021, the court of The Hague in the Netherlands ordered Shell to change its corporate policies to comply with "universally accepted" carbon dioxide emission reduction targets—direct dictation by a court of corporate strategy on climate change that is unprecedented.

Legal developments and issues regarding climate change, including the mitigation and greenhouse gas regulation, are discussed in further detail in Chapters 8, 15, and 20.

Governance-Based ESG litigation

As explored previously in Chapter 4, directors have duties to monitor and oversee in good faith the corporation's compliance with laws, commonly referred to under Delaware law as *Caremark* duties.[23] Corporations may only conduct lawful business by lawful means. And as the court in *Caremark* held:

> [I]t would ... be a mistake to conclude ... that corporate boards may satisfy their obligation to be reasonably informed concerning the corporation, without assuring themselves that information and reporting systems exist in the organization that are reasonably designed to provide to senior management and to the board itself timely,

---

23. *In re* Caremark Int'l. Inc. Deriv. Litig., 698 A.2d 959 (Del. Ch. 1996).

accurate information sufficient to allow management and the board, each within its scope, to reach informed judgments concerning both the corporation's compliance with law and its business performance.[24]

Sustainability and ESG principles are more frequently being enshrined in legislation and rules, with which the corporation must comply. And when corporations do not, stakeholders may ask, "Where was the board?" Claims that directors violated their duties of monitoring and oversight often have been filed by stockholders in response to corporate scandals for alleged violations of a wide assortment of criminal laws and regulatory rules. Many of these stockholder lawsuits squarely implicate sustainability and ESG laws, such as money laundering, bribery conduct, off-label marketing practices, human slavery in the corporate supply chain, mining accidents, cybersecurity breaches, serial sexual harassment by senior officers, and food safety failures. *Caremark* claims remain among the most difficult to plead and prove for plaintiff stockholders, who must demonstrate bad faith through intentional dereliction of duty or a complete and utter failure to act in the face of a known duty to act. While this presents a high hurdle for plaintiffs, it has been cleared for purposes of serving motions to dismiss complaints in the pleading stages in several recent Delaware cases involving prime risks for single-product companies or profoundly deficient corporate governance practices.

> More sustainability and ESG principles are being enshrined in legislation and rules, with which the corporation must comply. And when corporations do not, stakeholders may ask, "Where was the board?"

One such case, *Marchand v. Barnhill*,[25] arose out of a listeria outbreak that affected ice cream made by Blue Bell Creameries USA, Inc. The outbreak was caused by food safety failures at two of the company's three plants and resulted in the deaths of three people. After inspecting the books and records of the corporation, the plaintiff stockholder filed a lawsuit asserting that the Bluebell directors breached their duties under *Caremark*. Reversing the Court of Chancery's dismissal of plaintiff's claims, the Delaware Supreme Court held that the plaintiff's complaint pleaded particularized facts satisfying the standard established under *Caremark*. The court explained: "When a plaintiff can plead an inference that a board has undertaken no efforts to make sure it is informed of a compliance issue intrinsically critical to the company's business operation, then that supports an inference that the board has not made the good faith effort that *Caremark* requires."[26] To support the inference of bad faith in light of food safety failures at this one-product company, the court cited, among other things, the absence of any board committee to oversee food safety issues, the lack of regular processes or protocols requiring management to inform the board of food safety risks and practices (including of red or yellow flags known by management), and the failure

---

24. *Id.* at 970.
25. 212 A.3d 805 (Del. 2019).
26. *Id.* at 822.

by the board to regularly evaluate this mission-critical risk as evidenced by board meeting minutes being generally devoid of any such discussions.

Marchand does not represent a change in the scope of directors' oversight duties or a relaxation of the demanding standards to sufficiently plead a *Caremark* claim. However, the case does show the risk of *Caremark* claims for "central compliance risks" that are "essential and mission critical." Corporate failures to comply with sustainability and ESG laws and regulations that present sizeable risks—especially those identified as such in public statements and disclosures by the corporation—may result in substantial declines in the corporation's value and impairment of its brand and reputation, prompting stockholders to sue directors for violating their duties of monitoring and oversight. More positively, sustainability and ESG may be understood as an extension of the directors' *Caremark* duties: by exceeding the minimum that is legally required and embodying sustainable and ethical principles in how the corporation conducts business, directors will cause their corporations to meet both legitimate and reasonable expectations for sustainability and ESG, and reduce the risk of violating sustainability and ESG laws.[27]

Additional Trends and Concerns

The summary presented above amply demonstrates that a wide variety of sustainability and ESG issues may form the basis of ESG litigation against a corporation and its leadership. It is not exhaustive. As an initial matter, the summary above focused on litigation in the United States. Many European jurisdictions, while generally not as litigious as the United States, have been leaders in adopting ESG laws and principles of stakeholder capitalism, and litigation in those countries has similarly, if not more directly, sought to conform corporate behavior to legal requirements. Notably, as class actions become more prevalent in European countries, companies are findings themselves being sued in ESG litigation similar to that historically filed in the United States. For example, on July 7, 2021, Germany's largest consumer protection group filed a class action lawsuit in Stuttgart against an automobile manufacturer in the wake of the Dieselgate emissions scandal.

> Directors should also be mindful of the legal risks from governmental authorities' enforcement of ESG laws, and stockholders' demands to inspect corporate books and records.

Further, directors should be mindful of two other forms of ESG litigation. First, though the summary above focused on private litigation, many sustainability and ESG laws are being enforced by the United States and international governmental authorities under criminal or quasi-criminal statutes and theories. How to respond to a government or grand jury subpoena, let alone defend against criminal prosecution of a corporate defendant, is beyond the scope of this book. Importantly, governmental authorities' enforcement of laws embodying ESG issues often gives rise to follow-on civil litigation, including oversight claims against directors.

Second, to support ESG litigation and corporate governance strategies, stockholders have increasingly demanded ESG information from corporations through actions to inspect

---

27. Leo E. Strine, Jr. et al., *Caremark* and ESG, Perfect Together: A Practical Approach to Implementing an Integrated, Efficient, and Effective *Caremark* and EESG Strategy, 106 Iowa L. Rev. 1885 (2021).

corporate books and records. The Delaware Court of Chancery previously denied a motion to dismiss a stockholder's action seeking to inspect books and records of The Hershey Company for evidence of mismanagement and breaches of fiduciary duties in light of allegations of suppliers' use of child labor in West African cocoa farms. The court observed that public statements by the company supported an inference that it was aware of instances of child labor in the supply of cocoa and, if true, the company was required to report those violations to relevant government authorities under local law.[28]

More recently, in *AmerisourceBergen Corp. v. Lebanon County Employees' Retirement Fund*,[29] the Delaware Supreme Court addressed a request to inspect the books and records of AmerisourceBergen, a distributor of opioids subject to extensive regulation and requirements to maintain effective controls and reporting systems. Because of its alleged misconduct contributing to the opioid crisis, the company is the subject of multiple investigations by U.S. federal and state governmental authorities and a defendant in multidistrict class action litigation, and had expended more than USD 1 billion in opioid-related costs. The stockholder's four stated purposes for the request included to investigate potential mismanagement and breaches of fiduciary duties by the corporation's directors and management. The Delaware Supreme Court held that, at the books and records stage, a stockholder neither needs to commit to what it will do with the results of its investigation, nor demonstrate that the suspected wrongdoing by the board is actionable. Stockholders need to only show a credible basis from which the court may infer potential mismanagement or wrongdoing warranting further investigation. The court further explained that while formal board materials may be the starting point, a stockholder's inspection may extend to informal board materials including directors' emails with senior executives or other communications only among officers and employees. Stockholder demands to inspect books and records, and other forms of information-based ESG litigation, will be increasingly important as corporations defend themselves in other forms of ESG litigation and protect valuable global brands.

Take-Aways for Board Members

Practical Guidance for Managing the Risk of ESG Litigation

For the foreseeable future, ESG litigation will only become a larger legal risk for companies. Directors still must oversee the creation of value, even while navigating troubled waters churned by the specter and incidence of ESG litigation. There is no "magic bullet" for directors, but there are practical steps that they may take to help them and the corporations they serve succeed.

- Directors should understand the specific legal risks presented by various forms of ESG litigation. They should seek out and rely on input from corporate management, in-house legal and compliance departments, and outside counsel, advisers, and experts qualified to identify and explain the particular types of ESG litigation that pose significant legal risk to the corporation.

---

28. La. Mun. Police Emps.' Ret. Sys. v. The Hershey Co., Civ. Action No. 7996-ML (Del. Ch. 2014), https://law-professors.typepad.com/files/hershey-ruling.pdf.
29. 243 A.3d 417 (Del. 2020).

- Using the framework noted above, directors should ask corporate legal counsel to identify key ESG litigation risks particularly relevant to the corporation's commercial activities and business model (current and anticipated) in each of the following categories: (i) disclosure-based ESG litigation; (ii) conduct-based ESG litigation; and (iii) governance-based ESG litigation. Directors should also seek to understand the risk of enforcement of sustainability and ESG laws and regulations by governmental authorities in the United States and abroad in light of the corporation's commercial activities and business model. Directors should prioritize litigation risks to focus first on "mission critical" compliance and litigation risks arising from sustainability and ESG issues.

- Directors should keep informed of developments and trends in ESG litigation affecting the corporation's industry and its competitors. Often, plaintiffs and prosecutors will look for and find sustainability and ESG issues in one company, and then conduct an "industry sweep" to see if a similar shortcoming exists in competitor companies. By evaluating the ESG litigation within its industry, directors may not only be able to identify potential claims against the corporation before being named as a defendant in a lawsuit, but may also better plan corporate strategy to mitigate appropriately legal risk from ESG litigation. Doing so may result in a competitive advantage given the significant impact ESG litigation may have on the ability to pursue and profitability of commercial activities and business models.

- The board of directors should determine whether risk management relating to ESG litigation should be overseen by the full board of directors or a dedicated board committee. If oversight is assigned to a committee of the board, the committee's charters should reflect the committee having being allocated that responsibility. The board should also consider how any committee tasked with overseeing ESG litigation will collaborate with other committees that are responsible for evaluating and addressing other sustainability and ESG risks that give rise to ESG litigation.

- Directors also should seek to complete an annual risk assessment of ESG litigation, and ask for the preparation and presentation of heat maps to help guide the board's oversight of the various evolving forms of ESG litigation. In doing so, directors should ensure that management also considers risks arising from conduct by the corporation's supply chain and other business partners. For "mission critical" and other material ESG litigation, directors should request scenario analyses to understand how it will impact the corporation both at present and in the foreseeable future.

- The board of directors should integrate identified and prioritized risks from ESG litigation into the corporation's enterprise risk management process. After overseeing the identification of risks from ESG litigation, directors should understand management's plan to manage and mitigate risk. Directors should ask about the ability to mitigate risks from ESG litigation through insurance (including but not limited to Directors and Officers insurance and consideration of A-B-C coverage thereunder), charter provisions, and indemnification and advancement rights. Moreover, directors should ascertain how responsible corporate managers will monitor and periodically update their risk management strategy for ESG litigation.

- The board of directors should design and adopt a comprehensive strategy to address the risk of disclosure-based ESG litigation. Tactics to manage disclosure risk, such as including appropriate disclaimers, determining where and how certain disclosures are made, and establishing a due diligence process to confirm the accuracy of statements, are set forth in Chapters 14 (public company mandatory reporting) and 15 (voluntary reporting). Directors should also make sure that management is using a collaborative, cross-functional team to draft and review sustainability and ESG disclosures. Directors should also confirm that management is not inappropriately limiting its review to sustainability and ESG disclosures made in SEC filings, and that statements in CSR reports, press releases, and marketing campaigns are also being appropriately vetted. The board of directors should also establish channels by which select material changes in the corporation's ESG policy are escalated to the board of directors in advance of being announced to corporate stakeholders.

- Over a longer-term horizon, the board of directors should evaluate whether its members have the appropriate experience and expertise to oversee sustainability and ESG issues that are the basis of more material ESG litigation. Further, the board of directors should evaluate if the corporation's in-house legal and compliance departments and outside counsel have sufficient resources and an appropriate skillset to manage key ESG litigation.

- The board of directors or committees thereof should establish in standing agendas a regular cadence for discussion of legal risk arising from ESG litigation. Directors should attend meetings (in person or remotely) and actively participate by proactively asking questions of management and each other. The corporate secretary and/or general counsel should keep an appropriate written record of the directors' decision-making, including in regular minutes. In addition, directors and counsel to the board and/or the corporation should be mindful of maintaining legal privileges, including in how board packages and communications are made and where they are stored.

* * * * *

The author is grateful to Maria McMahon for her research assistance, and Reagan Demas, Mark Goodman, and Douglas Sanders for their insightful comments. The views expressed herein are the personal views of the author and do not represent the views of Baker & McKenzie LLP or constitute legal advice.

Additional Reading

1. Caitlin M. Ajax & Diane Strauss, *Corporate Sustainability Disclosures in American Case Law: Purposeful or Mere "Puffery"?*, 45 Ecol. Law Q. 703 (2018).

2. Andrea Bonime-Blanc, Gloom to Boom, Ch. 7 (*Metamorphosis: Achieving Organizational Resilience*, 2020).

3. Committee of Sponsoring Organizations of the Treadway Commission (COSO) & World Business Council for Sustainable Development (WBCSD), *Enterprise Risk Management: Applying Enterprise Risk Management to Environmental, Social and Governance-Related Risks* (Oct. 2018), https://www.coso.org/Documents/COSO-WBCSD-ESGERM-Guidance-Full.pdf.

4. David Hackett et al., *Growing ESG Risks: The Rise of Litigation*, 50 ENVIRONMENTAL LAW REPORTER 10849 (Oct. 2020).

5. Sara K. Orr & Bart J. Kempf, *Voluntary Sustainability Disclosure and Emerging Litigation*, 19 CLIM. CHANGE SUSTAIN. DEV. ECOSYST. COMMIT. NEWSLETT. (2015).

6. Veena Ramani & Hannah Saltman, *Running the Risks: How Corporate Boards Can Oversee Environmental, Social and Governance Issues* (Nov. 25, 2019), https://corpgov.law.harvard.edu/2019/11/25/running-the-risks-how-corporate-boards-can-oversee-environmental-social-and-governance-issues/.

7. Society for Corporate Governance & Gibson, Dunn & Crutcher LLP, *ESG Legal Update: What Corporate Governance and ESG Professionals Need to Know* (June 2020).

PART V

Chapter 18
Corporate Culture and Governance

Howard Brod Brownstein

As companies and their boards of directors pivot toward considering sustainability as a critical component of their strategy and its implementation, they inevitably run into a basic corporate "fact of life"—the importance of the company's culture. Peter Drucker, perhaps the most well-known business commentator of our time, is often quoted as having said, "Culture eats strategy for breakfast." While the provenance of that statement is unsettled, its widespread acceptance as truth is not. Companies have learned to their sorrow that their culture can easily outweigh the decisions, policies, and strategies made in the executive suites and boardrooms, such as the attributed cause of General Motors' infamous ignition switch failures.[1]

The good news is that boards of directors are increasingly recognizing the importance of understanding their company's culture in fulfilling their fiduciary duties, as well as determining whether that culture is consistent with the company's strategy, and staying tuned in to how the company's culture may be changing. Interest in corporate culture has escalated in recent years, culminating in the landmark *"Report of the Blue Ribbon Commission on Culture as a Corporate Asset,"* published in 2017 by the National Association of Corporate Directors (NACD).[2] Following NACD's BRC Report, interest in and attention to corporate

---

1. CNN Business, *GM's 'Culture' Blamed for Current Crisis* (June 28, 2014), https://money.cnn.com/2014/06/28/news/companies/gm-smerconish/index.html.
2. National Association of Corporate Directors, *Report of the NACD Blue Ribbon Commission on Culture as a Corporate Asset* (Oct. 2017), https://www.nacdonline.org/insights/publications.cfm?ItemNumber=48252.

culture have remained strong, and it is a regular subject on the agendas of governance conferences.

What has been learned about the importance of a company's culture to corporate governance, and how does it relate to the movement toward including sustainability as part of the corporate strategy which boards are charged with overseeing?

We might best begin by inquiring what company culture is, since a likely historical starting point is Milton Friedman's famous article, *"The Social Responsibility of Business Is to Increase Its Profits,"*[3] There is clearly an inertial legacy that must be overcome, suggesting that culture is a "soft" topic and not subject to the rigorous metrics that accompany maximizing shareholder value as an overriding corporate strategy. The NACD BRC Report begins with acknowledging this potential obstacle, and posits as a definition of company culture "the sum of the shared assumptions, values, and beliefs that create the unique character of an organization."[4] Other cited definitions reference the assumptions that company employees make about what they are expected to do or not do, and how their success will be measured. An important point is that a company's culture is defined by behaviors, which are of course informed by values and beliefs.

The BRC Report goes on to suggest that the topic of culture is not soft but is in fact "hard," i.e., that culture creates an important and tangible impact on a company's performance, and that it is likely less familiar as an assessable characteristic than the more conventional metrics that boards historically review regularly, and therefore less well understood.

As possible validation of this proposition, consider the above-mentioned unfortunate example of GM and its faulty ignition switches which resulted in multiple deaths, with successive failure both at the plant level to adequately report the problem, and at the executive level to treat the problem as sufficiently serious—both indicative of a company culture that, in retrospect, was bound to lead to problems, sooner or later. There have been many other examples of corporate scandals which, when the news broke, revealed longstanding weaknesses at one or more levels of the companies involved.

It does not require much imagination to describe a difference in culture that might well have prevented, or at least mitigated, the problems that corporate scandals have uncovered. Suppose that GM had had a truly vibrant and easy-to-utilize method for plant employees to notify the board—and perhaps even regulators–about potential safety hazards, created within a cultural context of "We want you to do this" and "You're being a loyal employee if you do this, helping us to avoid potential problems." Included would be protection from any blowback or retribution, including if the suspected problem proved not to exist as severely or even at all—that would in fact be good news, and not a black mark against an employee for raising an alarm unnecessarily. The cultural message would be, "Better safe than sorry" and "Thanks for being a good lookout!"

Skeptics and cynics might argue that underperforming employees would use this mechanism as "cover" for their shortcomings—filing reports when they anticipate an unfavorable performance review, or worse—and there are no doubt such examples. But these should be relatively easy for companies to parse, especially if there is a cultural context that

---

3. "A Friedman doctrine-- The Social Responsibility Of Business Is to Increase Its Profits", *THE NEW YORK TIMES MAGAZINE*, Sept. 13, 1970.
4. Quoting City Values Forum and Tomorrow's Company, Governing Culture: Risk & Opportunity? (2016).

has been created that everyone needs to be vigilant for the good of the company. (I hope that I am not naïve in wanting this type of culture to exist at nuclear power plants!)

Inevitably when the news of scandals break, the question is then asked, "Where was the board?" And while the immediate cause of the problem may be some financial or operational issue, once one inquires into how the issue might have been prevented, it often becomes apparent that the underlying cause was the company culture. "To clean the river, you must go upstream."

And if company culture has the power to help prevent problems, or at least help to reveal problems sooner and effectively address them, it follows that company culture should be a key element in a company's strategy formulation and successful implementation.

> Company culture is clearly a board issue, *Q.E.D.*

If the case has now been sufficiently made that (1) culture is critical to the success of a company, and (2) it therefore is a required topic for boards to importantly consider, the next question to address is how boards can fulfill this responsibility. Just as a company's possibly most valuable asset—its reputation—does not appear on its balance sheet, there is no traditional report, for example, one based on Generally Accepted Accounting Principles (GAAP) to which boards can refer in order to discern the company's culture, and then assess whether that culture is well-matched to the company's strategy. Nor is there any familiar roadmap—such was for when it is necessary to divest an unprofitable business or restate an erroneous financial statement—for addressing a possible need to change a company's culture, should that appear necessary.

How can boards meet their responsibilities in this area? As discussed elsewhere in this book, there is an increasing call by the Business Roundtable[5] and others for boards to pivot toward considering sustainability as an important part of the company's purpose. How can boards determine the existing culture of a company, and then work with management to help promote change in the culture, as necessary, to achieve desired sustainability goals?

A valuable conceptual starting point may come from the *ontology* branch of philosophy: the study of "being," in contrast to "doing." While there will no doubt be much to "do" if companies are to pursue strategies that include sustainability as a key component, that "doing" will no doubt be far more difficult if the company's "being" remains rooted in the pure pursuit of shareholder value maximization. It will be necessary for a company to "be" sustainable, not just to "do" sustainable things.

> A company's culture may be the best window into its being.

The inclusion of sustainability in a company's purpose has been characterized as a paradigmatic shift, and therefore it is likely that the successful incorporation of sustainability

---

5. Business Roundtable, *Statement on the Purpose of a Corporation* (Aug. 19, 2019).

will require boards to examine closely the existing company culture, discern what changes might be needed, and how to work with management to effectuate such changes.

A board's inquiry into the company's existing culture should begin with an explicit decision to make such an inquiry, so that it is intentional on the part of the board, with appropriate recordation in board minutes, possible assignment to an existing or special board committee, decision whether an outside advisor might be helpful, and expectation of a subsequent report to the board, with ensuing board discussion and determination of any necessary future actions. Harking back to the definition of culture from NACD cited above, the goal is for the board to get a clear understanding of the "shared assumptions, values, and beliefs" that exist within the company, how those line up with the company's existing strategy and purpose, and what changes might be needed for the company's "being" to incorporate sustainability. How to make any such changes presupposes a clear understanding of what changes might be necessary, and why.

Among the methods that have been utilized by boards to understand the company's culture are reviewing what the company says, internally and externally, and how they say it. What message is given to employees, as well as to the company's customers, vendors, shareholders, and the communities it serves, about what is important to the company? Some boards have conducted "town hall" meetings with employees, utilized surveys, monitored social media, and/or conducted exit interviews with departing employees, in an effort to stay informed about the company's culture.

And specifically, what can reasonably be deduced about the company's current attitude toward sustainability, from an inquiry into the above areas? Is sustainability mentioned prominently, and does the company go beyond "lip service" and actually include sustainability in the company's policies and decisions? Are there meaningful metrics by which the company measures its efforts and performance regarding sustainability?

First and foremost should be discussions by the board with management—what do *they* believe is the culture of the company, and what evidence can they produce for their belief? And following from those reports of scandals that might have been prevented had the company's culture been different, boards might well ask how their own company's employees might behave in a similar situation. What "shared assumptions, values, and beliefs" are generally in place within their company, and what results might they produce in the face of, for example, a safety or ethics issue?

It has been suggested that the culture at GM may have changed as a result of the above-mentioned scandal,[6] not only regarding the reporting of safety issues, but also regarding GM's overall strategy for producing gasoline automobiles.[7]

Among the elements of a company's policies and operations that the NACD BRC Report suggests may help boards in navigating their inquiry into culture, are the company's rules and codes of conduct, its compensation and incentive structures and practices, and its compliance and ethics policies. Compensation is a form of pricing, and pricing is a form of information—in this case, telling employees what is expected of them, and so just as

---

6. *GM: We Encourage Employees, Dealers to Tattle After Ignition Switch Crisis*, DETROIT FREE PRESS, Sept. 6, 2019.
7. Neal E. Boudette & Coral Davenport, *G.M. Will Sell Only Zero-Emission Vehicles by 2035*, THE NEW YORK TIMES, Jan. 28, 2021.

compensation should be aligned with a company's strategy, it can also be revealing about a company's culture.

To these more objectively definable areas are added others that are more subjective: how people behave generally in meetings and otherwise, how decisions are made, and the general style of leadership. Boards might also inquire into the level of employee engagement—how much do employees know or care about the company's activities, and how might this level of engagement be strengthened?

Regarding leadership styles, it is certainly true that the "tone at the top" set by a company's senior management is an important component of company culture. However, that is just one part of the whole, and it should not be assumed that company culture begins and ends with the tone set by leaders. The collection of shared values, beliefs, and assumptions that makes up company culture includes much more.

> Changes in culture will be needed to accommodate the "paradigm shift" required by including sustainability as a central component of a company's purpose.

The culture of companies that are large or multinational may be more complex than that of companies that are smaller or less diverse geographically. Boards need to take this into account, both in seeking to understand the company's existing culture and in overseeing the formulation and implementation of any changes in culture that will be necessary to accommodate a greater focus on sustainability.

Once a board feels that it has gained a good understanding of the company's culture, it follows that it should consider that culture as a useful context for the decisions that the board makes and the management activities that it oversees. Boards should be alert for proposed decisions or actions that might seem inconsistent with company culture and inquire further into how those decisions or actions will play out. At the very least, any such possible inconsistency might well be a source of risk that the planned decision or action will not be successful, or at least limited in its effectiveness, as well as a possible destabilizing influence in other areas, or to the company in general.

The likelihood that changes in culture will be needed to accommodate the "paradigm shift" required by including sustainability as a central component of a company's purpose cannot be overstated. A company that has been "slugging it out" every day in the marketplace, with its employees down to the plant level having short-term profitability and maximization of shareholder value present in their very drinking water, must assume that basic changes in mentality and practice will be needed from top to bottom. How sustainable are the company's products, including how they are disposed of? How does the company source its product and service inputs, and its power? How sustainable are its production processes? How does it deal with waste, including decisions that affect the amount of waste produced? These are just a few of the many questions that companies will face as they embrace sustainability as part of their corporate purpose, and it will be the board's duty to oversee this process, and to confirm that it has been comprehensive and accurate.

The foregoing is not meant to suggest in any way that sustainability and shareholder value are necessarily at odds or mutually exclusive. Indeed, it has been argued that incorporating sustainability into a company's strategy and purpose will help secure its long-term survival and success, and that the suggestion of necessary tradeoffs between profitability and sustainability is overestimated. And of course, the opinion of a company's customers about who it is "being" in the world may well affect their loyalty. This goes "way beyond optics" and how the company portrays itself, since the buying public is fed a tremendous amount of information about the companies from which it buys products and services, and has gotten more sensitive about negative publicity and abhors hypocrisy. The point is, there will be much work for companies to do in order to shift their "being," and it all begins with company culture.

Based upon the board having gained a good understanding of the company's existing culture, it can turn to specifically what changes in that culture might be necessary in order to successfully incorporate sustainability into the company's purpose and strategy. A good starting point would be an in-depth discussion with management, obtaining its input into what might have to be different about the company's culture so that sustainability would be an integral part of the company's "being." A spirit of open inquiry is helpful to this process, as well as resistance to any notion that this will be simple, or—worse—unnecessary. A management attitude of "Don't worry, we got this!" may not only spell danger in achieving whatever transformation may be necessary, but may bespeak broader challenges for board governance: insufficient management attentiveness to risk, a dismissive attitude toward the role of the board, etc.

What might a company culture that incorporates sustainability look like? How might sustainability show up in the company's day-to-day operations, offices, and policies? How will compensation and advancement properly reflect the addition of sustainability goals and objectives to those that already exist, and are there any tradeoffs? What new risks might arise, how might existing risks change as a result of a shift toward sustainability, and how will the board oversee management of those risks?

Culture, like strategy, must be pervasive in order to be effective, as well as consistent in order that its messaging be clear. A board must work with management to make sure its thinking is informed by, *inter alia*, the requirements of sustainability, and that sustainability is considered by them in all of their planning and decision-making. And for a change in culture regarding sustainability as a strategic goal to be successful, the board must be clear and unequivocal about its position.

And while the previous comment is true that sustainability and profitability need not be in opposition to one another, this does not mean that sustainability is without short-term cost. The challenge is to determine how to be both sustainable *and* profitable, at least in the long run, much as a board might look at any important investment in its future.

To better understand how their company can successfully cultivate a culture of sustainability, boards may investigate examples of companies that have successfully done so. Rankings and reviews abound,[8] and among the companies one sees mentioned are tech companies like Cisco and HP, retailers like Best Buy and H&M, apparel companies like Patagonia, manufacturers like Sony, and others.

---

8. See, e.g., Corporate Knight, *2021 Global 100*, https://www.corporateknights.com/reports/2021-global-100/; Leslie P. Norton, *These Are the 100 Most Sustainable Companies in America*, Barron's, Feb. 7, 2020.

One element of company culture that is sometimes overlooked is the culture of the board itself. How the board approaches such issues as its own effectiveness and responses to change are reflections of its culture, and how it views its responsibility. While discussions about "board culture" typically focus on such issues as how well differences of opinion in the boardroom are accommodated, the prospect of a shift in company strategy and purpose toward sustainability should give rise to the board reassessing its own readiness, for example, in terms of its composition, its committees, board processes, etc.

Perhaps, the board should add or substitute one or more directors who have had experience with companies that have successfully incorporated sustainability into their purpose. Possibly, a committee of the board—whether an existing or a new special or permanent committee—should be assigned to do a "deeper dive" into what the shift toward sustainability will require, with more frequent meetings, engaging advisors, etc. Explicitly taking up all of these questions and others—regardless of how they are resolved—may be reflections of a healthy board culture, and may improve the likelihood that the shift in the company's strategy and purpose will be successful.

> Consideration of company culture should not be merely "additive" to the board's agenda, but should be integrated into all of the board's duties.

The NACD BRC Report makes the important point that consideration of company culture—perhaps after an initial ramping-up—should not be merely "additive" to the board's agenda, but should be integrated into all of the board's duties. In other words, while the board's duties include many important matters such as CEO succession, risk oversight, etc., its review of company culture and determination to change it require a more extensive and persistent effort. Per above, the company's culture provides an important context for all company decisions and actions, and therefore consideration of company culture is critical to the success of any planned shift toward sustainability.

At some point, the shift in a company's strategy and purpose toward sustainability will result in a series of decisions and planned actions which may include budgets, timetables, and anticipated outcomes, involving operational and financial changes as well as intended changes in company culture that are perceived as necessary. The actual results may then require adjustments and revisions, and all of this will be within the scope of the board's oversight responsibilities. The company's culture—both before and during the shift toward sustainability—will provide boards with a valuable backdrop for understanding progress being made, as well as additional progress needed.

Throughout the process of any change in company strategy and purpose, boards will want to pay proactive attention to stakeholder engagement, since the expectations of stakeholders—as well as their potentially valuable support—can be an important element in the success of any company, and especially one that is going through important changes. Playing offense is usually better than playing defense! For example, shareholders will want to know how any planned changes may affect them in terms of earnings or dividends. Other stakeholder groups, such as customers, vendors, employees, and communities, also play an important role in the company's success, and so including them in the process will likely be valuable. Some boards have established a "Stakeholder Communication Policy" which governs who may speak to stakeholders on the board's behalf, in order to help ensure correct and consistent messaging.

Take-Aways for Board Members

- As boards consider whether and how to incorporate sustainability into their values, strategy, and purpose, understanding their company's culture is critical for determining what this will require and how to achieve it.

- Such understanding must then be followed with changes that will have strategic, operational, financial, and risk oversight implications, all of which will be long term in nature.

- Without a company culture that is consistent with whatever changes are pursued, there is a risk that the company may be "doing" without "being."

Chapter 19
Operations Management: Supply Chain, Employees, Customers

John Legaré Williams

Introduction

In the 1987 movie *Wall Street*, Gordon Gekko famously said, "Greed, for lack of a better word, is good." Throughout the movie, the ruthless corporate raider used this theory to justify his unethical stock trading practices. He seized control of target companies and created value for its owners with layoffs. Under this set of values, building a company was a simple equation of labor and capital. In 1759, the economist Adam Smith introduced the "invisible hand" concept of free markets in his book, *The Theory of Moral Sentiments*. His theory held that individuals acting in their own self-interest in a free-market economy would unintentionally promote the public good.

Another more modern economic theory, known as game-theory, looks at the market as a series of "games" that build upon previous competitive interactions and experiences. Within this multipart game, managers are rewarded for providing benefits to customers and employees that would not be profitable in a single-round game. Focusing less on short-term profits and more on the long-term well-being of all stakeholders benefits the bottom line. By having happy employees and company goodwill, recruitment becomes easier, productivity increases, and turnover is reduced. Wise managers aim to maximize the *triple* bottom line: people, planet, and profits.

Leaderships that value their company's employees and customers generally have greater chances of success. Business author Michael Leboeuf said, "A satisfied customer is the best business strategy of all." Some companies have adopted the position of Chief Experience Officer, or CXO, to maintain a positive brand image and a loyal customer base. Today's Human Relations officers are beginning to view their workforce as "employee entrepreneurs" who can be more productive and innovative when given an optimal environment and incentives. This sentiment often becomes even more important during times of economic prosperity, as the labor market becomes constrained with a lower unemployment rate.

Corporate directors have legal and contractual duties to provide for the long-term sustainability of their companies. Many directors previously dismissed early trends toward sustainability as pitting the interests of the public against those of shareholders. However, companies that were once seen as being enlightened or charitable now serve as industry standards for productivity and innovation with loyal customers and constituents. Operating a company as a short-term profit machine has raised concerns that it often comes at the cost of long-term performance and growth. Corporate governance has long been driven by a principle of shareholder primacy in which directors place the interests of shareholders above all others. Running a company with minimum costs and maximum profits overlooks the importance of stakeholder satisfaction and innovation. Theories centered around success through sustainability have shifted the focus away from shareholder primacy toward an approach that acknowledges the inherent value of a company's stakeholders. The stakeholder theory involves a holistic approach that considers all individuals in and around an organization.[1]

Consumers, employees, investors, suppliers, community members, and the environment are all included within a corporation's plan for sustainability. The corporation recognizes its ability to provide opportunities and promote growth within its market, the surrounding community, and the planet.

In this chapter, we summarize how corporations engage with their two most pivotal stakeholders: employees and customers. This is done by integrating sustainability within operations management. First, we delve into strategies utilized by leading corporations to ensure sustainability within their supply chains. We later go into detail about the key benefits that make a viable sustainability strategy absolutely invaluable to the operations of any corporation.

The Supply Chain

For many corporate directors and officers, the story of forced labor in some countries serves as a cautionary tale and reveals the ultimate challenge corporations face in their efforts for sustainable operations management. As the supply chain grows longer and more remote, the difficulty of maintaining the standards of each component in the chain expands to the origin of all inputs and raw materials.

1. Stacy H. Lee, *Achieving Corporate Sustainability Performance: The Influence of Corporate Ethical Value, and Leader-Member Exchange on Employee Behaviors and Organizational Performance*, 7 Fash. Text. (2020). Gale Academic OneFile, https://link-gale-com.udel.idm.oclc.org/apps/doc/A625896197/AONE?u=udel_main&sid=AONE&xid=089482ff.

In early 2020, the issue of Uyghur internment within China began to hit dangerously close to home for dozens of high-profile, multinational corporations. Beginning in 2017, the Chinese government expanded their initiative to root out supposed "religious extremism" and separatism among ethnic minority groups. This resulted in nearly two million Muslim peoples, including Uyghurs and Kazakhs, effectively disappearing over a two-year span when they were placed in re-education facilities located in Xinjiang. Experts believe this figure is the largest internment of a people since World War II.[2] Despite the documentation of these camps and subsequent human rights abuses, multinational corporations were able to remain blissfully ignorant of the fact that their supply chains benefitted from these forced labor camps for a number of years.

In February 2017, the Australian Strategic Policy Institute (ASPI) authored a policy brief detailing the transfer of over 80,000 Uyghur peoples from re-education camps in Xinjiang to factories located throughout China. In following the transfers of Uyghur workers from the re-education camps in Xinjiang to manufacturers throughout China, the ASPI was able to implicate some of the world's most prominent companies across several industries in this massive, forced labor scheme. From apparel brands such as Nike, Adidas, and Puma, to tech giants Apple and Google, it seemed as if every major corporation involved in American consumer life had either directly or indirectly benefited from this rampant exploitation. Even Patagonia, a company lauded as an early champion of sustainability and social responsibility, found itself on a list of fashion brands reported to have benefitted from Uyghur labor. In many cases, the multiple layers of the supply chain hid the abuse of Uyghur laborers. In July 2020, the State Department issued an advisory memo cautioning businesses of these threats to their supply chains and the possible repercussions.[3]

For some, the story may be disheartening. Directors may feel that maintaining sustainable environmental and fair labor practices across all of a company's operations, both foreign and domestic, is a losing battle. The truth is, however, the battle must be fought. Today, stakeholders no longer see ethical sourcing and sustainability as being extraordinary; rather, it has become to some an expectation. The struggles and failures of other corporations should not render the goal of sustainability as being unattainable in the eyes of any company. Maintaining sustainability within operations management requires both a nuanced approach and collective action. The onus of managing a corporation's operations falls upon its officers; however, it is up to the directors to implement a system of governance that serves to bolster accountability and overall sustainability among even the lowest tiers of the supply chain.

The glaring issue concerning sustainability within the supply chain of a multinational corporation is the chain's inherent size. As we saw in the example from China, most violations are perpetrated by the lower-tier suppliers of these companies. The nature of the products these manufacturers produce means that they have a broad and diverse customer base. As these competing interests and standards dilute one another, there becomes less incentive for manufacturers to follow any specific corporation's sustainability protocols. Oftentimes,

---

2. Nathan Ruser & James Leibold, *Family De-Planning: The Coercive Campaign to Drive Down Indigenous Birth-Rates in Xinjiang*, Australian Strategic Policy Institute (2021), https://s3-ap-southeast-2.amazonaws.com/ad-aspi/2021-05/Family%20deplanning%20v2.pdf?IO4rxtbW_Up5C6usSJ4EpMFHm6khL7uF.
3. Press Release, U.S. Department of State, Xinjiang Supply Chain Business Advisory (July 13, 2021) (on file with the U.S. Department of State).

these manufacturers operate in countries where environmental standards are either minimal or nonexistent. Due to the fact that they are not as well known, these manufacturers also enjoy less pressure from nongovernmental organizations (NGOs), the news media, and stakeholders of the corporation. Even if these manufacturers had the best of intentions and aspired to comply with sustainability standards, it is more likely than not that they lack the resources or the expertise required to adhere to these requirements.[4]

Perhaps, there is no better long-term example of industry-wide supply chain issues than the commercial shrimping industry. Americans are the largest consumers of shrimp in the world; however, approximately 80 percent of global shrimp supply comes from countries other than the U.S.[5] As global demand for shrimp rose sharply beginning in the 1960s and 1970s, consumer preferences shifted from shrimp being a delicacy, like shrimp cocktail at the country club thought of as a fancy treat, to shrimp being viewed as another protein source used in all types of meals. Supply grew with demand and resulted in scaling up from the local "Bubba Gump" shrimp boat to more large-scale industrial farming and fishing, putting downward pressure on prices. Because of overfishing shrimp, the aquaculture and sea floor near poorer coastal countries have suffered due to lack of oversight and lack of adequate fishing regulation.

Not unlike the Chinese government's recent abuses of their Muslim populations, the poorer residents of these countries have also suffered greatly. Countries like Bangladesh and Thailand are accused of relying on slave labor in their shrimp fisheries and impressing fisherman on shrimp boats. With the proliferation of Red Lobster and Calabash Seafood restaurants, consumers are more interested in quantity and low price over quality and ensuring that fisherman are paid fairly. Most consumers have no idea that slave labor may go into their low-price shrimp. Food service companies may have difficulty going down the line to the bottom of the production chain to ensure all suppliers meet even minimal standards for human well-being.

The growing need for ensuring sustainable supply chains in vulnerable industries like fishing has created a market for supply chain auditors and consultants. These companies follow similar processes of traditional management consulting firms, where for a six-month period, they inspect supplier documents, interview managers and key employees, and solicit customer surveys. They compile the data into a report and deliver recommendations to senior management for short- and long-term improvement The auditor industry however is susceptible to corruption. Issuing a bad audit can result in the auditor being replaced in a race to the bottom for auditing standards. Bribes or wining and dining auditors also can make audit results unreliable. For consumers of products labeled "green" or "fair trade," they may not have sufficient information to distinguish true benefits from "astroturf-green" policies without substance. This results in the corner-cutting companies getting an edge on the benevolent companies until they are called out for their practices by undercover investigations.

For a company to tackle systemic issues of accountability, transparency, and resource availability, it is necessary to launch an effort that is both well organized and collaborative

4. Veronica H. Villena & Dennis A. Gioia, *A More Sustainable Supply Chain*, Harv. Bus. Rev. (March–April 2020), https://hbr.org/2020/03/a-more-sustainable-supply-chain.
5. Accenture, *Exploitative Labor Practices in the Global Shrimp Industry*, Humanity United (2013), http://humanityunited.org/pdfs/Accenture_Shrimp_Report.pdf.

in nature. In observing the practices of industry leaders in sustainability, two things are made clear: a proper corporate governance structure and industry-wide collaboration are important to supporting efforts for sustainability.[6]

Ensuring Sustainability Through Corporate Governance

The weight of supporting sustainability throughout a supply chain cannot be placed squarely on the shoulders of middle managers. It is the responsibility of the board of directors to implement and maintain a sound structure in which sustainability goals are effectively communicated and components can easily be held accountable.

Before any sustainability measures can be taken, a board must ensure that there is buy-in not only among the board itself, but throughout the corporate structure. Directors must utilize the tools at their disposal to make sure that their policies and protocols are in line with their own sustainability requirements. Set sustainability milestones. Collect data. Analyze performance metrics. Seek out sustainability certifications and deal with other certified businesses. This peer-to-peer communication is appreciated by managers and reinforces that the company's highest-ranking individuals, the board of directors, are aligned with and engaged in the sustainability program.

> It is important that directors regularly review the progress of a company's sustainability efforts and communicate these updates to all middle managers and stakeholders alike.

In order to promote continuity within the sustainability operation, it is important that directors encourage cross-functional coordination between executives and managers from each unit of a company's operations. From product design, to legal, to human resources, to finance and logistics, each unit should have a representative who accepts the company's goals and carries the responsibility of maintaining and reporting upon the sustainability metrics of their respective sectors.

In 2015, the United Nations Global Compact, in collaboration with the global nonprofit Business for Social Responsibility (BSR), published a report detailing the supply chain governance structure of industry giant Hewlett-Packard (HP). Within its corporate structure, HP maintains a Supply Chain Board which works in tandem with its Ethics and Compliance Office to implement the company's Supply Chain Responsibility Program. The Supply Chain Board achieves cross-functional coordination by having VPs from each unit of HP's business structure serve as members. Extensive, third-party audits and the development of suppliers' audit programs for sustainability are key to the board's efforts of ensuring internal alignment within the company's operations. The Supply Chain Board meets monthly and reports directly to the company's executives.[7]

---

6. Alan S. Gutterman et al. THE LAWYERS CORPORATE SOCIAL RESPONSIBILITY DESKBOOK: PRACTICAL GUIDANCE FOR CORPORATE COUNSEL AND LAW FIRMS (American Bar Association, Business Law Section, 2019).

7. *Supply Chain Sustainability: A Practical Guide for Continuous Improvement*, UNITED NATIONS GLOBAL COMPACT with BSR (2015), https://d306pr3pise04h.cloudfront.net/docs/issues_doc%2Fsupply_chain%2FSupplyChainRep _spread.pdf.

Industry Collaboration

One of the most effective methods being utilized by corporations for tackling unwieldy supply chains is industry collaboration. This collective approach aims to perpetuate industry-wide standards for sustainability. By utilizing the same suppliers, major corporations within an industry are able to increase their leverage among low-tier suppliers and more effectively track sustainability protocols. Through resource sharing, manufacturers are also able to better equip suppliers to meet these standards.

One of the byproducts of the collective approach has been the creation of numerous industry associations. These associations comprise some of the largest corporations within their respective industries and function to create, impose, and maintain standards. The most notable of these coalitions is the Fair Labor Association (FLA), which serves as a multi-stakeholder initiative for improving global working conditions and promoting worker rights within the apparel and agriculture industries. The FLA comprises not only industry-leading corporations, but also universities and civil society organizations. These stakeholders come together to formulate and impose a code of conduct guided by international human rights protocols put forth by both the International Labor Organization and the United Nations.

Another example of this kind of collaboration is the Responsible Business Alliance (RBA). The RBA consists of giants of the technology industry such as Intel, HP, Apple, Dell, and Phillips. The coalition strives for resource efficiency and waste reduction within production and conducts standardized assessments of each member's operations. Industry-wide training for suppliers in both production streamlining and sustainability is also subsidized by members.[8]

The advantages of industry collaboration in regard to advancing sustainability are incomparable; however, there are certain risks that companies should consider before becoming involved in such initiatives. Collective action may serve as an unforeseen threat to a company's internal commitment to sustainability. If an organization views potential collaboration partners solely as competitors within a market, they may be inclined to retract some of their duties and put more onus on the other members. This is also due to the fact that industry collaboration is inherently resource-draining. The potential for both cost and time efficiencies does exist; however, many of these initiatives require heavy investment and sustainability results are not guaranteed. There also looms the potential for antitrust risks involving anticompetitive collaboration and taking precautions from making those associations overly cozy. These concerns mostly consist of inadvertent violations committed by representatives who may discuss prices or commercial strategy with other companies within the same sector.

Employees

Identifying and tending to the needs of employees is one of the most important aspects of a viable, sustainability strategy. The benefits correlated with an ethical and desirable working environment are crucial to the long-term growth of any corporation and a positive company image. Disclosure of employee statistics to the public is in some cases becoming a requirement. On November 9, 2020, the SEC, under a Disclosure Effectiveness Initiative, put

---

8. Villena & Gioia, *supra* note 4 at 198.

into effect amendments aimed to modernize and improve corporate disclosures by requiring SEC reporting companies to provide a description of their "human capital resources" on Form 10-K, to the extent the disclosures affect an investor's understanding of a company's business.[9]

As is the case with most components of the sustainability model, creating an ethical and desirable working environment stems from the supply chain. Employees who hold in high regard the sustainability practices of their employers exhibit improved confidence in senior management. This positive relationship encourages different types of organizational citizenship behavior, in which employees involve themselves in discretionary behaviors which forward the goals of the company. A peer-reviewed study on employee behaviors revealed that the recognition and subsequent rewarding of positive employee behaviors trigger a "butterfly effect" within an organization. If a manager were to promote an employee for being heavily committed to behavior, the employee would be more likely to engage with junior employees, adopting the role of a mentor. These relationships function to develop stronger, direct ties to management and ultimately produce a virtuous cycle begetting more positive behaviors. These sustainable relationships make employees feel that they are valued and that senior management is supportive of their innovative ideas.

The converse of organizational citizenship behavior is counterproductive work behavior. When employees feel dissatisfied with their work environment or find the operations of a company to be unethical, they tend to exhibit behaviors with the intention of hurting the interests of an organization. The negative impacts of counterproductive work behaviors stretch far beyond losses in productivity. According to one study, "employees engaged in high levels of negative behaviors tend to develop stress-related problems, a high rate of turnover intentions, lack of confidence at work, and physical or psychological pains".[10] Negative energy can bring down morale like a house of cards in a vicious cycle.

The most fundamental way to develop strong, employee–employer relationships is through engagement. An organization achieves true sustainability when its corporate values align with the personal values of its employees. Sustainability must be implemented within each dimension of the employee–employer relationship. Companies that successfully achieve sustainability are able to reconcile gaps between corporate and employee values within these three areas.

Formal Dimension

The formal dimension of the employee–employer relationship encompasses the employee's job description and any contracts, company handbooks, or performance agreements that the two parties agree upon. Sustainability measures and goals should be implemented into these descriptions and agreements. It is important that these reciprocal expectations for sustainability are established before the relationship even begins.[11]

---

9. Maj Vaseghi et al., *Incorporating Human Capital Management Disclosures into a Company's Annual Report*, HARVARD LAW SCHOOL FORUM ON CORPORATE GOVERNANCE (Oct. 31, 2020), https://corpgov.law.harvard.edu/2020/10/31/incorporating-human-capital-management-disclosures-into-a-companys-annual-report/.
10. Robert G. Eccles, *The Performance Measurement Manifesto*, HARV. BUS. REV. (Jan.–Feb. 1991), https://hbr.org/1991/01/the-performance-measurement-manifesto.
11. Vaseghi *supra* note 9.

Emotional Intelligence

Once expectations for sustainability are established, it is important that they are continuously reinforced. Directors should press managers to develop systems for identifying positive and sustainable behavior and subsequently rewarding it. Recognition not only functions to maintain these behaviors, but also encourages their growth and further development.[12]

The next step after recognition is incentivization. The progression of sustainable employment strategies has seen a rise in "pay-for-performance" models within corporations in which incentivization is tied to profitability. When it comes to pay-for-performance models, management practice professor Robert G. Eccles from Oxford University's Saïd Business School promotes individualized strategies determined by managers rather than standardized, company-wide policies. "I favor linking incentives strongly to performance but leaving managers free to determine their subordinates' rewards on the basis of all the relevant information," he says. "Then it is up to the manager to explain candidly to subordinates why they received what they did."[13] This open communication among employers and employees reinforces the foundation of trust between the two parties.

Social

The individual relationship between an employer and employee is not independent of the organizational culture surrounding the relationship. Employees are conscious of whether a company's actions are in line with its expressed values.[14] Whether it be a component of the supply chain, another employee, or even the board itself, any action that serves as being contradictory to a company's pledge to sustainability may be severely damaging to the trust that the company aims to maintain with its employees.

A corporation's sustainability practices also have significant effects on its ability to recruit talent. In a survey conducted by the William Mitchell Law Review, 69 percent of those surveyed said that they take into consideration the social and environmental track record of a company when deciding where to work. This sentiment is even stronger among those holding a Masters in Business Administration. In the end, a company that maintains a strong reputation for corporate social responsibility is viewed as being more attractive to prospective employees.

> 88 percent of MBA graduates claimed that they would be willing to take a pay cut to work for a company that exhibits sustainable business practices as opposed to one that does not.[15]

One industry leader in sustainable labor practices is the U.S.-based apparel company Levi Strauss & Co. The company puts the overall health of its employees at the forefront of its sustainability strategy by implementing several worker rights and well-being programs

---

12. Vaseghi *supra* note 9 at 201.
13. Eccles *supra* note 10 at 201.
14. Vaseghi *supra* note 9 at 201.
15. William H. Clark Jr. & Elizabeth K. Babson, *How Benefit Corporations are Redefining the Purpose of Business Corporations*, 38 WILL. MITCH. L. REV. (2012), https://open.mitchellhamline.edu/cgi/viewcontent.cgi?article=1451&context=wmlr.

throughout its operations, including its suppliers' factories. Although the purpose of these programs is to improve worker well-being and ensure worker rights, they also help suppliers achieve savings through increased productivity and reduced absenteeism. The company also strives to negotiate worker rights and workplace safety into all of its bilateral, regional, and multilateral trade agreements. Levi Strauss & Co. aims to legitimize its sustainability efforts by publicly advocating for the coupling of trade and labor. Representatives of the company meet with senior government officials and offer congressional testimony promoting workplace standards and worker rights provisions in regard to trade negotiations.

Customers

As consumers of products and drivers of sales, customers rival only employees in terms of importance to a corporation. As sustainability practices have progressed, increasing emphasis has been placed on the needs of customers. The title of customer has also been expanded to describe not only those individuals directly purchasing products, but the community members surrounding a corporation as well. With the advent of Benefit Corporations and the practice of stating the corporation's public benefit in its governing documents, known as a "mission lock," corporations have realized the inherent value in fostering growth in their surrounding communities. Adding policies to governing documents can prevent policy vacillation depending on the personalities of who is at the helm of the sustainability office at any given time.

As concern for environmental and social issues continues to grow, consumers are becoming increasingly aware of their ability to drive change not only within their own communities, but also within corporations. With each passing generation, more and more consumers are deciding to align their wallets with their values. The impacts for a company if it decides not to align itself with the values of its customer base can be devastating.

These consumer behaviors may be most apparent within the apparel industry. In a recent survey, 33 percent of customers claimed they had switched apparel brands due to concerns about sustainability, and 75 percent said that they consider environmental and social sustainability when shopping for clothing.[16] Additionally, a separate study found that 61 percent of millennials would be willing to pay more for ethically sourced and eco-friendly products.

An example of the integration of customer engagement into the sustainability strategy from a leading corporation is Unilever's Sustainable Living Plan. In 2010, the company launched the Unilever Sustainable Living Plan (USLP) with the purpose of pursuing several goals including the promotion of fairness in the workplace through inclusivity and providing opportunities for women. The plan also aims to cut the company's environmental impact in half by 2030 through reductions in greenhouse emissions and water usage and utilizing sustainable sourcing. A significant portion of the USLP however concerns promoting the health and well-being of its customers. The company undertook an initiative to improve the nutritional value of products across its wide range of brands. These efforts resulted in a reduction of sodium levels and unhealthy, unsaturated fats and an increase in

---

16. Michael Shellenberger, APOCALYPSE NEVER: WHY ENVIRONMENTAL ALARMISM HURTS US ALL (Harper, an Imprint of HarperCollinsPublishers, 2020).

essential fatty acids in numerous products. The company succeeded in reducing the caloric value of several of its ice cream products, including children's ice creams. Along with making beneficial changes to its products, Unilever has successfully commingled sustainability with its marketing strategy to help disseminate information about health and hygiene to people across the globe.[17]

Another example is SABMiller. According to the company's 2016 sustainability report,[18] not only does the brewing giant support over 175,000 small businesses through its value chain, it also undertakes meaningful initiatives to improve communities around the globe. Throughout Europe, the company maintains a campaign with the goal of reducing alcohol abuse and alcohol-related violence. The company has established or supported over 160 programs committed to taking on alcohol-related harm. In partnership with local institutions and NGOs, the company also sponsors prevention interventions for Fetal Alcohol Syndrome. In Poland, over 200,000 pregnant women have been reached due to the company's efforts.[19]

Achieving the Triple Advantage

For corporations capable of building successful frameworks for the maintenance of sustainability practices, the benefits are significant. The ultimate goal of perpetuating sustainability throughout corporate operations is the achievement of what is often called the "triple advantage." The triple advantage encompasses the business benefits that are concurrently realized alongside significant environmental and societal progress. In 2015, the World Economic Forum issued a report detailing the benefits experienced by companies that are leaders in sustainable operations management. Corporations capable of becoming leaders of sustainability within their industries are able to experience long-term improvement in four key areas: revenue growth, cost reduction, brand reputation, and risk mitigation.

Revenue Growth and Brand Reputation

According to the report, leading corporations may experience between a 5 and 20 percent increase in revenue growth for successful, sustainable products.[20] These spikes in revenue are possible due to the fact that companies are often able to charge a premium for products manufactured with clean technology or that are ethically sourced.

The report details that corporations may experience between a 10 and 25 percent increase in the popularity and image of their corporate brand through the legitimization of their sustainability practices. The benefits afforded to a company's brand reputation cannot be understated. Companies with established reputations carry a larger base of loyal customers who are willing to purchase a broad array of products. A sustained customer base functions to encourage confidence within the market, leading to higher price-earnings

---

17. *Sustainable Living*, Unilever, https://www.unilever.co.uk/sustainable-living/.

18. *Sustainable Development Report 2016*, SABMiller (2016), https://www.ab-inbev.com/content/dam /universaltemplate/ab-inbev/investors/sabmiller/reports/sustainable-development-reports/sustainable-development -report-2016.pdf.

19. Ibid.

20. *Beyond Supply Chains: Empowering Responsible Value Chains*, World Economic Forum (Jan. 2015), https://www3.weforum.org/docs/WEFUSA_BeyondSupplyChains_Report2015.pdf.

multiples and lower funding costs. Along with driving sales, a strong brand reputation also functions to promote success within the corporation itself. Brand reputation has significant effects on employee morale and retention of talent. As previously stated, employees are more effective at forwarding the goal of a corporation if they feel the values of the corporation are aligned with their own.

Cost Reduction

Corporations that commit to operating sustainable supply chains often find themselves mitigating their production costs. Proper streamlining of the production process through equipment and energy efficiency functions to both reduce waste and decrease production costs. In the face of diminishing resources and rising commodity prices, resource efficiency and waste reduction have become necessary for companies that intend on remaining profitable. The report claims that companies may experience an average 10 percent reduction in manufacturing costs and an average 17.5 percent reduction in material costs. Overall supply chain costs can be reduced by an average of 12.5 percent.

Take-Aways for Board Members

Sustainability practices function to promote an expectation for disciplined compliance with environmental, ethical, and health and safety standards; however, sustainability contributes to more than just the mitigation of legal risk. Through the operation of a diverse and responsible supply chain bolstered by sustainable substitutes, companies are able to mitigate source risk and ensure stability for their operations.

Improving sustainability and providing a benefit for customers and other stakeholders is not only altruistic. In fact, sustainable practices often, if communicated effectively, benefit the long-term bottom line. Improved customer satisfaction, new markets, and employee productivity help the company and are not simply charitable. Therefore, adopting sustainable workplace, customer and supply chain policies satisfy a director's fiduciary duty because they primarily benefit the company.

Chapter 20
Environmental Resources Management

Nancy S. Cleveland

Introduction

Environmental resources management broadly encompasses how a business uses natural resources—air, land, and water—in creating and protecting business value. When done responsibly, natural resources are used in ways that protect ecosystems for continued use. Sustainable management of natural resources relates not only to consumption, but also to how those resources become polluted by the waste products of extraction, business operations, and consumption.

Any business today that does not understand and work to minimize environmental impacts puts itself at risk in a variety of ways. From liability and fines for pollution to reputation risk; inefficiencies to resource scarcity; competitive disadvantage and lost market share to loss of a social license to operate, the consequences of poor environmental resources management can be significant.

> Any business today that does not understand and work to minimize environmental impacts puts itself at risk in a variety of ways.

Primary Concerns

Common to virtually all sustainability management systems, and the rating systems that evaluate business sustainability performance, are the primary ways in which a business impacts natural resources. While specific natural resources may be of greater concern in particular industries, the most existential impacts relate to energy, water, and waste. How a business addresses these concerns is primarily reflected in company data on energy and water consumption, and waste (including air, land, and water pollution). Reducing negative impacts in these three areas is viewed as the responsibility of everyone who lives on our small planet.

In today's business climate, the extent of business responsibility broadens as natural resources are depleted and populations grow. Board members should understand how management is performing in this regard. Extraction, depletion, and pollution are key concerns, and these concerns extend to a business's impacts all along its value chain.

> Systems thinking is the practice of understanding the world as a complex set of interconnected systems in which we live and do business. Sustainability as a business management tool is a framework for understanding where and how a business fits into this complex, interconnected system of systems.

Societal Pressures

The concept of living on a resource-limited, small planet is fairly new.[1] For centuries, enjoying Earth's bounty was limited only by human invention. As industrialization began harnessing Earth's resources in the 18th century, we embraced a take-make-waste mindset based on a belief that resources are plentiful and space for disposal of waste is seemingly limitless. These views began to change as humans traveled into space in the 1960s. Human-created boundaries disappear when Earth is viewed from space. What becomes apparent is the so-called Overview Effect, a realization that:

- we are one planetary community;
- our natural resources and ecosystem services[2] are all we have for survival; and
- there is no "away" for the waste and pollution we create on planet Earth.

Inherent in this evolving societal perspective is the concept of systems thinking, a fundamental element of sustainability and managing impacts on natural resources. Systems thinking is the practice of understanding the world as a complex set of interconnected

---

1. The realization that Earth is spherical, not flat, took hold over centuries, beginning in the 6th century BCE in some parts of the world and not appearing in others until the 17th century CE. See https://en.wikipedia.org/wiki/Flat_Earth#Alternate_or_mixed_theories (last accessed Nov. 30, 2020). Whether one viewed the Earth as flat or round, its natural resources were limited only by virtue of humans' understanding of their usefulness and ability to access and use them. Generally, resources were perceived as being plentiful, if only one could harness them.
2. Ecosystem services are the functions and benefits provided by the Earth's ecosystem, a dynamic and interdependent community of organisms that interact with each other and their physical environment. Examples of ecosystem services are food, raw materials, medicines, hydro-energy, clean air and water, natural pest and disease control, soil regeneration, shade, wind, tidal currents, plant pollination, nutrient cycles, and physical areas for human recreation and enjoyment. Sometimes, these benefits are grouped into four categories: provisioning, regulating, supporting, and cultural.

systems in which we live and do business. Sustainability as a business management tool is a framework for understanding where and how a business fits into this complex, interconnected system of systems. It is about recognizing when and the extent to which existing ways of thinking and doing business have become obsolete or even threatening to the viability of an organization. With respect to natural resources, this moves us away from the linear take-make-waste mindset and toward a circular borrow-use-return mindset that allows for innovative ways of solving complex, systemic problems and limitations.

It is not enough to tabulate and change a business's direct impacts. Businesses are expected to understand and change indirect impacts as well. To do this, companies must implement a systems-based sustainability management program that reflects an in-depth understanding of systems thinking. The sustainability management system should demonstrate a thorough understanding of the company's product and services supply chain, distribution processes, uses, and disposal activities. This is key to enabling management to fully address and excel at environmental resources management and meet a board's primary objective of value protection and creation.

Direct and Indirect Impacts

Impacts on Earth's ecosystem—both negative and positive—vary widely from business to business. For companies that make physical products, one must look for impacts from the extraction of a product's component parts all the way to disposal of the product at the end of its useful life, and every aspect of creation, distribution, and use in between. For services companies, there are impacts associated with the products they use (again, from extraction to disposal) and the processes of providing services. For example, an insurance company will have direct impacts on the energy and office supplies consumed by operating offices for its service providers, as well as indirect impacts by virtue of activities like business travel and investments it makes with capital reserves.

One tool for a deep understanding of impacts is called a lifecycle assessment (LCA). An LCA is the collection and examination of the overall impacts of a product or service from materials sourcing to production to distribution to disposal. LCA focuses on the energy inputs and outputs and materials used to gauge social, economic, and environmental impacts of the product or service.[3]

While LCA is a comprehensive way of calculating impacts, it is fairly expensive and out-of-reach for many companies to use on a wide-scale basis. With knowledge of what LCA is, however, businesses can better understand the broad scope of systems thinking required to assess sustainability risks associated with their products and services. Management will have to determine not only what impacts are significant, but also what products and services contribute most significantly to those impacts.

From the board's perspective, a good starting place is to understand what is considered significant at the industry level. The Sustainability Accounting Standards Board (SASB) is an independent 501(c)3 nonprofit organization with a mission to develop sustainability

---

3. One organization that provides a wealth of information and an LCA-based methodology for assessing product impacts is The Sustainability Consortium. The Consortium's focus is on impacts throughout a company's supply chain. See https://www.sustainabilityconsortium.org/ (last accessed Dec. 3, 2020).

accounting standards that help public companies disclose relevant, material information to investors. Through a consensus process, SASB created industry-based lists of material sustainability issues and metrics best used to quantify impacts.[4] Becoming familiar with this information for a company's industry will help both public and private boards focus the company on addressing significant impacts. It will have the added benefit of helping the board understand and prepare for sustainability inquiries from investors.

> From the board's perspective, a good starting place is to understand what is considered significant at the industry level. Becoming familiar with this information for a company's industry will help both public and private boards focus the company on addressing significant impacts.

Overview of Environmental Impacts

Below is an overview of how businesses impact environmental resources.

Air Pollution

For most businesses, risks associated with polluted air generally arise from two sources:

- noncompliance with law for emissions that are regulated by national, state, or local authorities; and
- indoor air pollution.

Noncompliance with environmental permit requirements and/or emissions limits is a typical risk. It will expose a company to substantial penalties and/or lawsuits.

Indoor air pollutants are of particular concern because of impacts on human health, which arise from dust, mold, allergens, and off-gassed chemicals. These impacts often result in productivity losses. In extreme cases, an unhealthy workplace has the potential to affect a company's ability to attract and retain talent.

Air pollution can result from operational processes, transport systems, and supply chains as well. Federal air quality standards such as the Clean Air Act and the National Ambient Air Quality Standards set maximum atmospheric concentrations for specific pollutants and regulate emissions to those standards.

Companies can reduce air pollution through eco-efficiencies and technology solutions. By incorporating environmental considerations into design, retrofit, and operating processes, products, buildings, and manufacturing systems can be made more efficient and sustainable in protecting the quality of the air we breathe.

Land Use and Biodiversity

Land uses that directly or indirectly degrade, exploit, pollute, or destroy land and ecosystem services can have cascading effects on the ecosystem. A loss of or damage to habitats and biodiversity can cascade into extinction, invasive species, predators and pests, resource

---

4. The SASB Materiality Map is a useful tool for at-a-glance information by industry groups. See https://materiality.sasb.org/ (last accessed Dec. 3, 2020).

scarcity, and changes in ecosystems like the water cycle. All of these have costs to society, and in many cases, they are illegal.

Businesses may not always see the impacts they have on biodiversity and land as significant. Individual business impacts often are not significant until they are added up with the direct and indirect impacts of many others. In such instances, companies are often expected to address relatively small impacts to take part in reducing a cumulative effect. For example, procurement or supply chain practices of many may support market demands that indirectly cause deforestation.

Championing and following changes in norms and practices to correct such deleterious results, and working to protect and restore natural resources and ecosystem services, can yield business benefits such as:

- Increasing revenue from responsibly produced goods and services
- Improving access to financial capital from socially responsible investors
- Improving sustainability reputation, credentials, and values of the organization
- Enhancing social license to operate

Energy

Energy management is the process of systematically planning, sourcing, and distributing energy resources to meet consumption needs, while taking into account environmental and economic impacts. To be most effective and resourceful, energy management systems work within a hierarchy (from most to least preferable) of preferred action. The first priority is to reduce energy use, and then meet the remaining demand with the most sustainable means possible. The hierarchy looks like this:

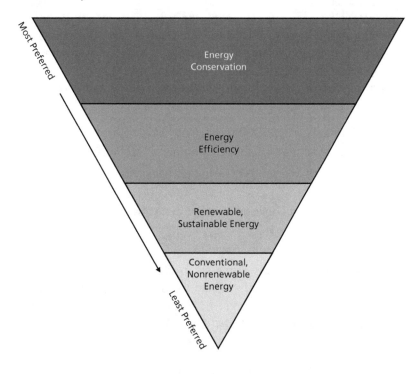

The primary objectives of energy management are:

- resource security,
- energy conservation,
- operating efficiencies,
- cost stabilization and savings, and
- pollution reduction.

Technological innovation continues to deliver new ways to improve efficiency and conserve energy consumption, even without behavioral changes, in facilities, operations, and transportation.

The amount and type of energy we use can also have serious implications for the natural environment. While every energy source has some impact on the natural environment, whether on air and water quality, wildlife and habitat loss, or climate change, fossil fuels—coal, oil, and natural gas—do substantially more damage to the environment than renewable energy sources—solar, wind, and hydro. Being part of the transition to renewables is an essential part of energy management today.

Materials

As increased consumption constrains the availability of natural resources, product-based businesses will suffer if not prepared. Materials essential to production may be affected by other factors like climate change and supply chain disruptions. Preparation means not only understanding the limits and stressors for materials, but also investing time and resources in creating the alternative processes and resources needed to avoid intractable problems and innovate product requirements.

Looking at materials management through the broad lens of systems thinking gets at root problems and helps direct resources toward solutions. When material issues affect an entire industry at an existential level, leadership in collaborative activities with business partners and suppliers can protect market share and industry viability.

Incorporating sustainable materials management into product development and sourcing practices can have significant benefits. These benefits include:

- savings generated by efficiency and reduced waste;
- better risk management as negative environmental and social impacts are addressed;
- preparedness for—or avoidance of—supply chain disruptions and resource scarcity; and
- value-driven research and development for more sustainable materials.

Waste

Businesses produce waste of all kinds. Some are in significant volumes, and some are hazardous. Our ecosystems can only absorb certain kinds of waste, and even then, in limited amounts. As the burden of waste becomes more critical, treatment and disposal become increasingly subject to regulation and related costs. And as natural resources dwindle and become increasingly more expensive to source, it behooves businesses to innovate more and better ways to recover those resources from products and manufacturing processes for reuse.

Waste management is the process of reducing the negative effects of waste on the environment and society, including human health and well-being. Best practices follow a hierarchy of preferred activities:

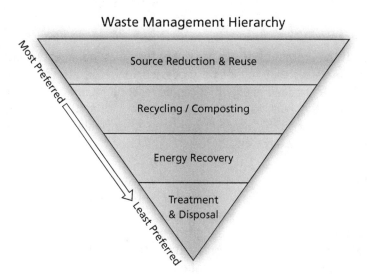

The basic concept of this inverted pyramid is first to avoid or eliminate waste, then reabsorb waste into productive reuse if possible, and lastly, properly handle what remains. This strategy helps businesses responsibly management the wastes they create, with an overarching goal of keeping viable and valuable resources in productive use, even after a particular product has reached the end of its useful life. To preserve ecosystems and reduce landfill burdens and improper disposal of waste that cannot be processed by ecosystems, businesses have a social and environmental responsibility to manage their waste in the most preferred and sustainable ways possible.

When businesses optimize waste management, they demonstrate a desire to protect, preserve, and sustain people and our limited and precious natural resources. The best way to do that is to understand and implement the waste management hierarchy. Here are some examples and explanations of how this is done.

Source Reduction and Reuse

- Salvage waste for use in other manufacturing processes or reincorporate it back into the same process.
- Redesign product packaging to reduce packaging waste.
- Use design that considers standard measures to get the full measure of materials and eliminate cut waste.

Recycling/Composting

- Use design to improve the ability to recycle or compost the raw materials incorporated into products.

- Reprocess materials and products that have reached the end of their useful life back into raw materials that can be put into further productive use.

Energy Recovery

Energy recovery is the process of extracting, rather than wasting, energy before disposing of products and materials that cannot be processed for reuse through recycling. Many types of waste have embedded energy that can be recaptured and used. Waste-to-energy is a method of doing this, such as incineration or recovery of methane gas that is created by anaerobic digestion of landfill waste. It can be used to create various forms of usable energy such as heat, steam, electricity, or fuel.

Treatment/Disposal

The graveyard for waste that cannot be recycled or reused in any way is the landfill or treatment facility. Even though this is the least preferred way to manage waste, these facilities are highly regulated for how they are designed, operated, and closed, including capping landfills and using them for surface recreational activities. Hazardous wastes are highly regulated to avoid environmental contamination.

When businesses optimize waste management, they demonstrate a desire to protect, preserve, and sustain people and our limited and precious natural resources. The best way to do that is to understand and implement the waste management hierarchy.

Water

Water risk refers to the potential for water scarcity, water stress, flooding, or drought that impacts the ability to conduct business. The severity of the risk corresponds to the intensity of the water challenge, as well as the vulnerability of the business. Water risks can be:

- physical (e.g., too little water, too much water, water that is unfit for use, or inaccessible water),

- regulatory (e.g., strict, lenient, or poorly enforced regulations), or

- reputational (e.g., how your business is perceived by the public with respect to water).

Many organizations and investors assume that water will remain cheap and readily available in years to come. But, based on global water projections, this assumption is short-sighted. Improper management and poor planning for water resources can negatively impact the bottom line. It can also create negative stakeholder perceptions of a company's commitment to water stewardship and its ability to anticipate and adjust to water conditions.

The primary objectives of water management are:

- security of water resources,
- water conservation,
- quality suited to use,
- efficient facilities,
- cost stabilization and savings, and
- pollution avoidance and reduction.

In an office environment, it is relatively inexpensive and easy to achieve water conservation. But for businesses that consume a lot of water, identifying water risks and prioritizing areas for action are more complicated and critical to business viability. The risk of water-related disruptions in supply chains may be even higher than at the company level. Businesses can address these issues by working with suppliers and external stakeholders to raise awareness and build capacity for water management.

Mitigating risks can be complex and challenging because there often are many competing interests in terms of access and availability. In any case, failure to mitigate and innovate to deal with water scarcity issues will be costly.

The appropriate mitigation response depends on whether water scarcity originates inside or outside a company. Water risk for high-consumption businesses originates from two primary sources:

- *Risks due to company operations, products, and services*: These risks originate directly from company and supplier operations, and how products and services affect local communities and ecosystems. Improved management within the facility and with suppliers (e.g., by switching to less water-intensive materials and processes) can help to mitigate these risks.

- *Risk due to basin conditions*: In contrast to direct operational risks, water basin risks are outside the direct control of a company. They cannot be addressed through changes in company or supplier operations. These risks require engagement outside the company via collective action, advocacy, and/or engagement at a policy level.

Green Building

The Green Building movement, spearheaded in the United States by the U.S. Green Building Council and its LEED certification programs,[5] is a movement to radically change the impact of buildings on natural resources and human occupants. The movement has had a major effect on the creation and expanded availability of environmentally friendly technology and products. It has provided significant, viable means for businesses to

---

5. For more information, see https://www.usgbc.org/ (last accessed Dec. 3, 2020).

reduce the negative impacts of the buildings they occupy and provide more healthy and welcoming workspaces.[6]

Businesses can demonstrate a commitment to improving sustainability performance by requiring that all relocation, new location, and renovation projects for their built environment needs use the well-tested and widely available technologies, products, and services underlying the USGBC's LEED programs, even if certification is not an objective.

Take-Aways for Board Members

- Understanding how a business uses natural resources—air, land, and water—in creating and protecting business value is fundamental to developing board policies to ensure that natural resources are used in ways that protect the business and the ecosystems on which it relies.

- Environmental resource management grounded in systems thinking is a key business function for identifying resource constraints, opportunities for more sustainable approaches to consuming natural resources, and related business risks in an increasingly resource-constrained world.

- Embracing environmental resources stewardship as part of board policy will help a company preserve the availability of resources that are essential to its products and services.

- Board policies that promote environmental resource management will ensure long-term success by providing a basis for research and development of alternatives to wasteful or damaging processes and essential resources that cannot be naturally replenished or protected.

---

6. As an outgrowth of the Green Building movement, the concept of Well Building has emerged to help businesses improve workforce attraction and retention by creating highly attractive and health-inducing buildings in which to conduct business. The International Well Building Institute leads this effort with a science-based building certification program for buildings that are designed and built to enhance human health and well-being. See https://www.wellcertified.com/ (last accessed Dec. 3, 2020).

Chapter 21
How to Leverage Benefit Governance

Frederick Alexander

What Is a Benefit Corporation?

This chapter investigates whether corporate form matters in building a more sustainable business (spoiler alert: the author believes it matters immensely). The most prevalent corporate form that purports to increase sustainability is the benefit corporation, which has been around since the early 2010s. Within ten years, over 10,000 benefit corporations were formed and over 300 collectively raised more than $4 billion in outside capital; by the middle of 2021, there were ten publicly traded benefit corporations in the United States and three additional public companies that had adopted benefit corporation governance, a form of private ordering available to companies in jurisdictions where the benefit corporation is not available. Many well-known brands belong to these companies including Dannon Yogurt, Silk Milk, Eileen Fisher, Avon Products, The Body Shop, and Allbirds Shoes. Financial services like Amalgamated Bank and Lemonade Insurance are included as well.

In the modern era, the importance of corporate form was highlighted in the 1980s, when management of publicly traded companies felt vulnerable to unsolicited bids that could lead to large premiums for shareholders, but also job loss and community stress. There was a belief that corporate law was in some sense responsible for this threat because corporate law focused directors on shareholders, but not other stakeholders. In response, many states adopted "constituency" statutes that allowed directors to consider the interests of other stakeholders, including workers, customers, and communities, when defending against a takeover bid, when selling the company, and in other situations.

Delaware, the preferred choice of corporate domicile for publicly traded companies in the United States, never adopted such a constituency statute, and only a few companies left Delaware to take advantage of the new provisions. Although these statutes allowed directors to consider other stakeholders, with one expired exception they did not require it, and some scholars who have studied the effect of those law changes say that the only constituency to benefit was management and that rather than making directors more accountable for stakeholders, they simply became less accountable to shareholders.

There the matter stood until 2010, when Maryland adopted a "benefit corporation" statute, which gave companies the option to choose a corporate form that *required* directors to consider the interests of stakeholders and to strive to create a material positive effect on the environment and society as a whole. Many states followed, and as of 2021, 42 jurisdictions in the United States have a benefit governance option, as do three countries and the Canadian province of British Columbia.

This chapter describes how benefit corporations differ from conventional corporations, and how a company might use the statute to operate more sustainably. The key point is very simple: directors of a benefit corporation have an obligation to consider the broad impacts of their decisions, whereas directors of a conventional corporation may (and in some jurisdictions must) put shareholders first, even if that priority means making decisions that degrade our natural environment, threaten social institutions, or exploit vulnerable communities. Corporations that adopt benefit corporation status are essentially putting sustainability into their legal DNA.

> Corporations that adopt benefit corporation status are essentially putting sustainability into their legal DNA.

As more jurisdictions adopt the form, more variations come into being. This chapter describes the form adopted in Delaware, except where otherwise indicated. Delaware is the corporate home of most publicly traded corporations in the United States, and it is also favored by many investors, so that entities looking to raise outside capital often incorporate there. The Delaware version (which has been partially or wholly adopted in Colorado, Kansas, Tennessee, Texas, and Kentucky) is called the "public benefit corporation" or "PBC."

Essential Elements of Benefit Corporations

Responsible and Sustainable Management: The Balancing Obligation

The Delaware law describes a PBC as a corporation intended to operate in a "responsible and sustainable manner." The law specifically requires a PBC to *balance* three considerations: (1) the shareholders' financial interests, (2) the best interests of those materially affected by the corporation's conduct, and (3) a specific public benefit identified in the corporation's charter documents. This balancing obligation distinguishes benefit corporations from conventional corporations: rather than focusing solely on economic wealth of shareholders, a PBC must balance the interests of stakeholders other than shareholders as ends in themselves.

The second part of the three-part balancing act is quite broad. The directors must account for employees, customers, and the communities where a corporation does business. In addition, where a corporation's actions affect the environment or social institutions, populations can become stakeholders who are "materially affected" by corporate decisions, so that directors should include these groups in its decision-making balance. In this particular, the law's reference to "sustainable" operations can be understood as requiring a corporation to consider what constitutes its fair share of any common resource, whether environmental or social.

While balancing shareholder interests and the interests of stakeholders generally, each PBC must also choose one or more specific public benefits. A public benefit is a specific positive effect on a defined group. Once established, the specific purpose can only be changed by a charter amendment that would require approval of both directors and shareholders. A corporation becoming a benefit corporation should take great care in selecting a specific purpose.

> Best practice for benefit corporations: provide a specific purpose that is broad enough to limit the need for future amendments but narrow enough to be meaningful.

It is a best practice to provide a purpose that is broad enough to limit the need for future amendments to the specific goal. For example, if a company's specific public purpose involves ensuring that school children receive nutritious meals, it may be best to refer to that generic but specific purpose, rather than articulating the specific means by which the company currently achieves that purpose since, as the company scales and evolves, its method for providing nutritious meals may also change.

The Effect of the Balancing Test on Director Decision-Making

As described above, directors of PBCs are required to balance the interests of shareholders with the best interests of stakeholders materially affected by the corporation, and the corporation's identified specific benefit. Therefore, the directors of a PBC must weigh concerns other than maximizing economic value for the shareholders of the corporation, and the directors must manage the corporation in a way that balances all of the relevant interests.

Of course, even in a conventional corporation, directors must consider myriad stakeholder interests to successfully manage a business. But conventional Delaware corporate law is clear that such consideration must be rationally related to shareholder value. While this provides conventional corporate directors some leeway as to social responsibility, they are still required to view all decisions through the lens of value maximization for shareholders. Under the PBC model, the opposite holds: directors *must* balance the interests of stakeholders other than shareholders, even when those interests collide.

While directors must engage in this balancing, no specific outcome is mandated; instead, boards are required to engage in a balancing *process*. As long as the directors act independently and in good faith, the courts will accept their balancing decisions. (This is not clear in every jurisdiction that has a benefit corporation law, so companies should carefully consult with counsel before choosing a jurisdiction.)

This broad discretion is known as the "business judgment rule," and is an important corporate law rule that protects business decisions from second-guessing by courts. The rule prevents shareholders from suing directors for "bad" decisions as long as the directors are independent and informed and act in good faith. Thus, if shareholders sue directors for failing to balance the three statutory categories of interests, the court will reject the claim unless the shareholders show that the board was conflicted, uninformed, or irrational.

This means that a shareholder challenging the board would have to claim that the directors failed to pursue one of the three interests entirely (or perhaps engaged in a level of pursuit so weak as to constitute "conscious disregard" of that interest). Thus, a plaintiff could allege that the directors were no longer pursuing shareholder return or were no longer attempting to act in the best interests of the stakeholders affected by its conduct. Alternatively, a plaintiff might allege that despite minimal consideration of all three goals, the board engaged in a trade-off that no rational person would engage in.

The Unique Role of Shareholders

Although benefit corporation law creates a duty to consider stakeholder interest, it does not give stakeholders rights. Instead, in order to maintain accountability for the new obligations, shareholders are permitted to bring claims that directors failed to balance shareholder and public benefit interests correctly.

> Although benefit corporation law creates a duty to consider stakeholder interests, it does not give rights to stakeholders.

This limitation makes the adoption of benefit corporation status more palatable to corporations and shareholders: if the law created new rights that allowed any stakeholder to bring a fiduciary lawsuit, the risk of litigation pitting stakeholders against one another would be intolerable. But the rule limiting rights to shareholders is more than a practical compromise: it reflects an idea that is a central theoretical underpinning of the benefit corporation: *shareholders have an interest in promoting the interests of all stakeholders and are adequate representatives for them.* Under benefit corporation law, after all, shareholders retain the power to elect directors, approve merger transactions, and bring legal challenges. Stakeholders have no voice in any of these matters.

Does this mean the new corporate form is just greenwashing, and that benefit corporations will continue to maximize shareholder value? There are several reasons to believe the new form can be a part of real change. First, by forming and investing in a benefit corporation, the shareholders and management have agreed to manage the corporation for the benefit of a broad group of stakeholders. Presumably, this means that the shareholders (or at least a majority of them) have determined that it is important that all stakeholders are accounted for in board decisions. Second, for widely held public corporations, most shareholders are broadly diversified investors who are dependent on a stable society and environment to support all of their investments and would be financially injured if some corporations create extra profits by externalizing social and environmental costs. Third, shareholders (or the beneficiaries represented by institutional shareholders like pension and mutual funds) are humans with broad interests—interests in a livable environment, interests in a stable society, and interests in a viable future for generations to come.

Disclosure

PBCs must provide shareholders with a report once every two years assessing the corporation's promotion of its stated public benefit or benefits. The law requires that the corporation provide such a report every other year. The report must describe the board's goals and standards with respect to stakeholders; specifically, the report must include four elements:

(1) the benefit *objectives* the board has;
(2) the *standards* the board has adopted to measure progress against those objectives;
(3) *objective factual information* based on those standards; and
(4) an *assessment* of the corporation's success in meeting its objectives.

Unlike some benefit corporation laws, the Delaware statute does not mandate that the report use a standard developed by a third party. Nonetheless, if a PBC chooses, it may include in its governing documents a provision that mandates that the corporation provide a report more frequently; that requires the report to be made public; or that requires the corporation to use a third-party standard in measuring its stakeholder performance.

Managing a Benefit Corporation

Starting with Transparency

The best starting point for directors considering broadened benefit corporation obligations is the statutory transparency requirements. In order to comply with these obligations, the directors must determine who is materially affected by the corporation's business, develop and maintain criteria for balancing both the interests of those so affected and any specific benefit identified in the corporation's charter, and measure progress against those criteria. The corporation may adopt a third-party standard to monitor its actions and progress, and while it is not required to do so, a third-party standard can be a useful tool for a board to use to understand its stakeholders and their concerns. Note that some benefit corporation statutes outside of Delaware do require the use of a third-party standard.

The exercise of maintaining a credible reporting function focused on sustainability will require the board and management to address important stakeholder issues and maintain a record of that work. Below are additional recommendations of procedures a benefit corporation board may adopt to ensure it is properly addressing stakeholder concerns.

Establish a Committee

A committee may be tasked with responsibility for sustainability issues. Assigning this responsibility to a committee should not be viewed as isolating the benefit purposes. Instead, assigning matters to committees is generally perceived as a recognition of the importance of the delegated matters. For this reason, vital functions, such as compensation and audit, are generally assigned to committees. Research suggests firms that adopt effective sustainability programs are more likely to form a separate board committee to address sustainability issues. The board can delegate this responsibility to an existing committee, such as audit or governance, or create a new, stand-alone committee. The committee that is responsible for sustainability issues should include in its committee charter oversight of and/or recommendations with respect to: third-party standards, if any; internally generated standards; choice of certifying body or bodies, if any; the benefit report; and sustainability objectives, standards, strategies, and policies.

Management Role

While the committee should oversee sustainability issues, management must fully integrate benefit purpose into its function. Notably, management should draft the benefit report and report progress toward the impact objectives to the board. Additionally, management should make recommendations on the following subjects: third-party standards and internally generated standards; certification issues; and sustainability objectives, standards, strategies, and policies. Many companies already have a sustainability function, such as a Chief Sustainability Officer. In a benefit corporation, this role will be heightened in importance, as sustainability shifts to being a primary purpose of the corporation. As discussed above, board decisions around benefit issues will be protected by the business judgment rule, but the rule requires that directors be fully informed. Accordingly, management and sustainability officers will have a critical role in providing the board and relevant committees with the information necessary to consider and balance the interests of all relevant stakeholders.

Periodic Activity

Certain activities should be conducted cyclically in accordance with the timing selected for production of the company's benefit report. Sustainability objectives should be established and assessed annually. The committee should meet regularly and report to the board.[1] Periodic reports to the board from the committee will allow the board significant opportunity to address stakeholder interests. Management and the committee should meet for an extended period of time, at least annually, regarding these sustainability objectives. Finally, the board should review the benefit report.

This is not meant to suggest that sustainability issues are separate from the operation of the corporation generally. Directors should keep the broad objectives of the corporation in mind and seek to understand the implications of all corporate decisions on important stakeholders. It is a best practice for directors to keep a copy of the corporation's benefit standards and goals at hand during board meetings and while doing board work, in order to reference the objectives and goals against any decisions being made.

> It is a best practice for directors to keep a copy of the corporation's benefit standards and goals at hand during board meetings and while doing board work, in order to reference sustainability objectives and goals against any decisions being made.

---

1. *See* B Lab Procedures, *supra* n. 458, at 2 (correlating board responsibility for sustainability with high-sustainability performance).

Nonperiodic Activity

Management and the committee should have different responsibilities with respect to issues that arise in a nonperiodic fashion. Management can be charged with bringing significant sustainability issues to the board that come up out of cycle and that are not covered by policies, such as the effect of a strategic change or product change on workers or customers, or the environmental impacts of significant building projects, fleet acquisitions, or other matters. Depending on magnitude, the committee should consider sustainability issues implicated by new developments, such as carbon emission policies or the effect of a sale transaction on workers' compensation or customers.

Of course, many individual decisions are made at the management level, and not brought to the directors' attention. For such delegated decisions, it is important that a corporation have adequate policies in place to guide management decisions that affect stakeholders.

With respect to director-level decisions affecting benefit purposes, the committee could make the decision or defer to the board if the particular inquiry is of great significance. Regardless, the committee should report any and all decisions to the board. In general, clear policies and record-keeping with respect to stakeholder concerns will preserve the protections of the business judgment rule for ordinary decisions.

Process Issues

Management's recommendations to the committee and the committee's recommendations to the board should be distributed well in advance of committee and board meetings in order to give directors adequate time for review. Meeting minutes should reflect sustainability issues discussed, resolution of those issues, and any direction given to the committee or management. Additionally, if a third-party standard or internal standard has been adopted, materials and minutes should reflect consideration of how the standard maps to the interests of those affected by the corporation's conduct. Standard meeting procedure should include reviewing of internal checklists to determine whether other sustainability issues should be added.

Company Sales
The Standard

Under conventional law, directors have an obligation or ability to obtain the highest price for shareholders when a corporation is sold in a transaction resulting in a change in control, and courts carefully scrutinize director conduct to ensure that standard is met. In a benefit corporation, directors have a broader mandate to consider all stakeholders. Nevertheless, because change-of-control transactions present unique risks, the heightened scrutiny applicable to such transactions will continue under benefit corporation statutes. However, because benefit corporation directors have an expanded duty to balance other stakeholder interests the scrutiny will take place through a different lens.

A benefit corporation board will be required to balance a multitude of interests in a sale of the company. Traditional directors already balance numerous shareholder considerations when financially valuing bids for a company and the broad stakeholder proposition of benefit corporation governance adds to the considerations benefit corporation directors should bear in mind when valuing bids.

Thus, the substantive conventional requirement—maximizing value for shareholders—is likely to change, and become an obligation to find the "best" transaction for all stakeholders as a group, so that if shareholders challenge a sale in court, directors are still required to show that they pursued a reasonable path toward maximizing *collective* value for all relevant stakeholders—that is, the total value to be received by shareholders, stakeholders affected by the corporation's operations, and specific beneficiaries, if any. For both practical and conceptual reasons, this is unlikely to be enforced on a mathematical basis where the sum of all benefits to all stakeholders is calculated, with the transaction having the highest sum being the one that must be chosen. First, such mathematical precision is not possible. Second, and more importantly, such an interpretation would run counter to the business judgment concepts inherent in the statutes with respect to balancing and considering stakeholder interests.

Instead, the court is likely to examine the same issues they look at in traditional sale situations to ensure a fair sale process, such as the effect of market checks and deal protections. On the other hand, a board's rational choice among bids that allocate value among stakeholders differently should not be subject to heightened scrutiny under Section 365(b), which mandates the application of the business judgment rule for all allocation decisions. Case law interpreting protective mechanisms involving corporations subject to constituency statutes suggests this will be the case. This is an area where the law may differ significantly under various benefit corporation statutes, so consultation with counsel is critical.

However, when a board does allocate value to stakeholder interests, the court could scrutinize the board's actual efforts to ensure that stakeholder value is achieved. For example, the court could focus on whether measures to protect stakeholders after the sale closes are enforceable. As with most non-conflict transactions however, a reviewing court is still most likely to focus more on process than on substantively reviewing the board decision. The next section offers guidance for selling a benefit corporation in compliance with the expanded fiduciary duties of a benefit corporation.

The Sale Process

Because sale transactions will be subject to heightened scrutiny and because the calculus of value will be so different, corporations will need to adopt clear procedures to reasonably address stakeholder interests. This task may be less onerous than it sounds. Presumably, a benefit corporation involved in a sale process has already established the standards by which it is addressing stakeholder concerns, including through adopting third-party standards, and setting objectives and standards. The task of the board of a benefit corporation being sold may well be to make sure the sale does not unduly interfere with those objectives, or negatively affect performance against the third-party standard. In this sense, the board will need to investigate the plans of the buyer, something that would be of very limited importance for a conventional corporation.

Confidence that the buyer will maintain the status quo may well be sufficient to meet a board's public benefit obligations, but that confidence may require some combination of due diligence, contractual obligation, and corporate governance structure. The critical concern during the sale process will be surfacing these issues and making sure that management and outside professionals involved in the process understand the importance of addressing stakeholder concerns.

It may also be the case that simply maintaining the status quo is not sufficient. This could be because (1) the buyer does not plan to treat the stakeholders as well or (2) the buyer is paying a large premium, some of which the board determines should be shared with stakeholders. An example can make this concrete: a buyer may plan to combine workforces, which will lead to large layoffs, and may be able to pay a large premium because of the efficiency gains from that combination. In a cash sale by a conventional corporation, all of that financial gain goes to shareholders—and the board does not even have an obligation to investigate what the transaction will mean for its workforce. In a benefit corporation, however, the board will need to determine how these stakeholders will be treated, and when learning of the layoffs, devise a strategy that takes their interests into account. This might mean any number of things, such as negotiating severance, retraining, and similar provisions. Where a large premium results from efficiencies that do not hurt stakeholders— such as the ability to use the salesforces to sell the products from the combined companies, the board might also consider asking that some of that premium goes to workers in the form of bonuses or other compensation.

Merger agreements may have to address post-merger conduct because of a need to protect stakeholder interests. In some situations, agreements will need to be drafted to assure both the continuation of the benefit provisions in the corporation's charter and continued implementation of the benefit principles.

There may be alternative means to protect stakeholders. For example, a benefit corporation being sold in a transaction that will result in a loss of jobs in a community might fund a trust to provide assistance to the community, including job training and local business development. Or a company may simply favor a buyer that has a strong reputation for operating in a responsible manner.

Defensive Situations

Benefit corporations, like traditional Delaware corporations, can take defensive actions in response to a takeover threat. These defensive tactics are likely to be evaluated against the same standard as conventional corporations, which requires that the defensive measures be reasonable in relation to the threat posed.

Significantly, however, traditional corporations can only deploy these devices to protect shareholders from a very specific threat: a situation that jeopardizes shareholder value. In contrast, because a benefit corporation board must account for a much broader range of considerations, the range of possible threats that can be addressed by defensive measures will be broader than in traditional corporations. In that sense, directors will be given greater discretion to employ defensive devices in order to protect the company and its sustainable mission. That said, it is unlikely that this discretion will extend to board action that limits the exercise of shareholder voting rights.

Take-Aways for Board Members

Readers should remember that benefit corporation governance is only the map, and not the territory itself. By shifting corporate purpose from shareholder wealth to shared value, this new corporate form can show the way for executives, directors, and shareholders to work together to build business models that derive sustainable profits from efficiency and innovation and that reject the business of extraction and exploitation. But that shift requires more than a change in corporate form. In considering a proposal to convert a conventional corporation to a benefit corporation, the board should:

- Work with shareholders and executives to reach a shared understanding of the unique nature of a benefit corporation.

- Establish a specific public benefit appropriate to the company's circumstances but flexible enough to accommodate natural business evolution.

- Consider what procedures the company will use to engage in the balancing required by the statute.

- Consider how the board will play its role in the balancing equation and whether there will be a modification in the committee structure.

- Review potential third-party standards the company may be able to use satisfying the balancing obligation.

- Consider how the company plans to be transparent about the new structure.

Chapter 22
Sustainable Development Goals and Other International Sustainability Initiatives

William Jannace

Background

In 2015, United Nations (UN) Member States unanimously adopted the 2030 Agenda for Sustainable Development, which provides an operational framework for attaining peace and prosperity for the world. The 17 Sustainable Development Goals (SDGs) serve as a clarion call for collective action by all countries—developed and developing—in a global partnership premised on the concept that poverty and other deprivations are interrelated and must be addressed holistically through comprehensive strategies that improve health and education, reduce inequality, and spur economic growth—all while mitigating climate change and working to preserve oceans and forests. The oversight and monitoring of progress of the SDGs is achieved through various UN organizations.[1]

The 17 SDGs are:

- GOAL 1: No Poverty
- GOAL 2: Zero Hunger

---

1. Department of Economic and Social Affairs: Sustainable Development, *The 17 Goals*, UNITED NATIONS, https://sdgs.un.org/goals.

- GOAL 3: Good Health and Well-being
- GOAL 4: Quality Education
- GOAL 5: Gender Equality
- GOAL 6: Clean Water and Sanitation
- GOAL 7: Affordable and Clean Energy
- GOAL 8: Decent Work and Economic Growth
- GOAL 9: Industry, Innovation, and Infrastructure
- GOAL 10: Reduced Inequality
- GOAL 11: Sustainable Cities and Communities
- GOAL 12: Responsible Consumption and Production
- GOAL 13: Climate Action
- GOAL 14: Life Below Water
- GOAL 15: Life on Land
- GOAL 16: Peace and Justice Strong Institutions
- GOAL 17: Partnerships to achieve the Goal

Global Public–Private Sector Initiatives

In 2020, MSCI Inc.'s Environmental, Social, and Governance (ESG) Trends to Watch noted the following important trends for investors: climate change; new terms for capital; revaluing real estate; the new human capital paradox; and keeping score on stakeholder capitalism.[2] In its 2021 ESG Trends to Watch, MSCI noted that investors committed to aligning with the Paris Agreement face more challenges: persuading companies to make radical changes or face a shrinking universe of qualifying investments; hype and skepticism about ESG giving way to a more nuanced understanding of when and how ESG has shown pecuniary benefits, and when it has not; policymakers and investors will heed the alarm on biodiversity loss, adapting methodologies established for measuring and managing climate risk; institutional investors may need to report on new ESG metrics for their portfolio companies (e.g., the European Union's (EU) Sustainable Finance Disclosure Regulation (SFDR)); and investors taking steps toward more creative, systemic approaches to reduce inequalities, with possible solutions such as social bonds.[3] In support of consistency and uniformity in ESG practices, the Open-Source Climate Initiative (OSCI) was established with the goal of creating an open-source data commons, providing easier access for anyone to access information on companies' environmental performance. It is planning to create a repository of tools that investors and regulators can use to perform climate risk "scenario analyses" and to help companies set a path to net zero emissions.[4]

---

2. MSCI, *2022 ESG Trends to Watch*, MSCI, https://www.msci.com/esg-trends.

3. MSCI, *2021 ESG Trends to Watch*, MSCI (Dec. 7, 2020), https://www.msci.com/www/blog-posts/2021-esg-trends-to-watch/02227813256.

4. Elena Johansson, *Is Open Source the Answer to the Climate Date Problem?*, Expert Invest Europe (Sept. 28, 2020), https://expertinvestoreurope.com/is-open-source-the-answer-to-the-climate-data-problem/; Open Source – Climate, *News*, OS-C, https://www.os-climate.org/news/.

Coupled with the SFDR is the Sustainable Finance Taxonomy Regulation (SFTR), which is in effect as of January 1, 2022, and provides an EU-wide glossary of environmentally sustainable activities. The impact of the EU's sustainability focus continues unabated and will affect all stakeholders in the SDG and sustainability ecosystem. For example, climate laws are being promulgated across the EU as legislators agreed on the European Climate Law, part of the European Green Deal,[5] which will see larger commitments to net zero goals. The establishment of a European Scientific Advisory Board on climate change has also been announced as well as sector-specific roadmaps to carbon neutrality. The European Commission (EC) proposed the EU Taxonomy Climate Delegated Act—a tool for investors to increase transparency by creating a common language to be used under the SFTR. (The Act will also require advisers to discuss sustainability when assessing their suitability for investments.) The new Corporate Sustainability Reporting Directive, will strengthen the rules introduced by the Nonfinancial Reporting Directive (NFRD), encouraging more sustainability reporting by simplifying it and aligning it with financial reporting, and eventually it will replace the NFRD beginning January 1, 2023.[6]

In the U.S., the legal and regulatory pace has accelerated under the Biden-Harris administration with the proposed 2021 ESG Disclosure Simplification Act;[7] the Federal Reserve establishing Financial Stability and Supervision Climate Committees;[8] the US Treasury Department's "Whole-of-Economy" approach and the creation of a Climate Hub to drive investments to clean sources;[9] and the Commodity Futures Trading Commission (CFTC)[10] establishing its Climate Risk Unit.[11] The Biden-Harris administration also issued an executive order to strengthen the US financial system against climate-related risks. The order instructs the US Treasury Department to work with the other members of the Financial Stability Oversight Council to report how they plan to reduce risks to financial stability, by improving climate-related financial disclosures to better measure their potential exposure. The order also

---

5. The European Green Deal takes a holistic approach to sustainability. Among the Green Deal's initiatives, those relevant to a sustainable food sector are the following: The Farm to Fork (F2F) Strategy, the Methane Strategy, the Circular Economy Action Plan, the Biodiversity Strategy, the Fit for 55 package, and related renewable energy initiatives and the Adaptation Strategy. Janusz Wojciechowski, The European Green Deal: Taking a Holistic Approach to Addressing Food Sustainability, BARILLA CENTER FOR FOOD & NUTRITION, https://foodsustainability.eiu.com/blogs/the-european-green-deal-taking-a-holistic-approach-to-addressing-food-sustainability/.
6. Natasha Turner, *EU Adopts Ambitious Package to Drive Sustainable Funding*, EXPERT INVEST EUROPE (Apr. 22, 2021), https://expertinvestoreurope.com/eu-adopts-ambitious-package-to-drive-sustainable-funding/; *NFRD vs. CSRD: What Are the Differences?*, ESG ENTERPRISE, https://www.esgenterprise.com/esg-reporting/nfrd-vs-csrd-what-are-differences/.
7. Corporate Governance Improvement and Investor Protection Act, H.R. 1187, 117th Cong. (2021)
8. Lael Brainard, Governor, Fed. Rsrv. Sys., Address at Ceres 2021 Conference: Financial Stability Implications of Climate Change (March 23, 2021); FEDERAL RESERVE BANK OF NEW YORK, *Kevin Stiroh to Step Down as Head of New York Fed Supervision to Assume New System Leadership Role at Board of Governors on Climate*, FEDERAL RESERVE BANK OF NEW YORK: PRESS RELEASES (Jan. 25, 2021), https://www.newyorkfed.org/newsevents/news/aboutthefed/2021/20210125.
9. Janet L. Yellen, Secretary of the Treasury, U.S. Dept. Treas., Remarks to the Institution of International Finance: Climate Change (Apr. 21, 2021).
10. In 2020, the CFTC published its Climate Risk Study, making it the first U.S. federal agency white paper on climate risk in financial system. It recommended imposing a price on carbon as important step to manage climate risk and focused primarily on financial stability in the face of climate change.
11. Press Release, Commodity Futures Trading Commission, CFTC Acting Chairman Behnam Establishes New Climate Risk Unit (March 17, 2021) (on file with CFTC).

provides for the development of a "Whole-of-Government" approach.[12] The U.S. Treasury Department issued Fossil Fuel Energy Guidance for Multilateral Development Banks (MDBs)—key guidance in response to Executive Order 14008 on Tackling the Climate Crisis at Home and Abroad. In its Guidance, Treasury advocates for MDB investments prioritizing clean energy, innovation, and energy efficiency, which will help achieve a clean and sustainable future consistent with the development goals of the Paris Agreement.[13] Further, President Biden and G7 Leaders launched the Build Back Better World (B3W) Partnership—a new global infrastructure initiative led by major democracies to help narrow the $40+ trillion infrastructure need in the developing world, which has been exacerbated by the COVID-19 pandemic. Through B3W, the G7 and others will coordinate in mobilizing private-sector capital in four areas of focus: climate, health and health security, digital technology, and gender equity and equality with investments from their respective development finance institutions.[14]

The U.S. state legislatures are also proposing more stringent climate legislation. California introduced mandatory climate disclosure requirements for large companies operating in California laying the groundwork for new climate legislation which will be the first of its kind in the U.S.[15] The U.S. Climate Finance Working Group, which includes 11 industry groups including the International Swaps and Derivatives Association (ISDA), also released a set of principles for financing the U.S. transition to a sustainable low-carbon economy. The principles provide a pragmatic approach to the transition and include a recommendation on the development and harmonization of taxonomies, data standards, and metrics.[16]

Global Initiatives

> The Principles for Responsible Investing (PRI)[17] with over 4,000 signatories globally representing approximately $120 trillion in assets under management (AUM) is a set of investment principles that offer a menu of possible actions for incorporating ESG into investment practice

The Principles for Responsible Investing (PRI)[18] with over 4,000 signatories globally representing approximately $120 trillion in assets under management (AUM) is a set of investment principles that offer a menu of possible actions for incorporating ESG into investment practice. These asset owners, asset managers, and global sustainability consortiums are helping to address climate change and its impact on the environment, civil societies, the potential for climate conflict, and global supply chains. Most recently, the PRI announced

---

12. Press Release, White House Briefing Room, President Biden Directs Agencies to Analyze and Mitigate the Risk Climate Change Poses to Homeowners and Consumers, Businesses and Workers, and the Financial System and Federal Government (May 20, 2021) (on file with The White House).

13. Press Release, U.S. Department of the Treasury, Treasury Announces Fossil Fuel Energy Guidance for Multilateral Development Banks (Aug. 16, 2021) (on file with the U.S. Department of the Treasury).

14. Press Release, White House Briefing Room, FACT SHEET: President Biden and G7 Leaders Launch Build Back Better World (B3W) Partnership (June 12, 2021) (on file at The White House).

15. See S. SB-260 (2021–2022), (Calif. 2021).

16. The U.S. Climate Working Group, *Financing a U.S. Transition to a Sustainable Low-Carbon Economy*, ISDA (Feb. 18, 2021), https://www.isda.org/a/qXITE/Financing-a-US-Transition-to-a-Sustainable-Low-carbon-Economy.pdf.

17. Principles for Responsible Investment, *About the PRI*, PRI, https://www.unpri.org/pri/about-the-pri.

18. Id.

that beginning in 2021 it will update its reporting obligations to include questions "about policies on shaping real-world outcomes" and how those relate to the UN's SDGs.[19]

> In September 2019, over 600 institutional investors with more than $37 trillion in AUM urged governments to increase efforts to tackle the global climate crisis and achieve the goals of the Paris Agreement.

In September 2019, over 600 institutional investors with more than $37 trillion in AUM urged governments to increase efforts to tackle the global climate crisis and achieve the goals of the Paris Agreement. The Global Investor Statement on Climate Change[20] urges governments to phase out thermal coal power, put a meaningful price on carbon pollution, end subsidies for fossil fuels, and update and strengthen nationally determined contributions to meet the goals of the Paris Agreement. The 2021 Global Investor Statement to Governments on the Climate Crisis calls for governments to raise their climate ambition and implement robust policies. This statement is signed by 457 investors representing over $41 trillion in AUM. The joint statement to all world governments urges a global race-to-the-top on climate policy and warns that laggards will miss out on trillions of dollars in investment if they aim too low and move too slow. The statement also sets out five actions governments need to undertake: strengthen Nationally Determined Contributions for 2030 in line with limiting warming to 1.5°C; commit to a mid-century net zero emissions target with clear sectoral decarbonization roadmaps; ensure ambitious pre-2030 policy action including strengthened carbon pricing, phasing out fossil fuel subsidies and thermal coal-based power, avoiding new carbon-intensive infrastructure (no new coal power plants) and developing just transition plans; ensure COVID-19 economic recovery plans support the transition to net zero emissions; and commit to implementing mandatory climate risk disclosure requirements.[21]

In September 2019, Amazon and Global Optimism announced The Climate Pledge, a commitment to meet the Paris Agreement 10 years early. Amazon became the first signatory of this pledge. The Climate Pledge calls on signatories to be net zero carbon across their businesses by 2040—a decade ahead of the Paris Agreement's goal of 2050.[22] Additional efforts include various networks subsumed under the Paris Aligned Investment Initiative[23] involving 110 investors worldwide representing $33 trillion in AUM; 22 of these investors representing $1.2 trillion in AUM are signatories to the Net Zero Asset Owners

19. Alastair Marsh, *Investors Must Consider Climate, Social Equity, Not Just Returns*, BloomBerg green, June 15, 2020, https://www.bloomberg.com/news/articles/2020-06-15/investors-must-consider-climate-social-equity-not-just-returns.

20. The Investor Agenda was launched in 2018 by the Asia Investor Group on Climate Change, CDP, Ceres, Investor Group on Climate Change, Institutional Investors Group on Climate Change, PRI, and UNEP Finance Initiative. It aims to accelerate and scale up investor actions worldwide critical in addressing climate change and achieving the goals of the Paris Agreement. Press Release, IIGCC, Record 631 Institutional Investors Managing More Than $37 Trillion in Assets Urge Governments to Step Up Ambition to Tackle Global Climate Crisis (Dec. 19, 2019) (on file at The Investor Agenda).

21. Press Release, IIGCC, 2021 Global Investor Statement to Governments on the Climate Crisis, (Sept. 14, 2021) (on file at The Investor Agenda).

22. Press Release, The Business Wire, Amazon Co-Founds The Climate Pledge, Setting Goal to Meet the Paris Agreement 10 Years Early (Sept. 19, 2019) (on file at The Business Wire) https://www.businesswire.com/news/home/20190919005609/en/.

23. Briefing, IIGCC, Paris Aligned Investment Initiative (Sept. 19, 2019) (on file The Investor Agenda).

Commitment,[24] while the Net Zero Investment Framework[25] is being utilized by 33 major investors managing a combined $8.5 trillion in AUM. Most recently, a group of banks, insurers, asset managers, and owners all made new net zero emissions pledges[26] as part of the launch of the $70 trillion (recently increased to over $130 trillion of private capital) Glasgow Financial Alliance for Net Zero.[27] While these pledges are seen as positive steps, there remain issues with respect to "greenwashing"[28] and asset owners aligning with the Two-Degree Climate Goal.[29]

Various corporations are setting goals to reduce their greenhouse gas (GHG) emissions, in part through a pledge with the global initiative Science-Based Targets.[30] The Science-Based Targets initiative advocates science-based target setting by companies as a way of increasing companies' competitive advantage in the transition to the low-carbon economy. The overall goal of signatories to the initiative is to limit global warming to below 2°C above pre-industrial levels. The initiative is a partnership between CDP, the UN Global Compact, the World Resources Institute, and the Worldwide Fund for Nature, with collaboration from the "We Mean Business Coalition" (which signed an open letter to President Biden indicating its support for the Biden administration's commitment to climate action, and for setting a federal climate target to reduce emissions[31]).

In addition, Climate Action 100+ involves more than 450 investors with combined AUM in excess of $39 trillion, who engage with 100 of the largest corporate GHG emitters and 60 other companies positioned to drive the transition to a net zero emissions economy. The Climate Action 100+'s engagement agenda includes three main goals: improving governance, improving disclosure of climate risk, and reducing GHG emissions across supply chains in alignment with the Paris Agreement goals.[32] State Street Global Advisors

---

24. PRINCIPLES FOR RESPONSIBLE INVESTMENT, *Net-Zero Alliance Members*, UNITED NATIONS ENVIRONMENT PROGRAMME, https://www.unepfi.org/net-zero-alliance/alliance-members/.

25. IIGC Investor Guide, *Net-Zero Investment Framework*, IIGC (Aug. 5, 2020), https://www.iigcc.org/resource /net-zero-investment-framework-for-consultation/.

26. UNEPFI: COLLECTIVE COMMITMENT TO CLIMATE ACTION, *Guidelines for Climate Target Setting for Banks*, UNITED NATIONS ENVIRONMENT PROGRAMME: FINANCE INITIATIVE (Apr. 21, 2021), https://www.unepfi.org/banking/bankingprinciples /resources-for-implementation/climate-target-setting/.

27. Press Release, United Nations Environment Programme, Mark Carney, UN Race Zero Campaign, COP26 Presidency Launch Net Zero Financial Alliance (Apr. 21, 2021) (on file at United Nations).

28. Chris Hall, *Carney's GFANZ an "Example of Greenwashing,"* ESG INVESTOR (Apr. 23, 2021), https://www .esginvestor.net/carneys-gfanz-an-example-of-greenwashing/.

29. Only 48% of asset owners have taken steps to align their investments with the Paris Agreement goal of keeping climate change well below a two-degree rise from pre-industrial levels, according to a new report on financial institutions' portfolio emissions. Chris Hall, Less Than Half of Asset Owners Aligning with Two-Degree Climate Goal, ESG INVESTOR (Apr. 28, 2021), https://www.esginvestor.net/less-than-half-of-asset-owners-aligning -with-two-degree-climate-goal-cdp/.

30. CSX, for example, aims to reduce GHG emissions intensity by 37.3% between 2014 and 2030 through investments in technologies and operational practices. It had already achieved its 2020 goal of reducing emissions intensity by 6%–8%. FreightWaves, *CSX Union Pacific, Canadian National Pledge to Reduce Emissions*, YAHOO: FINANCE (March 19, 2020), https://finance.yahoo.com/news/csx-union-pacific-canadian-national-205203924.html.

31. WE MEAN BUSINESS COALITION, *Business & Investors Call For Ambitious U.S. NDC*, WE MEAN BUSINESS COALITION, https://www.wemeanbusinesscoalition.org/ambitious-u-s-2030-ndc/?utm_source=twitter&utm_medium =social&utm_campaign=US_NDC.

32. Its resolutions filed during the 2020 proxy season were on six themes: (1) Independent Board Chairs; (2) Paris-Aligned Transition Strategy; (3) Stranded Assets from Natural Gas Infrastructure; (4) Disclosure of Direct and Indirect Lobbying; (5) Lobbying for Policy Framework Alignment with the Paris Agreement; and (6) ESG Metrics in Executive Compensation. Morgan Lamanna & Rob Berridge, *Climate Action 100+ Targets The Largest 100 Corporate GHG Emitters*, PROXY PREVIEW (March 17, 2020), https://www.proxypreview.org/2020/contributor -articles-blog/ climate-action-100-targets-100-largest-corporate-ghg-emitters.

indicated that it intended to vote against companies that score poorly on ESG metrics.[33] Aviva Investors[34] also stated that the firm will vote against companies considered to be climate laggards and against those in the Climate Action 100+[35] list of large emitters that do not commit to science-based targets. Climate Action 100+ recently released its first net zero benchmarking of the world's largest corporate emitters. The benchmarking seeks to define the key elements of a "net zero-aligned" business strategy. While the assessment shows that there is growing momentum around companies making ambitious climate commitments, the benchmark also highlights that companies have a long way to go in delivering on these promises. In particular, the assessment notes that no company has yet fully disclosed how it will achieve its goal to become net zero by 2050.[36]

Further, through Caring for Climate, the UN Global Compact, the UN Environment Programme (UNEP), and the secretariat of United Nations Framework Convention on Climate Change (UNFCCC) have helped shape the engagement of businesses with climate change. Caring for Climate signatories are committed to set GHG emissions reduction targets, to work collaboratively with other companies and governments, and to publicly report on performance on an annual basis. Some of the signatories have become carbon-pricing champions, increasing investments in renewable energy and low-carbon technologies.[37] Further, there is also the Oil & Gas Climate Initiative, whereby 13 of the world's largest energy producers support the goals of the Paris Climate Agreement to progress to net zero emissions by 2050.[38] In addition, over 200 companies have formally committed to RE100, a global corporate initiative to cover electricity usage with 100% renewables before 2050.[39] The Climate Majority Project was launched to eradicate carbon pollution at the US' largest power utilities.[40] In connection with these initiatives, the financial services industry has been pressured to cease financing fossil fuel development. It has slowly and steadily heeded the call of its shareholders and pressure by organizations such as Majority Action.

From the perspective of multilateral development banks, the Asian Infrastructure Investment Bank (AIIB) and Amundi[41] announced the establishment of a $500-million

---

33. STATE STREET GLOBAL ADVISORS, *Into the Mainstream: ESG at the Tipping Point*, STATE STREET GLOBAL ADVISORS (Nov. 2019), https://www.ssga.com/content/dam/ssmp/library-content/pdfs/insights/into-the-mainstream.pdf.

34. David Cumming, Why Asset Managers Cannot Be Passive on Climate Change, Financial Times (Jan. 30, 2020), https://www.ft.com/content/ac9c2345-ed98-4f03-a537-b9926819b675?shareType=nongift.

35. Climate Action 100+, http://www.climateaction100.org/.

36. Press Release, Climate Action 100+, Climate Action 100+ Issues First-Ever Net Zero Company Benchmark of The World's Largest Corporate Emitters (March 22, 2021) (on file at Climate Action 100+).

37. Press Release, United Nations Climate Change, United Nations Global Compact-Business Leadership Criteria on Global Pricing (Oct. 21, 2015) (on file at United Nations); UNITED NATIONS GLOBAL COMPACT, *Carbon Pricing*, https://www.unglobalcompact.org/take-action/action/carbon#champions.

38. OIL AND GAS CLIMATE INITIATIVE, https://oilandgasclimateinitiative.com.

39. Anna Shpitsberg & Eduard Sala de Vedruna, *Policy, Technology, Company Strategies, and the COVID-19 Wildcard: Seven Trends to Watch for in Global Power and Renewables in 2020*, IHS MARKIT (March 11, 2020), https://ihsmarkit.com/research-analysis/seven-trends-to-watch-for-in-global-power-renewables-in-2020.html.

40. Press Release, New York City Comptroller, Global Investors Launch Initiative to Wipe Out Carbon Pollution at Country's Largest Power Utilities (Feb. 28, 2019) (on file at New York City Office of the Comptroller).

41. European Investment Bank—EIB—and Amundi have announced the official launch of the "Partnership to Expand Green Finance in Europe". Press Release, Amundi, Launch of the Green Credit Continuum Programme (July 9, 2019) (on file at Amundi Asset Management); Michael Hurley, Green Bond Fund of the Year, Initiative of the Year: Amundi and IFC's Emerging Green One, Environmental Finance (April 2, 2019), https://www.environmental-finance.com/content/awards/green-social-and-sustainability-bond-awards-2019/winners/green-bond-fund-of-the-year-initiative-of-the-year-amundi-and-ifcs-emerging-green-one.html.

portfolio dedicated to Asia Climate Bonds, to accelerate climate action in the AIIB's members and to address the underdevelopment of the climate bond market. Amundi and AIIB have developed a Climate Change Investment framework, which considers several variables to analyze issuers' ability to cope with climate change.[42] In November 2019, the US, Australia, and Japan announced the establishment of the Blue Dot Network to serve as a globally recognized seal of approval for major infrastructure projects, bringing together governments, the private sector, and other organizations behind a set of high-quality global infrastructure development standards. The initiative aligns with the G20's Principles for Quality Infrastructure Investment, particularly on governance, environmental standards, and transparency.[43] Complementing this initiative is FAST-Infra (Finance to Accelerate the Sustainable Transition—Infrastructure) which seeks to accelerate the flow of private investment to sustainable infrastructure in developing countries, by developing a label for sustainable infrastructure.[44]

There have also been public pronouncements and initiatives by sovereign wealth funds (SWFs) highlighting the need to integrate ESG into investment decision-making, including the establishment of the One Planet Sovereign Wealth Fund Framework.[45] While a positive development, sovereign asset owners, such as SWFs have expressed doubt about the efficiency of financial markets and their capacity to maximize social welfare. Despite subscribing to ESG's financial benefits and managing roughly two-thirds of their assets actively, less than half are adopting ESG investing in a comprehensive way. Moreover, SWFs have lagged other public investors in terms of ESG adoption.[46] While this may be the case generally, the world's largest SWF—the Norwegian SWF—announced that it will begin to screen the hundreds of new companies it adds to its portfolio each year for ESG risks as it seeks to regain its place as one of the leading responsible investors in the world. This will entail screening about 500–600 companies that are added to its reference index annually and decide whether to invest in them or not or start active ownership measures such as monitoring. New screening will mainly impact smaller companies in developed markets such as the US and Europe.[47]

---

42. Press Release, Amundi, AIIB and Amundi Launch an Innovative Climate Framework, (Sept. 10, 2019) (on file at Amundi Asset Management).

43. U.S. Department of State: Development Finance, *Blue Dot Network*, U.S. Dept. of State, https://www.state.gov /blue-dot-network/.

44. FAST-Infra started under the auspices of the One Planet Lab as a collaboration between the HSBC Bank, the Organization for Economic Cooperation and Development (OECD), the International Finance Corporation, the Global Infrastructure Facility (World Bank), and Climate Policy Initiative and which has evolved into a broad-based private–public partnership involving banks, asset managers, governments, MDBs, National Development Banks, academics, and non-governmental organizations. Barbara Buchner et al., *FAST-Infra Overview*, Climate Policy Initiative (March 1, 2021), https://www.climatepolicyinitiative.org/wp-content/uploads/2020/12/FAST-Infra -Overview-Nov-2020.pdf.

45. Press Release, International Forum of Sovereign Wealth Funds, One Planet SWF Working Group Publish Framework on Climate Change (July 6, 2018) (on file at One Planet Sovereign Wealth Funds).

46. Elliot Hentov & Alexander Petrov, *How Sovereign Asset Owners Think About ESG*, State Street Global Advisors (Aug. 2019), https://www.ssga.com/library-content/pdfs/official-institutions-/how-sovereign-asset-owners-think -about-esg.pdf.

47. Richard Milne, *Norway's $1.3tn Oil Fund Broadens ESG Screening to Smaller Companies*, Financial Times (May 3, 2021), https://www.ft.com/content/f6649a49-03cb-47ef-89ab-2181ae9b30c2.

Human Capital and Human Rights

The Human Capital Management Coalition had submitted a petition to the US Securities and Exchange Commission (SEC or Commission) requesting that it adopt new rules, or amend existing rules, to require issuers to disclose information about their human capital management policies, practices, and performance.[48] In August 2020, the SEC adopted amendments to public company disclosure requirements under Regulation S-K.[49] One of these amendments is a new requirement to discuss any human capital measures or objectives that management focuses on in managing the business, to the extent such disclosures would be material to an understanding of the company's business.[50] Investors such as BlackRock and State Street Global Advisors are making human capital and company culture engagement priorities, and the Global Reporting Initiative and the Embankment Project for Inclusive Capital, among others, are identifying human capital as key value drivers.[51]

In addition, to mitigate climate risk, there has been added focus by shareholders to encourage companies to establish Climate Competent Boards[52] through the establishment of more diverse boards. Companies and boards have recognized albeit too slowly the need to embrace the benefits of diversity at the board level, particularly when transformational change is required such as the need to address climate change.[53] In this regard, the National Association of Corporate Directors (NACD) commissioned a Blue-Ribbon Commission to explore building and maintaining a strategic-asset board, focusing on issues such as board composition and diversity, and ongoing director-skills development.[54]

---

48. Letter from Meredith Miller, Chief Corp. Govn. Officer, Hum. Cap. Mgmt. Coal., to William Hinman, Dir. Div. of Corp. Fin., SEC (July 6, 2017) (on file with the Securities and Exchange Commission).

49. 17 C.F.R. § 229, 239-240 (2019).

50. Under new Item 101(c)(2)(ii) of Regulation S-K, public companies will be required to provide a description of their human capital resources, including the number of persons employed by the registrant, and any human capital measures or objectives that the registrant focuses on in managing the business (such as, depending on the nature of the registrant's business and workforce, measures or objectives that address the development, attraction, and retention of personnel). Disclosure is only required to the extent material to an understanding of the registrant's business taken as a whole, except that, if the information is material to a particular segment, a registrant should additionally identify that segment. See ibid.

51. Steve Klemesh et al., *How and Why Human Capital Disclosures are Evolving*, HARVARD LAW SCHOOL FORUM ON CORPORATE GOVERNANCE (Nov. 15, 2019), https://corpgov.law.harvard.edu/2019/11/15/how-and-why-human -capital-disclosures-are-evolving/.

52. CalPERS has publicly raised the need for climate change competence in the Boardroom. Hedge funds such as TCI Fund Management have indicated its expectations for the boards of the companies it invests in as well. CALPERS, *CalPERS' Governance and Sustainability Principles*, CALPERS (Sept. 2019), https://www.calpers.ca.gov /docs/forms-publications/governance-and-sustainability-principles.pdf; TCI FUND MANAGEMENT LIMITED, *ESG Investment Policy*, TCI FUND MANAGEMENT LIMITED (Nov. 21, 2019), https://www.tcifund.com/files/esg/TCI%20 ESG%20Policy.pdf?AspxAutoDetectCookieSupport=1.

53. Attracta Mooney and Jennifer Thompson, *Why the Focus is Shifting to Boards on Cyber Security*, FINANCIAL TIMES (Sept. 8, 2018), https://www.ft.com/content/c70caa94-2d88-3ece-b802-79e9bac2f32c.

54. Report of the NACD Blue Ribbon Commission on Building the Strategic-Asset Board, NACD (Sept. 15, 2016), https://www.nacdonline.org/insights/publications.cfm?itemnumber=35303.

Human Rights

The PRI published a human rights framework for institutional investors, entitled "Why and How Investors Should Act on Human Rights,"[55] expanding its own focus on human rights and establishing a program to embed the UN Guiding Principles on Business and Human Rights[56] into investment activities.[57] ESG-centric investors were supportive from its start. Mainstream investing, however, had been slower to embrace it, but several developments encouraged their receptiveness to it: (1) the exponential rise in ESG investing following the 2008 financial crisis, coupled with the increased recognition that many of the "S" factors in ESG are human rights related; (2) the tangible materiality of many human rights concerns;[58] and (3) the Pandemic, also focused attention on the "S" in ESG, including the unsustainable economic and social inequalities in the current economic system. Recently, there were updates to the Equator Principles to expand the scope of diligence required for projects to require borrowers and financial institutions to conduct greater levels of due diligence, with particular focus on issues such as climate change and human rights and the way in which these, and other environmental and social factors, are analyzed and reported.[59]

Most recently, a group of institutional investors, including Aviva Investors, Schroders, Brunel Pension Partnership, The Church of England Pensions Board, Boston Common Asset Management, and Mercy Investment Services led by the UK charity fund manager CCLA Investment Management Limited, have written to companies with significant operations in the Persian Gulf region, asking them to provide details on how they are protecting migrant workers—amid concerns over debt bondage and slave labor in the region, which have been exacerbated by the COVID-19 pandemic. More than 50 firms were targeted, including multinationals such as Shell, McDonalds, and Exxon Mobil.[60] In addition, the Investor Alliance on Human Rights (IAHR) has focused on supply chain ethical lapses involving, for example, modern slavery and has organized investors to scrutinize companies for possible supply chain concerns linked to Uighur forced labor.[61]

---

55. PRI: Human Rights, Why and How Investors Should Act on human Rights, PRI (Oct. 22, 2020), https://www
.unpri.org/human-rights-and-labour-standards/why-and-how-investors-should-act-on-human-rights/6636.article.
56. *UN Guiding Principles*, Business & Human Rights Resource Centre, https://www.business-humanrights.org/en
/big-issues/un-guiding-principles-on-business-human-rights/.
57. International "soft law," with a sustainability focus, has expanded through the OECD Guidelines for Multinational Enterprises, the Global Compact (voluntary initiative based on CEO commitments to implement uni- versal sustainability principles), and the UN Guiding Principles on Business and Human Rights. OECD, *OECD Guidelines for Multinational Enterprises*, OECD Publishing (2011), https://dx.doi.org/10.1787/9789264114515-en; United Nations Global Impact, https://www.unglobalcompact.org/.
58. The Australian Strategic Policy Institute noted that supply chains at 82 multinational companies such as Apple and Huawei were linked to factories using forced labor from China's Uyghur minority community. Vicky Xiuzhong et al., *Uyghurs for Sale: 'Re-education,' Forced Labour and Surveillance Beyond Xinjiang*, Australian Strategy Policy Institute (March 1, 2020), https:// www.aspi.org.au/report/uyghurs-sale.
59. Allen & Overy LLP, *Updated Equator Principles: Transition to Version 4*, JDSUPRA (March 24, 2021), https://www.jdsupra.com/legalnews/updated-equator-principles-transition-3825951/.
60. Paul Verney, Modern Slavery *Climbs Investor Agenda as $3trn Coalition Begins Gulf Engagement*, Responsible Investor (Aug. 5, 2020), https://www.responsible-investor.com/articles/modern-slavery-climbs-investor-agenda
-as-usd3trn-begin-gulf-engagement-and-guidance-on-uyghur-is-launched.
61. *Investor Action on the Human Rights Crisis in the Uyghur Region*, Investor Alliance for Human Rights, https://investorsforhumanrights.org/issues/investor-action-human-rights-crisis-uyghur-region.

Sustainable Finance and SDGs

The theme of the 2020 World Economic Forum (WEF) was "Stakeholders for a Cohesive and Sustainable World."[62] A global risks report published by the WEF noted that all the top long-term risks by likelihood are environmental, and that climate change is rated the biggest global threat.[63] The announcements and initiatives[64] that arose both before and after the WEF emphasize that asset owners, asset managers, investee companies and their employees, stakeholders, and governments are prioritizing sustainability through the integration of ESG factors into policies, practices, and investments. At the WEF, Larry Fink, CEO of BlackRock, announced that BlackRock would start redirecting its investments away from fossil fuel companies.

In its 2020 annual letter, BlackRock announced a number of initiatives to place sustainability at the center of its investment approach, including: making sustainability integral to portfolio construction and risk management; exiting investments that present a high sustainability-related risk; and strengthening its commitment to sustainability and transparency in its investment stewardship activities.[65] BlackRock's 2021 annual letter builds upon its prior one and reiterated its views with respect to climate change and the investment opportunities it presents.[66]

Although, a U.S.-based money manager, given the breadth of its international holdings, it is worth noting BlackRock's views on stewardship and sustainability. Further, the SFDR will potentially impact BlackRock and other U.S.-based money managers that have a presence in Europe and as such there is underway movement toward de facto global sustainability standards, being led by the EU. The Sustainability Accounting Standards Board (SASB) and the International Integrated Reporting Council (IIRC) merger, scheduled to be completed in 2021 resulting in the creation of the Value Reporting Foundation,[67] is another major step in simplifying the corporate reporting system which should also support the above trends. The

---

62. World Economic Forum Annual Meeting 2020, *About*, World Economic Forum, https://www.weforum.org/events/world-economic-forum-annual-meeting-2020/about.

63. *The Global Risk Report*, World Economic Forum (Jan. 15, 2020), https://www.weforum.org/reports/the-global-risks-report-2020.

64. Among other initiatives, the Task Force on Climate-Related Financial Disclosures (TCFD), the Vatican's 2019 statement advocating carbon pricing regimes, and the Climate Finance Partnership have been promulgated policies to address climate change and further sustainability.

65. In 2020, BlackRock engaged with numerous companies that face material financial risks in the transition to a low-carbon economy. Its engagements resulted in votes against directors where progress has been insufficient. It published many more vote bulletins, put more companies "on watch" due to their failure to fully consider climate risks, and advised companies that they could face consequences at 2021 shareholder meetings if they fail to make progress on reducing carbon emissions and moving toward a more sustainable business model. *Investment Stewardship Annual Report*, BlackRock (Sept. 2020), https://www.blackrock.com/corporate/literature/publication/blk-annual-stewardship-report-2020.pdf; Larry Fink, *Larry Fink's 2021 Letter to CEOs*, BlackRock, https://www.blackrock.com/corporate/investor-relations/larry-fink-ceo-letter.

66. Id.

67. *IIRC and SASB Announce Intent to Merge in Major Step Towards Simplifying the Corporate Reporting System*, Value Reporting Foundation: Integrated Reporting Framework (Nov. 25, 2020), https://integratedreporting.org/news/iirc-and-sasb-announce-intent-to-merge-in-major-step-towards-simplifying-the-corporate-reporting-system/.

sustainability standards frameworks are further consolidating into the new International Sustainability Board.[68]

In addition, there is also the WEF Active Investor Stewardship project established to mobilize the investor community as part of the WEF's broader efforts on long-termism, by identifying key investors and corporations who, driven by long-term risk and return considerations, engage actively with one another to mitigate risk and seek financial opportunity in addressing long-term challenges such as climate change, technological disruption, and corporate governance. The project utilizes the WEF's platform to connect investors with corporate leaders, drawing upon related efforts led by the Forum's Community of Chairmen, International Business Council, and signatories of the Compact for Responsive and Responsible Leadership.[69]

Global Regulatory Sustainability Initiatives

In October 2018, the International Organization of Securities Commissions (IOSCO) established its Sustainable Finance Network (SFN) to provide a forum for members to exchange experiences and gain a better understanding of various sustainability issues. The SFN has analyzed the context in which securities regulators are addressing sustainability efforts, the roles they can play, and the challenges they may face. It has focused on sustainable finance disclosure issues and their relevance for investor decision-making as well as on the development of industry-led initiatives. It built on previous IOSCO work: the 2019 IOSCO Statement on Disclosure of ESG Matters by Issuers and the Growth and Emerging Market Committee report on Sustainable Finance in emerging markets and the role of securities regulators.[70]

Its most recent report provides an overview of current initiatives, by both regulators and the industry, and an analysis of the most relevant ESG-related international initiatives and third-party frameworks and standards. It also identifies several areas where improvements can be made and articulates the need for IOSCO to play a key role in this area. To address these challenges, IOSCO agreed to establish a Board-Level Task Force on Sustainable Finance, to improve sustainability-related disclosures made by issuers and asset managers; to work in collaboration with other international organizations and regulators to avoid duplicative efforts and to enhance coordination of relevant regulatory and supervisory approaches; and to conduct case studies and analyses of transparency, investor protection, and other relevant issues within sustainable finance.[71]

In addition, the International Platform on Sustainable Finance (IPSF) was established in October 2019 with IOSCO as an observer. The IPSF covers the international cooperation

---

68. Michael O'Dwyer, *New Body to Oversee Global Sustainability Disclosure Standards*, Financial Times (Nov. 3, 2021), https://www.ft.com/content/3fb80e89-4ce6-4cc8-8472-ae4c8c99b12d; Andromeda Wood, *International Sustainability Standards: Levelling the Disclosure Playing Field*, CSRWire (Nov. 4, 2021), https://www.csrwire.com /press_releases/730901-international-sustainability-standards-levelling-disclosure-playing-field.

69. Oliver Wyman & World Economic Forum, *Enabling Investor Stewardship in the Global Public Equity Markets*, World Economic Forum (June 2021), https://www3.weforum.org/docs/WEF_Enabling_Investor_Stewardship_in _the_Global_Public_Equity_Markets_2021.pdf.

70. The Board of the International Organization of Securities Commissions, *Sustainable Finance and the Role of Securities Regulators and IOSCO: Final Report*, IOSCO (Apr. 2020), https://www.iosco.org/library/pubdocs/pdf /IOSCOPD652.pdf.

71. Id.

of regulatory tools and initiatives for the capital markets that are fundamental for private investors to identify and seize environmentally sustainable investment opportunities which are key to scaling up environmentally sustainable finance, in the field of: i) taxonomies, ii) financial products standards and labels, and iii) disclosures.[72]

At the Paris "One Planet Summit" in December 2017, eight central banks and supervisors (currently 83 members and 13 observers) established a Network of Central Banks and Supervisors for Greening the Financial System (NGFS), to help strengthen the global response required to meet the goals of the Paris Agreement and to enhance the role of the financial system to manage risks and mobilize capital for green and low-carbon investments in the broader context of environmentally sustainable development. In 2019, the NGFS published its first comprehensive report "A Call for Action" which proposed recommendations aimed at achieving these goals.[73] The NGFS published an "Overview of Environmental Risk Analysis (ERA) by Financial Institutions," which provides a list of examples of how environmental risks are transmitted to financial risks, and a review of the tools and methodologies for ERA used by financial institutions: including banks, asset managers, and insurance companies.[74]

In July 2020, the Sustainability Survey 2019 by the World Federation of Exchanges (WFE) was released reporting on the nature and extent of WFE member engagement with ESG issues.[75] Key highlight is that exchanges continue to develop sustainability efforts through strong engagement with WFE Sustainability Principles.[76] Among the exchanges with ESG initiatives, 80% had some form of SDG-specific initiative.[77]

Take-Aways for Board Members

A Multifocal-Time Horizon Approach to Sustainability

The SDGs have driven new initiatives for asset owners, asset managers, issuers and their boards, and various other stakeholders across the global sustainability ecosystem. It is an ever-increasing menu of options, opportunities, and initiatives to voluntarily embrace sustainability or alternatively to have regulation and/or shareholder activism imposed with

---

72. Id.

73. *Network for Greening the Financial System*, BANQUE DE FRANCE: FINANCIAL STABILITY – INTERNATIONAL ROLE, https://www.banque-france.fr/en/financial-stability/international-role/network-greening-financial-system.

74. *Overview of Environmental Risk Analysis by Financial Institution*, NETWORK FOR GREENING THE FINANCIAL SYSTEM (Sept. 2020), https://www.ngfs.net/sites/default/files/medias/documents/overview_of_environmental_risk _analysis_by_financial_institutions.pdf.

75. See also The EU Non-financial Reporting Directive (Directive 2014/95/EU) which requires large companies to disclose, as part of their annual reports, information on how they operate and manage social and environmental issues, for the benefit of investors, consumers, policymakers, and other stakeholders. *Corporate Sustainability Reporting*, EUROPEAN COMMISSION, https://ec.europa.eu/info/business-economy-euro/company-reporting-and -auditing/company-reporting/non-financial-reporting; The WFE Research Team, *WFE Annual Sustainability Survey 2020*, WORLD FEDERATION OF EXCHANGES (July 15, 2020), https://www.world-exchanges.org/storage/app/media/ WFE%20Annual%20Sustainability%20Survey%20 2020%20150720.pdf.

76. Sustainable Stock Exchanges (SSE) initiative is a learning platform for exploring how exchanges, in collaboration with investors, regulators, and companies, can enhance corporate transparency—and ultimately performance—on ESG issues and encourage sustainable investment. SSE focuses on SDG targets relevant for stock exchanges, such as Climate Action, and implicitly supports SDGs, such as Clean Water and Sanitation. SUSTAINABLE STOCK EXCHANGES INITIATIVE, https:// sseinitiative.org/.

77. WFE Research Team, *supra* note 76.

attendant costs. Given the plethora of options and stakeholder demands how should a board prioritize them (i.e., navigating the complex world of stakeholder capitalism). First and foremost, establishing climate competency for the board will not only satisfy shareholder demands, but also help the board guide policy with respect to the growing climate change and sustainability regulatory demands—a trend as noted that will only increase under the Biden-Harris administration and with more EU sustainability regulations coming to fruition.

Over above shareholder concerns and regulatory requirements, climate change presents potential national security risks which impact all and will undermine the foundation of prosperity and stability in society.[78] Board climate competency, be it technical, legal, regulatory, and accounting in nature, can help issuers focus on those most impactful to their business operations and help them discern from private sector aspirations, priorities du jour and attendant unstructured data overload (the OSCI perhaps may help), and actual long-term regulatory demands driven by empirical data.[79] The utilization of a "change control" mechanism at the corporate level to monitor these changes, whether embedded in the legal, investor relations, risk management, or corporate secretary's office, reporting to an independent board committee may be a means to monitor and respond to this ever-evolving legal–regulatory–financial paradigm. Failing to be proactive in this area will only entail more reactive measures at a higher cost to the corporation's value,[80] and given the interconnectivity in a stakeholder ecosystem, the costs borne may not be limited just to shareholders.[81] Investors value higher transparency with respect to climate change risks and that disclosure tends to benefit disclosing companies—investors dislike uncertainty and are willing to pay a premium for less opaque companies—the choice seems simple for companies—the devil is in the details.[82]

---

78. The National Intelligence Council recently released Global Trends 2040: A More Contested World, which describes five potential scenarios for what the world may look like in 20 years. In the report, climate change was mentioned 87 times. The National Intelligence Council, *Global Trends 2040: A More Contested World*, OFFICE OF THE DIRECTOR OF NATIONAL INTELLIGENCE (March 2021), https://www.dni.gov/files/ODNI/documents/assessments/GlobalTrends_2040.pdf.

79. Representing more than $27 trillion in market capitalization, more than 2,000 companies of the 6,000 surveyed disclosed that they currently use an internal carbon price or plan to implement one in the next two years, according to a new CDP study. This is an 80% increase since 2015. Emmy Hawker, *More Corporates Introducing Internal Carbon Prices – CDP*, ESG INVESTOR (Apr. 21, 2021), https://www.esginvestor.net/more-corporates-introducing-internal-carbon-prices-cdp/.

80. SASB released a Climate Risk Technical Bulletin to help companies better understand how they can disclose climate risk in a manner that would provide investors with helpful information. As part of this review, SASB found that 68 of 77 industries are significantly affected in some way by climate risk, totaling 89% of the market capitalization of the S&P Global 1200. Mike Schnitzel, *Sixty-eight Out of 77 Industries Significantly Affected by Climate Risk, According to SASB*, IR MAGAZINE (Apr. 22, 2021), https://www.irmagazine.com/esg/sixty-eight-out-77-industries-significantly-affected-climate-risk-according-sasb?utm_content=164350759&utm_medium=social&utm_source=linkedin&hss_channel=lcp-2464787.

81. Not addressing climate risks, including those associated with carbon prices, could prove costly. S&P Global Trucost data shows that major global companies face up to $283 billion in carbon pricing costs and 13% earnings at risk by 2025, under a high-carbon-price scenario. Esther Whieldon & Jennifer Laidlaw, *Path to Net Zero Riddled with Potential Pitfalls*, S&P GLOBAL (Apr. 22, 2021), https://www.spglobal.com/esg/insights/path-to-net-zero-riddled-with-potential-pitfalls.

82. Caroline Flammer et al., *Shareholders are Pressing for Climate Risk Disclosures. That's Good for Everyone.*, HARVARD BUSINESS REVIEW (Apr. 22, 2021), https://hbr-org.cdn.ampproject.org/c/s/hbr.org/amp/2021/04/shareholders-are-pressing-for-climate-risk-disclosures-thats-good-for-everyone.

Chapter 23
Diversity, Equity, and Inclusion in the Boardroom & Beyond

Katayun Jaffari and Sarah Schlossberg

Introduction

In the wake of George Floyd's murder in 2020, calls for social justice reform and equity reverberated throughout the United States. This momentum for positive change continues today as many organizations start to resume normal operations following the pandemic. Boards have a duty—legally, ethically, and morally—to take the lead on implementing equitable work policies that ensure diversity, equity, and inclusion (DEI) measures are being integrated and addressed within their organizations.

DEI as a collective term is used to describe policies and programs that promote the representation and participation of different groups of individuals, including underrepresented or marginalized groups due to race, ethnicity, religion, gender, sexual orientation, and disabilities. The term "DEI" runs the risk of becoming a cliché if organizations lose sight of the meaning behind each of the individual words, which are defined as follows:

- Diversity: The state of having people who are of different races or who have different cultures in a group or organization.

- Equity: Fairness or justice in the way people are treated.

- Inclusion: The act or practice of including and accommodating people who have historically been excluded (because of their race, gender, sexuality, or ability).

As Verna Myers, a leading diversity and inclusion expert, famously said, "Diversity is being invited to the party. Inclusion is being asked to dance." Taking this illustration one step further, equity means that everyone has the opportunity to dance.

There are many benefits to a truly diverse workforce. Diverse cultural perspectives inspire creativity and drive innovation. Cultural sensitivity and insight can lead to more successful marketing and customer relationships. But simply hiring more diverse individuals does not fix the problem, it is merely the beginning of the solution.

Diversity and Inclusion in the Boardroom

Diversity in the boardroom is being encouraged in some instances, and mandated in others, at both the federal and the state level. Institutional and individual investors have also become strong advocates in the movement to diversify the boardroom. Organizations need to follow suit and be mindful of their legal and ethical requirements pertaining to board diversity.

Federal Oversight

It was not long ago, in 2009, when the Securities and Exchange Commission (SEC) first began requiring companies to disclose how the board considers diversity when identifying director nominees. Though a good first step, because "diversity" was not defined, many companies had differing definitions of the term. Ten years later, the SEC issued guidance encouraging the disclosure of self-identified characteristics of board candidates. To the extent a company's board or its nominating committee considers diversity characteristics in forming its recommendation that such person should serve on the board, the company should identify the self-identified diversity characteristics of any such director in its proxy statement disclosure. It should also discuss how those self-identified characteristics were considered.

Nasdaq is also focused on improving diversity on corporate boards. On August 6, 2021, the SEC approved Nasdaq's board diversity rules. The rules include "diversity objectives" that require Nasdaq-listed companies to either have or explain why they do not have at least two diverse directors. The diversity objectives require that companies have at least one woman director and one director who self-identifies as Black or African American, Hispanic or Latinx, Asian, Native American or Alaska Native, Native Hawaiian or Pacific Islander, two or more races or ethnicities, or as LGBTQ+. Under the rules, companies are also now required to annually disclose their board diversity statistics using a prescriptive matrix, referred to as the "board diversity matrix." A company's repeated failure to comply with the rules would subject the company to delisting. In an effort to help companies comply with the rules, Nasdaq will offer listed companies access to a board recruitment service.

Approval of the rules came on the heels of the initial proposal by Nasdaq on December 1, 2020. This initial proposal was revised on February 26, 2021, to: (1) ease the requirement on companies with five or fewer board members (these companies are only required to have or explain the absence of a single diverse board member); (2) allow newly listed companies additional time to achieve compliance; and (3) provide a grace period to regain compliance for companies that fail to maintain compliance due to a board vacancy. The rules also provide flexibility for foreign issuers and smaller reporting companies, both of which may satisfy the diversity objectives by having two female directors. One caveat, Special Purpose Acquisition Companies are exempt from the diversity objectives until their acquisition or combination known as the initial business combination.[1]

Nasdaq-listed companies will have a transition period to meet the diversity objectives or explain why they do not meet such objectives:

- Nasdaq Global Select Market and Nasdaq Global Market companies are required to have or explain why they do not have one diverse director by August 7, 2023, and two diverse directors by August 6, 2025.
- Nasdaq Capital Market companies are required to have or explain why they do not have one diverse director by August 7, 2023, and two diverse directors by August 6, 2026.
- Companies with boards of five or fewer directors, regardless of listing tier, are required to have or explain why they do not have one diverse director by August 7, 2023.

A company must also meet the diversity objectives or explain why it has not met the objectives, by the later of the applicable compliance date described above or the date of filing of the company's proxy or information statement for the company's annual shareholders meeting for the calendar year of the applicable compliance date. This would mean that, for calendar year-end companies, compliance would be required no later than the date on which the company files its proxy or information statement for its annual meeting in 2023 and 2025, as applicable. If a company does not file a proxy or information statement, then it must meet the diversity objectives, or provide the reason why it does not, by the filing date of its Form 10-K or Form 20-F of that same year.

> Nasdaq-listed companies that do not currently have the requisite diverse directors and have not already initiated the process of recruiting diverse directors should quickly do so in order to comply with the new rules in a timely fashion.

Nasdaq-listed companies must also plan to include the board diversity matrix in future proxy and information statements. Of particular note, calendar year-end companies must provide the matrix in their proxy or information statements for their 2022 annual meeting of shareholders. Accordingly, companies must quickly consider how to obtain self-identifying diversity status of directors for the matrix, such as including self-identification questions in their annual director and officer questionnaires or interviewing directors to obtain this information.

---

1. Rachel Collins Clarke and Mehrnaz Jalali, *SEC Approves Anticipated Nasdaq Board Diversity Rules* (Aug. 10, 2021), https://www.cozen.com/news-resources/publications/2021/sec-approves-anticipated-nasdaq -board-diversity-rules.

State Oversight

Spurred by the loud calls to action following George Floyd's murder, state legislatures also began enacting or proposing legislation aimed at accelerating board of directors' DEI efforts.[2]

California

California was the first state to pass a law legislating board diversity, requiring publicly traded domestic and foreign corporations with headquarters in the state to have at least one female on their boards. By the end of 2021, companies must have three females for boards with six or more directors, two females for boards with five directors, and one female for boards with four or fewer directors.

In September 2020, California enacted a law that requires board representation from under-represented communities—Black, African American, Hispanic, Latino, Asian, Pacific Islander, Native American, Native Hawaiian, or Alaska Native, or who self-identify as gay, lesbian, bisexual, or transgender. By the end of 2022, the minimum number of directors from under-represented communities must be three if the board has nine or more directors, two if the board has five to eight directors, and one if the board has four or fewer directors.

Colorado

Though it does not come with specific diversity mandates or disclosure requirements, Colorado has passed a resolution encouraging "equitable and diverse gender representation on corporate boards." The resolution urges public corporations in Colorado with nine or more directors to have at least three women; with five to eight directors, two women; and with fewer than five directors, at least one woman on the board.

Illinois

Publicly held domestic and foreign corporations with principal offices located in Illinois are required to provide certain disclosures in connection with diversity in their annual reports to the Secretary of State. They include the self-identified gender of each board member; whether or not board members self-identify as members of a minority group and if so, which group; a description of the company's process to identify and evaluate board and executive officer nominees demonstrating how diversity factors into the process; and a description of the company's policies and practices for promoting DEI. In 2020, new legislation was proposed that closely tracks California's board diversity law.

Maryland

Maryland tax-exempt, nonstock domestic corporations with operating budgets of more than $5 million and domestic stock corporations with total sales of $5 million or more must include in their state annual reports the number of female board members as well as the total number of board members. Private companies with share ownership of at least

---

2. Kathy Jaffari and Paul Hallgren, *Roundup of Boardroom Diversity Legislation*, TODAY'S GENERAL COUNSEL (Apr. 28, 2021), https://www.todaysgeneralcounsel.com/roundup-of-boardroom-diversity-legislation/.

75 percent family members are exempt from this law. There is a sunset provision providing that it will remain in effect until September 30, 2029.

New York

New York's board diversity law mandates a study regarding women directors on the boards of New York-based companies. Both public and privately held domestic and foreign corporations authorized to do business in New York must report the number of female directors on their board, along with the total number of directors.

Washington

Effective from June 2020, Washington State passed a law requiring specific diverse board representation. The law generally applies to public companies incorporated in Washington and requires that these companies either have a "gender-diverse board" or provide shareholders with a "board diversity discussion and analysis" as to why not.

Massachusetts

Board diversity legislation has been proposed in several states. The proposed Massachusetts legislation requires that by the end of 2021, publicly held domestic and foreign corporations with principal executive offices in the state must have a minimum of one person self-identifying as female director on the board. Additionally, by the end of 2023, such companies would need three female directors if the board has six or more directors and two female directors if the board has five or fewer directors. Violations carry a $100,000 penalty.

Michigan

Michigan's proposed legislation would require that publicly held domestic and foreign corporations with principal executive offices in the state currently have at least one person self-identifying as female director on the board. Additionally, by January 1, 2023, such companies must meet numerical requirements that align with California's gender requirements. Violations carry penalties similar to California.

Pennsylvania

In 2019, a resolution was proposed in Pennsylvania encouraging equitable and diverse gender representation on boards, along with broadly calling for leadership opportunities for women. The resolution urges that by 2021 Pennsylvania companies meet the same requirements set forth in the California statute with respect to under-represented communities.

Institutional Shareholders and Beyond

Certain institutional advisors are also implementing policies to improve board diversity. Institutional Shareholder Services (ISS), a global provider of corporate governance and responsible for investment solutions, market intelligence, fund services, and events, is seeking details of the self-identified race/ethnicity of directors to provide to investors, corporations, and governance practitioners. Similarly, investment management firm State Street

Global Advisors is asking companies to disclose their diversity characteristics, including directors' racial and ethnic makeup, to provide to their clientele.

> BlackRock and Vanguard are encouraging companies to disclose the racial diversity of their boards and are using their proxy votes to push this initiative.[3] To the extent that boards have not adequately accounted for diversity, these asset managers have warned that they may take corrective action such as voting against members of the nominating/governance committee.

Legislation and rules are not the only way to inspire change, though. Several companies have been caught in the crosshairs of shareholder derivative lawsuits for their failure to have any racially diverse directors. "The allegations are largely the same: the boards of directors of these public companies allegedly breached their fiduciary duties by failing to include diverse directors on their boards, despite statements of commitment to diversity, equality, and inclusion."[4] The plaintiffs in these actions are seeking a variety of remedies including board reform, removal of existing board members, return of board compensation, investments in DEI recruiting and training, transparency in annual reports surrounding DEI, as well as attorneys' fees. While such lawsuits face an uphill battle, their primary motive is to spur social change.

How to Get There

There are inherent risks with failing to develop and maintain a diverse and inclusive board. These include reputational risks, legal risks, supply chain risks, employee risks, and fiduciary risks. However, board diversity is not something that can be changed overnight.

Board Term

Few board seats turn over in a given year, making meaningful change incrementsal at best. Even when new positions become available, there is excessive reliance on existing director networks and connections which often lack diversity. Further, when organizations require prior board experience—and nearly three-quarters of open board positions are filled by directors with prior experience—it proves even more difficult for diverse candidates to get a foot in the door.[5]

Succession and Recruitment

The clear long-term solution is to address the root cause of the problem: lack of diversity in the succession pipeline all the way up to CEO and CFO. Building a more diverse pipeline, however, can take years or even decades of cultivation. In the meantime, there are a number of shortcuts directors can take toward improvement. First, they should consider increasing the size of the board. Second, they can open discussions on board director turnover and

---

3. John Galloway, Harvard Law School Forum on Corporate Governance, *A Continued Call for Boardroom Diversity* (Dec. 19, 2020), https://corpgov.law.harvard.edu/2020/12/19/a-continued-call-for-boardroom-diversity/.
4. Samantha Burdick et al., *A New Wave of Board Diversity Derivative Litigation* (Oct. 21, 2020), https://jdsupra.com/legalnews/a-new-wave-of-board-diversity-89301/.
5. *Egon Zehnder 2020 Global Board Diversity Tracker*, file:///C:/Users/sschlossberg/Downloads/2020%20Global%20Board%20Diversity%20Tracker.pdf.

refreshment. Organizations can complete a board composition matrix to identify gaps or overcapacity of director skills. They can also amend their bylaws to include tenure limit policies. Board culture retreats and onboarding policies can also serve to educate and elevate the board and the organization.

Board Oversight

Here are six actionable steps that any board can use to progress toward becoming more diverse and inclusive:

1) Create and promote an inclusive culture in the boardroom by updating boardroom policies and procedures, or create an onboarding program for new directors.

2) Use the annual assessment process to evaluate the board's contribution, drive refreshment, raise performance, and monitor progress toward DEI goals. Consider whether the board is optimized for the strategic direction the organization is headed in.

3) Elect board leadership who understands how to and who wants to drive diversity and inclusion. The chairs of the nominating and governance committees and the lead independent director should be committed to prioritizing director diversity.

4) Hold leadership accountable for diversity. Boards should voluntarily disclose diversity metrics fully to investors. Consider ways for the board to oversee DEI metrics throughout the organization.

5) Reassess search approach and criteria. Recognize potential weaknesses in traditional networking as a recruiting strategy. Be open to candidates who don't have C-Suite roles. Allow more time for board searches and create a long-term plan for adding diverse voices.

6) Avoid defining seats as "diverse." Don't view diversity as a check-the-box response to external pressure. Embrace a mindset that views every director search as an opportunity to enhance boardroom diversity.[6]

DEI in Management and the Organization

One of the greatest challenges for the board is ensuring that DEI initiatives permeate throughout the organization from top management down to every employee. This involves creating effective systems and programming—and regularly monitoring, evaluating, and updating those programs—to ensure that real, positive, sustainable change is taking place within the organization. One way to accomplish this is by designating a DEI committee on the board to oversee DEI efforts. The following five best practices are a good starting point for supporting DEI growth.

---

6. *Spencer Stuart 2020 Board Diversity Snapshot*, file:///C:/Users/sschlossberg/Downloads/2020%20Global%20Board%20Diversity%20Tracker.pdf.

Start at the Top

Top management needs to make an authentic and visible commitment to diversity in order for DEI initiatives to be engrained within the organization. Leaders need to communicate internally and externally the importance the company places on DEI. Internally, this can be as simple as circulating emails celebrating and/or providing paid time off for major holidays celebrated by marginalized religions and cultures. Another example is taking a stance on significant traumatic events affecting minority communities like following the murder of George Floyd or the anti-Asian hate crimes that spiked following the pandemic. Communications supporting, and providing resources for, the affected communities increase the feeling of safety within the organization. Externally, organizations should incorporate information about their commitment to DEI on their websites, in recruitment materials, and in other external communications to consumers and clients.

In order for DEI initiatives to be taken seriously and to be effective within the organization, management needs to hold others accountable. It cannot excuse offensive behavior. Management must work closely with human resources to ensure that bias is addressed and eradicated. Conversations with insensitive employees are difficult, particularly when the offensive behavior is subtle and the employee is in a position of power or well liked within the organization. Under these circumstances, it is not uncommon to excuse the behavior as unintended—a careless or accidental mistake. But good intentions are no excuse for harmful impacts. Further, each of those harmful impacts opens up the organization to potential liability.

Ultimately, each member of management and the board has to make DEI a personal priority. Implementing DEI priorities and initiatives makes good business sense and is good for the organization's bottom line and its long-term value because the company becomes more attractive to consumers and can often flourish with a variety of perspectives. But DEI change cannot be driven only by dollars and cents. As DEI expert, Aiko Bethea, explains, as a black person it is insulting to have someone explain that they should be nice to you because that behavior is worth more money. This is dehumanizing. The organization should do DEI work because it wants to be equitable, because it does not want its employees coming to work feeling "less than" others. Bethea adamantly believes that in order for DEI work to be transformative it must be relational, not transactional. This can be done by shutting down valuation conversations and encouraging management to convey to others why DEI work is personally important to them and respected within the organization.[7] In 2021, a number of law firms have offered young lawyers hours of billable equivalent credit for working on DEI initiatives to advance diversity and inclusion.

To be done right, DEI work takes time, intentionality, and a lot of effort. Sustainable DEI change cannot be reactive and will not happen overnight. Management and the board need to take the time to listen and learn from their diverse constituents, and then to take action.

---

7. Dare to Lead Podcast with Brene Brown, *Creating Transformative Cultures with Aiko Bethea*, Feb. 8, 2021.

Have Dedicated DEI Personnel and Committees

Organizations need to designate a team of personnel dedicated to DEI. Regardless of the exact titles, ideally this should include some combination of a Chief DEI Officer, Chair of the DEI Committee, and DEI Mangers or Directors. These positions should be valued because they are doing important work within the organization. That valuation can take the form of additional compensation, bonuses, or allotting a particular percentage of time during the workday to dedicate to DEI. If it is simply a volunteer position that individuals are expected to do in addition to their full-time jobs at the organization, the DEI initiatives will suffer from lack of commitment.

In addition to leadership positions, organizations should have a DEI committee and Employee Resource Groups (ERGs). DEI committees are most effective when they comprise a cross-section of employees representing views from different offices, backgrounds, and positions within the company. ERGs are affinity groups that serve to foster community and mentorship within marginalized communities. Some examples include ERGs for employees who are black, Asian, LGBTQIA+, Hispanic, and those with disabilities. ERGs are a great way to build communities and support within the organization. Budgets should be provided to diversity committees and ERGs to be used to create educational and supportive programming, as well as to connect with one another for fun. ERGs should be empowered to help the organization identify strategies that support inclusion efforts. While committees and ERGs are helpful, management cannot simply delegate all DEI work to them. Value-driven leaders ask how they can best support their committees and ERGs. Their role, however, should be a supporting one. Management should listen, assist, support, and allow the leaders of these groups to speak and lead, as well.

Recruit and Develop Diverse Talent

Recruiting and developing diverse talent is crucial to creating lasting DEI change within an organization. Attention must be paid to each step of the experience: sourcing and recruiting, hiring, onboarding, culture, and feedback. The board should have a fulsome understanding of what is being done to diversify recruiting and hiring practices to construct an equitable pipeline. Some questions a board member may want to consider include:

- Is the organization sourcing from predominantly minority schools?
- Does hiring personnel have appropriate DEI training to combat implicit bias?
- Are there recruitment goals?
- Have advertisements been placed in minority publications?
- Would an executive search firm specializing in the placement of minorities be helpful?

Other ways organizations can improve recruitment is to be proactive. Minority internship or fellowship programs provide excellent training and recruitment opportunities for potential future talent. Organizations should also consider how they can become involved in programs, such as job fairs or academic competitions, within predominantly minority high schools and colleges.

Once diverse employees are hired, the DEI focus shifts to development, retention, and promotion. During the onboarding process, individuals should be provided with information about ERGs. Formal and informal mentorship is also crucial when onboarding. Diverse employees coming into a predominantly white organization may require more specialized training, coaching, or mentorship than their counterparts. Underprivileged minorities, in particular, often have to overcome a variety of obstacles simply to level the playing field when onboarding into organizations including unequal education, lower self-confidence, distrust, and stereotypes.

Train, Train, Train

In addition to providing support and, when necessary, targeted substantive training to diverse employees, all employees need to be provided with training that strengthens DEI awareness and communication skills. To inspire meaningful change within an organization, companies should avoid "parachute training" where someone comes to speak once on the subject and then is never heard from again. DEI training needs to be conducted intentionally, interactively, and often. Because people learn differently, encourage the use of a variety of educational formats, speakers, and topics. Try implementing training courses for different audiences. For example, one training session may involve everyone in a particular office, while another training session may be limited to just upper-level management, and yet another to a department or committee.

Organizations should also cultivate a community of practice. Progress can only be made when individuals feel psychologically safe in their environment, allowing them to be vulnerable. But people who are trying to do better will get things wrong, too. Bethea suggests that for constructive conversations to happen, we have to call others in rather than calling them out. Calling out immediately makes people defensive and often hampers growth. Instead, adopt a teaching mindset to call others in. True change does not happen by memorizing facts, but by absorbing the teachable moments and incorporating them into practice. For example, if an individual says something insensitive, teach them simply by asking, "What did you mean when you said that?" After the intention is understood, communicate the impact of the insensitive language. Then, turn the conversation back to them by asking, "Now that you know the impact, how would you reframe it?"[8]

Track the Metrics

Finally, boards need to monitor how their organization is fairing with their DEI goals by ensuring that the correct metrics are collected and analyzed through the right lens. Identify what metrics are most meaningful in relation to your goals. Is it turnover rates? Hiring rates? Promotion rates? Compensation? Be specific on what the board and the organization want to achieve and what is deemed a key milestone. Establish a timeline for when you expect those milestones to be reached.

It is helpful to collect and analyze metrics for specific subgroups. The organization may be successful with integrating and supporting some subgroups, but not others. In this respect, it helps to look at the context behind the numbers for maximum impact as numbers can be easily manipulated if there is a revolving door of diverse employees. Why are

---

8. *Supra* note 4.

people leaving? Why are diverse candidates being passed over for promotion? Find the common themes where they exist.

Conclusion

In order to survive and thrive in today's world, companies must become leaders in the DEI space. Directors can no longer abdicate their responsibilities in moving the needle forward, blindly relying on management and the company to act appropriately. Directors must supervise the progress of their organization so that DEI does not become a meaningless catchphrase, but rather a tool to achieve authentic goals and transformation.

Take-Aways for Board Members

- Ensure that your board is in compliance with state and federal diversity requirements.
- Consider ways to improve board diversity over time including adding term limits, cultivating a more diverse pipeline, encouraging board director refreshment, and reassessing recruiting strategies.
- Ask for regular updates, including metrics, from management and DEI committees to determine whether DEI initiatives within the organization are being successfully implemented.
- Review recruitment, onboarding, and development practices with a focus on hiring and supporting diverse candidates.
- Analyze whether training programs are being conducted intentionally, interactively, and often.

About the Editors

Katayun I. Jaffari

Katayun I. Jaffari is a shareholder at Cozen O'Connor. She is Chair of the Corporate Governance Group and Co-Chair of the Capital Markets & Securities Group and the ESG Practice Group. She devotes her practice to advising boards of directors and executive management teams on all aspects of corporate matters including governance as well as handling complex securities transactions for businesses in a variety of industries ranging in the billions of dollars. Kathy has broad experience in capital market transactions, compliance matters, mergers and acquisitions, and ongoing business counseling.

Kathy guides boards of directors and management teams through the laws, rules, regulations, and practical realities that arise when leading an organization. She counsels clients on complying with federal governance laws as well and assisting clients with responding to stakeholder interests such as boardroom diversity and sustainability. Kathy advises and counsels on a myriad of governance issues and helps clients develop compliance programs with respect to legislative, regulatory, and listing rule requirements. She also assists non-profit corporations with respect to all aspects of corporate governance matters. In addition, Kathy provides training programs for boards, management, and employees with respect to many diverse compliance and governance matters. She serves as Co-Chair of the ESG Joint Subcommittee of the Corporate Governance Committee and Federal Regulations of Securities Committees of the ABA's Business Law Section and launched and served as Chair of the Diversity in the Boardroom Taskforce for the Corporate Governance Committee of the ABA's Business Law Section. Kathy launched the Inside Scoop series for Cozen O'Connor, interviewing experts about the latest, most pressing governance topics of the day.

Kathy writes and lectures extensively in the areas of corporate governance, including stakeholder issues such as sustainability and diversity, equity and inclusion, fiduciary duty matters, securities law compliance, and entity formations and transformations. A believer in the power of mindfulness as a tool to optimize one's professional and personal capacity for excellence, Kathy has a particular interest in mindfulness in the practice of law as a way to support the needs of her clients.

Stephen A. Pike

Stephen A. Pike is a Toronto-based Partner at the Gowling WLG law firm and is co-leader of the Gowling WLG Canadian ESG Advisory Services practice. As a senior legal advisor to Canadian, American, and global businesses, Stephen regularly provides advice on corporate law and governance, ESG, transactional, operational, and risk management issues, including CSR, supply chain, regulatory compliance, product distribution, marketing, licensing, and manufacturing, as well as product liability matters. He also advises businesses outside of Canada on setting up or acquiring operations in Canada and bringing products and services into the Canadian market.

Stephen is a member of the Board of Directors of the International Commission of Jurists—Canada; a Co-Chair of the ESG Joint Subcommittee of the Corporate Governance Committee and the Federal Regulation of Securities Committee of the Business Law Section of the American Bar Association; and serves on the Finance, Audit and Risk Management Committee of the Canadian Cancer Society.

He writes and speaks frequently on ESG issues and how businesses can address the risk of modern slavery, forced labor, and child labor in their operations and supply chains.

He regularly speaks about modern slavery in supply chains to business and legal organizations and has spoken to meetings of the Prospectors & Developers Association of Canada (PDAC), Women Get on Board, the Ontario Bar Association, Governance Professionals of Canada Canadian Corporate Counsel Association, the American Bar Association, and the Canadian Center for Ethics and Corporate Policy.

Stephen has written a 13-part series on insights for Canadian CEOs and directors on addressing forced labour in their businesses and supply chains. He has also co-authored three chapters, namely "Managing Reputational Risk," "Enterprise Risk Management," and "Governing the Multinational Enterprise," of the Director's Handbook—A Field Guide to 101 Situations Commonly Encountered in the Boardroom, published by the American Bar Association.

He is a member of the Program Faculty of the Osgoode Hall Law School PD Certificate Course in ESG, Climate Risk and the Law.

Stephen successfully completed the Directors Education Program offered by the Institute of Corporate Directors and the University of Toronto Rotman School of Management, and received the ICD.D designation.

About the Contributors

Frederick Alexander is the CEO of The Shareholder Commons, a non-profit organization dedicated to helping shareholders use their power to protect common resources and vulnerable populations. Alexander practiced law for 30 years at the law firm Morris, Nichols, Arsht & Tunnell, LLP, including four years as managing partner. During that time, he was selected as one of the ten most highly regarded corporate governance lawyers worldwide and as one of the 500 leading lawyers in the United States. In 2015, Alexander became Head of Legal Policy at B Lab, where he worked to create sustainable corporate governance structures around the globe. He left that position in 2019 to organize The Shareholder Commons. Alexander is a member of the Delaware Corporation Law Council, the body responsible for maintaining the premier corporate statute in the United States, where he previously served as Chair, testifying multiple times in the Delaware General Assembly, and drafting and shepherding important legislation, including provisions prohibiting mandatory arbitration, enabling proxy access, protecting majority voting, and authorizing benefit corporations. He served eight years on the American Bar Association Corporate Laws Committee and was the chief draftsperson of its White Paper on Benefit Corporations.

Marie Elena Angulo is counsel at White & Case, resident in Miami. She has more than 25 years of experience advising U.S. and non-U.S. issuers and financial institutions in connection with securities offerings, reporting requirements, and corporate governance matters. She advises on a broad range of transactions, including initial public offerings rights issues, follow-on offerings, private placements, privatizations, and other equity offerings; project bonds, investment-grade, convertible, and high-yield debt offerings; and exchange offers, tender offers, and consent solicitations. She has worked on capital raisings in the United States, as well as in Africa, Australia, Europe, Hong Kong, and Latin America. Angulo is a member of the American Bar Association and serves as senior advisor to the International Finance & Securities Committee.

Sonia G. Barros is a partner in Sidley's Capital Markets group and chairs the group's Public Company Advisory subgroup focused on advising clients in corporate disclosures and governance matters. Formerly the Chief Corporate Governance Counsel in the Division of Corporation Finance at the U.S. Securities and Exchange Commission (SEC), Barros was the Division's senior advisor on corporate governance policy and disclosures. Prior to that, Barros served as the Assistant Director in the SEC's Office of Real Estate and Commodities, where she had oversight authority for thousands of transactions and reviews of corporate disclosures, including financial statements, under the Securities Act of 1933 and the Securities Exchange Act of 1934.

Howard Brod Brownstein is President of The Brownstein Corporation, a turnaround management and restructuring firm, and regularly serves as an independent corporate board member of publicly-held and privately-owned companies, as well as large nonprofits. He is a past Vice Chair of the ABA Business Law Section Corporate Governance Committee, and currently serves as its Co-Chair of Programming. He has been named by the National Association of Corporate Directors as NACD Directorship Certified, and a Board Leadership Fellow. He served as President and Chair of the NACD Philadelphia Chapter, and is a regular member of NACD's faculty for its national programs.

Nancy S. Cleveland is the co-founder of Sustrana LLC, a sustainability management software and consulting company. Prior to retirement, Cleveland provided consulting services and led content development for Sustrana's online sustainability management software, which enables businesses to manage and realize performance improvements through sustainability best practices. Cleveland co-chaired the Governance and Sustainability sub-committee of the American Bar Association's Business Law Section. She is an accredited FSA II (SASB) and former LEED® AP and is trained in GRI reporting and as a TSC Service Provider. Prior to her work in sustainability, Cleveland was a practicing real estate and telecommunications lawyer.

Kevin M. Coleman serves as Chief Corporate Governance Officer and Assistant Corporate Secretary for The Huntington National Bank (Nasdaq:HBAN) where he prepares materials and information for the Board of Directors and executive management on all aspects of Huntington's corporate governance framework. He monitors and analyzes changes in voting policies and positions of institutional investors and proxy advisors and engages with them on various governance matters. Coleman also coordinates the preparation of Huntington's proxy statement, including drafting, reviewing, and editing. He also assists Huntington with non-regulatory disclosures, including the annual ESG Report. Coleman was a finalist in 2017 and 2019 for the Corporate Secretary's Rising Star award. He has authored or contributed to multiple governance and legal publications, including as a working group member for the *Report of the 2020 Multi-Stakeholder Working Group on Practices for Virtual Shareholder Meetings*. Coleman earned his Bachelor of Science in Marketing from the University of Alabama at Birmingham and his Juris Doctor from Cumberland School of Law, Samford University. He also served as Editor-in-Chief of Cumberland's Law Review. He is a member of the Alabama State Bar.

Lawrence A. Darby, III is a corporate finance and securities lawyer whose practice has consisted mainly of mergers and acquisitions, securities offerings, corporate restructurings, corporate governance matters and financial derivatives regulation. Recently mostly retired from active practice for corporate clients, he was a partner in Kaye Scholer LLP's New York City and Hong Kong offices and a founding partner of Howard, Darby & Levin, a New York City law firm. He continues to devote considerable time to the work of committees of the New York State Bar Association's International Law Section (of which he was a founder) and its Business Law Section and committees of the American Bar Association's Business Law Section including the Federal Securities Law and Corporate Governance committees. He frequently contributes to the ABA's *Corporate Governance Insights* publication on new accounting and auditing developments. He was graduated from Harvard College with an A.B. *cum laude*, from Harvard Graduate School of Business Administration with an M.B.A. and from Tulane University School of Law with a J.D.

Bruce Dravis served as Chair of the Corporate Governance Committee of the ABA Business Law Section from 2017 to 2020. He is a former partner of Downey Brand LLP of Sacramento, California. He has written and spoken extensively on corporate governance matters.

Rebecca Grapsas is counsel in the Corporate Governance and Executive Compensation practice at Sidley Austin LLP. She counsels U.S. public companies (including U.S. filers incorporated outside the U.S.) and foreign private issuers, private companies, private equity firms, state-owned enterprises, professional services firms, institutional investors, financial market utilities, and not-for-profit corporations (including universities, sports governing bodies, trade groups, and charitable organizations), operating in a wide range of industries, at all stages of their life cycle, with respect to complex corporate governance, securities regulation, and compliance issues, including fiduciary duties (including conflicts of interest and confidentiality obligations), board and committee leadership, composition and structure, board evaluation processes, CEO transitions, risk oversight, environmental, social, and governance matters, shareholder engagement and activism, proxy access, relationships with proxy advisory firms, executive and director compensation, special committee investigations, disclosure and compliance with corporate and securities laws, regulations and listing rules, including in the context of transformative transactions such as initial public offerings and spin-offs.

Claire H. Holland is special counsel in the Corporate and Capital Markets practice group in Sidley's Chicago office. Since joining the firm in 2003, Holland has assisted with a variety of public securities offerings and corporate transactions, including public and private mergers, acquisitions, and dispositions. In recent years, she has focused her practice on corporate governance matters, SEC disclosure requirements, and other federal securities law issues. Holland regularly gives advice to public company clients with respect to SEC reporting obligations, exchange listing standards, the requirements of the Sarbanes-Oxley Act and Dodd-Frank Act, and proxy advisory firm voting policies. She also advises corporate management, boards of directors, and board committees on their corporate governance policies and practices and counsels them on fiduciary duties, takeover defenses, legal compliance, and board and committee best practices.

William Jannace has worked over 35 years in the securities industry at the American and New York Stock Exchanges, FINRA and several investment banking firms. He currently serves as an expert witness for The Bates Group on securities litigation matters. He is a member of the faculty advisory group of ESG Competent Boards which provides professional development and advisory services on ESG and Sustainability to boards, investors, and executives globally. He is also an adjunct professor/lecturer at Fordham School of Law, the U.S. Army War College, the Global Financial Markets Institute, Baruch University, and Metropolitan College, where he teaches courses covering: Broker-Dealer Operations and Compliance; Investment Adviser and Investment Company Regulation; Capital Markets and Corporate Governance; Corporate Social Responsibility, ESG and Impact Investing; AML/FCPA; and Geopolitics, Climate Change, National Security, U.S. Foreign Policy, and Grand Strategy. He is also a research affiliate with the Fletcher Network for Sovereign Wealth and Global Capital, and a member of the: Bretton Woods Committee, NGO Committee to Stop Trafficking in Persons, and International Institute for Strategic Studies. Jannace has also conducted training programs in: Russia; Uganda; Burundi; Tanzania; Kenya; Saudi Arabia; India; Ukraine; Romania; Jordan; Turkey; Albania; China; Taiwan and Spain.

Hana Lee is an associate in the Corporate group of Sidley's Palo Alto office. Her practice spans domestic and cross-border corporate matters, including mergers and acquisitions, capital markets, shareholder activism defense and preparedness, venture capital transactions and corporate governance. Prior to Sidley, Lee was a Graduate Public Interest Law Initiative Fellow at the Institute for Justice Clinic on Entrepreneurship, where she assisted in the representation of community entrepreneurs and businesses with corporate governance, regulatory compliance and other transactional legal services. Lee received her J.D. from Harvard Law School, where she served on the board of the Harvard Legal Entrepreneurship Program, as a member of the Community Enterprise Project and as a teaching assistant for Innovation in Legal Education and Practice.

Kai H.E. Liekefett is a partner and co-chairs Sidley's Shareholder Activism & Corporate Defense Practice. He has over 20 years of experience in New York, London, Germany, Hong Kong and Tokyo. In the last 5 years, Liekefett has defended over 85 proxy contests, more than any other defense attorney in the world. Under Liekeffet's leadership, Sidley rose to the top of all activism defense league tables, including the No. 1 rankings by Bloomberg, FactSet, Refinitiv (formerly Thomson Reuters) and Activist Insight for 2020 and H1 2021. In 2021, Chambers USA ranked him as a Top 3 leading attorney for "Takeover Defense". In 2020, Liekefett was elected as a fellow of The American College of Governance Counsel, the honorary association of lawyers widely recognized for their achievements in the field of governance. Liekefett has been named "2019 Dealmaker of the Year" by The American Lawyer. Liekefett sits on the board of the New York Chapter of the National Association of Corporate Directors (NACD) and the Law360 Mergers & Acquisitions Editorial Board. He speaks regularly on panels and at universities around the world, including Harvard University and Frankfurt School of Finance & Management.

Hope Mehlman is Executive Vice President, General Counsel and Corporate Secretary for Bank of the West and is a member of the Bank's Executive Management Committee. Mehlman oversees the Bank's legal activities and regulatory relations functions. She leads the design and execution of the Bank's legal and regulatory strategy while fostering a culture of risk awareness and accountability. In addition to her responsibilities at Bank of the

West, Hope also serves as Corporate Secretary for BNP Paribas USA, Inc., and is a member of the BNPP USA Executive Management Committee. Mehlman serves as member of independent Oversight Committee for Best Practices Principles Group for shareholder voting research. She was the recipient of the Corporate Secretary's 2019 Governance Professional of the Year (Large Cap) Award. Additionally, Global Proxy Watch recognized Mehlman in its 2019 Stars list of ten people around the world who have had a breakthrough impact in governance. Mehlman previously served as Co-Chair of the Board of Directors of the Council of Institutional Investors, a member of Broadridge's Independent Steering Committee and President, Southeastern Chapter of the Society for Corporate Governance. Before joining Bank of the West, Hope served as Executive Vice President, Corporate Secretary, Chief Governance Officer and Deputy General Counsel for Regions Financial Corporation. Prior to Regions, she was a partner in a private practice focused on a full range of corporate governance, regulatory, compliance, and other issues affecting financial institutions' operations. Mehlman holds a Bachelor of Arts degree from Cornell University, a juris doctor degree from Seton Hall University Law School and a LL. M. in Taxation from NYU School of Law.

Jessica Mendoza is an associate at White & Case's Miami Office. Her practice focuses on domestic and cross-border finance transactions. She regularly represents financial institutions, project sponsors, developers, and corporate borrowers on cross-border lending transactions in Latin America, including project finance and bilateral corporate finance transactions. She advises project sponsors and developers on engineering, procurement, and construction contracts, operations and maintenance contracts, and other project documents.

Beth-ann Roth is a Certified Corporate Governance Professional® and shareholder of R|K Invest Law, PBC, a Public Benefit Corporation law firm. She counsels on SEC defense, ESG compliance and shareholder advocacy, and on the regulation and business of importing organic, biodynamic, vegan, and fair trade wine, beer and spirits. Roth is also President of ESG Legal Services, a 501(c)(3) public interest law firm, where she launched the Corporate-Shareholder Communications Initiative to establish a legal framework for non-adversarial dialogue outside the shareholder proposal process. She serves as pro bono General Counsel of Die Jim Crow, a non-profit record label giving voice to fighting racial injustice in the US prison system. Roth was previously an appellate litigator in the Office of the General Counsel at the SEC, and then joined the rulemaking section of the Division of Corporation Finance. After serving as a lobbyist, she joined the Calvert family of responsible mutual funds, and was concurrently the first lawyer for Calvert Impact Capital. She was with the law firms of Katten Muchin Rosenman and Dechert, served as counsel to Rev. Leon Sullivan (author of *The Sullivan Principles*) on impacting investment initiatives both domestically and in Africa, and later served as Deputy GC for FINCA, providing microfinance services in 21 countries.

Sarah Schlossberg is an attorney in the Commercial Litigation Department at Cozen O'Connor. Her practice is focused on a wide variety of complex commercial litigation matters. In addition to Sarah's legal practice, she manages the firm's Commercial Litigation Department, supporting the attorneys and staff in the department. On a more global level, she serves as the co-chair of Cozen O'Connor's Women's Initiative and as lateral integration coordinator for new litigation attorneys. Sarah is committed to giving back to the community and has handled numerous pro bono matters throughout her career. She currently sits on the Board of Directors for Philadelphia's Anti-Defamation League and the Wolf Performing Arts Center. Sarah is passionate about DEI issues, and has a regular column in the ALI CLE's The Practical Lawyer entitled "Life, Liberty, and the Pursuit of Equity."

John H. Stout is an officer and shareholder with Fredrikson & Byron P.A., a law firm headquartered in Minneapolis, with other Minnesota offices in St. Paul and Mankato. Fredrikson also has offices in Iowa, North Dakota, Mexico, and China. Stout advises executives, boards, directors, and officers of for-profit, nonprofit, and benefit corporations on a wide range of governance, finance, sustainability, ESG and CSR matters. Recently, he has worked with start-up and early stage businesses on organizational, finance and governance matters. Stout co-chairs Fredrikson's Corporate Governance, Corporate Sustainability and Social Responsibility, Artificial Intelligence and Sports and Entertainment Groups. Stout also co-teaches a governance course at the University of St. Thomas Law School. Stout is very active in the Business Law Section of the American Bar Association. From 2011 to 2014, he chaired the Section's Corporate Governance Committee and served on its Governing Council. Currently, he co-chairs the Section's Working Group on the Rule of Law and its Corporate Social Responsibility Committee. Stout is a member of the American College of Governance Council. In 2017, he received the Twin Cities Business Outstanding Directors Lifetime Achievement Award for his corporate governance accomplishments.

Peter P. Tomczak is a partner with Baker McKenzie, and serves as Chair of the firm's North America Litigation and Government Enforcement Practice Group. He has conducted sensitive internal investigations, in particular those arising under the US Foreign Corrupt Practices Act, for multinational corporations in more than 25 international jurisdictions. He counsels clients and their boards of directors on corporate compliance and corporate governance matters, including ESG trends and developments. Tomczak regularly publishes and presents on anticorruption, compliance and corporate governance issues, including having coauthored The Foreign Corrupt Practices Act Handbook (5th ed. 2018) with Robert W. Tarun. He was recognized in the National Association of Corporate Directors (NACD) Directorship 100—Governance Professionals and Institutions (2018-2021). Prior to joining Baker McKenzie, Tomczak clerked for Vice Chancellor John W. Noble of the Delaware Court of Chancery. He received his Juris Doctorate degree, Magna Cum Laude, Order of the Coif, from the University of Michigan Law School, and was awarded the Daniel H. Grady Prize for graduating first in his law school class and the Emmett E. Eagan Award for excellence in the study of corporate law.

Paul Wehrmann has been practicing law for over 30 years and is a member of Weaver Johnston Nelson, PLLC, in Dallas, Texas, specializing in corporate, securities, and transactional law. He has extensive experience in corporate governance, venture capital, mergers and acquisitions, securities regulatory compliance, and entity formation and regulation. He holds a Juris Doctorate from the Dedman School of Law at Southern Methodist University, where he served on the Board of Editors of the Journal of Air Law and Commerce and received the Sumners Foundation Scholarship. He also holds a Bachelor of Arts, magna cum laude, from Southern Methodist University, and was the first graduate of its liberal arts honors program. He is a member of Phi Beta Kappa, the American Bar Association, the State Bar of Texas, the College of the State Bar of Texas, and Mensa. Within the Business Law Section of the American Bar Association, he has worked on the Policy Initiative on Sustainability Financial Reporting Working Group; the Sustainable Development Task Force of the Sustainability and Governance Subcommittee; the Deal Points Study on Carveout Transactions; and the Committee on Corporate Documents and Process, Private Company Forms Task Force. He is married with three children.

John Legaré Williams is President of The Williams Law Firm, P.A. in Wilmington, Delaware, where for the past 20 years his practice has focused on business transactions and litigation. Williams received his B.A. from Williams College and his juris doctor from Emory University School of Law. Williams is also the President of IncNow.com, an ecommerce Delaware registered agent. In 2019 and 2021, IncNow received B Corp's Best for the World Award in Corporate Governance. Williams was appointed by the ABA to serve as an advisor to the Uniform Law Commission for the Drafting Committee of the Uniform Protected Series Act. He has been engaged as an expert witness on the series LLC. He is Past-Chair of the American Bar Association's Partnerships and LLCs Committee for the Real Property Trust and Estates Section. He is a frequent speaker nationally on the topic of the Delaware Series LLC. He also is the inventor of an issued US patent for a "System and Method for Processing and Dynamically Segregating Business Assets" utilizing the Delaware Series LLC.

Derek Zaba is a partner and co-chair of Sidley's Shareholder Activism practice. He counsels companies on activism defense/proxy contests, activism preparedness, takeover defenses, shareholder engagement and corporate governance matters. Over the past two decades, he has been involved in dozens of activist campaigns and proxy contests in advisory and principal capacities. Prior to Sidley, Zaba was the head of the activism defense practice at a leading shareholder engagement and corporate governance advisory firm. Zaba has been recognized by Chambers USA as a leading lawyer in "Takeover Defense." He is a highly sought-after speaker for panels on the topics of shareholder activism and related matters and regularly speaks on the topic of shareholder activism, including at Stanford University Law School and on public radio.

Reuben Zaramian is a senior associate in Sidley's New York office where his practice focuses on shareholder activism and corporate governance. He frequently advises public companies on complex board matters and special situations, as well as activism preparedness, ESG issues, investor engagement and disclosure obligations. Prior to Sidley, Zaramian was an associate at a law firm with a prominent shareholder activism practice, where he represented investors in high-profile activist situations. Zaramian has been involved in over 75 shareholder activism and related special situations matters and has represented public companies and investors in dozens of proxy contests. He received his J.D. from Osgoode Hall Law School in Toronto.